Centripetal Forces in
the Sciences

Centripetal Forces in the Sciences

VOLUME II

Edited by
Gerard Radnitzky

An ICUS Book

PARAGON HOUSE
NEW YORK

First edition, 1988

Published in the United States by

Paragon House Publishers
90 Fifth Avenue
New York, NY 10011

Copyright © 1988 by Paragon House Publishers

Library of Congress Cataloging-in-Publication Data

Centripetal forces in the sciences.

   Papers from a meeting of Committee I of the
Thirteenth International Conference on the Unity
of the Sciences, held in Washington, D.C. in
Sept. 1984.
   Bibliography:
   Includes index.
   1. Science—Philosophy—Congresses. 2. Science—
Methodology—Congresses. 3. Science—Social aspects—
Congresses. 4. Reductionism—Congresses.
I. Radnitzky, Gerard. II. International Conference
on the Unity of the Sciences (13th : 1984 :
Washington, D.C.). Committee I.
Q174.C463   1987   501   86-30389

ISBN 0-89226-048-3

Manufactured in the United States of America

Contents

Acknowledgments

This second volume of the Series APPROACHES TO THE UNITY OF THE SCIENCES grew out of a workshop that held a preparatory meeting in Paris and then formed Committee I of the Thirteenth International Conference on the Unity of the Sciences, which took place in Washington, D.C., in September 1984. This volume presents a selection from the papers and comments delivered at that meeting. The manuscripts have been revised and rewritten after the Conference.

On behalf of the participants I thank, in particular, Alvin M. Weinberg not only for acting as Honorary Chairman but also for taking an active part in the discussions. Again, we—the participants of the Conference—wish to acknowledge our indebtedness to the International Cultural Foundation, its Founder, its Board of Directors, and its officers. Last, and not least, my personal thanks go to the paper writers, the paper discussants, and the general discussants for their contributions to what, I trust, will prove to be an improvement of our knowledge about the sructure and the growth of knowledge.

Foreword

The Unity of the Sciences can be approached on many levels. To the philosopher, the term "Unity of the Sciences" refers to the underlying structure of the scientific edifice—the relation of one part of science to another. To the practicing scientist, it means the application of a scientific result from a science outside his specialty to the clarification of specific problems within his own specialty. To the sociologist, it implies scientific truth itself being the result of negotiation between competing power centers—that all science, in a way, is a branch of sociology. To the scientific administrator, trying to manage a multidisciplinary team working on a single large project, the Unity of the Sciences connotes the welding of disparate viewpoints into an effective mechanism for research.

Professor Gerard Radnitzky has brought together in this volume a brilliant collection of essays, each of which illuminates one or another aspect of the Unity of the Sciences. The authors and commentators are scholars of impeccable reputation and profound insight, and they are to be congratulated for their efforts. The essays were first presented at the Thirteenth International Conference on the Unity of the Sciences in Washington, D.C.

As honorary chairman of Professor Radnitzky's committee, I listened to all of the papers as they were presented and discussed. Not being a professional philosopher, I was not always able to appreciate some of the subtleties of the arguments; however, I understood enough to want very much to read the lively exchange at leisure. Now that I have re-read all of the papers, I can say that I have learned much from them. I hope that other readers of these papers will enjoy these intriguing insights as much as I did.

The world of science owes much to Professor Radnitzky for organizing this symposium, and to the International Cultural Foundation for sponsoring the International Conferences on the Unity of the Sciences. The unity of the sciences is a subject that always brings nods of bemused assent to practicing scientists, humanists, and philosophers—but no one seems to do much to bring this unification about. The annual International Conferences on the Unity of the Sciences is the only forum where the subject is dealt with seriously and continuously. I hope that this volume will be widely read, and widely appreciated, by all we scientists and scientific administrators who feel guilty because our day-to-day specialization contributes to the dis-unity of the sciences when, deep in our hearts, we realize that the unity of the sciences is an ideal to which we all aspire.

ALVIN M. WEINBERG

Introduction

Gerard Radnitzky

This volume constitutes a sequel to the collection entitled *Centripetal Forces in the Sciences*. Yet, it is completely self-contained. It illuminates the problem cluster of the Unity of the Sciences from new angles and sometimes also from the same angle but with a different focus.

UNIFICATION, REDUCTION AND INTERTHEORETIC RELATIONSHIPS

In intellectual history the unification of knowledge has been a perennial theme. Probably the first great advance was made in antiquity by the atomists, and later by Epicurus and Lucretius, who developed a dynamic, and strikingly modern, world view. They postulated a thoroughgoing homogeneity in nature: everywhere in the cosmos the same laws apply, and the basic structure of nature is everywhere the same. Also the cosmological model of cluster formation and the corpuscular theory of light was anticipated by these early thinkers, who speculated about the unity of nature. The unity that these thinkers postulated was an ontological unity, *i.e.*, they claimed that behind the apparent diversity of phenomena—of things and processes—there is, on ultimate analysis, only one or a very limited number of basic entities. Newton was the first who proposed the idea that gravity formed the matter, which originally was spread out homogeneously, into clumps which we see as stars. In the dynamic universe projected by the Pre-Socratics the various structures and clusters are more or less stable: they change continually so that new clusters are formed and old ones fall apart. The cosmos is in a perpetual flux.[1] In this respect Aristotle, in the wake of Parmenides and Plato, constitutes a great regression. His distinction between a sublunar sphere and an upper "eternal" and static sphere was particularly unfortunate.

Normally, 'unity' in the expression 'unity of science' refers to science as an ensemble of theories. The theories are changing, but they change in such a way that, if a particular theory contains a kernel of truth, that kernel is preserved. For instance, when a theory is being replaced by an improved version of it or by a successor theory that is incompatible with it, the achievements of the older theory are retained. (For instance, Einstein's and Newton's theories are incompatible; but for velocities far below the speed of light, the test statements derived with the help of Newton's theory are very close approximations to the test statements derived with the help of Einstein's theory.) "Unity" in the weakest sense means compatibility of the various pieces of knowledge. The most ambitious interpretation of the idea of "unity of science" is a quest for a grand unifying theory. The attitude underlying this quest is *reductionistic.* One first makes an ontological or metaphysical assumption, *viz.* that there are different "levels of reality" that form a hierarchy of strata; then one assumes that different branches of science deal with different levels of reality. The idea of unification then takes the form that a theory about entities that are considered to be on a certain ontological level can be deduced from another theory that is about entities that are considered to be on a "deeper" level. However, it is doubtful whether in the history of science we find any cases of a successful *complete* reduction in this sense.

Hence, it appears advisable to follow Noretta Koertge's advice to concentrate on the *relationship* between the various sorts of theories (Chapter 2 of this volume). Such an investigation will *improve our knowledge about the knowledge constituted by these theories.* Theories are basically linguistically formulated expectation. The knowledge that they may contain is knowledge in the objective sense, *i.e.*, the truth-value of a descriptive statement as well as the validity of an argument are independent of any questions about who, if anyone, believes them and independent of any questions about how that statement or argument originated. Man transcends himself, once he has acquired descriptive language, with the help of his theories. The theories become objects that lead a partially autonomous life; they may be criticized, and a particular theory may be rejected while its carrier survives. An improved understanding of knowledge in the objective sense results from the competition between theories. The competitive market of ideas elicits not-yet existing knowledge, and it enables us to discover more and more of the potentialities of extant theories (see Bartley 1987b and Bartley 1987c).

METHODOLOGICAL REDUCTIONISM VERSUS METAPHYSICAL REDUCTIONISM

Any terminology is a matter of convention. Nonetheless, clarifying a few key terms may help to avoid misunderstandings. *Reduction* in the strong sense makes the reduced theory dispensible. A theory T_1 is reduced by a theory T_2 if and only if (1) the two theories belong to disciplines that represent different provinces of knowledge, and (2) T_2 logically entails T_1. For instance, what often, erroneously, is regarded as the deduction of Galilei's law and Kepler's laws from Newton's theory and, in fact, is the deduction of an improved successor of these laws (which contradicts the original law-statement) with the help of Newton's theory constitutes a systematization or unification, but not a reduction in the sense in which the term 'reduction' has just been defined. Of course, 'reduction' is used in various senses in the literature; and the above definition is nothing more than a proposal of how to use the term in the present context.

Following Popper, I find it helpful to distinguish between methodological reductionism and philosophical reductionism (Popper 1982a). A *methodological* reductionist proposes a reductionistic research program because he considers such a program to possess heuristic value. Making such a proposal does not necessarily imply any ontological commitments. On the other hand, *philosophical or metaphysical* reductionism is based on a particular world view or ontological posit. It assumes essentialism, *i.e.*, the view that ultimate explanations in terms of essences or substances are possible, and that one province of knowledge may be completely derivable from another province. The philosophical reductionist even predicts that, eventually, such a reduction will become possible. Postulating the possibility of ultimate explanation is tantamount to claiming that nothing intrinsically new enters at higher levels. Popper has argued (in my opinion rightly so) that methodological reductionism may, in certain cases, facilitate intellectual progress, while philosophical reductionism is basically mistaken (Popper 1982, 113–174). There cannot be any ultimate explanations since why-questions never lead to an ultimate answers. Rather, solved problems create new problems; this is an unintended consequence of problem solving and, hence, scientific research, like criticism, is an open-ended process. As our knowledge grows, the range of our (as-yet) unsolved problems will expand. We cannot know in advance which of the unsolved problems will turn out to be solvable.

There are various arguments for the *incompleteability thesis* of science or the thesis of problem propagation. A well-known pictorial illustration is the image of a man who draws a map of his writing desk that includes the map he is drawing; this reproduction would have to include that reproduction, and so *ad infinitum* (Popper 1982a, 129; Hayek 1952, 194). Obviously, the drawer cannot complete his task. This image may also illustrate the thesis of the pervasive fallibility of all scientific knowledge, of all knowledge about the empirical world. The map that is included in the other maps becomes smaller and smaller, and the smaller it becomes the greater must be the relative imprecision and the more unpredictable and indeterminate the next small stroke. Another illustration that is often used and is very suggestive is Gödel's theorem of the incompleteability of formalized arithmetic. In every axiom system for number theory, there are some problems that are decidable only in a stronger system; and in this stronger system new but exactly analoguous problems arise. Hence, the view that eventually a complete reduction of one system to another will be possible is mistaken.

Philosophical reductionism is a blind alley. However, it does not follow that our attempts at reduction have necessarily brought only costs and no intellectual gains. We may have learnt something from the partial successes of attempted reductions, and there is a good chance that we may have learnt something from our partial failures. These failures may have led to new and interesting problems. "The quest of science is, therefore, by its nature a never-ending task in which every step ahead with necessity creates new problem." (Hayek, 1952, 194). As Kant emphasized, scientific research has no boundary in the sense of a final, ultimate description or explanation of the world, because solved problems create new problems. Intellectual progress occurs whenever these new problems are "deeper" than the old problems, *i.e.*, the problems that we have been able to solve up to now.

MICROREDUCTIONS

The discussion of the problem of reduction usually refers to microreduction. If so, it hinges on a few central questions. (1) Considering only theories about inanimate nature, is it possible to reduce one of these theories to another theory that deals with entities on a "deeper" or "lower" level of phenomena? For instance, can we reduce chemistry to physics? (Chapters 8 and 9 are devoted to this question.) Is it really the case that the so-called reduction of chemistry to physics turns out to be a reduction to a physics that assumes evolution—cosmogeny—and, hence, also assumes the existence of emergent properties? (2) Is it possible to reduce the life sciences to physics? If the origin of life is a unique event, then biological theories cannot be fully successfully reduced. Following Popper, I submit that with the emergence of life, purpose and problem solving emerge also, because all life involves problem solving (which need not be conscious), and only organisms pursuing some purpose (which need not be done consciously) solve problems for themselves (computers don't). (cf., *e.g.*, Radnitzky 1987b.) (3) Is it possible to reduce theories in animal psychology to biological theories? If animal consciousness is an emergent property, then such reduction cannot be fully successful. (4) Can theories about human consciousness of self be reduced to theories about animal psychology—and then, finally, to chemistry and physics? (Chapter 12 and 13 will deal with these and related problems: "Mind and brain–reduction or correlation?")

A consistent *philosophical* reductionist must deny the existence of phenomenal (mental) entities; and he must also deny the existence of abstract entities such as the contents of thoughts, hypotheses, problems, arguments, etc., apart and beyond their physical embodiment in statements, figures, diagrams, and so forth (*i.e.*, in entities that belong to the world of material phenomena). However, if one denies the existence of abstract entities (Popper's World-3), one must also deny the possibility that a physical theory is invented, that the invention leads to technological changes which, eventually, through the intervention of deliberate human action, produces certain changes in the physical world around us. From such a denial it would follow that these changes must be predestined. Hence, if philosophical reductionism is applied to the mind-body problem, it leads to philosophical behaviorism, a view that is patently false, even absurd. Philosophical reductionists therefore resort either to panpsychism or to denying the existence of consciousness altogether (metaphysical behaviorism or identity theory).

MICROREDUCTION, DOWNWARD CAUSATION, AND CONSCIOUSNESS OF SELF

The stock-taking of the various approaches to the problem of unity and the problem of unification of science has led to the following list. (1) The unity of *aim* and the unity of *method* (*i.e.*, of the global method of problem solving) appear to be unproblematic. These sorts of unity have nothing to do with reductionism. (2) Unification through *language, i.e.*, the program that all results of scientific research should be formulated in a canonical language—essentially a positivist approach—has proved to be a blind alley. (3) Unification through *laws* may be either a program of methodological reductionism or a program of philosophical reductionism. Insofar as it is only a heuristic strategy, it may be useful, at least in certain cases. However, usually it is interpreted as a program of microreduction, and such a program appears to presuppose (4) that there is an *ontological unity*. The corresponding heuristic program advises us to attempt to explain everything in terms of molecular or other elementary particles, finally to reduce all branches of science to elementary particle physics. In this program, statements about the micro-world play a role that is analoguous to that of observation sentences in the positivist program. Its appeal appears to be due to the fact that we think that we understand upward causation, *i.e.*, how substructures of a system cooperate to affect the whole system. According to this program even human consciousness and its manifestations are assumed to be explainable in terms of biology or, finally, in terms of chemistry and physics.

Popper has given strong arguments against that program.[2] Consciousness of self has emerged from a give-and-take process between mental entities on the one hand and abstract entities (theories, problems, arguments, etc.) and also material entities on the other. These abstract entities—linguistically formulated ideas, theories, arguments. etc.—are man-made and have emerged with the emergence of language. However, they possess a partial autonomy, which may be seen as another example of the unintended consequences of action. We have already hinted at one aspect of that partial autonomy when emphasizing that solved problems create new problems. For example, when man invented calculating with natural numbers, he discovered the problem of whether or not there is a highest prime number. Such problems are discovered, not invented. Or to take a more modern example: when attempting to reduce rational fractions to ordered pairs of natural numbers, the reduction turns out to be one to *sets* of equivalent pairs. It made necessary modern set theory—a development which, again, is an example of unintended consequences of action. It also illustrates how attempts at reduction can lead to new and "deeper" problems; in the example, to problems that arise from the antinomies of infinite sets. Thus, the reduction turns out to be a reduction to axiomatic set theory.

But let us return to the argument about the non-reducibility of mental life to biological phenomena. Our mental life is in part shaped by the theories, the abstract entities, which it has created. If the autonomous part of the realm of abstract entities can interact with our mental life, then that mental life cannot be reducible to the physical world or, more accurately speaking, theories about that mental life cannot be reduced to physiological theories. Consciousness of self is based on the theories that the individual develops about himself and about his environment, on the memory of such theories, on theories about the connection between such memories and a unique body and, in particular, on theories about the geno-identity of consecutive items of conscious experience (inspite of interruptions through sleep and periods of unconsciousness). Each individual is biologically unique, and the set of his experiences is likewise unique. What would it mean to reduce statements about a *unique* event at the level of consciousness of self or of human creativity to statements about biological or physical entities? Also this line of thought suggests that we should focus our attention on the problem of intertheoretic relationships rather than on the various programs of reduction. It also prompts us to devote more attention *to downward* causation, *i.e.,* to processes whereby a higher structure operates upon its substructures, and higher-level phenomena have a downward effect upon lower-level phenomena. The choice example of downward causation is a voluntary action within the human organism; another example is the so-called cellular control of molecular activities, which completes our knowledge about the "molecular control of cellular activities". Popper has made the interesting proposal that downward causation can sometimes be explained "as *selection* operating on the randomly fluctuating elementary particles. The randomness of the movements of the elementary particles—often called 'molecular chaos'—provides, as it were, the opening for the higher-level structure to interfere." (Popper 1978, 348). A selection then occurs at the level of higher-level structures: from the repertoire of possible movements or random movements those are whittled away that do not "fit" into the processes occurring at the higher-level structure. (Chapter 10 "Order and Chaos" by Roman Sexl deals with the corresponding problems for physical science.)

The new discipline called *synergetics* examines how throught the interaction of subsystems spatial, temporal, and functional structures are created at the macroscopic level, where they assume properties that are not exemplified at the level of the subsystems—emergent properties. Synergetics focuses on situations in which those structures exhibit a form of self-organization. It does so with a view to discovering the laws that govern those processes of self-organization—laws and processes that are independent of the nature of the subsystems (Haken, 577). Synergetics possesses a unifying potential, because these processes of self-organization occur not only at the level of atoms, molecules, cells, photons, organs, etc., but also on the level of animal behavior and human organization. Hayek's concept of spontaneous order helps us to understand the evolution of order at the level of human organization.

METHODOLOGICAL INDIVIDUALISM VERSUS METHODOLOGICAL HOLISM OR COLLECTIVISM

Downward causation as a voluntary action was mentioned as an example where a kind of behavior is selected from a set of possible behaviors by higher-level structures, by the conscious human being. Humans are "creatures which make, and which cannot but make, choices" (Flew 1985, 5; see also 93–95, 98 f., 103–107). A very high proportion of all behaviors are actions, where it is characteristic of an action that whatever we do, we could have done otherwise. A selection process may select from a repertoire of random events, without being random in its turn. Action in the full sense can be predicated only of human beings. Hence, the properties of collectives and institutions as well as their behavior (their "quasi-actions") are, in principle, explainable by the behavior of individual agents. All social collectives are composed of individuals, and can act only through the actions of their components. "Whatever is said about any mass movements, organized collectivity, or other supposed social whole, must at some stage be related and in some way reduced to discourse about the doings, beliefs, attitudes, and dispositions of its components." (Flew 1985, 43). This assumption is the basis of the approach that usually is labelled *methodological individualism.* (Chapter 14 of this volume critically examines the dispute between Methodological Holism or Methodological Collectivism and Methodological Individualism.)

DISCIPLINARY AND EDUCATIONAL CONSEQUENCES OF SOME FORMS OF REDUCTIONISM

If one predicts that, finally, it will become possible to "reduce" one branch of science to another branch—in particular, if one predicts that microreductions will become possible—then one thereby suggests or appears to suggest that the reducing discipline is "deeper", *i.e.*, deals with a level of reality that is ontologically more fundamental than the level with which the reduced discipline deals. Thus, Koertge points out that "Even when an attempted reduction is not completely successful, the disciplinary and educational consequences can be enormous . . . Practitioners of the secondary science often have reason to fear that their prestige and funding will also be reduced." (Chapter 2 of this volume). The effect will be a cartelization of the institutions that carry scientific research: the universities, the learned journals, and so forth. Cartelization is essentially an attack on competition; and, since competition is not only a selection mechanism but also a discovery process, cartelization in academe hampers scientific progress. Cartelization in the form of protection against criticism in the field of ideas is the intellectual counterpart to protectionism in economic life. Economic protectionism necessarily leads to reduction in national income and in growth; it hampers economic progress and eventually ruins the economy.

In academe, protectionism may, however, also take the form of erecting fences between branches of science and, in particular, of declaring disciplines to be completely independent from each other[3] or even theories to be incommensurable.[4] Because of the connection between positions with respect to the problem of the unity of science (in particular, with respect to the reductionism-emergentism debate on the one hand and science policy on the other) it appeared apposite to place at the beginning of this work a general overview of the problems of science policy and of the values that underlie the scientific enterprise (Alvin Weinberg in Chapter 1). The existence of that connection provides yet another recommendation for focussing on intertheoretic relationships rather than on the problems of reductive unity and ontological unity.

INTERACTIVE UNITY

The program of investigating inter*theoretical* relationships—a program that belongs to the methodology of research—has a counterpart in the program of exploring inter*disciplinary* relationships, which is a program in science policy. It concerns both a science policy that is internal to science and a science policy that is external to science, *i.e.*, it is of interest both to the individual researcher and to the science administrator. Sometimes the label *interactive unity* is used to refer to the fact that two areas of science that have so far appeared to be quite independent of one another are shown to "interact" in unexpected ways. Specialization is necessary, and the division of labor is a prerequisite of efficiency. But specialization should be accompanied by the search for fruitful interactions between fields of studies. If one has experience of one kind, it is rational to attempt to use it as resource when doing something else. This may sometimes result in a new discipline: an example is biochemistry. We may speak of *vertically* connected disciplines. For example, biologists have to know a lot of chemistry, while chemists do not need to know much of biology. Hence, in that case, the flow of epistemic resources tends to be "upward". Certain disciplines are *horizontally* connected. They too can profit from a flow of epistemic resources, but often don't. For instance, botanists and zoologists tend not to read each other's journals. The consequence is that, *e.g.*, work on sex-switches in plants lagged considerably behind work on sex-switches in animals (see Michael Ghiselin, Chapter 1 of Radnitzky and Bernholz, 1987). Scientific progress in the former field would have been faster if the botanists had known more about the work of zoologists; it would have been facilitated by the flow of epistemic resources from zoology to botany.

What hinders that flow of epistemic resources are the costs. Most specialists have enough to do just keeping up with their own field. The acquisition of epistemic resources that might be applicable to his own field causes the researcher both opportunity costs (*i.e.*, the gains in knowledge foregone—gains which would have accrued to him if he had invested his time and effort in research in his own speciality along the same lines as he did before) and resource costs (*i.e.*, the effort of learning new techniques, the time invested in reading journals from neighboring fields, etc.). Hence, the practical problem is *how to reduce the costs of horizontal interaction or unification.* Ghiselin suggests that the costs could be reduced by emphasizing fundamentals and by proposing a group of exemplary problems that could serve as a focus of attention for those with diverse backgrounds. Also a common methodological language might help, paying attention to how key terms, such as 'explanation', 'emergent property', and the like are being used in order to avoid talking past each other. If the opportunities of intellectual progress become generally known, it will be possible to attract intellectual capital to an enterprise that promises high return in new knowledge upon investment of scarce resources of time and effort. However, for this, special institutional arrangements are needed. Multidisciplinary conferences can provide a starting point and a forum. These reflections, again, suggest that it is worthwhile to open this volume with a paper on science policy and on the values underlying the scientific enterprise.

PRE-SUMMARIES

The brief summaries which follow, provide a first orientation regarding the issues discussed in the essays contained in this, the second,
volume on the Unity of the Sciences.

Alvin M. Weinberg begins his essay by making a distinction
between the "practice" of science, *i.e.*, problem solving, and the
"administration" of science, *i.e.*, science policy in the wide sense, in
particular, risky investment decisions. The individual researcher has
to decide in which problems to invest time and effort (cf., *e.g.*,
Radnitzky 1987a), and government agencies or firms have to allocate
scarce resources between disciplines (Radnitzky 1986a). Each of these
branches of activity underlie different values or regulative principles.
The regulative principle that governs research is the quest for getting
closer to the truth, for discovering interesting truths. The utility
function of the science administrator is to realize as much as possible
of the goals set by national policy or by the policy of a firm. Weinberg
then proposes and clarifies criteria that may govern a science policy
that is external to science. They apply primarily to applications-
oriented research. Then he develops the theme of "unity as a value
in administration of pure science". Eventually, Weinberg examines
the question of whether or not his criterion of scientific choice (the
criterion of scientific merit, which he first proposed twenty years ago
and which since then has become well-known and is widely used and
often referred to in the literature) may be generalized in such a way
that it can serve as a model for a criterion of human choice.

In her essay "Is Reductionism the Best Way to Unify Science?"
Noretta Koertge questions the assumption that reduction is a most
important intertheoretical relation. The extreme division of labor in
the scientific enterprise has at the same time brought about a strengthening of the interdisciplinary connections between previously disparate
sciences. It might appear that the ancient metaphor of *the* single,
unified tree of knowledge is about to be realized. What would be the
structure of the tree? And how does the tree of knowledge grow?
Koertge first shows that the positivists' approach failed: by clinging
to the term 'reduction', while clandestinely re-defining it, the positivists
tended to obscure the changes in our understanding of the structure
and the growth of science. Their metaphysical reductionism turned
out to be a blind alley. What about methodological reductionism?
Koertge is able to show that methodological reductionism as a heuristic
approach is *not* always recommendable. She illustrates this claim with
examples culled from the history of chemistry where progress was

made either by ignoring the putative primary science (physics) or by developing theories that were inconsistent with the physics of the time. Thus, the founding of modern chemistry came about by treating problems in chemistry in an autonomous fashion, not by borrowing concepts from physics.

Hence, cognitive progress in the methodology of science is achieved when we move from the various reductionist programs to *intertheoretic criticism*. This is the central thesis of Koertge's essay. Whenever an intertheoretic situation that vaguely approximates "reduction" occurs, the secondary science generally forces changes in the primary science, and at the same time the primary science is correcting the low-level laws. To understand the growth of knowledge, it is essential that we compare and critically assess the results of various theoretical and metaphysical approaches. "Intertheoretic criticism allows us to seek out the exact relationship between mutually relevant scientific theories without prejudging, as does the reductionist program, which one is basic or more apt to be correct."

The second part of Koertge's essay illustrates the benefits of comparing different theoretical approaches. Having discussed problems of the methodology of science in the first part, she turns to different approaches to social science, in particular, to the problem of explaining the origins of a new tradition and of explaining why and how a group adopts an innovation. The approaches that are compared are Skinner's operant conditioning, Marvin Harris's "cultural materialism" (which has certain affinities with Hayek's cultural-evolution-approach), and Popper's rational problem-solving approach (usually labelled 'situational logic'). By comparing the three approaches to the same explanatory problem or to similar explanatory problems, we discover whether they overlap; and we also can produce good reasons for preferring one theory to another. The principal fallibility of every theory is another reason to regard non-dogmatic reductionism as a special case of intertheoretic criticism. However, the methodology of intertheoretic criticism, of course, includes other varieties of theory comparison such as, for instance, the search for inconsistencies between quasi-complementary theories or the attempt to unify purportedly disjoint sciences.

In his comments on Noretta Koertge's essay, Walter B. Weimer agrees that it is time to redirect attention toward the problems of how theories are related and how they succeed one another. He contrasts reductive explanations with other types of explanations such as, *e.g.*, Hayek's *"explanation of the principle"*. Like Hayek, he sees the evolving ensemble of scientific knowledge as basically a spontaneous order. Useful methodological rules restrict themselves to limiting the manoeuvre space of the researcher, but basically they aim at increasing his freedom of decision rather than reducing it. Eventually, Weimer argues that in certain cases reductionistic programs can, nonetheless, add to the growth of knowledge.

In "The Change of the Concept of Reduction in Biology and in the Social Sciences" Werner Leinfellner approaches the general problem of intertheoretic relations from the point of view of the logician. Hence, his essay is bound to be somewhat technical, at least in certain parts. He argues that the "received view" of reduction should be replaced by a comparison of structures, in particular a downward and an upward comparison of structures and functions at different levels. In this way it should become possible to find out how theories that, in their original form, were incompatible theories may, later on, merge into a new theory. He illustrates his theses by examples culled from biology and social science. By analyzing case studies from biology and the social sciences, he wishes to prove that the so-called reductions in biology and in the social sciences are in reality structural comparisons that replace fully what has been called *reduction*. Among his examples are the so-called "reduction" of microeconomics to the Individual's Preference Behavior, the so-called "reduction" of Collective Choice Theory to Individual Choice Theory, the question of the reducibility of the concept of life, and the so-called "reduction" of culture to genes, *i.e.*, the central reduction problem of sociobiology. His main contention is that the various changes in the meaning of *reduction* together with the newest developments of holism in biology force us to rethink, and possibly to replace, the whole method of reduction as well as its materialistic program with a new method of structural comparison and integration.

In his comments on the preceding essay, Larry Briskman critically examines Leinfellner's proposal rather than attempting to reduce levels, to attempt to bridge the gap between upper-level holistic systems and their lower-level parts (subsystems) "by searching for similarities" and by building up "a network of theories or models". Briskman asks, in what sense, the search for, the discovery of, structural similarities or identities is explanatory at all? He raises the searching question: What exactly does the discovery of structural similarities explain? The method of structural modification and comparison appears to consist in attempts to "merge" (or, perhaps, "map") partial aspects of each theory, or model, with (or into) the other. This will usually involve modifying either, or both, of the initial theories so as to produce the potential for "matching". We cannot hope to answer the above-mentioned key question: "What exactly does the discovery of structural similarities explain?" unless the problem situation is specified. "For similarity to bite we must be supplied with some point of view, or problem, or interest from which to judge the question." (L. Briskman). In the absence of a problem we can always find *some* "structural similarities" between theories or models describing different "levels".

Hence, Briskman proposes that, instead of using Leinfellner's approach, we investigate the relation between different theories, or between different "levels", by investigating whether or not reductive explanation can be achieved with respect to them. This attempt can at least lead to failure and so it can offer us the opportunity to learn something. Briskman concludes his comments by stating good reasons for recommending the search for reductive explanations: such searches can fail and probably they will fail, and thereby they will allow emergentism to pass some severe tests. If there should be cases in which the search for reductive explanations succeeds, this will lead to a non-arbitrary modification of the theoretical knowledge that was available before the attempt and thereby to intellectual progress.

The next two essays deal with the problem of the unification of physics. If one wishes to reduce some other discipline to physics, the chances of success of such an attempt at reduction will, to a considerable extent, depend upon the "state of the art" in physics itself.

Bernulf Kanitscheider starts from the problem of how the thesis of the unity of method, *i.e.*, the claim that there is only one global method of problem solving, namely the interplay of creativity and criticism in various forms (cf., Andersson 1984, 1–14), can be combined with the metaphysical assumption that physical reality constitutes a hierachical structure of different layers. By means of examples from the unified theories of physics he attempts to show that his *explicata* of the concepts of "level" and "hierarchy" are fruitful, *i.e.*, that they help us to answer the above-mentioned question.

Kanitscheider argues that theoretical reflections as well as experimental findings in physics support the metaphysical conjecture that nature is stratified. Nature appears to contain a level structure, where each level appears to have certain properties of its own and particular laws governing processes. Insofar as the metaphysical hypothesis that nature can be regarded as an interacting whole divided in several layers in which the forces among the particular constitutents engender emergent qualities is accurate, physical science must attempt to devise explanations of the material relations obtaining between the interacting layers. Kanitscheider contrasts two epistemological approaches: "methodological separatism" and "methodological unificationism". The former recommends that physical science should concentrate on intra-level explanations; the latter recommends that we also take into account inter-level explanations, because they are indispensable for a deeper understanding of nature. With the help of many examples culled from the history of physics as well as from current theoretical physics, in particular, from elementary particle physics and cosmology, Kanitscheider shows that "methodological separatism" as a research program would have to leave unaccounted for many items of information about the world that are contained in the surplus meaning of the stronger unified theories. He comes to the conclusion that unification is not an aesthetic luxury, but a global research program without which a deeper understanding of nature is not possible.

The unification of physics exhibits the following main features: It is concerned only with "mild" reductionism, because a structure can be real, even if it is not basic. It is concerned with coherence, because it is the connexity of the level structure of nature that renders it intelligible. The micro-world of elementary particles (strong and weak interactions), the molar world of bulk matter (electromagnetic interactions) and the world of megaphysics (ruled by gravity) would be separated if there were no interconnexity. Unification is concerned with surplus meaning. A host of phenomena would be unknowable, if we renounced the stronger unified theories. Unification is connected with simplicity. In physics, unification means going up to a domain of higher energy. The gauge theory description reveals that the world becomes more "simple" at extreme energies. Kanitscheider shows that certain fundamental puzzles of classical cosmologies get a new, interesting solution if analyzed with the help of the grand unified theories. Unification is also concerned with evolution. At a late stage of development the universe, which in the beginning was very simple and symmetric, evolved into a hierarchy of systems with growing complexity. Unified physics should explain why and how these different levels emerged. For this task, morphogenetic theories like synergetics (see Chapter 10), non-linear thermodynamics, and catastrophe theory are needed.

In his comments on Kanitscheider's essay, Max Jammer begins by pointing out that all great breakthroughs in science were coupled with unifications: Newtonian theory originated from a fusion of terrestrial and planetary motions into a unified theory of mechanics; the emergence of field theories led to a unified treatment of electricity, magnetism, and light; special relativity theory produced a unified notion of space-time; and quantum mechanics may be viewed as a formalism unifying the corpuscular and the ondulatory aspects of physical reality. From the system-theoretical viewpoint, unity of science is granted, not by an utopian reduction of all sciences to physics and chemistry, but by the structural uniformities of the different levels of reality. Max Jammer is in general agreement with Bernulf Kanitscheider's paper; he elaborates and illuminates several of the subthemes, some of them from the viewpoint of the history of physics.

Hans Primas analyzes the alleged reduction of chemistry to quantum mechanics in "Can We Reduce Chemistry to Physics?" Within the formation of quantum-mechanical theories, holism is in harmony with reductionism. Quantum mechanics is a well-defined holistic theory, and non-Boolian theory reduction represents a sophisticated variant of reductionism. In the classical domain there are a few rigorously worked-out examples that show that the emergence of essential novelty in a higher-level description is a compelling consequence of quantum mechanics. (A property is an "emergent" property in the weak sense if it is a novel property that a system possesses while its parts, or subsystems, do not possess it. A property is "emergent" in the strong and interesting sense if it is in principle impossible to predict its coming into existence from any knowledge about previously existing entities, however complete and accurate that knowledge may be.)

Primas argues that (1) quantum mechanics as a holistic theory describes the world as an undivided whole, and any analysis of it into parts requires an abstraction from some factually existing Einstein-Podolsky-Rosen correlations; (2) most of the theoretical concepts of chemistry have not (yet) been reduced to quantum mechanics, and that it is doubtful whether a completely successful reduction will ever be achieved; (3) some of the theoretical concepts of chemistry have been related in a rigorous way to quantum mechanics; (4) all known cases of (partially) successful reductions of chemical theories hinge upon singular assymtotic expansions that accentuate particular viewpoints. Thus, it may be held that chemistry can be reduced to quantum mechanics only if we adopt the research program of methodological reductionism. However, this may constitute a fruitful research program only if one does now allow it to degenerate into metaphysical reductionism, which is dogmatic. In this way Primas endorses Kanitscheider's position that, when attempting a "reduction", one does not need at the same time to deny ontological status to the entities of the reduced theory. (Cf. hereto also Popper 1963, 115.)

Marcelo Alonso comments on Primas's essay. Then Primas replies to Alonso's comments in the form of a rejoinder. One of the bones of contention is the question of what exactly is to be understood by 'quantum mechanics', i.e., a fruitful explication or programmatic delimitation of a particular problem cluster or discipline. The debate provides some deep insights into the methodological aspects of the problem of the "reduction" of chemistry to quantum mechanics. Since such a discussion is bound to be somewhat technical, at least in parts, it is impossible to do justice to it by the few sentences that can be devoted to it in this Introduction.

Classical physics saw the world as a regular, deterministic clockwork, ruled by Newtonian laws. This view changed dramatically, even as far as classical mechanics is concerned, with the discovery of chaotic systems. The problems that dominate the textbooks of mechanics, *i.e.*, the harmonic oscillator or the planetary system, have turned out to be rather special and singular cases of a calculable physical system in the midst of a world of chaos. Chaotic systems are so sensitive to small pertubations from outside that they cannot be meaningfully separated from the rest of the universe, and their behavior cannot be predicted in detail. Thus, chaotic systems, which have unpredictable properties due to their violent response to slight external perturbations, turned out to be a general and characteristic case of mechanical systems.

In his essay, Roman Sexl shows that behind the chaos there is a new type of order, the "soft order". It is a spontaneous order, the order exemplified, for instance, by the delicate balance of regularity and individuality in snowflakes. These soft orderings unite regular and individual traits. Mathematically, soft order can be dealt with with the help of non-linear differential equations that were studied by Prigogine, Eigen (both Nobel Laureates, who have been chairmen of working groups at previous International Conferences on the Unity of the Sciences), by Schuster, and by Hermann Haken, who coined the name 'synergetics' for the new discipline.

Roman Sexl outlines these three approaches to the understanding of how spontaneous orders emerge from chaos. For Haken the laser was the prototype of a spontaneous transition to order. Synergetics provides us with a terminology and with models for the *emergence of genuinely new properties*—emergent properties in the strong sense—of a system, properties that cannot be predicted from the properties of its subsystem, because they arise from amplification of small perturbations. What we find is that instable dynamical systems possess completely new properties, that these properties emerge in systems far from equilibrium; and that we, in principle, cannot predict the new type of property that emerges. At best we can explain its emergence, a fact which is of great importance for all disciplines that deal with entities that have a strong historical component, and that deal with contingent processes. Roman Sexl outlines the implications of these new phenomena for the relationship between physics, biology, philosophy, and the reduction problem.

In his comments on Sexl's essay, Erwin Schopper reminds us that it was essential for the development of physics that it began by studying systems that represent fairly good idealizations of the classical two-body system. Weakly disturbed two-body systems can, in many problem situations, be treated *as if* they were closed systems (like free fall planetary motion). Schopper also points out that, for instance, snowflakes can be made identical in the laboratory, but under natural conditions minute differences in density and temperature preclude such qualitative identity.)

Although unification of physics has not been achieved, important progress has been made toward the unification of forces. There are limits to unification, because in complicated systems it is not so much the forces that predominate, but rather the initial conditions. This applies in particular to all systems that have a history as well as to all contingent processes. Although the stars and the earth have a history, this insight is of particular importance for *biological* systems and for the explanation of *human* phenomena. Moreover, a unification does not lead to a reduction in the technical sense, because all theories are modified when they are reduced to a more general theory.

These reflections pave the way for addressing the problem of how to relate disciplines at different levels of phenomena, in particular, when confronted with the problem of the mind-brain interface. Percy Löwenhard's essay explicitly raises the question: Mind and brain—reduction or correlation? He leaves it unanswered, in part because certain results of psychophysics suggest that more than simple correlation is involved. The first part of his paper examines the role of matter, energy, and entropy in self-organizing living systems. Living systems are conceived as hierarchically organized systems, biochemical systems that are largely self-sustaining, and which have in common such properties as metabolism, reproduction, mutability, and interaction between functional elements (proteins) and carriers of information (DNA, RNA). Different organisms, then, vary with respect to additional characteristics such as activity, reactivity, locomotion, program-controlled growth, behavioral modifications through learning, consciousness, etc.

Löwenhard conceives mind as a manifestation of the brain. The central phenomenon in the realm of "mind", *i.e.*, consciousness, presupposes life. For the intuitive concepts of "life" and "consciousness", different explicata are offered in studies that deal with phenomena at different levels of phylogenetic evolution. In certain contexts consciousness may be viewed as a mode of information-processing in the brain, whereby the brain is conceived as an autoanalytic instrument, which is capable of detecting its own states. At least human beings have in their conscious states access to two sources of information: internal information gained from introspection and external information, which is derived with the help of scientific theories from a study of electrophysiological and biochemical recordings. Löwenhard argues that the situation can be analyzed with the help of a model in which the manifestations of mind (phenomenal entities like mental events and contents, feelings, and so on) are correlates of certain brain states.

If the emergence of consciousness has evolutionary significance, it should be possible to show that consciousness provides an adaptive advantage for the organisms that possess consciousness, especially consciousness of self. In his comments on Löwenhard's paper, Franz Wuketits emphasizes the difficulties associated with the various explicata that have been proposed for the concept of "emergent property". Wuketits's essay also shows that the empirical and the methodological study of the problem of the mind-brain interface eventually leads to ontological problems. Those who view mind as basically an epiphenomenon thereby have implicitly opted for a materialist ontology, a position that may appear even less attractive than an idealistic position, *i.e.*, a position that would grant full ontological status only to phenomenal or mental entities. After all, a mental event can be located only through other mental events, and this way of locating it is distinct from the way in which physical events can be located; hence, it appears impossible in principle to "reduce" one side to the other.

The papers dealing with the life sciences also provide a bridge to the study of the problem of the unity of science as it poses itself in the social sciences. 'Social sciences' is a label for a heterogeneous group of studies that range from empirical investigations that would qualify as *science* even in the restricted Anglo-Saxon use of the word, through interpretations, to "social science as public opinion" (in Edward Shils's apt formulation). In the methodology of the social sciences the problem of inter-theoretic relation poses itself in the form of the competition between the holistic or collectivist approach and methodological individualism. The research program of methodological individualism is based upon the fact that only individuals can act in the full sense of acting and that, therefore, the social scientist should attempt to explain collective phenomena like the emergence of collectives (such as families or societies) and their properties and behavior in terms of the actions of individuals and the relations between individuals. Thereby a considerable number of social phenomena (collective phenomena) can be explained as *unintended* consequences of the actions and interactions of individuals. Such typical sociological questions as, for instance: Why does the suicide rate vary between nations? Why are all societies stratified? These can be adequately answered by explanations in terms of individual actions.

Karl-Dieter Opp contrasts the basic model of methodological individualism with the collectivist research program (exemplified by Marxism and functionalism). In the literature, the basic model of methodological individualism is often referred to as the "Rational Choice Model," the "rational problem-solving approach," or the "economic approach". In economics it is often called the *REMM-model: R*esourceful, *E*valuating, *M*aximizing *M*an (Karl Brunner). The key idea is that human beings strive to improve their lot, and, since they always operate in a situation of scarcity, economizing scarce means is imperative. The model does not attempt to explain the origin of a particular preference structure. Karl-Dieter Opp investigates what reasons sociologists could have for not making use of the Rational Choice Model. He finds the reasons that can be extracted from the literature to be not satisfactory. He then confronts the Rational Choice Model with a widely accepted sociological model and assesses the achievements of each of these approaches. He also lists certain areas of problems where the application of the Rational Choice Model has met with certain difficulties. It turns out that with the help of the Rational Choice Model we can explain why the "sociological model of man" ('SM'-model for short), *i.e.*, the model that depicts man as essentially a rule-follower, is successful in a limited range (e.g., life in a tradition-governed tribe, conventional manners, etc.). It can also explain why the SM-model is not successful outside that particular area. Hence, the Rational Choice Model has a considerable unifying potential for the social sciences and even for all of the human sciences[5].

In his response to the above essay Angelo Maria Petroni criticizes the expected utility theory, which he claims to be the foundation of the individualist research program in the form in which it is outlined in Opp's essay. Petroni points out the the original expected utility theory is confronted with many difficulties and that some reformulations have been produced with a view to accommodate the discrepancies between observed choice behavior under uncertainty and the axioms of expected utility theory. He then goes on to examine some of these reformulations and also supplies ample references to the relevant literature. He suggests that what Opp's individual research program presupposes is an unformalized and "broad" utility theory, not one of the family of expected utility theories in the technical sense. Petroni then raises the problem of the so-called Rationality Principle: "*Any* utility theory presupposes this principle in one of its versions, and therefore also methodological individualism as it has been presented by Professor Opp needs it." (A.M. Petroni). Karl Popper's and Herbert Simon's version of the rationality principle are discussed.

The topics discussed by Opp and Petroni suggest that a closer look into the ecology of rationality in the social sciences is called for. Raymond Boudon embarked on this task in his essay "Explanation, Interpretation and Understanding in the Social Sciences." The methodological concepts of explanation and interpretation have several meanings in the social sciences. Among the adequacy criteria of scientific explanation is the requirement that all statements of the argument that constitutes an explanation be "true", or more realistically, be sufficiently corroborated. If a sequence of staments is called an *interpretation*, it is thereby suggested that subjective opinions of the analyst influence its content.

Raymond Boudon claims that interpretations play an important role in actual social science research, but that they are often mistaken for explanations and that, therefore, it is important to make a clear distinction between explanations and interpretations. While Boudon thus recognizes the importance of interpretations in social science research, he emphasizes that the aim of social science is to provide explanations. Boudon explicates the distinction between explanation and interpretation by introducing the concepts of strong explanation and weak explanation. A sequence of statements in the form of an argument qualifies as a strong explanation if the general statements in the premises are "acceptable" or plausible or sufficiently corroborated and no rival law-hypotheses are available. A weak explanation or interpretation has the same logical structure as a strong explanation, but some of its premises are *ad hoc* or lack empirical corroboration and/or there exist attractive rival law-hypotheses, which offer themselves as alternatives. Boudon then provides examples of each of these types of arguments from the literature in the social sciences, in particular, examples from Tocqueville and from Max Weber. Some of his examples also illustrate the thesis that success in the sociological sense (*i.e.*, increase in the researcher's reputation) and intellectual success (*i.e.*, scientific progress achieved) do not always correlate. For example, Max Weber's thesis on the influence of Protestantism on capitalism is an example of an explanation in the weak sense, and it is beset with many insufficiencies. Yet, it is famous. In contrast, Weber's work *Protestant Sects in America* provides a strong explanation of high validity; yet it has received relatively little attention by the scientific community. Boudon also shows that intellectuals and the public often mistake ideological doctrines for strong explanations, in particular if these doctrines are presented in the form of an explanation. For example, R. Nurske's "theory of the vicious circle of poverty" (which got even more prestige when the Nobel Laureate Samuelson formalized it) can be shown to have primarily an ideological function. Its key premises look like analytic truths, but upon analysis they turn out to be based upon implicit assumptions that are patently false. The ideological function of many of such pseudo-explanations may explain why "interpretations" are often given more validity and credibility than they deserve.

In his comments on the above essay, Alain Boyer agrees with the individualistic research program advocated by Boudon and also with his emphasis on the concept of unintended consequences. He draws attention to certain methodological problems associated with Boudon's approach. For instance, he points out that interpretations suggest that a general law has been discovered while, in fact, the explanation is weak precisely because it fails to explain the singularity of the case. He also points out that the difference between a weak and a strong explanation is more one of degree than of quality. The role of models in historiography is also illuminated in Boyer's essay.

Many of the examples in both Boudon's and Boyer's essays were culled from historiography. 'History', like 'social science', is a label for a heterogeneous group of studies. These studies range from criticism of sources, which are often close to being "scientific" in the restricted Anglo-Saxon sense, to global interpretations with important aesthetic and dramatic dimensions. As a specialist in time-related changes, the historian has a privileged position in the unity of science, for all explanations must have a historical, i.e., a narrative character. This assertion is one of the key theses in Peter Munz's essay. Explanations in history must be distinguished from explanations of history. The former deal with parts of a narrative; the latter with the totality of everything that has happened and which is, as such, not amenable to explanation. Munz gives a tentative list of the major adequacy criteria of an explanatory strategy. He then gives a survey of competing strategies of explanation used in history. He describes and criticizes six strategies and one program in which historical events are considered to be so unique that explanations become impossible. He comes to the conclusion that only the so-called Covering Law Model of explanation meets the adequacy criteria which he has proposed. This model has unexpected uses outside the narrow field of explanation. It provides a structure for narration; it underpins the intelligibility of narration; and it provides a useful heuristic tool for the historian.

Munz then examines the major objections that have been raised against the Covering Law Model. He comes to the conclusion that

the Covering Law Model has withstood criticism better than the other
models have, and that by throwing light on the traditional hermeneutic
problems it makes an important contribution to the unity of scientific
method. It can solve the alleged antithesis between *Verstehen* and
Erklären (understanding and explanation); it improves on the theory
of situational logic, and it obliges us to set up two postulates in order
to guard the empirical content of the general laws employed in the
Covering Law Model.

In her response to the preceding essay, Eileen Barker elaborates
aspects of reductionism in history and draws attention to the limited
realm of applicability of certain types of covering laws used in historical
and culturological explanations. Barker's essay helps one to recognize
the importance of self-reflection of science. Thus, it paves the way
for the two final essays in this volume, and it also makes us see how
important the self-reflection of the methodologist is. Her paper achieves
this by first pointing out that to understand the individual (psychology)
one has to understand the whole culture. In order to understand how
the particular culture works, it is necessary to see it as a Gestalt, and
also to understand the extent to which people throughout history
have seen the world through culturally specific spectacles. To look
at "what they really see" *without* being aware of these spectacles is
to miss out on a crucial element in explaining what they are doing.
(Incidentally, this influence of "spectacles" might be viewed as a
special form of downward causation.) By introducing these issues
Barker makes it imperative to examine the well-known theses of
Thomas Kuhn, a theme dealt with in the following essay by Ian
Jarvie.

Ian Jarvie in his essay, "Explanation, Reduction and the Sociological Turn in the Philosophy of Science or Kuhn as Ideologue of
Merton's Theory of Science," explores the way in which ideas are
received by the scientific community. (In the phrase "the sociological
turn in the philosophy of science" it would be appropriate to place
the expression 'philosophy of science' in scare quotes, since those
who have executed that turn have practically abandoned the philosophy of science.) Jarvie's essay invokes the distinction between success
in the abstract sense (*i.e.*, scientific progress) and success in the sociological sense (*i.e.*, in the sense of recognition by the scientific
community, increase in reputation, and the like)—a distinction that
has been mentioned in connection with Boudon's essay. Success in
the sociological sense depends not only and often not even primarily,
on the scientific merit of the product, but essentially on the marketing
and, last but by no means least, upon whether at the time there exists
a receptive market for certain ideas. Jarvie illustrates some of his

main theses by the case of Thomas Kuhn, whose work has been enormously influential in the philosophy of science Establishment, but has not received much favor from natural scientists or economists.[6]

Jarvie asks: can ideas be eliminated from sociological reductions of science? He argues that they cannot without those reductive explanations becoming incoherent. His essay focusses on the work of Robert Merton, who has tended to overlook ideas in his search for social variables that will explain the rise of science. His overlooking them may have encouraged such extreme views as those of the contemporary Edinburgh School, who acknowledge no barrier to explaining scientific ideas as mere sociological epiphenomena. Less extreme than these, Merton nevertheless in his recent study of the rise of the science of the sociology of science, through the particular careers of Popper and Kuhn, does not refer to their ideas. Jarvie analyzes his arguments. Merton sees the possession of talent and the production of ideas that are not ahead of their time as being crucial to explain Popper's lack of influence in the sociology of science and Kuhn's immense influence. But Popper does not lack talent; and the concept of being ahead of one's time is vague. Yet, Popper failed to gain the "communicative advantage" that Kuhn did. To give a better explanation of this differential success, Jarvie's paper makes the functionalist point that the reception of ideas may be explained by their capacity to serve a social formation. Kuhn's ideas—which legitimated "normal science" as a respectable intellectual activity which was hence deserving of funding—served the growing profession of science and its desire for funding. Popper's ideas, by contrast, presented a challenge to the authority of science and raised fundamental questions of the legitimacy of its growth and its funding. This test case illustrates the need to treat ideas as an independent variable in sociological studies of science.

In the closing essay, Peter Munz sets the problem in a wider historical perspective: he explains the extraordinary success of Kuhn's sociological theory of knowledge by placing it in its historical context. In the Age of Enlightenment, philosophers became as sceptical of scientific thought as they had become of religious thought. They realized that it was easier to acquire knowledge than to explain the method of acquisition. Theories of empiricism proved as inadequate as theories of innate ideas.

In the decades that followed the French Revolution, the study of society had moved into the foreground, and philosophers began to wonder whether knowledge might be explained as a function of social experience. This quest was reinforced by the notion that social experiences are more accessible than natural phenomena. The recourse to society recommended itself because it seemed able to explain the acquisition of knowledge and the maintenance of knowledge where all other theories had failed. The grip of sociology on the theory of knowledge was further strengthened by the belief that the value of knowledge depends on the quality of its sources (the so-called "genetic fallacy"). The recourse or retreat to sociology would have been less persistent if only that belief had been abandoned (*i.e.*, if the "genetic fallacy" would have been recognized for what it is) and if people had also recognized that the scientific merit of a piece of knowledge and hence its value as an epistemic resource, depend on the degree to which it can withstand criticism, *i.e.*, on what happens *after* the formulation of the statements under consideration.

As it was, the recourse to sociology can be divided into three phases. In the first phase, society was invoked as an explanation of knowledge in order to "emancipate" mankind from false beliefs. In this stage, the purpose of the sociology of knowledge follows in the footsteps of the Enlightenment. In the second phase, specific features of social order were invoked in order to explain knowledge and to account sociologically for standards of plausibility. In the third phase, the phenomenon of society itself was taken to explain any knowledge we have, because all meaning was taken to be determined by the fact that language, like society, is a rule-following habit—a "language game." Building upon the later philosophy of Wittgenstein, Kuhn's theory dominates the third phase. Kuhn, being less of a historicist than Foucault, conceives "paradigm changes" (roughly) as due to changes of fashions.

Peter Munz ends his survey with a consideration of factors in the acquisition of knowledge that can be accounted for by the *absence* rather than by the presence of certain social institutions. Thus, the recent development in the sociology of ideas began with the emancipatory turn, and through the explanatory turn it led to the "relativistic" or deterministic turn. The latter is inspired by the later philosophy of Wittgenstein, in particular, by his idea of forms of life that are "incommensurable" and hence can be criticized only from within. Munz sees Michel Foucault and Kuhn as representatives of this last phase, the Wittgensteinian turn in the so-called "sociology of knowledge", which, more correctly, should be called 'sociology of belief '.

Concluding Remarks

Thus, this volume ends with the self-reflection of the methodology of research or the philosophy of science. The spirit of the early Greek philosophy of nature, which was invoked in the opening section of this Introduction, was scientific and realistic. They searched for truth;

and they operated with the commonsense notion of truth, according to which a true statement is one that accurately describes a particular state of affairs. They were epistemological realists, *i.e.;* they believed that the structure of the external world and the processes in nature were not influenced by knowing processes, that, for instance, the planets move as they do without being influenced by our knowing or not knowing about them. They embraced both methodological reductionism and metaphysical reductionism. Eventually, man came to learn that it was extremely unlikely that a completely successful reduction of one discipline to another discipline (on a "deeper or higher level of reality") would ever become possible. Some would hold (in my opinion rightly so) that that is impossible in principle, because of the phenomenon of emergence.

The last two essays show that, if you make a *tour d'horizon* of contemporary intellectual trends or schools or fashions, you will find some intellectual and scientific progress, but also some regressions. Certain schools of thought like the so-called "sociology of knowledge" (or more accurately speaking, the "sociology of belief") operate with a consensus criterion of "truth" (scare quotes around the word 'truth'). That school and many others have opted for various sorts of scepticism such as, for instance, the instrumentalist view of theories, the Incommensurability Thesis (of theories or paradigmata), sociological or historical relativism, and so forth. The roots of this widespread tendency of relativism appears to be the fusion of truth and certainty combined with a craving for certainty, a utopian concept and ideal knowledge according to which genuine knowledge is certain knowledge.[7] If one recognizes that such knowledge cannot be provided by empirical enquiry, yet is unable to free oneself of the utopian ideal of knowledge, then one concludes that scepticism is the only intellectually respectable position. However, there is a third option: to retain the concept of absolute truth as a regulative principle, while at the same time admitting that the methods for ascertaining the truth value of particular statements are, in principle, fallible, and that, hence, all human knowledge is fallible. The task is *not to prove* our knowledge, *but to improve* it. Our philosophical knowledge cannot be improved if we do not take into account developments in science; on the other hand, our scientific research continuously involves methodological appraisals and decisions. (Cf., *e.g.*, Bartley 1987a, Radnitsky 1988.)

It is hoped that this series of volumes devoted to the approaches to the unity of the sciences and the unity of knowledge will stimulate both scientists and philosophers to reflect on the interface of science and philosophy. As already mentioned, the present volume is the second in a series of several volumes on the Unity of the Sciences. The first two volumes pay special attention to the methodological aspects of the problem; the first focusses on the unifying potential of the evolutionary perspective and of the economic approach[8]. The third volume attends to organization and change in complex systems, in particular, to the problem of how the universe proceeds slowly up the staircase of complexity. The fourth volume illuminates other aspects of the theme of the Unity of the Sciences by exploring the concepts and theories of symmetry, energy and entropy (queen and shadow of the universe) and of space-time. The third and fourth volumes are edited by Marcelo Alonso. Other volumes are in preparation.

NOTES

1. Some of the problems thrown up by this line of thought such as, *e.g.*, the question of the origin of large structures in the universe and the problem of the origin of order in the universe will be dealt with in detail in the third volume in this series on the Unity of the Sciences.

2. Cf., *e.g.*, Popper "Natural selection and the emergence of mind", Chapter 6 of Radnitzky and Bartley 1987 (originally in *Dialectica* 32 (1978):348); see also Petersen 1983.

3. This form of protectionism in academe has been criticized by W.W. Bartley, III in Chapter 5 of *Centripetal Forces in the Sciences*, the first volume in this series Approaches to the Unity of the Sciences.

4. A decisive criticism of the "Incommensurability Thesis" is given in Andersson 1988, in particular, in section 5.3.2.

5. Related problems are dealt with in Chapters 12 through 17 in the above-mentioned volume *Centripetal Forces in the Sciences;* and the unifying potential of the economic approach is in detail explored in Radnitzky and Bernholz 1987.

6. In the opinion of this author, Kuhn's work has been extremely overrated. Andersson in Andersson 1988 shows that Kuhn's criticism of falsificationism is based on two methodological problems: the problem of the theory-impregnatedness of experience and the problem created by the thesis of the alleged immunity of theories or paradigmata from criticism, at least during periods of "normal science", which thesis eventually leads to the Incommensurability Thesis. The thesis of the theory-impregnatedness of experience and of the principal revisability of basic statements is in full agreement with pervasive fallibilism, the view that the methods of ascer-

taining the truth value of a statement are in principle fallible. It need not lead to relativism, if it is possible to solve the problem of how basic statements can be criticized—and this problem has been solved. Insofar as Kuhn's research strategy (for "normal science") consists in recommending slight modifications of the falsified theory, it is in agreement with falsificationism. If so, many of the examples from history of science, that Kuhn provides turn out to be irrelevant: they do not show what they purport to show. In the above-mentioned work, Andersson shows that the choice examples of Kuhn (*e.g.*, the alleged incommensurability of the Copernican and the Ptolemean theories) can be analyzed with the help of a falsificationist methodology and that that analysis is by far superior to the interpretation offered by Kuhn. See also Radnitzky 1988.

7. The so-called "sociology of knowledge" is critically examined in more detail in Radnitzky and Bartley. eds. 1987, Part III, entitled "Rationality and the Sociology of Knowledge".

8. The expanding domain of the economics is investigated in detail in Radnitzky and Bernholz, eds. 1987.

REFERENCES

Andersson, G., ed. 1984. *Rationality in Science and Politics.* Volume 79, *Boston Studies in the Philosophy of Science.* Dordrecht: Reidel.

Andersson, G. 1988. *Kritik und Wissenschaftsgeschichte. Kuhns, Lakatos' und Feyerabends Kritik des kritischen Rationalismus.* Tübingen: Mohr.

Bartley, W.W., III. 1984. *The Retreat to Commitment.* New York: Alfred A. Knopf, 1962, Second Edition with 100-pp. Appendix, LaSalle: Open Court.

Bartley, W.W., III. 1984. "Logical Strength and Demarcation." In Andersson, *Rationality:* 69–94.

Bartley, W.W., III. 1987a. "Philosophy of Biology *versus* Philosophy of Physics." In Radnitzky and Bartley, *Evolutionary Epistemology:* 7–45.

Bartley, W.W., III. 1987b. "Alienation Alienated: The Economics of Knowledge versus the Psychology and Sociology of Knowledge." In Radnitzky and Bartley, *Evolutionary Epistemology:* 423–451.

Bartley, W.W., III. 1987c. "The Division of Knowledge." In Radnitzky, *Centripetal Forces:* 67–102.

Bég, M. 1984. "Teorie unificate." *Enciclopedia del Novecento.* Volume VII: 550–572. Roma: Istituto della Enciclopedia Italiana.

Diemer, A. *et al.*, eds. 1971. *Der Methoden—und Theorienpluralismus in den Wisenschaften.* Meisenheim am Glain: Verlag Anton Hain.

Egidi, R. 1979. *Il Linguaggio delle Teorie Scientifiche.* Napoli: Guida Editori.

Flew, A. 1985. *Thinking about Social Thinking. The Philosophy of the Social Sciences.* Oxford: Blackwell.

Haken, H. 1984. "Termodinamica irreversibile e sinergetica." *Enciclopedia del Novecento.* Volume VII: 573–591. Roma: Instituto della Enciclopedia Italiana.

Hayek, F. 1952. *The Sensory Order.* Chicago: University of Chicago Press.

Hirshleifer, J. 1985. "The Expanding Domain of Economics." *The American Economic Review.* 75:53–68

Hirshleifer, J. 1987. "The Economic Approach to Conflict." In Radnitzky and Bartley, eds. *Economic Imperialism:* 335–364.

Hoyningen-Huene, P. und Hirsch, G. eds. 1988. *Wozu Wissenschaftsphilosophie?* Berlin: W. de Gruyter.

Jarvie, I. 1988. "Evolutionary Epistemology." *Critical Review* 2:92–102.

Munz, P. 1985. *Our Knowledge of the Growth of Knowledge.* London: Routledge and Kegan Paul.

Petersen, A. 1983. "On Downward Causation in Biological and Behavioral Systems." *History and Philosophy of the Life Sciences* 5:69–86.

Popper, K.R. 1963. *Conjectures and Refutations.* London: Routledge and Kegan Paul.

Popper, K.R. 1972. *Objective Knowledge. An Evolutionary Approach.* Fifth Revised Edition. 1979, London: Oxford University Press.

Popper, K.R. 1982a. *Postscript to The Logic of Scientific Discovery.* Volume II: *The Open Universe. An Argument for Indeterminism.* Edited by Bartley, W.W., III. LaSalle: Open Court.

Popper, K.R. 1982b. "Indeterminism Is not Enough: An Afterword." In Popper 1982a, *Postscript II:* 113–130.

Popper, K.R. 1982c. "Scientific Reduction and the Essential Incompleteness of all Science." In Popper 1982a, *Postscript II:* 131–174.

Popper, K.R. 1984. "Against Induction: One of Many Arguments." In Andersson, *Rationality:* 245–249.

Popper, K.R. 1978. "Natural Selection and the Emergence of Mind." *Dialectica* 22:339–355, repr. in Radnitzky and Bartley eds. 1987, pp. 139–161.

Radnitzky, G. 1968. *Contemporary Schools of Metascience.* New York: Humanities. Revised and enlarged edition. Chicago: Regnery, 1973.

Radnitzky, G. 1971. "Theorienpluralismus-Theorienmonismus: Einer der Faktoren, die den ForschungsprozeB beeinflussen und die selbst von Weltbildannahmen abhãngig sind." In Diemer, *Der Methoden- und Theorienpluralismus:* 135–184.

Radnitzky, G. 1983. "Science, Technology, and Political Responsibility." *Minerva* 21:234–264.

Radnitzky, G. 1985. "Réflexions sur Popper. Le savoir, conjectural mais objectif, et indépendent de toute question: Qui y croit? Qui est à son origine?" *Archives de Philosophie* 48:79–108.

Radnitzky, G. 1986a. "Responsibility in Science and in Decisions about the Use or Non-use of Technologies." *The World & I. A Chronicle of Our Changing Era:* 649–675.

Radnitzky, G. 1987a. "Cost-Benefit Thinking in the Methodology of Research: The "Economic Approach" Applied to Key Problems of the Philosophy of Science." In Radnitzky and Bernholz, *Economic Imperialism:* 283–331.

Radnitzky, G. 1987b. "Erkenntnistheoretische Probleme im Lichte von Evolutionstheorie und Ökonomie." In Riedl und Wuketits eds. *Die evolutionare Erkenntnistheorie:* 115–132.

Radnitsky, G. 1987c. *Entre Wittgenstein et Popper: Détours vers la decouverte— le vrai le faux, l'hypothèse.* Paris: Urin.

Radnitzky, G. 1988. "Wozu Wissenschaftstheorie? Die Falsifikationistische Methodologie im Lichte des Ökonomischen Ansatzes." In Hoyningen-Huene und Hirsch eds. *Wozu Wissenschaftsphilosophie:* forthcoming.

Radnitzky, G. ed. 1987. *Centripetal Forces in the Sciences.* New York: Paragon House Publishers.

Radnitzky, G. and Andersson, G., eds. 1978. *Progress and Rationality in Science.* Volume 58, *Boston Studies in the Philosophy of Science.* Dordrecht: Reidel.

Radnitzky, G. and Andersson, G., eds. 1979. *The Structure and Development of Science.* Volume 59, *Boston Studies in the Philosophy of Science.* Dordrecht: Reidel.

Radnitzky, G. and Bartley, W.W., III eds. 1987. *Evolutionary Epistemology, Theory of Rationality and the Sociology of Knowledge.* LaSalle: Open Court.

Radnitzky, G., and P. Bernholz, eds. 1987. *Economic Imperialism: The Economic Approach Applied Outside the Field of Economics.* New York: Paragon House Publishers.

Riedl, R. und F. Wuketits, eds. 1987. *Die evolutionäre Erkenntnistheorie.* Hamburg: Parey.

Part 1

PROBLEMS OF THE UNIFICATION OF SCIENCE AND OF REDUCTIONISM IN THE LIGHT OF METHODOLOGY OF RESEARCH AND OF SCIENCE POLICY

1

Values in Science: Unity as a Value in Administration of Pure Science

ALVIN M. WEINBERG

THE TWO ASPECTS OF SCIENCE

Science is both its Administration and its Practice. By Administration of science, I mean not the housekeeping of science, but rather the art of choosing, among the infinitely many possible questions answerable by science, which questions to ask. By the Practice of science I mean the actual conduct of the research: theorizing, observing, measuring, interpreting results, and communicating results. (Note that I shall use Administration and Practice in a somewhat specialized sense. I therefore capitalize these words.) Otherwise put, Administration is concerned with *what* to do, Practice is concerned with *how* to do it; or with less accuracy, Administration is, roughly, strategy, Practice is tactics.

This distinction between scientific Administration and scientific Practice holds at every level. The individual scientist must decide which research he ought to carry out next; he must then carry out the research. He is therefore both a scientific Administrator and a scientific Practitioner. A scientist's proficiency as Administrator is a measure of his scientific taste—for what is scientific taste but the knack of choosing worthwhile problems? The Administrative facet of a scientist's work, his "taste," rarely intrudes explicitly—good scientists have it, poor ones don't; and I suspect most scientists would take offense at being described as Administrators.

Some scientists excel as Administrators, others as Practitioners. Thus James Conant, in comparing the scientific styles of Lavoisier

3

and Priestley, says "Lavoisier's lasting contribution was made because he placed his experiments in the framework of an ambitious attempt to explain a great many facts in terms of a grand conceptual scheme. It would not be too misleading to call him a master strategist in science. Priestley, on the other hand, probably excelled Lavoisier as an experimenter, but he failed to appreciate fully the significance of his results in terms of the great question of the day—combustion and calcination . . . he was a great tactician, but a poor strategist."[1]

The individual scientist working at his bench (more likely today, his Apple computer) epitomizes "Little Science." In Little Science, Administrator and Practitioner are the same person. As the size and complexity of the questions addressed increases, that is, as the science becomes Big Science, the split between Administrator and Practitioner becomes more pronounced. Since much more is at stake in Big Science than in Little Science, the strategic choices must be made much more explicitly and self-consciously in the former than in the latter. The director of a large laboratory must, at least in theory, devote most of his time choosing between competing claimants on his always-limited budget. At the highest level of scientific activity—that is, the allocation of a nation's total scientific effort between say, high energy physics, molecular biology, environmental science—and the carrying out of the national policy, the separation between Administration and Practice is practically complete. The President's Science Advisor spends all his time worrying about allocation; he has no time left over for the details of how the science pie he has cut is actually eaten.

Scientific values underlie criteria by which we decide upon the "worth" or "validity" of scientific activities. Values underlie both the Administration and the Practice of science; these values therefore constitute a meta-science. But the values that underlie the Practice of science and the values that underlie the Administration of Science are different. In other words, corresponding to the separation of science into its two aspects, Practice and Administration, there are two separate meta-sciences or sets of values—one for scientific Practice, another for scientific Administration. In speaking of Values in Science, I shall therefore have to speak of the two sets of values separately.

THE VALUES OF SCIENTIFIC PRACTICE

The primary question asked of every scientific discovery is "Is this discovery true?" Indeed, science is usually regarded as a search for truth: truth is the criterion by which every scientific assertion is judged, and it must therefore be regarded as the underlying value of scientific Practice.

I have fudged a bit speaking of scientific Practice, not of science. Yet this is an essential point, since we know that two scientific discoveries may be equally true—equally valid as judged by the criterion of truth—yet the one may be far more "significant," "worthwhile," or "valuable"—than the other. In applying the criterion of truth we are considering not whether the question purportedly answered by our research was a good or useful or important question; we are simply asking whether the question was answered correctly and convincingly. In short, truth is a value, a criterion of choice, only the Practice of science, not the Administration of science.

I find puzzling that the philosophy of science, insofar as I understand it, is preoccupied primarily with epistemology and logic—in establishing a basis for deciding whether a scientific finding is true or is not true. It must, to the degree that I describe it fairly, be regarded as the Philosophy of Scientific Practice, since it deals hardly at all with the other aspect of science, its "Administration."

Many authors have been much intrigued by the notion of truth as a value, perhaps the primary value, in science—notably Jacob Bronowski[2] in his *Science and Human Values,* Anatol Rapoport[3] in his *Science and the Goals of Man,* and Abraham Maslow[4] in *The Psychology of Science.* My observation that truth is a value that underlies only the Practice of science, not its Administration, must not be taken to betray a disparagement of these authors. Science certainly aims for truth; and truth must therefore be regarded as a value of science, though it cannot be regarded as the only value.

But even truth cannot always be regarded as a fully operable or applicable criterion of merit for the Practice of science. There are many important questions that are isomorphic with bona fide scientific questions and that might therefore be regarded as scientific, but which, in principle, *cannot be answered by science.* I have called these questions "trans-scientific" since they transcend the proficiency of science. Examples of such trans-scientific questions are the prediction of extremely rare events, or the prediction of trajectories for systems close to instability—e.g., Thom's catastrophes. Among rare events, perhaps the most relevant are those concerned with the response of animals, whether mice or human beings, to extremely small physical or chemical insults. We know that, on average, 50 rems of radiation delivered to each of 1000 mice is very likely to double the mutation frequency in each of the mice. What we cannot say, and possibly can never say, is whether 1 millirem delivered to each of 50 million mice, for the same 50,000 mouse-rem exposure, will also cause the same aggregate number of mutations. Thus, the two questions are iso-morphic, yet the one involving the rare events is trans-scientific, the other is scientific.

As an example of the other kind of trans-scientific question, I mention attempts to predict the future—whether of the economy, our energy demand, or the climate—where the underlying phenomena are so complicated as to be subject to Thomian instabilities—or simply to demand more knowledge than we now possess. It was my frustration with these extremely important, and all-but-unanswerable questions, that led me to characterize most of social science (with the possible exception of economics) as being "trans-scientific."

Alice Whittemore in a paper, "Facts and Values in Risk Analysis for Environmental Toxicants,"[5] argues that where the issue involved trans-science—in this case, the danger to humans of very low levels of chemical insult (much below the level at which harm can be detected)—truth can no longer be used as a criterion of merit since the sought-for effect is always lost in the noise. *In principle*, it is impossible to decide whether or not such low levels of exposure are or are not harmful; the proposition is intrinsically undecidable. Never-theless, scientists are always asked to make such judgments since the regulatory agencies are by law required to set standards. Professor Whittemore points out that in these circumstances, values other than truth enter into the scientists' judgment. A scientist working for the Dow Chemical Company is likely to interpret findings as to the toxicity of dioxin differently than is the scientist working for the Environ-mental Defense Fund. Both scientists would undoubtedly claim to be invoking a criterion of truth; but since the truth criterion, in principle, does not apply, each scientist is actually applying some other criterion of validity—a criterion that reflects his prejudices about big business or participatory democracy.

My separation between science and trans-science is probably too extreme, too schematic. The line between the two is surely fuzzier than I have implied in the foregoing discussion. Many, if not most, of the problems that evoke violent public reactions—like the existence or non-existence of a threshold for biological damage from exposure to toxic agents, or the biological basis for alleged racial differences in intelligence, or the existence of the so-called nuclear winter—possess genuinely scientific as well as trans-scientific components. Thus, one finds scientists argue violently as to the proficiency of science in giving answers to these questions; and these arguments generally reflect the value system and social or political orientation of the antagonists. Such controversy, in which one's commitment to truth is modified by his social and political values, must be contrasted with controversy over genuinely scientific issues where social and political values intrude far less. The struggle between Mach and Ostwald on the one hand and Boltzmann on the other as to the reality of atoms was often bitter—but I don't think the positions of the antagonists reflected more than a commitment to scientific ideals. On the other hand, some recent arguments about the genetic basis of intelligence, or even the effects of extremely low levels of radiation, surely have been powerfully influenced by the psychological if not political attitudes of the adversaries.

All of this by no means casts doubt upon the efficacy of truth as a criterion of merit in genuinely scientific, as opposed to trans-scientific, Practice. All scientific practitioners profess a commitment to truth; their individual values encroach on, or supersede, truth only where the latter is an inefficient criterion of validity, and that is in trans-science, not in science.

THE VALUES OF SCIENTIFIC ADMINISTRATION

Scientific Administration, in the narrow sense in which I use the term, asks not "Is this science true?", but rather "Of two equally true scientific activities or findings, 'Which is more worthwhile?' " Both findings may be equally valid as measured by the criterion of truth, but one might be regarded as being more important than the other. The discovery of fission in uranium-235, and the discovery of a new energy level in the U-235 nucleus are equally true; the former is obviously much more important than the latter. How do we know that one is more important than the other or, in the administrator's terms, how can we establish priorities between competing scientific activities?

Such judgments after the fact of the relative importance of different scientific discoveries of course has always been an intrinsic part of science. They give science an internal hierarchical structure, which scientists find, at the least, to be pleasing. Such judgments are the very essence of scientific Administration. Every Administrator at whatever level is always deciding what science to support, what science not to support. Unfortunately, he must make these judgments before, not after, the science is practiced, and this requirement has given rise to a search for criteria of scientific choice. The ensuing debate on scientific priorities has attracted considerable attention, especially among those formulating national scientific policy. Here is an instance of a rather philosophic question. How to judge the relative value of competing scientific activities, which, at least in principle, has urgent practical application.

The debate itself was greatly encouraged by Professor Edward Shils, the editor of *Minerva;* most of the more philosophic writings on the subject have appeared in that journal. The modern debate began with Michael Polanyi's famous paper, "The Republic of Science: Its Political and Economic Theory," which was published in 1962,[6] though the question of how scientists choose among possible researches was raised as early as 1939 by the sociologist, Robert K. Merton.[7] Merton insisted that values arising from outside of science underlay such choices: ". . . The foci of scientific interest are determined by social forces as well as the immanent development of science. We must therefore examine extra-scientific influences in order to comprehend . . . why scientists applied themselves to one field of investigation rather than another."[8] I contributed to the 1963 debate in *Minerva* with two papers entitled "Criteria for Scientific Choice,"[9] a title suggested to me by Professor Shils. Other papers in the *Minerva* series were by C.F. Carter[10] and by Stephen Toulmin.[11]

The sharpest difference in outlook was between Polanyi and me: he regarded the Republic of Science as being governed by a free market in which the direction of scientific development resulted from the interplay of innumerable, decentralized decisions made by myriad individual scientific "Administrators." He thus regarded science as a self-organizing structure guided by an "Intellectual Marketplace" (to use Harvey Brooks' phrase)—that is, by the unplanned competition between different scientific activities, each claiming greater scientific worth than the others. I, on the other hand, argued that though Little Science progressed without explicit planning, the course of Big Science could be, and was being, planned, and the planning could be based on "Criteria for Scientific Choice." If Polanyi's "Free-Market" Republic of Big Science claimed Adam Smith as its patron, my vision of the Republic of Science owed much to Karl Marx. My scientific economy was a planned one, his an unplanned one.

My criteria of choice were of two kinds, internal and external. Internal criteria arose from within the Administration of science, and answered such questions as "Are the scientists competent?" and "Is this field at a point where progress can be expected—*i.e.,* is it ripe for exploitation?" If such internal criteria are not met, than the effort spent is likely to be fruitless. In other words, the internal criteria are criteria of "efficiency," since they are aimed at judging how likely a given allocation of resources will actually yield positive results. The underlying value here is "efficiency."

The external criteria arise from outside science or from outside the specific field being judged. Whereas the internal criteria are intended to test whether a proposed scientific activity is likely to be conducted efficiently, the external criteria are intended to test whether the activity is likely to be judged important, useful, or worthwhile. Now it is a principle of philosophy, which undoubtedly goes back to the Greeks, that the worth or value (as opposed to the truth) of an activity or proposition cannot be judged except from without the given universe of discourse. Thus, to judge how worthwhile is a given scientific undertaking, we must go outside the undertaking itself. I therefore proposed three external criteria of merit, which arise from the outside: technological merit, social merit, and scientific merit. By technological merit I mean the technological relevance or usefulness of a scientific activity: for example, research on high temperature plasmas obviously has great technological merit since it might lead to controlled fusion energy, though some might have claimed in the early days of the research on fusion that useful points of departure were lacking.

By social merit I meant the direct social impact of a scientific activity. For example, high energy physics, largely conducted as an international collaborative enterprise, plays a role in furthering international understanding. Or again, the social sciences must be rated high in social merit—they bear the same relation to social engineering as the physical sciences do to civil engineering or the biological sciences to medicine. (That I consider them too often lacking in fruitful points of departure is undoubtedly my problem, not the social sciences'!)

Both of these external criteria arise from outside sciences; they are mainly relevant to applied, or better, "applicable" science. The value underlying them may be regarded as utility: we choose that science which is socially or technically *useful*. My third external criterion of merit, by contrast, arises from within science, but outside the scientific field or activity under scrutiny; it alone is relevant to "pure" science. It was suggested to me by John Van Neumann's beautiful statement about the necessity for a pure mathematical discipline, if it is to avoid fragmenting into a mass of incoherent detail, to return regularly to its antecedents in earlier, more classical branches of mathematics. I argued that the same consideration ought, *mutatis mutandis,* to apply to empirical science. I therefore defined "scientific merit" of a given pure scientific activity in the statement, "The scientific merit of an activity in pure science is to be measured by the degree to which it interacts with and illuminates the neighboring scientific disciplines in which the activity is embedded."

Twenty years have passed since the debate began on priorities in *Minerva*. During this time National Science Policy has been a recurrent concern of many governments and governmental advisory bodies. Thus the U.S. National Academy of Sciences in the late 1960s, on through the 1970s, has examined entire fields of science; among these were reports on physics, the first by a committee headed by G. Pake[12] and the second, by A. Bromley;[13] chemistry, by F. Westheimer;[14] biology, by P. Handler,[15] to mention a few. These studies reviewed the prospects and accomplishments of the fields under study, and, in at least some cases, attempted to suggest priorities among the various sub-fields. The philosophic debate on scientific choice figured fairly prominently in some of the studies, perhaps most notably in the Bromley study of physics, which appeared in 1973. Bromley and his colleagues set up a system of criteria by which each of eight subfields of physics and some 69 "program elements" within the subfields were judged; they also assigned to each sub-field and program element a numerical rating on each of thirteen criteria so that the "worth" of each sub-field and program element was a "thirteen-component" vector. Bromley then suggested that priorities in funding ought to go to those fields whose "criterion vector" was longest. The criteria themselves were, with a few modifications, closely patterned after those discussed in the *Minerva* debate. The major modification to the *Minerva* criteria of choice had to do with Bromley's recognition that certain very large and expensive pieces of equipment, like the National Accelerator Laboratory, required funding in competition with sub-fields of physics, yet could hardly be judged by the same criteria. Instead, he constructed "structural" criteria, which took account of the importance of these facilities to the pursuit of whole fields of endeavor. As a matter of historic interest, I have reproduced the ratings proposed by the Bromley committee for the eight sub-fields of physics (Figure 1–1).

Though I have not followed all of the more recent attempts to allocate public funds among different scientific fields and within scientific fields, the studies I am familiar with seem to invoke these or related criteria of choice—at least when they discuss the question of priorities, if not in the actual assignment of priorities.

For example, the 1983 report on *Opportunities and Challenges in Research with Transplutonium Elements*[16] repeatedly refers to the importance of research on transplutonium elements to the chemistry of all the transition elements, not simply to the chemistry of the transplutonics. To quote from this report (page 62), "Chemistry is based on establishing interrelations in the behavior of the different elements. Each element, with its unique features, when its chemistry is compared with that of others, helps knit the fabric of theory that transforms a compilation of observations into a science." And in order to arrive at these judgments as to the relevance of transplutonic chemistry to chemistry as a whole (its "scientific" merit in my terminology), the panel sought advice from scientists in adjacent branches of chemistry and physics. So insofar as the debate on scientific priorities has provided a language, or an underlying structure for the actual allocation of effort within science, I would say that the philosophic debate has been applied practically.

On the other hand, I don't think one can claim too much for the criteria of choice as practical recipes for making actual choices. Scientific choices at the highest level, involving as they do many millions, even hundreds of millions of dollars, often become political choices. These are determined not so much by abstract criteria of merit as by interplay of competing political power. This was seen particularly in the Bromley panel's recognition that existing large facilities simply cannot be turned on and off. Moreover, the external criteria of merit can much easier be applied to scientific activities *after*, rather than before, they have been completed. But in a way this is a deficiency of any criterion of choice, whatever the choice. (For example, we can decide on the wisdom of a decision to go to war in Vietnam much better after the fact than before.) Nevertheless, decisions must be made: that our criteria of choice for scientific Administration are no better or no worse guides for actual administrative choices in science than are criteria of choice in any human endeavor must be regarded as a reflection of our inability to foresee the future, not necessarily a deficiency of the criteria themselves. And, of course, the criteria were conceived mainly to help make the largest choices, the choices of Big Science. If they also are relevant for choices in Little Sciences, where choices are less explicit, this is rather an incidental benefit of the criteria.

UNITY AS A VALUE IN ADMINISTRATION OF PURE SCIENCE

The internal criteria are criteria of efficiency, measuring how efficiently resources are brought to bear on science. The external criteria of social and technological merit, often overriding in practice, are criteria of utility. They measure the usefulness, in a practical sense, of a scientific activity, but they affect the structure of science only in an adventitious way. When we measure neutron cross-sections in order to build better nuclear reactors, we hardly worry about rounding out our general picture of nuclear matter. Hence, we measure only those cross-sections relevant to the technological task, whether or not these particular cross-sections are of intrinsic importance to the rounding out of our picture of the nucleus. Thus, one can speak of efficiency and utility as values underlying these criteria of choice.

On the other hand, of the external criteria, I would regard the criterion of scientific merit as occupying the most fundamental theoretical position: it alone arises from within science and deals with the underlying structure of science—the relation between the parts of science to each other. It alone imposes an orderly structure on science. Remember that we propose to judge the merit of a pure scientific activity by the illumination that this activity throws on the neighboring fields in which it is imbedded. This criterion therefore stems directly from a perception that a unified science, one in which the different parts of science are related to each other, are consistent with each other and illuminate each other. Such science is in some very fundamental sense better—more pleasing, more powerful, more beautiful—than a science that is not so unified. If this is our perception of what constitutes a more worthwhile science, our criterion of scientific merit is simply a restatement of this perception: pure scientific activities that unify are better (*i.e.*, are more valuable and therefore merit more support) than pure scientific activities that do not tend to unify. (And indeed, what is the search for unity except a restatement of Occam's razor: that science must be parsimonious, that it seeks to explain more with less?) Thus to summarize, *utility* is a value underlying the Administration of applied Science, and *efficiency* is a value for the Administration of both pure and applied science. I would suggest that *unity* is the unique value underlying only the Administration of pure science. (To help the reader follow my argument, I have illustrated, with the help of Dr. William C. Clark, the structure of science and its values in Figure 1–2).

To recognize unity as a value in pure science is hardly new: Jacob Bronowski, in *Science and Human Values,* speaks of the search for unity as being almost indistinguishable from the search for truth in science. Yet I have proposed a fundamental distinction between truth and unity: truth *and* unity are underlying values for science, but they apply to the two different aspects of science. *Truth* is the underlying value for scientific Practice, *unity* is the underlying value for the Administration of pure science. Each pure scientific discovery or activity must satisfy a criterion of truth if it is to be recognized as science; but the *value* of the discovery or the activity is measured by the unity that it imparts to the entire scientific edifice.

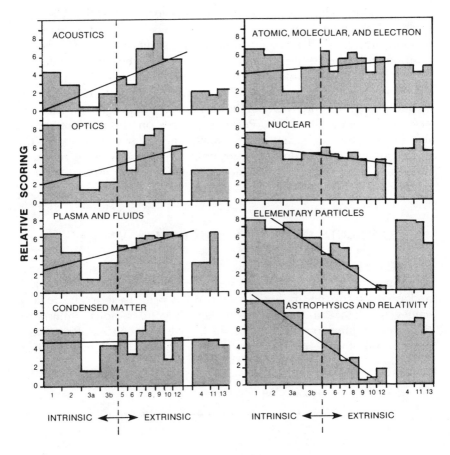

CRITERIA

1— RIPENESS FOR EXPLORATION
2— SIGNIFICANCE OF QUESTIONS ADDRESSED
3a- POTENTIAL FOR DISCOVERY OF FUNDAMENTAL
     LAWS
3b- POTENTIAL FOR DISCOVERY OF GENERALIZATIONS
     OR BROAD SCIENTIFIC APPLICABILITY
4— ATTRACTIVENESS TO MOST ABLE PHYSICISTS
5— POTENTIAL CONTRIBUTIONS TO OTHER
     SCIENCES
6— POTENTIAL STIMULATION OF OTHER AREAS OF
     SCIENCE

7— POTENTIAL CONTRIBUTION TO ENGINEERING,
     MEDICINE, APPLIED SCIENCE
8— POTENTIAL CONTRIBUTION TO TECHNOLOGY
9— POTENTIAL FOR IMMEDIATE APPLICATIONS
10- POTENTIAL CONTRIBUTION TO SOCIETAL GOALS
11- CONTRIBUTION TO NATIONAL PRESTIGE AND
     INTERNATIONAL COOPERATION
12- CONTRIBUTION TO NATIONAL DEFENSE
13- CONTRIBUTION TO PUBLIC EDUCATION

Figure 1-1: Histograms of the Survey Committee average jury ratings of the core physics subfields in terms of the intrinsic and extrinsic criteria developed in this Report. The straight lines superposed on the histograms are drawn simply to provide a characteristic signature for each subfield. It is interesting to note that these signatures divide naturally into three classes, with emphasis shifting from intrinsic to extrinsic areas as the subfield matures.

I suppose what I say displays an unbecoming hubris. After all, truth as the underlying value for science has always been accepted without argument. To propose that truth ought to share this prime position with unity—but the one in relation to scientific Practice, the other in relation to Administration of pure science—may appear to some to be pedantic or hair-splitting. Yet, on reflection, I see nothing so odd about the underlying values for the two aspects of science not necessarily being the same. Perhaps the reason this distinction has not been taken as a matter of course in the past is because the profession of science Administrator, unlike that of scientist, is relatively new—too new to have commanded much attention among philosophers of science.

VALUES IN SCIENCE AND HUMAN VALUES

Peter Caws in his admirable book, *The Philosophy of Science*[17], dismisses value in science as a matter of style, it involves a sense of proportion and a feeling for the "fit" of theory to the world. In short, he regards values in science as being intrinsically beyond serious philosophic discussion. Philosophy of science, in his view, is epistemology, logic, possibly ontology—but never axiology. I hope that I have at least

Figure 1-2: Science and Its Values.

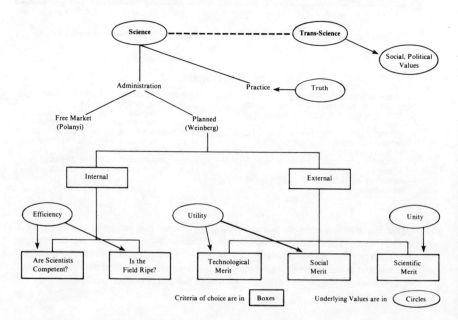

made plausible that values (that is, criteria of choice), possibly even "Absolute" values, do underlie science—truth being the underlying value for scientific Practice, and unity being the underlying value for the Administration of pure science.

Can all of this have anything to do with human values (that is, criteria of choice for human actions)? Here I must confess to be embarking on a road strewn with much larger boulders than the one I have already traversed. I am aware of Moore's statements about the naturalistic fallacy: that from a proposition about "is" we can never logically derive a proposition about "ought." Nevertheless, since I have no philosophic credentials to lose, I shall indulge in speculation as to possible connections between human values and values in science.

My lesser speculation has to do with the extent to which human values affect both scientific Practice and scientific Administration. We have already seen that in situations where truth is an ambiguous criterion of choice, other human predilections and biases tend to fill the void. But this can occur only where one deals with trans-scientific questions (that is, questions that are intrinsically beyond science's proficiency). For, although human predilections sometimes try to intrude in the course of bonafide science—as, for example, Lysenko's attack on Mendelian genetics, or the Nazi attack on relativity—the working of Polanyi's Republic of Science extirpated these false heresies, and they are now forgotten.

On the other hand, human values certainly underlie my external criteria of choice. Thus, if one accepts social merit, or even technological merit as a criterion, then one must ask *who* is to determine social merit? Is better national defense meritorious? Is lengthening of life-span meritorious? Is the development of nuclear power meritorious? I happen to believe each of these is meritorious; but there are many who would regard at least some of these as being without merit.

Thus, one can hardly doubt that underlying human orientations, beliefs, biases, often manifested in sheer political power, affect the course of scientific Administration. Indeed, this was the main point made by the sociologist Robert Merton more than 45 years ago.

What about the inverse question: can the values we have identified in scientific Practice and scientific Administration somehow serve as human values in a much more general sense? That is, are the criteria for scientific choices transferrable to human choices?

The professional philosopher will say no—that even if the criteria of scientific choice are valid, or even practically useful, there is no logical connection between the criteria for deciding on the valuable or good or beautiful in science and the criteria for deciding these characteristics in human relations generally. Nevertheless, the non-professional must be tantalized by the realization that in science, and particularly in scientific Administration, one is confronted with the necessity for choice in a particularly explicit manner and in a circumscribed universe. Perhaps therefore the experience we gain in analyzing the problem of value within science may serve as a model for analysis of the broader problem of value. Value in science might therefore be a model for human value, even if the values in science do not *imply* human values.

Actually, there is a literature devoted to the "derivation" of human values from scientific values. I have in mind the writings of Bronowski, Maslow, and Rapoport, all of whom come to pretty much the same conclusion. For them the underlying scientific value is *truth:* it is this value which governs Polanyi's Republic of Science, or Bronowski's "Society of Scientists." Here is a polity dedicated to the pursuit of truth, and by almost any criterion, it works: that is, science is successful, perhaps the most successful of man's undertakings. Let us therefore model the human polity, say these writers, after the Republic of Science—dedicated always to truth, and somehow organized, as is science, to extirpate falsehood.

One cannot help but be sympathetic with such a lofty ideal—a community of humankind, not merely a community of scientists, dedicated to truth. But one must recognize the enormous practical difficulty in creating, and conducting, a Republic of Humanity that is isomorphic with the Republic of Science. Who is to determine truth? If truth is an inadequate criterion of choice in trans-scientific questions (which at least are structurally similar to bonafide scientific questions) how much less adequate is it as a criterion in ordinary human intercourse? Who shall decide where truth lies in the struggle between competing religions, or political systems, or economic systems?

For these reasons, I am attracted more to the idea of using the underlying criterion of the Administration of pure science, unity, as a more reasonable, or perhaps more practical criterion of choice, *i.e.,* a value, for human relations. Again, this is by no means an entirely new idea—Bronowski himself urges unity as an underlying value. And he quotes Coleridge: "When Coleridge tried to define beauty, he turned always to one deep thought: beauty, he said, is 'unity in variety.' Science is nothing else than the search to discover the unity in the wild variety of nature—or in the variety of our experience."

Thus, I would suggest that my criterion of scientific merit might be generalized along some line such as this: Just as every basic scientific activity is embedded in a broader scientific matrix, and just as its merit is to be judged by the unity it brings to that underlying scientific matrix, so every human activity is embedded in a broader human matrix. And the merit of that activity is to be judged by the degree to which that activity contributes to the unity and illumination, and ultimately to the harmony, of the many activities with which it interacts.

Almost twenty years have passed since I first proposed using this criterion of scientific choice as a model for criteria of human choice. I have since been taught by professional philosophers about the naturalistic fallacy, perhaps even the impossibility of establishing any convincing, let alone unique, value system.

Despite the professionals' disavowal, the problem of value is surely the most fundamental question both in science and in human affairs. And indeed, the difficulty of applying a broad criterion of value, *unity*, to actual human decisions must be formidable. Probably the difficulty is just as formidable as the difficulties I mentioned in applying a criterion of truth to the judgment of human decisions. Yet one cannot but be intrigued that whenever we encounter strife in our imperfect world—between religious groups, between nations, between individuals—a resolution appears in discovery and exploitation of common aspirations, beliefs, and understandings of the contestants. Switzerland once was a battleground; its unification led to peace. Western Europe 40 years ago fought World War II; today Europe is a unity, and war between Germany and France is unthinkable. Today, East and West, Communist and non-Communist seem to be in irreconcilable struggle; yet can we not eventually find common elements and aspirations—in this case the common desire to avoid thermonuclear annihilation—that provide sufficient overarching unity to avoid this awful disaster?

The analogy between our problem of scientific choice and the problem of human choice is too tantalizing to be ignored. Perhaps I overwork the analogy in these admittedly tentative attempts to illuminate the deep questions of human values with perspectives gained from the far narrower question of scientific values. But—tentative and halting as such an attempt may appear to the initiated—the questions themselves, if not my answers, are powerfully important. I hope, in analysis and criticism of these ideas drawn from the ethics of science, one can find ever more convincing approaches to the formulation of a credible ethical system for humankind.

NOTES

1. James B. Conant, *On Understanding Science*, New Haven, CT: Yale University Press, 1947.

2. Jacob Bronowski, *Science and Human Values*, NY: Harper Torchbooks, 1959.

3. Anatol Rapoport, *Science and the Goals of Man*, NY: Harper, 1950.

4. Abraham Maslow, *The Psychology of Science*, NY: Harper and Row, 1966.

5. Alice S. Whittemore, "Facts and Values in Risk Analysis for Environmental Toxicants," *Risk Analysis 3* (1): 23–33, March 1983.

6. M. Polanyi, "The Republic of Science—Its Political and Economic Theory," *Minerva 1* (1): 54–73, 1962.

7. Robert K. Merton in *The Sociology of Science*, N. Storer, ed., University of Chicago Press, 1973. (Especially Part 2, "The Sociology of Science.")

8. Robert K. Merton, *Interactions of Science and Military Technique* (1938), reprinted in *The Sociology of Science*.

9. Alvin M. Weinberg "Criteria for Scientific Choice," *Minerva 1:* 159–171, Winter 1963.

10. C.F. Carter, "The Distribution of Scientific Effort," *Minerva 1:* 172–181, 1962–1963.

11. Stephen Toulmin, "The Complexity of Scientific Choice: A Stocktaking," *Minerva 2:* 343, 1964.

12. George E. Pake, Chairman, Physics Survey Committee, *Physics: Survey and Outlook*, National Research Council/National Academy of Science, Washington, D.C., 1966.

13. D.A. Bromley, Chairman, Physics Survey Committee, *Physics in Perspective*, National Research Council/National Academy of Sciences, Washington D.C., 1972.

14. F. Westheimer, Chairman, Chemistry Survey Committee, Committee on Science and Public Policy, *Chemistry: Opportunities and Needs*, National Research Council/National Academy of Sciences, Washington, D.C., 1965.

15. P. Handler, Chairman, Committee on Research in the Life Sciences, Committee on Science and Public Policy, *The Life Sciences*, National Research Council/National Academy of Sciences, Washington, D.C., 1970.

16. *Opportunities and Challenges in Research with Transplutonium Elements* National Academy of Sciences, Washington, D.C., 1983.

17. Peter Caws, *The Philosophy of Science*, Princeton, NJ: Van Nostrand & Company, 1965 (pp. 13, 264, 334).

2

Is Reductionism the Best Way to Unify Science?

NORETTA KOERTGE

INTRODUCTION

It is easy to document the fact that scientific research is becoming more and more specialized. Thirty years ago in America an ambitious young analytical chemist would most likely publish in the general periodical *Journal of the American Chemical Society*. Failing that there was *Analytic Chemistry* or *Industrial Engineering Chemistry*. Today, good work in analytical chemistry appears in specialized periodicals such as *Journal of Chromatography, Journal of Liquid Chromatography, Journal of Electroanalytic Chemistry and Interfacial Electrochemistry, Journal of Magnetic Resonance*, etc.

   Surprisingly, there accompanies this extreme division of labor a strengthening of the inter-disciplinary connections between previously disparate sciences. For example, at my university, students take *chemistry* courses with names such as "Biogeochemistry" or "Enzymology," while the *biology* department offers courses in "Molecular Genetics" and "Biochemical Analysis of Growth and Development." Sometimes the boundaries seem to have disappeared completely. Our *psychology* department lists P511, "Social Psychology"; the *sociologists*, on the other hand, teach S435, "Social Psychology of the Self." Even the traditional gaps between natural science, social science, and moral science are apparently being bridged—E. O. Wilson's book with the bold title, *Sociobiology—The New Synthesis*, proposes a biological account of ethics and aesthetics. And many people working in artificial intelligence, cybernetics, or brain neurophysiology are even less modest.

It might appear that the ancient metaphor of *the* single, unified tree of knowledge is about to be realized. Faced with these numerous blendings and borrowings between traditional disciplines, the philosopher of science must ask: Exactly what is the structure of the tree? Is physics the basic trunk from which unfolds first chemistry, then biology, then psychology, etc.? Or is the topology of knowledge more complex? And how does the tree of knowledge (or is it a forest?) grow?

FROM REDUCTION TO INTER-THEORETIC CRITICISM

Historical Background

There was already a basic disagreement about the structure of scientific knowledge amongst the Greeks. Aristotle proposed what we might dub a coalition model of the sciences. Each individual science was to be axiomatized; the explanation of particular or lower-level facts would be given through syllogistic deduction; the higher level first principles were to be learned directly through a method of collection-analysis-and-intuitive-apprehension, which Aristotle called *induction*[1]. (His meaning is significantly different from what Bacon or Hume later understood by that term.)

There were certain first principles that were common to all sciences (*e.g.*, if equals are taken from equals, equals remain). But other principles were special to the scientific subject-matter. Thus for Aristotle, geometry and arithmetic were distinct sciences because one studies points and lines; the other is about units.

On this view the sciences are loosely unified through the shared first principles, but because of their disparate subject matters, each requires its own special or proper axioms. A bit of hierarchical structure is introduced through his notion of *subaltern* science—harmonics is subaltern to arithmetic because numerical ratios must be used to explain the consonance of intervals. Nevertheless, there is no question of reducing harmonics to arithmetic—one is about sounds, the other about numbers. All sciences retain their individuality, and things are more or less what they seem.

A sharply contrasting theory about the structure of knowledge originated with the Greek atomists and was worked out by Lucretius[2]. On this view there were no essential differences between animals, vegetables, and minerals or body and mind, (Lucretius thought mind atoms were just unusually small and mobile.)

All aspects of nature, from meteorology to sociology, were to be understood in terms of the same basic principles of matter and motion. Aristotle's separate sciences stemmed from the irreducibly different qualitative aspects of the world. But for the atomists, strictly speaking, there were no colors, odors, tastes, or sounds. Rather there were complex interactions between the atoms emanating from objects external to us and the atoms of our sense organs. (Most of our sensations are veridical, but if surface films from a horse and a man should happen to collide, we may form the idea of a Centaur.)

Lucretius' program was one of thorough-going reductionism. Everything was to be explained in terms of changing arrangements of atoms—everything from the shape of the earth to the evolution of species, to sexual desire, to creativity, to religious beliefs. One can't imagine a more unified, nor a more hierarchical, picture of scientific knowledge.

As science itself developed, both the Aristotelian and the atomistic programs encountered set-backs. Many of the sciences Aristotle thought were qualitatively distinct became integrated into new composite disciplines. Galileo's unified account of terrestrial and celestial motions, Descartes' discovery of analytic geometry, Wohler's synthesis of urea (an organic chemical) from inorganic materials—each blurred one of Aristotle's qualitative distinctions.

The Mechanical Philosophers of the 17th Century on the other hand, although inspired by the atomistic reduction program, revised it in many ways. To the solid, massy, impenetrable, moving atoms, Newton added forces—first gravity and repulsions between neighboring atoms, then chemical forces to explain fermentation and cohesion, forces that acted between light and matter, etc. And Descartes, although a thorough-going reductionist as far as the natural sciences were concerned (remember the comparison of a dog yelping in pain to a rusty door hinge), severely truncated the Lucretius program by his theory of mind-body dualism.

But let us now turn to 20th Century philosophical views about the overall structure of scientific knowledge and the proper role of reductionism. We will see that philosophers have given the term *reduction* a precise, technical definition.

Russell and the Attempt to Reduce Mathematics to Logic

Russell's description of the logicist program in the concluding chapter of his *Introduction to Mathematical Philosophy*[3], provides a clear example of the modern notion of reduction (although he does not use the term):

"Mathematics and logic, historically speaking, have been entirely distinct studies. (However) . . . in fact, the two are one . . . (S)tarting with premises which would be universally admitted to belong to logic and arriving by deduction at results which as obviously belong to mathematics, we find there is no point at which a sharp line can be drawn, with logic to the left and mathematics to the right." (p. 194)

It is customary to call the subject that provides the premises the *primary* science and the historically distinct subject that is now derived from it the *secondary* science. However, there is certainly no hint in Russell's account that the reduced science (mathematics) is in any sense inferior to the primary science (logic). If anything, the evaluation is reversed: "They differ as boy and man: logic is the youth . . . and mathematics is the manhood of logic." (p. 194) However, we will see that often the reduced science is considered to be diminished, either ontologically or epistemologically. Of course, mathematics cannot be derived from logic unless each concept in mathematics, such as *natural number*, is defined in terms of concepts within Russell's logic theory, such as *class of all classes similar to . . ..* Philosophers sometimes speak of *term reduction* when such definitions can be carried out. Theory reduction presupposes term reduction, but not *vice versa*.

The Positivists' Reduction Program

Logicists felt that they could make mathematical concepts more clear by attempting to reduce them to logic. Logical positivists hoped to make the propositions of science more certain by constructing them (through definitions and derivations) from statements expressed in an epistemologically privileged primary language[4].

But what should this basic language be like? In his famous *Aufbau*, Carnap tried to begin with people's elementary, unitary experiences, which he considered to be more basic than Mach's sensations because the latter already presupposed a certain amount of analysis. However, as the difficulty of the reduction became apparent, positivists compromised their program in various ways. First of all, they strengthened the primary language enormously, moving eventually from protocol sentences to observation languages that included rather esoteric terms such as *pressure, sulfuric acid,* and *half-life*.

But even with a beefed-up base, it was still impossible to produce adequate definitions of terms such as *electromagnetic radiation*, or *ideal gas*. And so again they retreated, this time by dropping the formal requirement that the concepts in the secondary science be strictly defined in terms of the primary vocabulary and by admitting that the theorems in the secondary science could not all be strictly derived from the primary science. Thus, for example, we have Carnap's *reduction* sentences (which, despite their name, do not allow us to replace theoretical terms by observation terms). What is generally not admitted is that these retreats totally vitiate the original epistemological program. If electrons cannot be defined in terms of sensations or pointer readings, then it no longer makes sense to claim that they are just a convenient conceptual shorthand for complicated arrays of sense experience.

Even if the positivists' epistemological reductionist program had been totally successful, it would have left totally open questions about the ontological structure of the world. Although Carnap claims to describe *Der Aufbau der Welt* (the construction of the *world*) unless we are idealists, we want to say that the world (as opposed to our *knowledge* of it) is composed of things like electrons and energy, not built out of my or your experiencing of red patches or pointer readings.

Reduction vs. Explanation

Often when contemporary scientists speak positively of reductionism, they have little more in mind than the search for theoretical explanations. Here they follow the example of the pre-Socratics who wanted to reduce the wildly fluctuating variety of experience to a few originative principles, which behaved in a law-like fashion. Recall also how Plato urged astronomers to build up the complicated retrograde motion of planets from a combination of uniform circular motions, and how Galen tried to explain the wide variety of physiological and emotional states in terms of a shifting balance between only four humors.

Whereas Mach (and other positivists) took human sensations to be primary and tried to reduce everything else to them, the Greeks tried to explain our ordinary experience of the world in terms of conjectural primary starting points. Aristotle is very explicit about this pragmatic inversion—he stresses that what is better-known-to-us may not be the same as what is better-known-(primary)-in-Nature. (In a Lakatosian rational reconstruction of the history of philosophy, Aristotle would, of course, come well after Mach.)

In the search for explanation, we should not be surprised or disappointed if any particular conjectural explanatory theory turns out to be false or incomplete—we simply revise it freely and try again. Or so one might expect from my account so far. However, neither modern scientists nor their predecessors generate their conjectures randomly. As non-positivistic historians and philosophers of science have stressed, most scientific conjectures originate in meta-physical world-views that are defended with philosophical arguments. Thus, Aristotle did not propose his four-quality theory of matter just because it looked like a promising explanatory hypothesis. He also supported it with a variety of plausibility considerations. Likewise, for the Mechanical Philosophy of Descartes, 19th Century Naturphilo-sophie, Ostwald's Energetics, and Popper's Rationality Principle Approach.

When scientists who are searching for explanations in one domain have fairly definite and fixed ideas about which concepts and laws should appear in the explanans, and when they attempt to define the explanandum concepts in terms of concepts within another previously determined domain, we shall say they are looking for reductive explanations.

Having a pre-established metaphysical or theoretical context for our proposed scientific explanations facilitates the process of hypothesis construction in many ways, but it also means that there may be some motivation to gloss over reduction failures.

If magnetism cannot be reduced to complicated collisions of corpuscles, then Cartesianism is dead. If language learning cannot be explained in terms of Skinnerian reinforcement schedules, then behaviorism is no longer a viable metaphysics of human behavior. If institutions have latent functions that benefit the group as a whole, but which have no direct discernible impact on individuals, then methodological individualism would be weakened.

On the other hand, opponents of the world-view of the primary science may be predisposed to over-estimate the difficulty of the proposed reduction. Although some so-called "anti-reductionists" are against scientific explanations of any kind (some phenomenologists seem to fall into this category), more often the opponents of reduction are really complaining about the limited explanatory resources of the prevailing mataphysics. (See, for example, the papers in *Beyond Reductionism*, the proceedings of a 1968 Alpbach Symposium on the Life Sciences.[5])

Even when an attempted reduction is not completely successful, the disciplinary and educational consequences can be enormous. For example, according to the logicist program, mathematics is *nothing but* logic. As Russell points out, his system shows that it is doubly erroneous to describe mathematics as the science of quantity or number. In addition to the traditional counter-examples of topology and projective geometry, after the reduction we see that even arithmetic is about sets, not about numbers as primary, unanalyzable entities.

Even though Russell's original program was unsuccessful, it had a profound impact on education. Not only must graduate students in mathematics now learn logic and set theory (which is *prima facie* a good thing), even elementary school education in mathematics has been "logicized" (at best a mixed blessing). There is, of course, no *a priori* reason why the pedagogical order in which we approach a science should mirror the logical order of the subject. (As a first approximation, the historical order would be a better candidate.)

Practitioners of the secondary science often have reason to fear that their prestige and funding will also be reduced. My friends in zoology complain because their labs, library resources, and stockrooms are inferior to those of the molecular biologists. In chemistry, on the other hand, folks who synthesize and describe the properties of molecules may have less prestige than the atomic and nuclear chemists.

Again, there is no *a priori* reason why the secondary science should be less intellectually challenging or valuable than the primary science. And given the historical fact that there has never been a single successful reduction (in the classical Russellian sense), it is truly ironic and unfortunate that there should be so much historical basis for the paranoia of the scientists in the "secondary" field.

Methodological Reductionism

I have given a variety of reasons why reductionism may have unpleasant connotations: it is often associated with positivist epistemology, metaphysical chauvinism, or disciplinary imperialism. Furthermore, I have boldly conjectured that there has never been a successful case of strict reduction so far in the history of science. Sometimes the secondary science is only *approximately* derivable from the primary science. (cf. the relation of Kepler's Planetary Laws to Newtonian Mechanics.) Sometimes only *part* of the secondary science can be derived—the phenomena or generalizations, which cannot be reduced, tend to be uncritically discredited or forgotten. (cf. both Kepler's and Bode's "laws" concerning the distances between planets.) Sometimes the primary science has to be significantly *altered* or extended before any version of the original secondary science is derivable. (cf. the logicists' extension of traditional logic to include set theory.)

Nevertheless, it could still be the case that *trying* to reduce one theory to another is the best way to make scientific progress. A teacher of mine used to point out that it is the radical dualists who should most welcome research into artificial intelligence and computer problem-solving. It is only by sincerely trying to simulate mind on a machine that we will discover what the differences are. And even though chemistry hasn't *really* been reduced to physics, still they are very intimately related sciences, and perhaps it was only by trying to perform the reduction that these connections have been established. I have much sympathy with both of these arguments, but it is also important to point out that pursuing a reductionist program is not always the best methodology.

Let me illustrate this claim with brief examples from the history of chemistry where progress was made either by *ignoring* the putative primary science (physics) or by developing theories that were *inconsistent* with the physics of the time.

First, it may not be at all clear beforehand which science is most likely to be primary. According to Aristotle's system, the laws of motion were dependent on the chemical composition of bodies. Those materials that were predominantly fire and air tended to go up. Conglomerates of the cold elements, earth and water, tended to go down. The natural motion of the celestial element (or quintessence) was circular. Light, on the other hand, traveled in straight lines in all directions. So in Aristotle's system, chemistry seemed to be at least as fundamental as physics.

Two thousand years later, in his textbook[6] Mendeleev speculated that the contemporary physical definition of mass might have to be replaced by a chemical one:

> ". . . in the future when chemistry shall have reached the age of mechanics . . ., some kind of compromise will be arrived at, and the quantity of a substance will be calculated in a manner quite different from the present one, although the conceptions of mass and atomic weight will be retained." (*Principles of Chemistry*, Volume II, p. 33)

Neither Aristotle's or Mendeleev's approaches survived in the long run, but both made important interim contributions. There are many other examples of controversies over which science is more fundamental. In opposition to the logicists, people such as Boole and Brouwer believed mathematics to be more basic than logic. And in the social sciences, there are controversies over whether the dominant causual arrows go from infrastructure (material, economic conditions) to superstructure (ideas, institutions) or *vice versa*.

Even when it is fairly clear which science is most likely to be primary, methodological reductionism can be scientifically sterile. In a famous query to the *Opticks*, Newton laid down a reductionist program for chemistry: was it not true that matter was composed of hard little atoms, which acted on each other via short-range forces? Given the success of Newtonian mechanics, it seemed reasonable to extend it to chemistry. Newton himself tried to reduce Boyle's Law (PV = const) to physics. He proposed a static model of gases in which adjacent particles repelled each other according to a 1/r force, but the force acted only on nearest neighbors. His hypothesis was completely *ad hoc* and untestable. There followed a hundred years of sterile reductionist model building.[7]

Experimental work based on the Newtonian paradigm was also barren. Stephen Hales, in *Vegetable Staticks*, a work whose very title reflects his Newtonianism, performed destructive distillations of every imaginable natural substance and carefully weighed the products, which he classified as tar, oils, and ash. Alas, his quantitative work was all useless. Newtonian physiologists experienced similar failures.

There was much progress in chemistry during the 18th Century, but it came not from the Newtonian program, but from chemists who were asking chemical questions and were proposing testable solutions to them that employed distinctively chemical concepts. I am thinking of Stahl's work on combustion and metallurgy, the Swedish chemists' systematization of displacement of reactions (e.g. iron displaces copper which displaces silver), and Black's and Priestly's discoveries of different "airs" (they are using a quasi-Aristotelian notion), etc.

Lavoisier, of course, revolutionized chemistry by the end of the 18th Century with his oxygen theory of combustion. Since weighing products and reactants is such an important part of Lavoisier's methodology, it is sometimes claimed that Lavoisier's success comes from borrowing methods from physics. Well, this is just nonsense—we could just as well say that he borrowed the accounting methods of merchants or government bureaucrats.

The important thing to note is that Lavoisier's famous Conservation Law is not just about the Conservation of Matter or Weight. He also proposes that *elements* are conserved. (On the Newtonian "nutshell" model of matter, transmutation was possible.) Remember that for Lavoisier, elements can only be individuated by their *chemical* properties. There was no known way at that time of characterizing them in terms of physical parameters. The founding of modern chemistry came about, not by borrowing concepts, theories, or methods from physics, but by treating problems in chemistry in an autonomous fashion.

In the 19th Century, the relationship between chemistry and physics became much more intimate. Dalton characterized elements in terms of their atomic weights. It was very productive for organic chemists to visualize atoms in space—one recalls Kekulé's benzene ring and Van't Hoff's tetrahedral carbon atom. The kinetic theory of gases at last provided a derivation of the various gas laws.

But lest we view this period as an unalloyed triumph of reductionist methodology, let me make three brief points about the era:

It was not the physics of Newton that chemists of the 19th Century found especially useful. Rather, it was the theories of electrochemistry and thermodynamics, which had been developed, in part by chemists. Reduction certainly won't work if the primary science isn't rich enough.

In working with molecular combinations of atoms, chemists found they had to introduce structural relationships that were quite different from anything encountered on the level of individual atoms. For example, Pasteur discovered left-handed and right-handed molecules whose biological properties are quite different. So the secondary science may need to introduce structural or other macroproperties which, even if they can be formally defined in terms of the primary science, would never be dreamt of by scientists working only in the primary domain.

Throughout this period, chemists continued to use ideas that were formally inconsistent with the best theories available in physics. Consider *valence:* why should carbon attract only four adjacent atoms and no more? This seemed contrary to everything physicists knew about forces. And even in the early period of Quantum Mechanics, physicists insisted on producing orbiting electron theories, such as the Bohr-Sommerfeld model, which may have accounted fairly well for the spectra of atoms but made absolutely no sense to chemists, who knew that the electrons had to be localized if we were to understand valence and chemical bonding. Lewis and Langmuir proposed their static theory in full recognition that they were going against the "best" physics of their time. G. N. Lewis says:

> "These two views (seem) to be quite incompatible, although it is the same atom that is being investigated by chemist and by physicist. If the electrons are to be regarded as taking an essential part in the process of binding atom to atom in the molecule, it (seems) impossible that they could be actuated by the simple laws of force, and traveling in the orbits required by the planetary theory. The permanence of atomic arrangements even in very complex molecules is one of the most striking of chemical phenomena. Isomers maintain their identity for years, often without the slightest appreciable transformation." (*Valence and the Structure of Atoms and Molecules,* 1923, p. 55).

Eventually, of course, physicists extended and corrected the old quantum theory so that it could be applied to the phenomena Lewis describes. Once again we see that chemistry (and physics!) progressed because the chemists retained a certain degree of autonomy.

From Reductionism to Inter-Theoretic Criticism

Agassi has argued that Boyle's Rule is dogmatic. (Boyle's Rule says that whenever theory and observation clash, it is always the theory which must give way.) In a similar vein, I have argued that reductionism, of either the epistemological, metaphysical or methodological variety is dogmatic. We can never know which science is primary, and history tells us that whenever an inter-theoretic situation that vaguely approximates reduction occurs, the secondary science generally forces changes in the primary science at the same time that the primary science is correcting the lower-level laws.

What is essential for the growth of knowledge is *not* that we always attempt to reduce all sciences to one Ur-parent system, but that we constantly *compare* and critically assess the results of various theoretical and metaphysical approaches. And when I speak of *comparison,* I do not mean the sort of pragmatic weighing of research program successes that Lakatos had in mind. I mean that we should actively look for logical inconsistencies between claims in disciplines, that we may have hitherto assumed to be complementary, rather than competing.

In my critique of reductionism, I praised G. N. Lewis for daring to develop a theory of chemical bonding that was inconsistent with the best physics of the time. But in so doing, I did not mean to laud (as would Feyerabend) the proliferation of pseudo-scientific proposals, which contradict our best current science. First, Lewis' proposal had high empirical content—it was open to experimental falsification. Second, both the chemists and the physicists were well aware of the inconsistency and made no attempt to cover it up. Instead, it was a pressing problem for all concerned.

This is not always the prevailing attitude. Sometimes, motivated in part by what I think is a legitimate reaction against reductionism, scientists tend to stifle inter-theoretic criticism by dividing up the pie—"You do the external history of science, I'll do the internal . . . We do sociology of science so we needn't worry about the intellectual content . . . The best approach to crime is multidisciplinary, using economic, sociological, psychological, and biological perspectives." Evolutionary biologists speak of proximate *vs.* ultimate explanations of inherited behavior as if they were quite independent. Psychologists distinguish various levels of behavioral analysis: micro, molar, individual, social, etc.

But are the stories we're telling on each level, or from each perspective, mutually consistent? If so, which one(s) is (are) causally primary? Exactly how do they fit together? I would hate to see the imperialistic expansionism of the reductionist replaced by disciplinary Balkanization, where inter-theory conflict is carefully avoided by the claim that advocates of apparently conflicting theoretical approaches are really only playing different language games. The philosophers of incommensurability, Kuhn and Feyerabend, were right to emphasize the fact that scientific concepts undergo radical transformations as science grows. Where they went wrong was in concluding that it was therefore impossible to compare competing theories in a rational way.[8]

Inter-theoretic criticism allows us to seek out the exact relationship between mutually relevant scientific theories without prejudging, as does the reductionist program, which one is more basic or more apt to be correct.

SACRED CALVES, PIGEON RESPONSES, AND THE RATIONAL PROBLEM-SOLVING APPROACH

In order to illustrate the benefits of actively comparing different theoretical approaches, I wish to juxtapose what I take to be Popper's general approach to the understanding of human behavior with B. F. Skinner's research program for psychology and Marvin Harris' attempts to explain cultural patterns in terms of their beneficial material consequences. I will proceed by first stressing the apparent conflict between Popper's theory and the other two views. Lest one simply opt for Popper's account, however, closer examination reveals that each of the three programs has positive aspects as well as obvious weaknesses. The paper ends with a call for a more sophisticated philosophical anthropology.

Popper's Approach to Social Science

Much of Popper's writing on social science is framed as a criticism of older political and social philosophies. However, in the course of arguing against unacceptable views, he also offers positive suggestions. These form the starting points for a distinctive approach to the understanding of human behavior. Other helpful hints can be found in his later works on evolutionary epistemology and objective knowledge. Here is my attempt to summarize some of Popper's fruitful ideas:

1. Humans are problem-solving animals. (There is a formal similarity between the evolution of species through variation-and-selection and the trial-and-error methods we use in science and everyday life.)

2. Unlike other animals, humans can use language both to articulate theories and to criticize them. (This makes us much more efficient at problem-solving and permits us to solve more problems per lifetime.)

3. We inherit our ancestors' solutions to problems through World-1 transmission of genes and through World-3 transmission of ideas. These provide us with basic expectations, which may be modified through experience.

4. The primary clue to understanding human behavior is the Rationality Principle (RP): People always act appropriately to their problem situations. To explain any behavior, no matter how bizarre, one describes the logic of the agent's situation *as she perceived it.*[9]

5. Although the sense of *rational* that figures in the RP is a minimal one, Popper also at times recommends a stronger sense, at least as an heuristic. According to his Transference Principle (TP), what's true in logic is also true in psychology. Although the TP is invoked primarily in discussions of induction, it would presumably also warn us against too facile an adoption of ideological analyses. In logic, our interest in a proposition is irrelevant to its truth—perhaps the same is true for beliefs.[10]

6. To understand the *effects* of a human action (as opposed to the reasons for it), we must look at the agent's overall *objective* problem-situation. Many of the bad things in society are the unintended consequences of our behavior, not the results of evil conspiracies.

7. Implicit in all the above is a methodological focus on the individual person (MI). Vague talk about class interests, the needs of society, or a pervasive Zeitgeist are at best shorthand statistical summaries of the goals, problems, and theories of individual human beings. (British English furnishes a nice homey example of MI when one says "the Government *are* considering . . ." as contrasted with the American use of the singular tense.)

8. The ability of social science to predict the future is limited in a way that is qualitatively different from anything found in pure physical science (even those branches dealing with open systems evolving indeterministically). Human activity is a result of World-3 problem-solving. Our problems and our best solutions are influenced by the theories of the world, that we accept at the time. But our knowledge of the world is constantly changing. And we cannot predict today what will only first be thought of tomorrow. There is a kind of radical

openness in World-3, which I believe has no analogue in physical science.

This concludes my attempt to condense several books and articles into an Eight-Fold Way, which I will call the Rational Problem-Solving Approach to Social Science.[11] Now, let's look at two attempts to explain human behavior, which either ignore or minimize the importance of the individual's beliefs about his or her problem situation. We'll start with Skinner.

Skinnerian Operant Conditioning

In Skinner's theory, one explains the present behavior of an animal by describing the history of rewards and punishments associated with similar behavior in the animal's past. Although Skinner has tried to extend his system to cover verbal behavior and intentional problem-solving, it clearly has the greatest appeal when applied either to lower animals or to cases in which higher animals are unaware of what they are doing. The success of animal trainers in getting animals to do tricks by a judicious schedule of rewards and punishments is well-known. Skinner claims that people's behavior can be modified in exactly the same way, especially if they don't notice what the conditioner is doing. In his autobiography, Skinner claims to have modified Chomsky's hand gestures during a debate by smiling and nodding at appropriate times. Presumably, Chomsky did not know that he was gesticulating more and more wildly—and if he did, he certainly was unaware of the link to Skinner!

My purpose here is not to give a comprehensive evaluation of the success of Skinner's research program, but simply to contrast it with the Rational Problem-Solving Approach. In Charts 2–1 and 2–2, we roughly schematize Skinner's theory of operant conditioning as happening in two big stages. (Each sub-process is numbered so it can be referred to later.)

As Skinner himself emphasizes, the parallels between his model and evolutionary theory are numerous. Consider process-1: Just as Darwinism gives no account of the causes of variation, so learning theory does not explain the repertoire of possible behaviors. (Skinner refers to an innate habit family hierarchy.) In process-2, the response of the environment to the various behaviors (or genetic variations) is again governed by laws outside of our central theory. What both theories purport to do is explain the *increased* tendency for B' to occur in the second stage (or for an inherited trait to occur in the second generation).

In early Darwinian theory (before the discovery of chromosomes), the mode of transmission of the selected characteristic was totally

Figure 2-1:

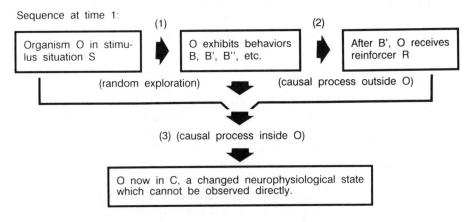

Sequence at time 1:

(1)		(2)
Organism O in stimulus situation S	O exhibits behaviors B, B', B'', etc.	After B', O receives reinforcer R

(random exploration)   (causal process outside O)

(3) (causal process inside O)

O now in C, a changed neurophysiological state which cannot be observed directly.

Figure 2-2:

Sequence at time 2:

(4)		(5)
O (in C) again in S	O exhibits B'	O again receives R

(propensity)   (same as 2)

unknown. Likewise, in Skinnerian theory. While I have alluded to a neuro-physiological change in process-3, Skinner himself would generally prefer to speak of the history of the organism without speculating on the details of the mechanism by which that experience is encoded.

Let us now contrast the Skinner scenario with a Rational Problem-Solving Approach. Whereas Skinner's model cannot even formally be applied unless the behavior in question is a repetition, the problem-solving model can—in principle—explain the very first occurrence of B. A rough sketch of such an explanation is as follows:

Figure 2-3:

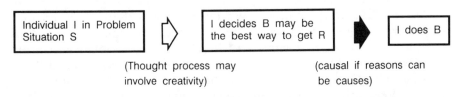

Individual I in Problem Situation S	I decides B may be the best way to get R	I does B

(Thought process may involve creativity)   (causal if reasons can be causes)

Because of its applicability to novel behavior, the Popperian model handles smoothly the cases of insightful behavior and learning by imitation that are troublesome for Skinner. One can, of course, add a second sequence in which the individual takes into account the actual outcome of the "experiment" of trying to get R through B. If B then becomes I's customary way of getting R in situation S, the observable differences between the Skinner account and the Popper account will be quite subtle.

Note that the RP approach cannot be applied if the individual is not consciously aware of either S or B. For example, it cannot be used to explain why a teacher unknowingly begins to spend more time standing to the right of the lectern if the students conspire to smile and look more attentive when she or he happens to wander over there. Here Skinner's theory works best.

On the other hand, conditioning theory has difficulty explaining why the teacher scrupulously avoids the right side as soon as he or she is *informed* of what the students are doing. However, here the RP model works quite well. One is tempted to conclude that the two theories are complementary. However, I doubt if either Skinner or Popper would be pleased with this result. In particular, Skinner would probably try to account for the teacher's behavior, after being told of the plot, in terms of higher-level rules (such as, "Don't let people manipulate you"). Supposedly, such rules themselves have been learned through operant conditioning. Popper, on the other hand, wants to extend his problem-solving approach to amoeba and stresses the importance of the objective problem situation. Both theories place high importance on trial and error, both deal with individuals, and both have some striking explanatory successes. Yet their conceptions of human nature are vastly different. Clearly, a more comprehensive view that reconciles their differences needs to be worked out.

But let us now turn to a third approach, one which focusses on social patterns of behavior. Since Harris' work may be unfamiliar to some philosophers, I will introduce it by means of an example—the case of the poor little sacred calves.

Harris' Explanation of Calf Mortality Rates

I can think of no jollier introduction to anthropology than Marvin Harris' *Cultural Materialism*.[12] Whatever one may think of Harris' own research strategy, it is impossible not to take delight in his wicked attacks on common enemies, such as Marxists, sociobiologists, and functionalists. (The criticism of Lévi-Strauss in a section called "The Raw, The Cooked, and The Half-baked" is especially wonderful.)

Very briefly, Harris' approach assumes that the basic problems that any society must solve are those of subsistence, production, and sexual reproduction. Furthermore, there are always problems of maintaining order and allocating resources. In analyzing any puzzling phenomenon, be it religious food taboos in New Guinea or the patterns of warfare in the Amazon, Harris' basic strategy is to see how the practice relates to cost-effective solutions to basic problems on what he calls the infra-structural level. In particular, he recommends that we take most seriously what people do. But what people *say* about what they are doing (their theories of their problem-situations) is of little direct interest to Harris.

One of Harris' most debated analyses concerns the sacred cow taboo in India. In opposition to reformers who wanted to promote a beef-slaughter industry, Harris stressed the material benefits of the traditional system. I certainly do not wish to raise here this very complicated controversy over social policy. However, I would like to report one intriguing side issue arising out of the extensive livestock censuses, that were taken.

In most of India, oxen (male cattle) outnumber cows (females) by ratios ranging from 100 to 70 all the way up to 100 to 47 in the northern plains.[13] The birth ratios are approximately equal, but fewer females reach maturity. However, in a certain district in Kerala, a state in southern India, the ratios are reversed. Female calves outnumber male calves by a ratio of 100 to 67.[14] When asked about the differential mortality rates, the Kerala farmers said that male calves were weaker, got sick more often, ate less. They all insisted that they would never deliberately shorten the life of any cattle and ardently affirmed the Hindu prohibition against doing so.[15]

How then are we to understand these skewed mortality rates? Is there a strange sex-linked disease that attacks males in Kerala and another one that debilitates females elsewhere? Harris, of course, looks instead at the different material conditions in the districts concerned. In India, cattle provide dung (for fuel), milk, and traction (for plowing). In Kerala's agricultural system, there is little demand for plow oxen and the males obligingly die off. In other districts of India, however, breaking up the hard, thin soil is the top priority, so milk cows become less valuable, and as if by an invisible hand, up to twice as many female babies die.

Harris' proposal is certainly testable. One predicts that the introduction of tractors (keeping other variables such as the need for cows' milk constant) would tend to increase male bovicide. It also follows from his theory that given limited resources for the production of cattle, any alternative source of fuel, milk, and traction will place female calves in jeopardy because that is the easiest way to control population growth. And sure enough, Harris reports that, in the cool plains of northern India where it is more feasible to produce water buffalo, the ratio of males to females reaches a maximum value. Yet this area, the headwaters of the sacred Ganges, is also a religious center for Hindus.

Harris' account seems to show that at least in this case, the agents' perceived problem situations and their more-or-less appropriate responses to them are quite irrelevant to the real explanation of their behavior.

A Response from the Rational Problem-solving Theorist

I think the common-sense reaction to Harris' story is also the one sanctioned by Popper's methodology: If all of these calves are being killed (no matter how subtle the means), don't the farmers actually know what's going on? Harris' example in no way eludes the Popperian approach if we hypothesize as follows:

Farmers in Kerala are in the following problem-situation: they have too many baby calves. Furthermore, milk cows are more valuable than draft animals. However, there is a religious taboo against killing cattle. The best solution to this multi-faceted problem is the following: cleverly manipulate the situation so that male calves are disadvantaged. Then, if they should happen to die, no one (neither God nor the neighbors) can blame you—you didn't kill them. And in no case does it make sense to tell a visiting anthropologist what really goes on.

This hypothesis is also testable and, as a matter of fact, Harris himself reports some data that supports part of the proposed scenario. In Kerala, a couple of farmers under questioning ". . . suggested that the male calves ate less because they were not permitted to stay at the mother's teats for more than a few seconds."[16] While in other cases, "a triangular wooden yoke is placed about the unwanted calves necks so when they try to nurse they jab the cow's udder and get kicked to death."[17]

The Rationality Approach seems vindicated. By trying to fill in the details of the way the farmers perceive their problem situation, we learn more interesting things about them. In fact, we are now faced with a new question: How do the villagers reconcile their religion with their quite blatant bovicide? In solving this problem, we will probably learn a lot about villager theology, ethics, and maybe even their theories of animal husbandry.

However, an advocate of cultural materialism might very well remonstrate as follows: Some social scientists are undoubtedly fascinated by the exploration of the webs of self-deception and mystification that people weave, but these thought systems are mostly ephemeral and without much real effect. Note that the villagers kill the calves *despite* the taboo. And their methods of killing them are so unsubtle that one can hardly find an influence of the taboo on their choice. It's mainly their verbal behavior that is influenced by their belief system.

Furthermore, there are many other parallel cases where the people concerned either aren't acting deliberately or aren't even aware of the effects of their behavior. In such cases, Harris might argue, a rational problem-solving approach cannot work; yet the cultural materialist can offer the exact same sort of explanatory analysis.

An example is the case in which infants sleeping with their mother accidentally die. Demographic studies show that female child morbidity rates go up in castes or classes where dowries are high and nothing is to be gained by daughters marrying "down." The explanation does *not* assume that the infanticide is deliberate.

Harris, of course, is not the only social scientist to employ what Merton called latent functional explanations. One must not confuse what philosophers call a *functional explanation* (in which the explanation describes the *effects* of a puzzling phenomenon) with the functional*ism* of a Parsons or Malinowski (which assumes that societies are in equilibrium). Perhaps a better name for this form of explanation is Skinner's term, *"selection by consequences."* When the people involved do not recognize the causal connection between a certain pattern of behavior and its beneficial effect, one speaks of a *latent* function.

One can even try to provide a functionalist explanation of mythological systems by showing how they increase the material well-being of the folks who hold them. By definition, any *latent* functional explanation has nothing to do with intentional problem-solving or World-3. How then do they fit in with the Popperian approach described above? Let us look at this type of explanation in more detail. I will concentrate on Harris, but my proposed critique applies to all attempts to explain by latent functions.

An Analysis of Harris' Explanatory Schema

Not all of Harris' explanations involve group selection, but some do so I will present his model that way. It can easily be adapted to the case where a single individual makes the innovation which is then picked up by the entire group.

Let us now look in more detail at latent functional explanations. Harris' scheme is not limited to cases in which the members of G are unaware of the connection between behavior B and material

Figure 2-4:

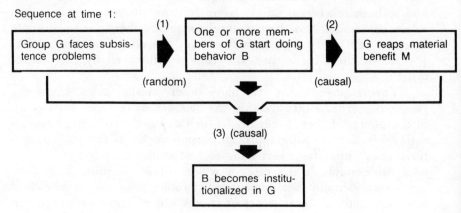

Sequence at time 1:

Figure 2-5:

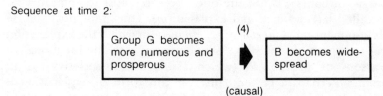

Sequence at time 2:

outcome M, but in many of his most dramatic explanations, especially those of taboos, the beneficial consequences are not recognized.

Thus, the sacred cow taboo has the unintended and unrecognized consequence of preserving breeding stock of draft and milk animals during times of famine. The pork taboo in the Middle East at one time encouraged populations to remain nomadic. (Pigs, though wonderful to eat, would tie people to a very limited part of the countryside.) And the institutionalized violence and female infanticide of the Yanomamo contributes indirectly to the maintenance of their tapir supply. (The connections in this case are so complex that neither the Yanomamo nor most anthropologists can sort them out!)

In each example, it is argued that the group benefits from the puzzling institution, and this fact is supposed to play a key role in the explanation of why the behavior originally became institutionalized. (Harris recognizes, of course, that the food practices of New York Jews or London Hindis require other explanations.)

Like Skinner, he does not provide a detailed mechanism for the *transmission* of the acquired behavior pattern, and like both Skinner and Darwin, he gives no story at all about how the behavior arose the first time. However, I wish to insist that we must raise both the problem of origins and the problem of transmission. I want to argue that at least in some cases there is *no* plausible hypothesis (at least I can't think of any) that would permit these processes to occur in the way which they must for a latent functionalist account to work. My line of argument is similar to those critics of Darwin who argued that it was impossible that the eye could have arisen by natural selection because in its primitive stages it would have conferred no reproductive advantage. Those critics turned out to have been factually mistaken, but the *form* of their attack was appropriate.

I think my point is easiest to see in the case of the Kongi. (I have used a simplified, somewhat artificial, example. Most of Harris' favorite examples are more complicated, but I think the same objection can be raised there.) The Kongi domesticate sows, but keep no boars. Every spring their pigs go for a ritual run in the forest where they mate with wild boars. The Kongi, however, know nothing about reproduction, swine or human, and they explain the ritual as offering the pigs to the gods, who luckily generally send them back. The latent functionalist would say that the practice (and indirectly, the myth) is to be explained in terms of the material benefits of having the sows fertilized.

Now, let's speculate about how the ritual might have originated. Perhaps one spring by accident one woman's sow got loose in the forest. *We* know that the ten squealing pigs, which arrived some weeks later, were a direct result. But the woman doesn't know this. So why should she ever let the sow out again? It can't arise from Skinnerian conditioning, for the reward does not follow closely on the behavior. In fact, the short-term effects of her behavior are negative—she has to go chase the lost sow.

But let's hypothesize that purely by accident, on her way to find the sow she has a religious vision and finds an especially big mushroom and decides God likes playing with pigs once in a while. We have now explained why the woman will continue to turn her sow out, but our explanation has nothing to do with the fertilization of the sow—with the latent function of the practice! It depends entirely on her religious beliefs. Even if there had been no boars in the forest we would expect her to turn out the sows in the spring.

We now turn to a second question, that of how the group came to adopt the woman's belief. Perhaps they too turn out their pigs and also find heavenly mushrooms—in which case, again, the latent function is irrelevant. Or maybe they notice that the woman is particularly successful at pig husbandry and so they copy all her pig practices. But in this case, they do realize there is some causal connection between turning sows out and raising lots of baby piggies, although their theory is different from ours. It might go as follows:

> How can one be a successful pig farmer?
> You have to keep the gods happy.
> How do you keep the gods happy?
> Well, you let them play with the sows every Spring, you never kill a sow (only boars), and you give them a food offering whenever you butcher a boar, you do pig dances every winter, etc. How do you know whether the gods are pleased? Well, if they are displeased, the crops fail, we have storms, and *there are no baby pigs in the spring* [my italics].

But in this scenario, the function is obviously not *completely* hidden from the people although their understanding of the connection is not completely correct. Again, the best explanation of the practice would include the agents' theories about what's going on.

There are two other types of scenario, but I think they can be dismissed quickly. The first hypothesizes a process of Darwinian natural selection: Individual Kongi who release their sows in the forest every spring can plausibly be said to increase their reproductive fitness because they have a more reliable food source. However, it seems unlikely that there is an inherited tendency to turn pigs loose. Also, biological evolution is much too slow a process to account for most cultural changes.

The second scenario postulates cultural evolution through group selection. Perhaps by sheer accident, plus the well-known human proclivity towards superstition, the Kongi as a group happen to adopt the institution of spring sow runs, while other tribes who are competing with them don't. The Kongi prosper while their rivals are all killed off, chased away, or assimilated. There is nothing impossible about such a scenario, but I wonder how widely applicable it is. First of all, how often does it happen that rival groups differ on only one (or a small number of) cultural parameters? To the extent that the Kongi are victorious not only because of pig fertility, but also because they historically had the richest hunting grounds and the best water supply, our explanation is diluted:

> Why do the Kongi have ritual pig runs?
> Because they fell into doing it and it led to pig prosperity which led to their cultural supremacy in the region. (Of course other contributing factors were their rich lands and good water supply.)

However, the main objection I have to this scenario is that it provides no mechanism for subtle changes in the institution under study. How, for example, could we use this kind of gross cultural evolutionary scenario to explain the differences in behavior between farmers in Kerala and farmers in the Himalayan plains? Must there be cultural conflict between rigidly-held ideologies in order for group selection to take place?

My overall argument can be summarized as follows: There seem to be only four ways in which the *fact* that behavior B leads to material benefit can cause B to become habitual:

One cognizes the connection (cf. Popper).

Skinnerian conditioning (works only if B leads quickly to M).

Darwinian selection (works only if B is genetically transmitted, and M increases reproductive fitness; also requires many generations).

Cultural evolution through group selection (works only if B is part of the group definition, and M increases cultural survival; requires group-group competition).

In *latent* functional accounts, by definition the first mechanism (rational analysis of the effects of one's behavior) is ruled out. My guess, however, is that further probing of actual cases would reveal that the natives *do* theorize that there is some connection between B and M although their theory may differ from ours. And in cases where Skinnerian conditioning, Darwinian inheritance, and cultural group selection are inoperative, without this cognitive mechanism, Harris' explanatory account won't work.

My conclusion is stronger than I anticipated: namely, that there are no latent functional explanations! However, perhaps with hindsight, this conclusion is not so surprising and is to be welcomed. Maybe latent functions are too easy to find.

Consider the following somewhat parallel case: Many people love to collect examples of successful folk medicine, ranging from rauwolfia (now known to contain reserpine) to herbal teas (some of which contain traces of useful drugs). It is sometimes claimed that although old-timers may have been in the dark about the exact nature of the beneficial effects of these home remedies, nevertheless, through trial and error they managed to select materials which, by and large, are efficacious. I am quite prepared to grant that folk medicinals are unlikely to be virulent poisons (though a surprising number, *e.g.*, penny royal, are mildly dangerous). What I am skeptical about is the claim that the explanation of why these remedies were adopted rests on their latent medicinal function. My bet is that even in the cases where they are functional, the real explanation of their popularity lies in their soothing taste or the sheer blind force of tradition. Again, my reason is that when the good effects are subtle and not immediate, there exists no mechanism by which the practice can be selected.

Methodological Morals of This Case

I have not attempted a complete analysis of the relationships between Popper's, Skinner's, and Harris' approaches to the understanding of human behavior. But even our partial preliminary comparison illustrates some of the general methodological morals, argued for in Part I.

It would not be productive to try to force any pair of these theories into a reduction relation—even an approximate one. Cultural materialism, operant conditioning, rational problem-solving—each have distinctive heuristic principles that guide our searches for explanation; each have paradigm cases in which they seem to work naturally. On the other hand, it would *not* be wise to try to divide human behavior into little intellectual fiefs. We must not simply say, "Let the Skinnerians have unthinking or habitual low-level behavior, and Popper have high-level decision making, and give Harris general cultural mores."

By actively comparing the three theories, we discover whether they overlap. (In which case they must either be inconsistent or partially redundant.) In particular, by raising a question external to Harris' research program, namely the problem of whether an institution whose primary function is latent could ever get started, we arrive at an interesting criticism of Harris' approach. Although he would like to exclude the beliefs of people from the explanation of their behavior, it seems that he cannot.

As to the rational problem-solving approach, in this paper I have presented the Eight-Fold Way as a research strategy for the explanation of *all* human behavior. Popper himself recognizes that it covers neither habitual "automatic pilot" behavior (riding a bicycle without thinking about how to do it) nor irrational perseverative behavior (trying to open a door with a key we know doesn't fit). We should perhaps add to the list certain kinds of "blind" Skinnerian conditioning.

I also think there is an important line of thought in Popper's work that goes beyond the approach outlined above. I am thinking of his emphasis on *objective* problem situations when discussing the history of science and also his stress on the objective existence of institutions.[18] Perhaps further development along these lines would narrow the gap between him and Harris. In any case, comparing the two approaches seems to be a productive exercise while seeking to eliminate one by reducing it to the other does not.

CONCLUSION

When Kuhn first presented his account of "normal science" (routine puzzle-solving or parameter measurements in which the "paradigm" is never questioned), Popperians were quick to point out its dangers.[19] Although Lakatos' theory of research programs offered a somewhat more rational account of scientific activity, it quickly became clear that the most effective way to criticize the "hard core" was from *outside* the framework of the research program.[20]

There are certain parallels between reductionism and normal science. One takes the primary science as given, either because of its past theoretical success or because of its metaphysical attractiveness, and then one tries to fit the phenomena described by the secondary science into that framework. If the reduction succeeds, clearly we have gained a deeper understanding of the "secondary" phenomena. (Successful normal science also extends the explanatory power of the paradigm.)

But if the reduction does *not* go through smoothly (and history teaches us it rarely does), there is a temptation to truncate or diminish (dare I say "reduce"?) the secondary science, to declare the unreduced phenomena as unimportant, or too complicated to deal with, or anomalous.

If the reduction attempt is carried out in a flexible, critical spirit in which one is quite as ready to modify the "primary" science as the the "secondary" one, then the exercise can be a valuable way to foster the growth of knowledge. But if both sciences are considered equally fallible, it becomes more accurate to speak of *intertheoretic criticism*. Non-dogmatic reductionism is a special case of intertheoretic criticism, but the latter methodology includes other varieties of theory comparison as well, such as the search for inconsistencies between quasi-complementary theories or the attempt to unify purportedly disjoint sciences.

NOTES

1. Aristotle, *Posterior Analytics.*
2. Lucretius, *De Rerum Natura.*

3. B. Russell, *Introduction to Mathematical Philosophy.* London: George Allen and Unwin, 1919.

4. A detailed analysis of both programs is found in J. Coffa, *To the Vienna Station: Epistemology, Semantics, and the A Priori from Kant to Carnap,* (forthcoming).

5. A. Koestler and J. Smythies, editors. *Beyond Reductionism: New Perspectives in the Life Sciences.* Boston: Beacon Press, 1969.

6. D. Mendeleev, *Principles of Chemistry.* Third English edition. London: Longmans, Green and Company, 1905.

7. For a history of the "nutshell" approach, see A. Thackray, *Atoms and Powers: An Essay on Newtonian Matter-Theory and the Development of Chemistry.* Cambridge: Harvard University Press, 1970.

8. For methods of comparing "incommensurable" theories, see my "Theoretical Pluralism and Incommensurability: Implications for Science and Education," *Philosophica* 31, 1983, pp. 85–108.

9. Cf. the critique of the "pure logic of choice" in Austrian economics.

10. See my "On Explaining Beliefs," *Erkenntnis* 22, 1985, pp. 175–186.

11. The above account improves on my "Popper's Metaphysical Research Program for the Human Sciences," *Inquiry* 18, 1975, pp. 437–462.

12. M. Harris, *Cultural Materialism: The Struggle for a Science of Culture.* New York: Vintage Books, 1980.

13. M. Harris, *Cows, Pigs, Wars, and Witches: The Riddles of Culture.* New York: Vintage Books, 1978, pp. 22–23.

14. M. Harris, *Cultural Materialism,* p. 35.

15. *Op. cit.,* pp. 32–33.

16. *Ibid.*

17. M. Harris, *Cows,* p. 23.

18. See my "Beyond Cultural Relativism." Edited by A. Musgrave and G. Currie in *Popper and the Human Sciences.* Dordrecht: Martinus Nijhoff, 1985, pp. 121–131.

19. See K. Popper, "Normal Science and its Dangers" and J. Watkins, "Against 'Normal Science.' " Edited by I. Lakatos and A. Musgrave in *Criticism and the Growth of Knowledge.* London: Cambridge University Press, 1970, pp. 25–37 and pp. 51–58.

20. See my "Inter-Theoretic Criticism and the Growth of Science." Edited by R. Buck and R. Cohen, in *Boston Studies in the Philosophy of Science,* Volume VIII. Dordrecht: Reidel, 1971, pp. 151–173.

3

Comments on Koertge's Essay

WALTER B. WEIMER

Like Koertge (in this Volume) I am bored by the topic of reduction and the thesis of reductionism when they usurp discussion of the growth of knowledge. As she asserts, there has never been a single instance of the successful reduction of one theory and its domain to another—all candidates for the title turn out—upon close examination—to be cases of theoretical *explanation* (of one theory by another) and *enrichment* (of both the secondary or reduced domain and the primary one). Thus, despite its bulk in traditional philosophy of science literature, I propose that it is more fruitful to ignore reductionism (which is, after all, a desideratum only from the standpoint of a metatheory of science, which requires a unified ontology, methodology, and epistemology as an *a priori* constraint) because it is not a genuine problem for understanding the unity in diversity of human knowledge. Instead, we should focus attention upon genuine problems in the domain of "theoretical relations." For example, we should be more concerned to understand what is involved when a theory *explains* something (either a data domain or another theory), what constraints our knowledge of epistemology places upon ontological speculation, the problems posed by attempting to understand complex phenomena, what constraints are imposed by our methodology, and so on. We will make no progress in understanding the growth of knowledge by rehashing the excellent "classic" arguments against reductionism provided by, *e.g.*, Feyerabend (1962), Kuhn (1970), Radnitzky (1970), among others (after all, the positivists and their intellectual descendents have either failed to read them or failed to understand them).

It is time to redirect attention toward the real problems of how theories are related, and how they succeed one another. If we follow this latter course, the issue of reduction will be seen correctly: As an empirical issue concerning the relationship of particular theories and domains, not as an overarching methodological constraint upon research or a metatheoretical issue forcing all theories into one type of mould.

The remarks that follow list several points that will require much thought if we are to understand inter-theoretic relations in sufficient detail that we can put reduction(ism) in its place. One must realize that in this brief commentary my remarks are sharp and simplified statements designed to provoke discussion rather than the full fledged defenses that my claims ultimately require.

EXPLANATION ISN'T REDUCTION, AND NEITHER ONE IS DEDUCTION

The first part of this claim is familiar enough that it requires almost no comment: To explain something means to offer a theory as to why the phenomenon must be what it is, not to reduce it to something else (least of all to something "familiar"). But the second contention is not commonplace, and is disturbing to Popperian sensibilities. Historically, the positivistic equation was that explanation equals reduction, which equals deduction. Against this tripartite identification, Popper (and others) have argued that to explain is not to reduce. But Popper (who, with Hempel, is the father figure for the "covering-law" model of explanation) identifies explanation with deduction. In this sense the Popperians have become unwitting allies of the positivists and other reductionists, because the reductionists argue (plausibly, I believe) that "If explanation is deduction, and if a reduction (which is deduction) explains, then there is no difference between us except Popper's aversion to the word reduction."

Against both Popperians and positivists I wish to deny *all three* identifications: Reduction is not explanation (except in the illegitimate sense of "explaining away"), and explanation cannot be deduction (even though Popper is correct that the only logic is the theory of deducibility). Instead of deduction, explanation is a matter of argumentative claiming: Theories assert that their models of reality are true. Explanations are argumentative models of the structural properties of a domain. It is to the domain of pragmatics and the province of rhetoric (rather than to syntactic structuring and/or logic) that we must turn in order to understand explanation (Weimer, 1977, 1984). When we do so, when we look at the nature and functioning of explanatory reasoning in actual scientific activity, it is clear that no explanation is "nothing but" logical deduction.

This negative thesis has been argued persuasively by Fries (1828), Körner (1966) and Feyerabend (1962). All have pointed out that empirical reality is never the last step in, to use Körner's terminology, the "deductive unification of experience," and that all genuine explanations change the meanings of the terms involved, and thus commit the equivalent of the logical fallacy of four terms (Feyerabend). This appears to be one reason why Popper has been forced to remove explanation from actual science and restrict it to a matter of after the fact reconstruction in World 3. But even if such a retreat to a purely logical realm is made, one cannot retain the equation of "explanation equals deduction" without saying that there are no explanations in domains of essential complexity (as I have used the term: See Weimer, 1982). This is because such domains range over infinite particularity, and the theories thereof cannot "deduce" infinite empirical particulars, only specify abstract rules that generate infinite particulars. Such realms employ what Hayek (1967) called explanation of the principle (rather than explanation of the particular, which is all that the "covering law" account can acknowledge). Such principles are part of an explanatory structure that is rhetorical and argumentative, but they cannot be deduced from it nor do they allow for the deduction of particular events.

But what about the "hard" sciences for which the covering law theory was developed? Perhaps complex domains are simply not scientific, and that (in part) because they cannot supply deductive explanations? This sort of scientistic reasoning fails because there are no deductive explanations in the hard sciences either. As Körner has shown, no empirical particular is ever the "last step" in any deductive unification of experience. The link between theory and experience is always one of *identification*, which is to say argumentative claiming, rather than deduction (Körner, 1966; Weimer, 1979). Thus if *no* theory deduces any empirical particular, it is clear that no explanation of any empirical domain is ever "nothing but" deduction, and that is true even though deductive logic is used in theoretical reasoning.

Another point, although tangential, may be added here. Bartley (1982) has argued that criticism (and hence the property of criticizability for a theory) need not pass through deducibility, that it need not be based upon what he called the (logical) transmissibility assumption. I mention this to caution Popperians, since it constitutes an existence proof that one indispensable property for scientific theories need not involve logic. I hope this puts them in a more receptive mood to entertain the seemingly heretical thesis that explanation is not and cannot be just deduction. Indeed, I think that the identification of explanation with logic is residual justificationism, just as the transmissibility assumption appears to be.

If we admit that explanation is argumentative and rhetorical rather than logical, we sweep one more prop out from under the diehard reductionist, and at the same time open up for critical scrutiny the previously closed problem of what constitutes an explanation. I think both consequences are quite desirable.

EPISTEMOLOGY CONSTRAINS ONTOLOGY

Put another way, what we think we know about how we know what we know forces us to be ontological agnostics and epistemic dualists. Reductionism (toward any form of monism) is incompatible with epistemology, and cannot be "known" to be correct in ontology. This thesis can be developed by straightforward examination of human knowledge and experience.

How we know is a matter for cognitive and neuropsychology: At issue is how knowledge results from the structuring and restructuring of patterns of neural activity. But *what* do we know? Here dualism is inescapable: On one hand we have phenomenal experience or acquaintance (in Russell's [1912] sense), on the other hand we have knowledge by description, discursive knowledge, of the nonmental realm with which we are not directly acquainted. Acquaintance is not and cannot be description, and vice versa (despite the fact that we can [sometimes] know by acquaintance the referential basis of a description, and can describe experience with which we are acquainted.) Although knowledge by description and phenomenal acquaintance may sometimes have the same reference, they can never have the same sense. As Russell (1948) and Maxwell (1972) have argued, our only knowledge of the nonmental realm, including our own bodies, is purely by description of its structural properties. The only *intrinsic* or nonstructural properties of objects, which we can know (if indeed we can know any at all), are those of the events in our brains and nervous systems comprising our phenomenal experience. Knowledge by description, whether commonsensical or scientific, always transcends experience. Thus arises the mind-body problem of sentience: We do not know the intrinsic properties of any nonmental entity, and therefore we cannot say whether the "mental" is or is not intrinsically identical to the "physical" (see Weimer, 1976).

This puts the cluster of mind-body problems that traditionally relate to reductionism in a new, and inherently problematic, light. What we know about the human epistemic predicament, as disclosed by the inescapability of a sharp acquaintance-description distinction, forces us to be dualists (I presume no one today is foolish enough to deny that human acquaintance is real, and that solipsistic Bishop Berkeleys who deny the realm of description are known to be acting inconsistently when they tell *us* anything of the sort). This leads to ontological agnosticism: Any claim that the "mental" is or is not the same stuff as the "physical" must rest on conceptual (metaphysical or otherwise) arguments alone, for no contingent knowledge claim can address the issue. No scientific theory can ever tell us whether the intrinsic properties of any object are the same as those with which we are acquainted. The mere existence of acquaintance, the "raw feels" of experience, forever precludes the tenability of any physicalistic monism. Likewise, the mere existence of knowledge by description precludes idealistic monism. Reduction of one to the other can never be known to be tenable.

PROBLEMS POSED BY COMPLEX PHENOMENA

The thesis that all science should be conducted upon the model of "classical" physics, and/or produce results of the same form, is widely recognized to be scientism. What we find when we examine domains of essential complexity (defined, following von Neumann, as being reached when the simplest adequate model of a phenomenon is as or more complex than the phenomenon itself) is that there are compelling reasons for why complex phenomena can never be understood on the simple science model. Indeed, the type of "progress" that is often lamented for its absence in the social sciences by the physics-is-the-only-genuine-science advocates can never be achieved. This is not because the moral sciences are "immature" or not yet scientific, but because science must take on a fundamentally different character when one deals with essential complexity. One such change was noted above in discussing explanation—understanding a complex phenomenon entails knowing the abstract rules generating indefinite surface particularity rather than being able to deduce particulars. Many other factors are involved: For more adequate discussion one must see other sources (Hayek, 1967, 1978; Weimer, 1980, 1982, 1988). But the import for reductionism of such arguments is obvious:

The quest for the reduction of complex phenomena to either the ontology or methodology of even Utopian physics is chimerical.

REDUCTIONISM HAS BECOME A "HAUNTED UNIVERSE" DOCTRINE

While it may have had a testable and refutable status when initially introduced, reduction(ism) has become something quite different for later day positivists and their descendants. In the terminology of Watkins (1958) it has become a confirmable and influential metaphysical doctrine that is immune to falsification and hence not empirically criticizable. Consider the proposition that a castle on a hill is haunted. There is "evidence" that is compatible with this (*e.g.*, hearing what one takes to be moans or chains rattling at midnight) that an advocate will take to be confirmation of the thesis. Likewise, such "partial success" at reduction is evidence in its favor to the metaphysical reductionist. But there is no evidence that can disconfirm or falsify the proposition that the castle is haunted. Even if we listen for 1000 years and hear no moans or chains, it cannot falsify the hypothesis that the castle is haunted. Such theories Watkins called confirmable and influential (influential because if you believe the castle is haunted it will affect your behavior—especially at midnight during a storm in its presence) even though they can never be falsified. Reductionism has ceased to be testable and has become a haunted universe doctrine. Its proponents are searching for ghosts.

How can one criticize a haunted universe metaphysical doctrine if it is not falsifiable? One way is by opposing it with another doctrine and adducing arguments in the latter's favor, preferably simultaneously showing that the doctrine to be discredited is inelegant, clashes with other well corroborated (not: justified) knowledge, *etc.* (see Bartley, 1982; Popper, 1983). The next section provides one more opposing argument that makes reductionism pale (indeed quite ghostly) by comparison.

DO NOT BLOCK THE DIVISION OF LABOR AND KNOWLEDGE

All useful methodological rules are negative constraints that tell us what mistakes to avoid rather than what particular actions must be achieved (Weimer, 1988). Reductionism violates this, because it (scientistically) tells us what particular result must be achieved: theoretical (ontological) and/or methodological unity. Against the reductionist goal is the brute fact of the superior power of specialization in a catallactic (abstract market) order. The division of labor that creates disciplinary divisions can produce far more than a single discipline (or single individual). The argument for the superiority of the division of knowledge is a straightforward extension of the situation for labor, which was clear to Ricardo over one hundred and fifty years ago in his law of comparative cost or association.

As Mises (1949) put it,

> The increase in productivity brought about by the division of labor is obvious whenever the inequality of the participants is such that every individual or every piece of land is superior at least in one regard to the other individuals or pieces of land concerned. If A is fit to produce in 1 unit of time 6 p or 4 q and B only 2 p, but 8 q, they both, when working in isolation, will produce together 4 p + 6 q; when working under the division of labor, each of them producing only the commodity in whose production he is more efficient than his partner, they will produce 6 p + 8 q (p. 158).

When we produce the commodity of scientific knowledge, the result is the same: superior productivity with individual (disciplinary) specialization. (And this holds even though knowledge cannot be quantized into units.) Thus over a period of time, in trial and error fashion the division of labor and its resultant, the division of knowledge, will displace isolated industry when the two compete. With the aid of these twin divisions we produce science, the arts, and technology—indeed everything that transcends the capacity of a single individual.

The Ricardian law of association is a fail-safe mechanism: It insures that we can continue to evolve and grow, even though no single individual (or plan, or theory, or discipline) can equal the productive capacity of the spontaneous order of human interaction, or even predict its course. Adherence to reductionism is equivalent to advocating central planning or a single locus of control (or allocation) for the market order: Such programs attempt to restrict the output of a complex spontaneous order (science or society) to a single plan thought out in advance, and all such attempts fail to allow for novelty and the unforeseen—for the unanticipated growth of knowledge.

In contrast, the lesson to be learned from the division of labor is that specialization—in individuals, disciplines, and resultant knowledge—will be never ending so long as we do not restrict the power of the catallactic order. Thus if we attempt to adhere to C. S. Peirce's supreme maxim for philosophy, *Do not block the way of inquiry,* we must not block specialization in the production of knowledge. Reductionism, far from advancing scientific understanding, is in fact an impediment to its achievement. In this respect it is exactly analogous to the "scientific" socialism that positivistic philosophers naively believed in— an attempt to force the abstract order of society (or science) to conform to the simple, superficially rational and desirable principles of operation that can work only in the face-to-face or tribal society that the civilized world abandoned thousands of years ago.

IN DEFENSE OF THE STRATEGY OF REDUCTION

Since I have been quite critical of reductionism, it is worth brief mention to note that the strategy of attempting to reduce (*e.g.,* the program of materialism in psychology) is often a very useful strategy for research. There is no paradox here at all: Reductionist strategy can be used to sharpen the points of agreement and disagreement between competing theories and research programs. (As a dualist I do indeed welcome computer based A. I. research, as Koertge's example indicates, because it gives me a sharper target to refute.) In this sense *trying* to reduce is one excellent way to make scientific progress, because it is likely to uncover errors very quickly. On this point I am an unrepentant Popperian: Learning is a matter of weeding out error, and I am in favor of all strategies that permit us to learn from our mistakes.

But this strategy works only in periods of what Kuhn (1970) called normal science, when there is a sufficiently strong shared framework of both tacit and explicit factors to permit puzzle articulation and solution to occur. At some point a "revolution" will occur, and then the reductive strategy is as (or more) likely to hinder as to help. Indeed it sometimes occurs that a new discipline will be created by following a reductive strategy (witness sociobiology, which attempted to reduce sociology to a "firm" biological basis). Then the revolutionary figures who created the new domain will retard progress if they push reductionism too hard (as E. O. Wilson appears to be doing).

In any event, however, one cannot blindly advocate this (or any other) strategy. When normal science breaks down, it becomes impossible to say when an anomaly will be "reduced" or, instead, become the basis of a revolutionary new theory. All strategies are fallible. Nonetheless, in situations that are far easier to describe in the abstract than to ascertain in the concrete, reductionistic programs can indeed aid the growth of knowledge.

A SCIENTIST'S UNDERSTANDING OF REDUCTION HAS NOTHING TO DO WITH TRADITIONAL PHILOSOPHICAL PROBLEMS

When a practicing scientist (especially one in a complex domain) advocates reduction, he or she is invariably not endorsing reductionism. The researcher has in mind a "simple minded" or ordinary language conception that does not carry with it the philosopher's excess baggage. My discussions with practicing researchers indicates that what they mean by "reducing to basics" means nothing more than searching for the fundamental explanatory principles involved in a phenomenon, and clearly specifying the essential (basic in a nonatomistic sense) entities which those principles utilize. What the researcher means by 'reduce' is what the philosopher means by 'explain' or 'understand.' Thus scientists are all for reduction (since it means explanation), and find it hard to imagine how (otherwise right-headed and competent) philosophers could seriously be opposed to 'reductionism.'

What I have found, in other words, is that the support for "reduction" by practicing scientists hinges upon the ambiguity of the term. When one explains to them what reductionism connotes to the philosopher, they either disavow it entirely, or endorse it on the basis of metaphysical or ethical reasons, which they clearly recognize to be independent of the epistemological and methodological constraints upon scientific knowing. Their actual practice searches for (deep or full) explanations rather than reductions. And this is, I contend, exactly as it should be—not only in science, but in the philosophy that attempts to understand it.

REFERENCES

Bartley, W.W., III. 1982. The philosophy of Karl Popper: Part III: Rationality, criticism, and logic. *Philosophia* 11, pp. 121–221.

Feyerabend, P. 1962. Explanation, reduction, and empiricism. Edited by H. Feigl and G. Maxwell in *Minnesota Studies in the Philosophy of Science*, Volume III. Minneapolis: University of Minnesota Press.

Fries, J. 1828. *Neue oder anthropologische Kritik der Vernunft*, Volume I. Heidelberg: Christian Friedrich Winter.

Hayek, F. 1967. *Studies in philosophy, politics, and economics.* New York: Simon and Schuster.

Hayek, F. 1978. *New studies in philosophy, politics, economics, and the history of ideas.* Chicago: University of Chicago Press.

Korner, S. 1966. *Experience and theory.* New York: Humanities Press.

Kuhn, T. 1970. *The structure of scientific revolutions.* Revised edition. Chicago: University of Chicago Press.

Maxwell, G. 1972. Russell on perception. Edited by D. Pears in *Bertrand Russell.* Garden City: Doubleday.

Mises, L. 1949. *Human action.* New Haven: Yale University Press.

Popper, K.R. 1983. *Realism and the aim of science.* Edited by W.W. Bartley, III. Totowa: Rowman and Littlefield.

Radnitzky, G. 1970. *Contemporary schools of metascience.* New York: Humanities Press.

Russell, B. 1912. *Problems of philosophy.* London: Oxford University Press.

Russell, B. 1948. *Human Knowledge: Its scope and limits.* New York: Simon and Schuster.

Watkins, J. 1958. Confirmable and influential metaphysics. *Mind* 67, pp. 344–365.

Weimer, W. 1976. Manifestations of mind: Some conceptual and empirical issues. Edited by G. Globus, I. Savodnik and G. Maxwell in *Consciousness and the brain.* New York: Plenum Press.

Weimer, W. 1977. Science as a rhetorical transaction: Toward a nonjustificational conception of rhetoric. *Philosophy and Rhetoric* 10, pp. 1–29.

Weimer, W. 1979. *Notes on the methodology of scientific research.* Hillsdale: Lawrence Erlbaum Associates.

Weimer, W. 1980. For and against method: Reflections on Feyerabend and the foibles of philosophy. *Pre/Text* 1–2, pp. 161–203.

Weimer, W. 1982. Hayek's approach to the problems of complex phenomena: An introduction to the theoretical psychology of *The sensory order.* Edited by W. Weimer and D. Palermo in *Cognition and the symbolic processes.* Volume II. Hillsdale: Lawrence Erlbaum Associates.

Weimer, W. 1984. Why all knowing is rhetorical. *Journal of the American Forensic Association* 20, pp. 63–71.

Weimer, W. 1988. "Spontaneously ordered complex phenomena and the unity of the moral sciences. Edited by Gerard Radnitsky in *Centripetal Forces in the sciences.* New York: Paragon House.

4

The Change of the Concept of Reduction in Biology and in the Social Sciences

WERNER LEINFELLNER

Traditional holists in biology and sociology (Driesch, Wertheimer, Köhler, and Durkhein) and modern system theorists (Bertalanffy, Miller in biology; Ackoff, Rapoport, Simon in economics; Parsons in social sciences; Heisenberg, Bell in physics and finally Leinfellner, Laszlo, Philips, Radnitzky, Day, Ruse in philosophy) share a strong opposition to the reductionist's tendency to explain the whole solely in terms of its parts. The downfall of the deductive, materialistic reductionism of the received view of reduction (Hempel and Oppenheim, Kemeny, Nagel) and the step by step demolition of the methodology of reductionism by Kuhn, Feyerabend, Sklar, Schaffner, Causey, Nickles and Wimsatt has led to a recent upsurge of antireductionism and finally to the abandonment of the idea that we reduce one theory to another (Hull and Wimsatt). It has resulted in a deep skepticism of any kind of reductionism, based on one-sided materialistic and analytic decomposition of wholes into parts. The whole idea of understanding and explaining holistic systems solely by the properties of the parts has suddenly become a dead end for research and scientific progress.

1. HOLISM VERSUS REDUCTIONISM OR THE RISE AND FALL OF REDUCTIONISM

Holists have always attacked what Watkins[1] (1965) has called "methodological individualism" or materialistic atomism of the reductionists.

It is exactly the materialistic search for ultimate particles or atoms in physics, for basic genetic units (genes) in biology and the foundation of societies on the individuals in the social sciences. In all cases the physical properties of the basic units build up the physico-chemical compounds, the biological, the economic, social and cultural wholistic systems. In Watkin's words, reductionism means to reduce our world to the ultimate constituents of the physical world, to the impenetrable last particles, which only obey simple mechanical laws. According to the reductionists, complex holistic systems are solely the result of a particular configuration of the properties of its individuals, of their dispositions, beliefs, *etc.*, *e.g.*, in sociobiology evolution of genes (lower level) should explain and determine the evolution of culture (higher level). But does it make sense to explain the upper level functions of a human body of 75kg by its 7.10^{28} u-quarks, the 6.10^{28} d-quarks and the $2.5 .10^{28}$ electrons? Could, as reductionists demanded it, the dispute between "mechanistic" and "vita-listic" schools be reformulated as the question whether biology could be reduced to physics (Oppenheim, Kemeny).[2] Also the question, as to whether there are emergent properties constituting the upper level organisms, was for Nagel[3] "just a matter of reduction." Reductionists used for their support the dynamic growth of theories, the fact that many theories included other theories has been interpreted as the claim that theories are reducible to their predecessor-theories, such as Relativistic Mechanics to Mechanics, Quantum Biology to Quantum Chemistry, Quantum Chemistry to Quantum Mechanics, Collective Choice Theory to Individual Choice Theory, Darwin's Theory and finally Mendel's Phenotypical Laws of Inheritance to Molecular Biology (hence to the Evolution of Genes, Dawkins, 1976).

The good news was that once scientific growth could be connected with reduction, reductionism seemed to become the methodology of scientific progress (Nickles, 197),[4] which promised a possible unification of theories by explaining and even replacing higher level laws by lower level laws. According to reductionists this method would permit the reducing of higher level laws, L_2 to the lower level laws, L_1 of the theory, T_1. But, the bad news was that the question remained unanswered as to what the real nature of the assumed reduction relation was. Further, it remained open whether we had actually reduced one theory to another $(T_2 \rightarrow T_1)$ or merely compared similar, partial structures of T_2 and T_1. It was no wonder that it was proven very early by Sklar, Schaffner, Causey, Nickels, Day, that the reduction relation was no simple, deductive relation at all. Rather it turned out to be a "comparing" relation, *e.g.*, the so called intralevel reduction (Wimsatt, 1976, 1976a, 1978, 1980) is in reality an iterated analogy or pattern-matching method and the interlevel reduction (Darden, Maull, 1977) ceased to hold between theories at all. These puzzling changes in the meaning of reduction occurred always, when scientists tried-in order to explain the whole by the parts—to reduce theories about wholistic systems to theories about their parts. Thus, to put it into a paradox: reductionism foundered, when it began to reduce "irreducible" social and biological wholistic systems.

2. THE RECENT DEVELOPMENT OF HOLISM

But not only reductionism changed; holism changed too, partly under the reductionists attacks, partly because of the revolutionary holistic development of physics and biology in the last decades. The traditional philosophical form of holism stated simply that: 1) The whole is more than the sum of its parts. 2) The parts cannot be understood in isolation from the whole, because they will lose their holistic inter-relations and 3) The whole determines the parts. When applied in biology it created the organicistic dynamic view (Haldane, 1926)[5] by incorporating principles of evolution (selection) and the mutual (causal) interdependency of evolving systems with the environment.

Finally, under the influence of molecular biology, population genetics and system theory, holistic systems came to be viewed as dynamic systems, which one can only adequately describe by models, provided that; 1) the evolutionary dynamics of a system S can be formulated in terms of time dependent differential equations of Haldane-Fisher type or of non-linear Eigen-Schuster type, (Leinfellner, 1984)[6]. 2) The system is open, exchanging matter and energy with the environment. 3) The evolving systems stay away from the deadlock of an internal equilibrium, and 4) the systems are order preserving and replicable.

The most astonishing and recent version of a global holism culminated in Bell's theorem (Leinfellner, 1980)[7] Primas (Essay 8 in this volume). It is a general consequence of quantum mechanics and states, expressed in a simple form, that all systems interact with all other systems in a non-local, statistically causal sense. It introduces a panholism, based on statistical mutual-causality and interaction of all subsystems, systems, environmental systems, (Leinfellner, 1984) into our universe and rejects the existence of truly isolated and independent units in nature. It puts a final end to the materialistic search for ultimate units whose properties and laws would explain all the higher complex holistic systems.

Thus, modern dynamic holism rests on three formidable assumptions: 1) on Bell's theorem, which assumes throughgoing statistical and fluctuating causal interactions between all systems, 2) on the ontological assumption that higher and complex (living) systems repeat in their specific construction the simple hierarchical global order of lower levels (as Plotkin and Baer's law suggest), and 3) on the assumption of an interaction and evolution of hierarchical levels. The presently known hierarchical global order consists so far of the energy level, the elementary particle level, the atomic level, the molecular level, the level of living macromolecules, the cell level, the multicellular level, the level of intelligent individuals and finally the social-cultural level.

3. WHAT HAPPENED WITH REDUCTION? OR THE CHANGES OF THE MEANING OF REDUCTION FOR HOLISTIC SYSTEMS

1) Since downward directed reduction (the received view) changed to a "mutual reduction," i.e. to a structural comparision between different levels, with the goal to explain how theories (T_1) or models (M_1) of the lower level with theories (T_2) or models (M_2) of the higher level are interconnected, it hardly deserved the label "reduction" any longer. 2) It is obvious that the first victim of new holism and of system theory was the ontological reduction, which wanted to reduce higher levels of holistic systems to lower ones (see sections 4–9). In spite of Schaffner's (1974) and Sklar's (1967) criticism of ontological reduction, there exists still the common view among reductionists and scientists that any methodological form of reduction (e.g., theoretical, intertheoretical, or interlevel reduction) is simply nothing else than a formal, mathematical or even a logical representation of an ontological reduction, i.e. an elimination of the higher level. The ontological reduction view would lead to the wrong conclusion that both the scientific progress and the unification of theories could be achieved only by "reducing" higher levels to lower levels. If that were true, then ontological reduction would be just a hidden materialistic reduction of the early logical empiricism. But, in spite of the fact that reduction changed its meaning to correlation and comparison of different level structures of a wholistic system, the label "reduction" survived. In reality structural comparisons began to explain the synergetic of different levels and became an explanation of how lower level structures (models) interact with higher level structures (laws), vice versa.

Finally, ontological reduction has always been identified with a bottom-top directed causation, in the sense that the lower level systems determine in a causal way, the upper level systems. This is untenable, because the mutual statistical causation between the two levels (Leinfellner, 1984) forbids simply one-sided bottom-top deterministic causation as well as one-sided (100%) top-bottom causation, (see section 3).

3. To understand fully this change in the meaning of reduction for holistic, biological and social systems we have to regard the unification of two isolated theories or models (T_1 or M_2 and T_2 and M_2) to a new theory T_3 as a new method which defines and simulates a temporal (historical) evolutionary process which consists basically of three steps; 1. The theory T_1 (or M_1) is modified ($\approx$) by a scientist to a theory or Model T_1^* (M_1^*) 2. the initial theory T_2 (or M_2) is modified too, or changed to T_2^* (or M_2^*) with the purpose to make out of the two isolated theories or models, describing different levels of one and the same holistic system, one new theory T_3 (or model M_3).

Thus, the whole process turned out to be a heuristic or inventive process to explain the complicated interactions of holistic multilevel systems. We assume that the domain D_2 of the theory T_2 and the domain of the theory T_1, D_1 at least overlap, i.e. D_1 and D_2 have a common intersection: ($D_1 \cap D_2$). In the following diagram, where modifying is symbolized by the matching relation "$\approx$" and comparing or correlating by the "$\rightleftharpoons$" relation, we get the following scheme for this unification method or trend:

$$
\begin{array}{lll}
 & & \left.\begin{array}{c} T_2^* \ (M_2^*) \\[4pt] \downarrow \uparrow \\[4pt] T_1^* \ (M_1^*) \end{array}\right\} T_3 \ (M_3) \\
\text{Upper level} & T_2 \ (M_2) \approx \\
\text{Lower level of a holistic system} & T_1 \ (M_1) \approx
\end{array}
$$

Schaffner (1974) and Wimsatt (1976, 1978, 1980) proved that this method is iterable and is in fact a method that explains how biological and social theories grow and merge to a new one, but they forgot that this method works only if the theories under investigation describe the same holistic system. Since it is the first task of the biological and the social sciences to explore the complicated interactions of living and social holistic systems, this method is certainly a valuable new tool to build up and develop new theories to understand holistic systems. How this can be done will be explained with the aid of some examples.

4. CAN WE REDUCE ECONOMICS TO A PSYCHOLOGICAL THEORY?

Often it has been said that the market is nothing else than the behavior of individuals explained by psychological laws. This looks like a complete reduction of a higher level collective behavior M_2 to a lower level individual behavior M_1. We know that individual preference behavior is dictated by maximization of the individual's utility: $M_1 = v(i) \geq 0$, but this alone cannot explain, for example, the demand and supply behavior of individuals at the market. But, we may try to find out which conditions (constraints) modify M_1, the individual preference behavior, to M_1^*, the psychologically-based behavior of diminishing marginal utility. For that reason we have to find a property which the "private" individual at the lower level shares with its higher level "holistic" market behavior, the demand and supply structure of the market ($= M_2^*$). Thus, under the modifying condition or constraint (C_1=consumption of successive units of goods by a single individual), we get the modification M_1^* of the individual's preference pattern M_1. For an empirical example of M_1^* we watch an individual drinking his morning coffee, and we will observe that, if the individual's need for more coffee is satisfied, his utility (preference) for the next cups will drop rapidly. By generalization we get our Model M_1^* of diminishing marginal utility. If we regard now the individual not as an isolated person drinking coffee, but as a participant in the market (at the higher level), we will see that he not only maintains this robust individual property M_1^* but it is reinforced by the market. We actually regard now solely the demand and supply behavior of the participants on the market (given a fixed income of the participants) and forget about competition, cooperation and all the other factors which determine simultaneously the market. Thus M_2^* is only a partial model or aspect of microeconomics ($M_2^* \subset M_2$). This partial model expresses the fact that the quantity demanded varies inversely in relation to its price. M_2^* matches ideally with our individual model of marginal utility (M_1^*): $M_2^* \rightleftharpoons M_1^*$. But, did we really, as Rothbard assumed, reduce the whole higher level market behavior to the psychological, lower level individual behavior? or economics to psychology? Certainly not. But what did we do? We simply picked out a salient and robust individual preference behavior under the condition (constraint) C_1 = marginal utility M_1^* and found that the same behavior appears reinforced in the model M_2^* as the law of supply and demand on the higher level. Thus, we did not reduce microeconomics to psychology but showed that there is a same salient, robust behavior (structure) of individuals on both levels if the holistic system: the market is activated. Careful analysis of this example shows clearly that we cannot regard it as an example of reduction of economics to psychology. It tells us: 1) under which condition (constraints) an individual's preference behavior will be reinforced by the market and 2) how we have to modify individual behavior (M_1) to $M\,\overset{*}{_1}$, when we want to integrate individual behavior into the holistic system—which we call a market.

5. HOLISM REVISITED, OR THE IRREDUCIBILITY OF HOLISTIC PROPERTIES

The problem of whether a class or group of our society is an irreducible holistic system or just a reducible aggregation of individuals touches the central issues of holism: is a whole more than the sum of its parts? Reductionists would try to reduce holistic properties, whereas antireductionists would try to prove that holistic properties are irreducible and irreplaceable by lower level properties. We will bring a proof why and how complexity-increase in wholistic systems inhibits reduction. Decision theory distinguishes between individual decision making (M_1) and group decision making (M_2). Individual competitive decision making is defined by a set of strategies, (sequences of actions or decisions): St_1, St_2, . ., St_n. There is for each decision maker an evaluation (utility U) of its strategies: U_1, U_2, . ., U^n. There are, or course, the rules of the decision process, which describe the permitted moves or sequences of moves. Winning, (the solution of a social conflict), against the other individuals, where each individual chooses his own strategies, means maximizing one's own utility $u(i) \geq 0$, by choosing one of the permitted optimal strategies or an optimal mixture of them, following the well-known minimax compromise. Here each individual follows his inherited, individual instinct of maximizing his utility in an optimal sense, given full insight in the dependency on the other's moves.

Now consider the cooperative "holistic" version of decision making, M_2, either in an economic or in a social or political scenario. Here the individual has to adopt (now as member of the whole (group) a modifying subsidiary condition, the complexitity-increasing group rationality, expressed by the superadditivity of group formation: $C = v(i) + v(i) < v(i \cup j)$. This means that the group utility (utility of the whole) $v(i \cup j)$ should always be greater than the sum of the individual utilities that the individuals can gain alone as isolated individuals. It is clear that we cannot reduce the superadditivity of the whole, of the group formation to the sum of the individuals utility because if we were to do so, the group utility for individuals would become zero, for the limiting case $v(i) + v(j) = v(i \cup j)$. Such a condition would never create cooperation, and no wholes or groups would form in reality and in experimental games. Thus, we may use for a workable cooperative union, group, class or holistic behavior the mathematical condition $C = v(i) + v(j) < v(i \cup j)$, which represents mathematically the traditional slogan, "the whole is more than the sum of the parts." It expresses the oldest social principle: "United we are stronger", and explains (because of its advantage for the individuals) even the historical formation of hordes, great families, clans, *i.e.*, primitive social wholistic systems. This condition is clearly irreducible. Because, if the greater sign changes to the equivalent sign, then group formation stops automatically.

On the other side, in experimental games, done at the University of Nebraska-Lincoln, it took an average of five to ten games until the individual gave up his noncooperative, lower-level individual behavior and adopted, i.e., learned, the higher level group behavior. A winning group is exactly a complex holistic system as already described, which perpetuates itself, because of its advantage and stability *ceteris paribus*, of course in iterated sequential games. This example tells us clearly that reduction of group behavior to "single individual behavior" does not work. It shows clearly that the individual utility behavior (M_1) changes by adopting the superadditivity constraint or condition C_1 to a cooperative "emergent" behavior of the individual as a member of a whole. This is expressed by the model M_1^* which matches with group behavior: M_2, thus we get $M_1 \approx M_1^* \leftrightharpoons M_2$. Here we cannot at all reduce the holistic dynamic group behavior to individual behavior, but we can again show under which subsidiary conditions or constraints C_1 the individuals become cooperative. (For more details see Leinfellner, 1986)

The superadditivity principle has been widely applied even for explaining holistic cooperation (symbioses) of DNA molecules with proteins (Eigen, Schuster, 1979), or for holistic cooperation between animals and finally for evolution of intelligence (Leinfellner, 1984, 1986). Recently, Axelrod has given additional "socio environmental" conditions (Leinfellner 1986) for the transition of competitive single individual behavior to cooperative holistic group behavior. We see clearly that reduction in the old sense is a redundant operation if we deal with real holistic systems. Nothing hinders us from defining superadditivity as an "emergent" holistic property in the transition from model M_1 to M_2 via M_1^*. (Holistic emergence is, of course, no

(Neo)-vitalistic concept), but is solely triggered by the complexity increase.

6. DID WE LOSE THE MEANING OF REDUCTION BY A SYMMETRICAL REDUCTION RELATION?

Looking back at the reductionism-antireductionism controversy we find that (according to Day 1977, 1985) the unidirectional ontological reduction of higher to lower level systems has lost its meaning in biology and social sciences. We also find that the intratheoretical reduction (called "transformatory" reduction by Nickles (1973), or "successional" reduction by Wimsatt (1974), which should reduce a (historically) following theory T_2 (e.g., Relativity Theory) to a predesessor Theory T_1 (Mechanics), if the subsidiary conditions permit it, is actually a comparison and merging of two robust partial structures (or partial models) of one theory T_2 (M_2) with a partial structure of another theory $T_1(M_1)$, given the same Domain $D_1=D_2$ of application or at least a common intersection of the domains $(D_1 \cap S_2)$ in a unified new third theory T_3 (M_3).

For such a partial comparison of structures we neither need Nagel's criterion, that T_1 is logically derivable from T_2, nor is it a hindrance if the two theories or their partial models M_1 and M_2 are incompatible (Kuhn, Feyerabend). For a better understanding we give a more detailed discussion of the so-called reduction of Special Relativity Theory to Classical Mechanics. We find immediately that only a part of the Special Relativity Theory, the impulse model, $M_2 =_{df} m_o v / \sqrt{1-v^2/c^2}$, over a certain domain of application D_2 can be modified, for the sake of structural comparison to: M_2^* $=_{df} m_o v / \sqrt{1-v^2/c^2}$, plus the subsidiary conditions or constraint, $c = v$ approaches 0, or $v \rightarrow 0$. We get the classical impulse model $M_1 = mv$, when the domain of D_2 shrinks to D_2^* and the limit case of this shrinking or matching is the model M_1. This so-called reduction has the form $M_2 \approx M_2^* = M_1$ and the alleged typical reduction relation, which should be asymmetrical according to the received view of reduction, is the identity relation! In this and many cases the "reduction" relation is symmetrical, since $M_1 \rightleftharpoons M_2^*$ and $M_2^* \rightleftharpoons M_1$ are equivalent, and $D_1 c D_2^* c D_2$. Thus, the identity relation, as in most cases, turns out to be a special case of an approximative comparison of partial structures between two theories T_1 and T_2 or between two models. But, why should we call it a reduction since we have lost its original asymmetric meaning? (Day, 1985)

7. (CAN WE "REDUCE" COLLECTIVE CHOICE THEORY (M_2) TO INDIVIDUAL CHOICE THEORY (M_1)?

It is widely believed that collective behavior can be reduced to individual behavior, but if we try to reduce the model of collective choice (M_2) to the model of individual choice (M_1), we will see that this is impossible. If the structure of M_2 is given by $(OA)^C$ = collective order axioms, where $(OA^C) =_{df}$ (Axiom of Connexity & Axiom of Transitivity & Collective Choice Axioms) and M_2^* is obtained by adding the Arrow condition C_2 for democratic holistic systems, here: C_2 = (U & I & P & D), where U is the independence Axiom *i.e.*, free choice among alternatives; I is Independence of irrelevant alternatives; P is Pareto-optimality, and D is non-dictatorship. What Arrow here actually imposed on the Collective Choice axioms (OA^C) is our basic idea of a free democracy. Practically he modified M_2 to M_2^* = $(OA^C$ & UPID). Now we should be able to amalgamate individual choices into collective ones and should be able to prove that the collective choices are reducible to, or are based on individual choices or preferences.

It was one of the greatest surprises in collective choice theory, i.e. of models of our free democratic society, that this "reduction" generated an inconsistency by yielding the famous Arrow paradox, better known as Arrow's Impossibility Theorem: $D \supset \bar{D}$ or D & $\bar{D}$, which means the flat contradiction that the model M_2^* = $(OA^C$ & UPID) is dictator free D and at the same time contains a dictator-$\bar{D}$. "Dictator" is intended here in the general societal sense, that the individual's choice P^1 (preference) is not free, contrary to Arrow's conditions, but dependent on someone else's choice. The impossibility of the reduction of collective choice to individual choice yielded the Arrow paradox which has shaken collective choice theory in its foundations. Its consequences are: 1) collective choice theory cannot be reduced, 2) either M_2^* is inconsistent or our democratic society based on the ideals of the French Revolution, Freedom (U,D), Equality (I), and Brotherhood (P), (Arrow, 1966), cannot be theorized free of contradictions, or 3) the society as a whole possesses superior emmergent properties, (due to its complexity-increase) which the individuals outside of society do not use or possess. Later D. Black tried to circumvent Arrow's paradox by the single peak condition, C_2^{**} = SP, which for individual choices or preferences is an almost utopian subsidiary "uniformity condition" (constraint). It demands that in any society there should exist or should be introduced a heritable, invariant, consistent underlying basic preference order for all individuals. This underlying consistent order actually matches the individual to the collective preference and could be achieved, e.g. by education, etc. Thus, we get a modification of M_2^* to $M_2^{**} = {}_{df}(OA_C)$ & UPID + (SP). If $M_2^{**} = {}_{df}(OA_i)$ & UPID & (SP) holds, the Arrow paradox disappears, i.e. our societal model becomes contradiction free and the "dictator" vanishes. Of course, D. Black's condition C_2^{**} introduced the idea of an "ought" to achieve an uniformity of preferences for all individuals and to match their preferences with the collective preferences and consequently under this strong constraints the upper level model M_2^{**} becomes one whole with the lower level model M_1^{**}, thus forms a contradictory free model M_3 of collective choice.

There have been other modifications, one of them is Skala's modification, SM (Skala, 1978)[8]. Skala modified M_2^* to M_2^{***}, by letting increase the number n of the members of the society. With this equally utopian, but not unrealistic condition: $n \to \infty$, the contradiction and the dictator vanish again.

This example shows clearly that we cannot reduce collective choice theory to individual choice theory, except by introducing voluntarily imposed constraints or uniformity-conditions such as Black or Skala's condition on the individual's preference patterns. Thus, we get the iteration model

$$
\begin{array}{ccccccc}
M_2 & \approx & M_2^* & \approx & \begin{array}{c} M_2^{**} \\ \Updownarrow \end{array} & \approx & \begin{array}{c} M_2^{***} \\ \Updownarrow \end{array} \\
M_1 & \approx & M_1^* & \approx & M_1^{**} & \approx & M_1^{***}
\end{array}
$$

which shows very clearly how initially incompatible theories or models M_1, M_2 and M_1^*, M_2^* can be modified to compatible new theories or models (the two and three starred ones). Here again, we have lost completely the idea of a rigid reduction as it was defined by the received view.

8. CAN LIFE BE REDUCED TO PHYSICS OR CHEMISTRY?

In this section we will analyse a case of a so-called reduction of a primitive biological model, M^B of self-replicating RNA strands, of Eigen-Schuster type, to Thermodynamics, $M^{Th.}$ M^B will refer to the sensational discovery by Cech (1982, 1986) of a highly unusual type of a single-stranded RNA. The findings support Eigen and Schuster's idea that single strand RNA, rather than double strand DNA may have been the most important carrier of genetic information as life began on this planet. This type of single strand RNA lives inside a creature, called *Tetrahymena*, a single cell organism found in pond water. This Tetrahymena type of an RNA strand is able to rearrange its internal structure by cleaving itself at specific locations and then joining the fragments in a specific new sequence. In other words, this newly discovered DNA can replicate itself "parthogenetically" without the help of proteins and enzymes and can thus alter its genetic informations (Cech, 1984). This example should demonstrate the heuristic non-reductive character of newest theories about life.

If we compare the model M^B with the M^{Th} model, or a model of life in its simplest form, $M^{B.}$ with the thermodynamic model which explains the chemism of life, we see immediately that they are incompatible. The most incompatible, widely known dissimilarities are: 1) the law of entropy, governing thermodynamics $M^{Th.}$ and 2) the concept of a thermodynamic equilibrium. As Friedman already showed (Friedman, 1982)[9], the so-called heterogeneous reduction, "reducing wholes (ensembles) to individuals," does not work, since, if the lower level macromolecules are subjected to the laws of thermodynamics, it does not follow that the holistic living system (our Tetrahymena-DNA) will follow those laws.

We first have to be aware that an average cell is an enormously complex system: This could be 1000 different enzymes (each existing in 100 exemplares) i.e. 100,000 enzyme molecules, each performing a particular job, regulating the metabolism and controling about 10,000 chemical reactions (syntheses) per minute. Such a complex dynamic, self-replicating system cannot be "reduced" at all in a literal sense to simpler units, without losing its holistic order because the higher-level systems in M^B are order-preserving, or negentropic, whereas the lower-level inorganic systems are order-decreasing (entropic). Reduction and structural comparisons are impossible because of the incompatibility of M^B and $M^{Th.}$ But, if we compare modifications recently proposed by Prigogine, *e.g.*, the modified entropic and modified equilibrium models of M^B and $M^{Th.}$ according to the scheme:

$$M^B \approx \left. \begin{array}{c} M^{B*} \\[2mm] \updownarrow \\[2mm] M^{Th*} \end{array} \right\} \begin{array}{l} \text{New Model or Theory} \\ M_3 \quad (T_3) \end{array}$$

$$M^{Th} \approx$$

we may find astonishing similarities ("$\leftrightharpoons$") between primitive life (M^B) and thermodynamics M^{Th} within a new unified model M_3 (or theory

T_3). Now, the structure of thermodynamics (M^{Th}) can be informally described by 1) the conservation of its energy, 2) the steady increase of the entropy of its equilibrium states, and 3) any relaxation of the constraint on a system leading to an increase of entropy.

We want now to modify the model M^{Th} (or classical thermodynamics) to the model M^{Th*} the famous Onsager-Prigonine model. Onsager (1931), Prigogine (1962, 1982). By including the environment its complexity increases and a new wholistic system: organism-environment is formed. But, the most important modification is the change of thermodynamics to a non linear version. This model is based on some invariance, or stability, conditions for the non-linear differential equations, which describe the dynamics of the Onsager-Prigonine thermodynamic systems $S \subset D^{Th*}$. Its most astonishing new property is: Its lower-level inorganic and lifeless systems can generate spontaneously and sustain order, like upper-level systems, e.g., our Tetrahymena RNA, if the following constraints hold: 1) the dynamics of the systems, their behavior, has to be described in terms of the non-linear differential equations of thermodynamics (of model M^{Th*}); 2) the system is an open system, exchanging matter and energy with the environment as living systems do; 3) the system stays always far removed from a state of internal equilibrium (equilibrium modification); and 4) autocatalytic and cross-catalytic reactions with feedback occur (Friedman, 1982).

We know now from thermodynamics (from M^{Th}) that any final state, any equilibrium state of lower-level systems must have a higher entropy than the initial ones. But, such an increase of entropy would increase disorder, uniformity, and that would be incompatible with the order-preserving tendency of our upper level living Tetrahymena-RNA macromolecule of the model M^B. But, using Prigonine and Onsager's "subsidiary constraints," we can modify M^B to M^{B*}. Then, we are able to compare more successfully M^{B*} with M^{Th*}. When we modify the linear thermodynamic model M^{Th} to a non-linear thermodynamic model M^{Th*} we have to preserve the most important robust property of entropy increase in both models. For such a purpose, we use the already mentioned constraint on the lower level and split up the total entropy S or dS of lower-level systems (the entropy increase) into two parts: 1) $dS = DS_i + dS_e$, where S_i is the internal entropy of the lower level system; 2) and S_e the external entropy of the surrounding environment. Since the lower-level systems in D^{Th*} are open, it is evident that even an internal-entropy decrease (equal to order increase) would not any longer violate the second law of thermodynamics, if it is compensated by an equal increase of the external entropy.

Thus, the lifeless lower-level systems in D^{Th*} can even be "ne-gentropic" order preserving, without violating the thermodynamic law of entropy! But, how can we change from classical thermodynamic equilibrium to non-equilibrium or disequilibrium? Quite generally, each strict equilibrium would be the deadlock, the death of any evolutionary process, the final stop; and such a system would stay forever in this final state. Again, Onsagers and Prigonine's model will help us. It is well known, that for lower-level systems not far away from the internal equilibrium, the changes or deviations from the equilibrium are getting smaller and smaller, or the gradient (the rate of changes with respect to the distance) is approaching zero.

Now, all the changes within our new holistic system: organism-environment consist of flows F of energy and heat (expressed by their gradients G), and since each flow F_i is mutually dependent on all the other flows F_j, we get for the total flows (changes) $F_{ij} = F_{ij}x_ix_j$. If the lower-level inorganic system is near the inner equilibrium, then the external losses F_j and internal gains F_j are the same $F_{ij}=F_{ji}$. According to Onsager (1931a, b), we get some kind of an invariantly stable state of the dynamic internal process if dG/dt is a minimum or the internal entropy production approaches a minimum, irrespective of the sum total of the entropy of the whole system—internal system and environment. Therefore, our inorganic lower-level systems in D^{Th*} may strive towards a steady state by increasing their order, just like any living upper-level systems in D^B. e.g., our Tetrahymena-RNA.

Since there are always disturbances, molecular fluctuations, Brownian molecular movements, random events, coming from the environment and the inner lower-level system, the steady state of the lower-level system near equilibrium will, if it oscillates symmetrically either stay steady near the equilibrium or, if it is disturbed in an asymmetrical sense, it will leave its "near-the-equilibrium state$_1$," in favor of a new "near-the-equilibrium state$_2$." It all depends on two conditions: 1) If the asymmetric disturbances or fluctuations disappear, the lower-level systems will stay stable, near the old equilibrium state$_1$; 2) if the asymmetric disturbing fluctuation prevails, it will automatically change over to a new near-the-equilibrium state$_2$. That means, if it suddenly becomes unstable, it will change from equilibrium state$_1$ to the new equilibrium state$_2$. If now the new, near-the-equilibrium state$_2$ has a smaller entropy production, it has increased, therefore, its internal order (organization).

In such a manner, a higher-ordered inorganic state can be generated from an inorganic state of lower order and organization, provided: 1) that the whole lower-level system is open, i.e. reacts like living systems with its environment; 2) that the lower-level system is far from the internal deadlock of an equilibrium and; 3) that it possesses auto- and cross-catalytic reactions, which again are necessary to create negentropy (Friedman, 1982, p. 32). Such systems will very quickly behave like biological mutants in great numbers, and the more stable and better adapted will "survive." The modified extension of thermodynamics M^{Th} to a non-linear, non-equilibrium thermodynamics M^{Th*}, ($M^{TH} \approx M^{Th*}$) will permit an explanation of the interaction between lifless and living matter, without "reducing life."

To sum up, we get some interesting philosophical and ontological consequences: 1) We cannot and do not reduce in biology any more life to inorganic, physical levels, but compare solely salient "robust" (or similar) common structures and functions of higher and lower levels if they are interacting within living holistic systems. 2) Ontology is not a description of a static, exclusive hierarchy in which two different levels are completely separated. It is rather, a dynamic ontology of becoming and explaining the function of multilevel wholistic systems (*i.e.*, the ontological barriers break down only within living systems, but not in the sense of the materialistic reduction that the lower level replaces the higher level). 3) One can demonstrate how and under which conditions upper-level systems influence lower-level systems and why lower-level systems are structurally and functionally weaker than upper-level systems. There is a strong similarity here with Prigogine's idea that even lower-level quantum physical operators are changed significantly in "living systems," by the addition of higher-level superoperators influencing the quantum physical operators "*in vivo*." 4) This empirical interaction is described theoretically by the formation of a new theory where former separated theories T^B (M^B), T^{Th} (M^{Th}) are modified and united in a new theory if they deal with the same holistic system.

9. REDUCTION OF CULTURE TO GENES?—A REDUCTION PROBLEM OF SOCIOBIOLOGY

There remains one open issue with respect to the received view of reduction. Maybe reduction reveals how lower-level systems influence and control in a direct causal sense higher-level systems. Then, any reduction program would require finding the primary lower-level causes that effect and influence totally the higher-level systems. Lumsden and Wilson have indeed linked in a new causal way cultural evolution with genetic evolution in their recent books "Genes, Mind, and Culture" (1981)[10] and in "Promethean Fire" (1982). Many critics have regarded it as a causal reduction of cultural evolution to genetic evolution, or a genetic explanation of culture and mind, but as will be shown in this chapter, that is certainly not the case.

Lumsden and Wilson's Gene Culture Theory M^{GCT} has many forerunners, but their theory is not only the best and most elegantly written work in this field, but uses the first time mathematically and empirically supported models.

On the one side Dawkins (1976), in his "selfish-gene" theory tried to reduce radically in a causal sense, biological evolution as a whole to the evolution of genes. (In his last book (1986)[12] he changed his reductionism to a "hierarchical reductionism" which is a mere explanatory method.) On the other side Maynard-Smith (1983) explained the evolution of social animal behavior and of inheritance of properties (acquired in an almost Lamarquian sense) by a game-theoretically based phenotype-genotype coevolution, which has been mathematized successfully in a new version of game theory, the theory of differential dynamic games. Finally, Eigen and Schuster (1981) extended this idea to lower-levels. They could prove that the historical evolution of RNA-strands, their struggle for survival, and their co-operation with proteins (enzymes) can be explained by and integrated into the new theory of the dynamic differential games, which includes even cooperative game theory. A detailed analysis is given in Leinfellner (1984, 1986).[12]

One may suspect that Lumsden and Wilson's two-level gene-culture theory would, in a certain sense, link Popper's World-3 with its second, and its second with its first by a bottom-top causality. Of course, such a bottom-top causality would vindicate the materialistic received reduction program. Our analysis of the Gene Culture Coevolutionary theory will prove that this is not the case. For that purpose, we have to give a short survey of the main concepts of the Gene Culture Coevolutionary theory M^{GCT} to understand the importance of Lumsden and Wilson's view. We have to understand why Lumsden and Wilson modified what we usually understand under culture and under a traditional theory of culture $M^{TC.}$ Our normal traditional theories of culture regard culture as the sum of all artifacts, behavior, institutions, and mental concepts, transmitted solely by learning among the members of a society. Since this view of society is typically static, Lumsden and Wilson modified this static character to a dynamic, evolutionary one. Thus, we get a typical modification in the sense already discussed, $M_2 \approx M_2^*$. The next decisive modification (or constraint) used the model of epigenesis, i.e. the holistic-dynamic concept that evolution on the lower-gene level and the higher-cultural level is one process of interaction between the genes, culture, and the environment.—It is called Gene-Culture-Coevolutionary Theory

(M^{GCT}) and includes the external and the cultural environment. Thus, gene evolution (level 1) ultimately causes directly the evolutionary generation of the distinct anatomic, neurophysiological, cognitive-behavioral, and indirectly the mental, relatively stable patterns in human cultures, (level 2). Epigenesis as a holistic process begins with the cells and stretches over the animalic, psychic, and mental levels, and it expands until it includes all aspects of culture. But, how does the coevolution of lower-level genes and higher-level culture work? Do genes cause cultural, or does culture cause genetic evolution, or are both equal partners? Firstly, M^{GCT} is a two-level theory in an ontological and in a theoretical sense; and secondly, its step-by-step construction in Wilson and Lumsden's fascinating book resembles more and more the enfolding unification of two theories of different levels into one.

The causal interaction of the two levels is introduced by the interactive model of epigenetic rules $M^{EP.}$ Epigenetic rules are partial, causal links which exist between the evolution of genes and the evolution of culture. This is done by the constraints of the model of epigenetic rules $M^{EP.}$ which show how culture depends on the DNA developmental blueprints, the genes. For a better understanding of the following, we have to de-anthropomorphize the concept of a rule. An effective rule is simply a one-to-one, or a many-to-one (causal) function, or a statistical one-many or many-many (causal) function, which regulates the interactions between genes G and culture C, in such a sense that for every gene g_i^{ε} G or group of genes, there exists a culturally invariant trait, called culturegene c_i^{ε} C. The function has the simple form: $g_i f c_i$. Much will depend on the empirical meaning of f and c. We don't need it for genes g_i, since there exists already an excellent bio-chemical interpretation of the genes, namely strands of DNA molecules, which determine an evolutionarily stable or invariant biological trait (phenotype or behavior).

Epigenetic rules come in two versions: primary and secondary epigenetic rules. Both channel (according to Wilson and Lumsden), create, and in a causal sense regulate invariant traits (patterns) of our culture. The primary rules regulate neurophysiological, statistically-invariant patterns of human behavior, which occur in all humans in the same invariant way; e.g., they regulate the early life of individuals, and they are cross-culturally invariant, such as invariantly recurring patterns of smell, color classifications, taste, (e.g. ideosyncrasies in all individuals). The secondary epigenetic rules are causally responsible for higher cultural patterns, called culturegenes (c), such as patterns of probability evaluation under uncertainty, risk behavior, phobias, cognitive patterns, fashions, etc. They are, invariantly (i.e. in the same form) recurring patterns of cultural behavior. A set of culturegenes (C) consists of simple culturegenes c_i, $C=(c_1, c_2, \ldots c_n)$. The epigenetic rules (f in our simplified interpretation) connect each higher level culturegene c_i with one or more lower level genes g_j. For the sake of simplicity, we take a simple one-to-one functional dependency, f, the strongest classical causal relation;

$$(g_1, g_2 \ldots , g_n) f(c_1, c_2 \ldots , c_m)$$

Interestingly, epigenetic rules resemble Freud's contributions from the unconsciousness, and the culturegenes have been anticipated somehow by Jung's archetypes, which manifest themselves in invariantly occurring and recurring cultural, behavioral patterns, attitudes, artifacts and mentifacts in mythology, poesy, and even in religion. The upper-level set C is relatively homogeneous for a specific epigenetic rule f_i, and the $(c_1, c_2, \ldots c_m)$ form a polythetic set C_1 which means that the divergent members of the set C_1 show only family resemblances.

At this state of reconstruction, Lumsden and Wilson's theory links the lower with the upper level by mapping the lower-level model of gene evolution M^{GE} onto the higher-level model of culture gene evolution M^{GCT} in the following way: for each change in the frequency of the genes within a gene population, there is a corresponding change of the frequency of our culturegenes. If α, β, γ, are frequencies (in terms of probabilities), then cultural change is a change in the frequency distributions from C_1 to C_2.

$$C_1 = \alpha_1 c_1, \alpha_2 c_2, \ldots, \alpha_n c_n : \alpha_1 + \alpha_2 +, \ldots, + \alpha_n = 1$$

If: $\alpha > \beta$ or $\beta > \alpha$

$$C_2 = \beta_1 c_1, \beta_2 c_2, \ldots, \beta_n c_n : \beta_1 + \beta_2 +, \ldots, + \beta_n = 1$$

The causal impact of the lower level M^{GE} on M^{GCT} the higher level, is achieved by two subsidiary conditions (constraints) of the Gene Culture Coevolutionary theory (GCT) namely: 1) that changes in the gene distribution have a causal effect on the culture gene distribution and 2) vice-versa. If we have two levels, we get a simplified version of the causal interaction of the lower level M^{GE} with M^{GCT} the higher level, by the following scheme:

Socio cultural (higher level) $\alpha_1 c_1$, $\alpha_2 c_2$, $\ldots$, $\alpha_n c_n$ Model M^{GCT}

$$\uparrow\downarrow \ \ \uparrow\downarrow \qquad\qquad \uparrow\downarrow$$

Epigenetic rules f   f   f   f

$$\downarrow\uparrow \ \ \downarrow\uparrow \qquad\qquad \downarrow\uparrow$$

Gene Level (lower level) $\gamma_1 c_1$, $\gamma_2 c_2$, $\ldots$, $\gamma_n c_n$ Model M^{GE}

Once we have arrived at this point, we have to use Wilson and Lumsden's concept of "translating." Translation is the causal effect of the epigenetic rules on the evolution of individuals and their development of individual cultural patterns (observed and measured by the usage-bias curves, which display and represent mathematically the probabilities γ_i that an individual $_i$ (organism) will use one or the other of various culturegenes c_i, given that it possesses a certain genotype and lives in a particular environment), f.i.. $_i$ follows a new cultural custom, prefers a new living style or a new fashion. To establish a statistical correspondence of the theoretical terms (g_i) of the lower level model M^{GE} with the upper level model's (M^{GCT}) theoretical terms (c_i), the average frequency of a culture-gene (c_i) within the whole population is obtained from the ethnographic curve, a sociometric concept of the higher level M^{GCT}. Ethnographic curves define a cultural, statistically invariant pattern, i.e. a pattern that remains stable for a relatively long time, but not forever, f.i., fashion trends. The ethnographic curves represent the proportion of individuals in the society that possess one or the other culturegenes as opposed to another (previous) distribution. It can be used as an ideal intrasocietal measure to compare different culturally invariant patterns even in different cultures.

Now, Wilson and Lumsden can argue that the usage bias curve of any individual in a certain culture gives the actual probability that this individual selects a given culture gene c_i from its culture, i.e. from the available pool of culturegenes C. Hence, given the usage bias curve for each individual, the distribution of the culturegenes and the rate of gene-culture coevolution can be determined. The matching of M^{GE} with M^{GCT} is achieved if the following additional subsidiary conditions (constraints) are observed, taken of course, from lower-level population genetics: 1) If genes, or small portions of genes, or polygenetic groups really cause and control the impact of epigenetic rules on cultural, relatively stable patterns, the culturegenes (bottom-top causality). 2) If no uniform epigenetic rules exist. 3) If variations *e.g.*, mutations in the epigenetic rules are inherited, i.e. the interactions between the two levels is of statistical causal nature. 4) If the epigenetic rules have the supposed causal effect on the individual's cultural development of its cultural patterns (gene culture translation). And 5) if culture genes differentially effect the genetic fitness of the next generation by altering the frequencies of the culturegene distribution in a population and are thus able to influence the evolution of culture in a causal sense by the coevolution of the genes (top-bottom causality).

Without going into the formal and empirical details of the sociometric support of the Gene Culture Coevolutionary theory (M^{GCT}), we may now summarize our results in the following five paragraphs.

1) The Gene Culture Coevolutionary theory (M^{GCT}) is obtained by a heuristic unification process, not by a reduction. Given the theory of gene evolution (M^{GE}) and given a statistical matching of the lower-level gene evolution theory (M^{GE}) to the higher level gene culture Coevolutionary Theory M^{GCT}, ($M^{GE} \leftharpoondown M^{GCT}$,) then the rectangles re-represent the synthesis, or the "modifying unification" of previously incompatible theories or models, which deal with the same holistic system, (here cultural and genetic evolution). Thus we get:

$$
\begin{array}{l}
\text{Traditional} \\
\text{Theory of} \\
\text{culture } M_2 \approx
\end{array}
\left|
\begin{array}{c}
M_2^* \\
\uparrow\downarrow
\end{array}
\right|
\begin{array}{c}
\text{Evolution} \\
\text{of culture } M_2^* = \\
\end{array}
\left|
\begin{array}{c}
M^{GCT} \\
\uparrow\downarrow
\end{array}
\right|
\left.
\begin{array}{l}
\text{New theory} \\
\text{of} \\
\text{coevolution}
\end{array}
\right\}
$$

$$
\begin{array}{l}
\text{Traditional} \\
\text{Genetics } M_1 \approx
\end{array}
\left|
\begin{array}{c}
M_1^*
\end{array}
\right|
\begin{array}{c}
\text{and: Evolution} \\
\text{of Genes } M_1^* =
\end{array}
\left|
\begin{array}{c}
M^{GE}
\end{array}
\right|
\left.
\begin{array}{l}
\text{of genes} \\
\text{and culture}
\end{array}
\right.
$$

From a metatheoretical point of view this scheme symbolizes a heuristic, inductive or statistical method of inventing and modifying, f.i. previously incompatible theories of different levels having the same or similar domains (applications) and describing one and the same holistic system to a new compatible theory. This method is by no means a reduction of culture to genetics; rather it correlates, or matches, two formerly incompatible theories (models) of evolution to a new single theory or model. Thus, Lumsden and Wilson have used an unifying and integrating method, which, since it is iterable, could merge and unify our knowledge by fusing theories (models) of different levels, dealing with the same holistic system, to more and more complex supertheories.

2) Since the Gene Culture Coevolutionary theory is an intrinsic statistical theory, it can explain only group or average behavior of individuals within a society, but never the exact cultural patterns of a single individual. Therefore, the concept of causality (used within M^{GCT}) is that of a statistical causality (see Leinfellner, 1981, 1984)[12] where the concept of statistical causality in social sciences is discussed in more detail). Moreover, the transitional probabilities, for example, in cultural-pattern-changes and in changes of the ethnographic curves have to be Markovian. Therefore, since statistical causality and the nature of transitional probabilities do not permit classical deterministic causality and throughgoing transitivity of causal chains, we have to reject for M^{GCT} a deterministic bottom-top causality. Thus, we have to assume for the whole of gene culture coevolution a partial, statistical, mutual causality of many-many type, which permits only that many (weighted) partial causes effect many (weighted) partial effects.

Therefore, between upper levels and lower levels there are only mutual, statistical causal relations (Leinfellner, 1981, 1984). This has the tremendous advantage that we are able to include into the partial causes the free will (the freedom of choice) of a single individual which becomes one of the partial causes, which influence cultural patterns *i.e.,* the ethnographic curves. Therefore, there exists neither a "materialistic" deterministic causation from bottom to the top levels nor a one-one deterministic causation from the top to the bottom!

3. Statistical causation has further the advantage that the higher the complexity of a level, the more likely is its impact on less complex levels. Or, given this mutual interaction of genes-culturegenes, the changes in the genes will be caused with higher probability by the higher-level units, the culturegenes. Thus, we have a predominance of statistical top-bottom causality. Therefore, in the main extent, cultural coevolution can be influenced only by a lower probability by the lower-level units (genes). This again makes it unlikely—contrary to the usual interpretation of Wilson and Lumsden's Gene Culture Coevolution theory—that individual genes or small polygenetic groups have a direct deterministic effect on today's cultural levels of organization. But, higher levels of cultural evolution have a predominant evolutionary, social, political, and perhaps ethical autonomy and regulating influence. Since the predominance of the higher level units is only a statistical causation its "statistical" autonomy should, of course, never violate fundamental basic chemico-physical conditions of existence and functioning of the lower level, for example, by pollution, atomic genocide.

4) Therefore, we agree, albeit cautiously, with Lumsden and Wilson that because of the mutual dependency of genes and cultural evolution, genetic engineering could be used only as a partial therapeutical, preventive measure. The same holds for gene manipulations for creating healthier designs and patterns for better human societies. But, this again will depend solely on the upper-level ethical standards and the upper-level ethical evaluation of the scientific research strategies used for genetic engineering and changes. But, we disagree that these changes could be done solely by bottom changes, *i.e.,* changes in our hereditary genetic material.

5) Given (1) and (4), we may better regard the interaction between genes and culturegenes as a sequence of alternating gametheoretic, competitive (Dawkins games) and cooperative, conflict solutions (Axelrod's games) (see Leinfellner, 1984)[13]. This could be done without violating the basic conditions of the Gene-Culture-Coevolutionary Theory and has the tremendous advantage that the periodically ocurring ups and downs of cultural trends could be explained as evolu-

tionarily stable, but cyclic solutions of a conflict between the genes and our culture or between our animalic heritage and our intelligence.

The analysis and reconstruction of Lumsden and Wilson's Gene Culture evolutionary theory M^{GCT}, ($M^{GE} \leftrightarrows$ makes it very unlikely that even exact knowledge of the structure of individual genes (small strings of DNA) alone would be the decisive tool in sociocultural engineering programs as it is expected by adherents of Wilson and Lumsden. But, the astonishing result that higher levels of organization may have a greater evolutionary statistical causal significance and impact than lower-level units may lead to important social, political and ethical implications.

A metatheoretical analysis of Wilson's and Lumsden's theory then shows how our views of scientific theories have changed. Scientific theories are no longer static but are dynamic and evolving units. Since the method of modification and unification of former incompatible theories (models) creates compatible supertheories or supermodels, it is no longer appropriate to use the label "reduction" for such a unifying method. This evolutionary, self-improving unification process is rather an innovative and new interdisciplinary method. If it continues, it has the enormous future chance to heuristically unite scientific theories or models of different levels and different disciplines (if and only if they deal with the same holistic systems) into gigantic, hierarchically ordered networks of theories or models about these holistic systems, as, for example, our culture. Its potential future lies in its possibility to connect and build up step by step a holistic, cognitive network of theories (models) about our society and could prove that our society is (in a global sense) really a dynamic, interwoven holistic system of culture, life and inorganic levels.

NOTES

1. J.W.N. Watkins, 1953. "Historical Explanation," p. 509.

2. P. Oppenheim, and J.GG. Kemeny, 1956. "On Reduction," *Philosophical Studies* 7, pp. 6–19.

3. E. Nagel, 1960. "The Meaning of Reduction," p. 310.

4. T. Nickles, 1973. "Two Concepts," p. 280.

5. J.S., Haldane, 1926. The Science, pp. 74–75.

6. W. Leinfellner, 1984. "Evolutionary Causality," pp. 260–262.

7. W. Leinfellner, 1980. *Grundtypen,* p. 129.

8. H. Skala, 1978. "Arrows Impossibility Theorem," p. 224.

9. K. Friedman, 1982. "Intertheoretic Reduction," pp. 17–20.

10. H. Lumsden and E. Wilson, 1981, p. 119.

11. R. Dawkins, 1986, pp. 13–14.

12. W. Leinfellner, 1986. pp. 138–147; 1984, pp. 233–246.

13. W. Leinfellner, 1984. p. 253.

REFERENCES

Arrow, K. 1966. *Social Choice and Individual Values 2.* New York: Wiley.

Axelrod, R. 1984. *The Evolution of Cooperation,* New York: Basic Books.

Causey, R. 1972. "Attribute-identities in Micro-reductions." *Journal of Philosophy* 69, pp. 407–422.

Cech, T.R.; e.a. (1982). "Self-Splicing RNA: Autoexcision and Autocyclization of the Ribosomal RNA Intervening Sequence of Tetrahymena", Cell, Vol. 31, No. 1, pp. 147–157.

Cech, T.R.; e.a. (1986) "The Intervening Sequence RNA of Tetrahymena is an Enzyme", Science, Vol. 231, No. 4737, pp. 470–475.

Darden, L. and Maull, N. 1977. "Interfield Theories." *Philosophy of Science* 44, pp. 43–64.

Dawkins, R. 1976. *The Selfish Gene.* New York: Oxford University Press.

Dawkins, R. (1986). *The Blind Watchmaker,* Essex.

Day, M.A. (1977). *Aspects of the Reduction of Thermodynamics to Statistical Mechanics,* Diss. UNL Lincoln.

Day, M.A. 1985. "Adams on the Theoretical Reduction." *Erkenntnis* 23, pp. 161–184.

Eigen, M., Schuster, P. (1979) *The Hypercycle.* New York, Springer.

Friedman, K. 1982. "Is Intertheoretic Reduction Feasible." *British Journal of Philosophy of Science* 33, pp. 17–40.

Haldane, J.S., *The Science and Philosophy,* London, 1926.

Kemeny, J.G., and Oppenheim, P., "On Reduction," Philosophical Studies, Vol. VII (1956), pp. 6–19.

Leinfellner, W. and Leinfellner, E. 1978. *Ontologie, System Theorie und Semantik.* Berlin: Dunker and Humblot.

Leinfellner, W. 1980. "Grundtypen der Ontologie" Edited by Haller, R. Grassl, W. in *Language, Logic, and Ontology*, pp. 124–133, Hoelder-Pichler-Tempski: Vienna.

Leinfellner, W. 1981. "Kausalität, in den Sozialwissenschaften". Edited by Posch. G. in *Kausalität, Neue Texte* pp. 221–260. Stuttgart: Reclam.

Leinfellner, W. 1984. "Evolutionary Causality, Theory of Games, and Evolution of Intelligence." Edited by Wuketits, F. in *Concepts and Approaches in Evolutionary Epistemology.* pp. 233–276. Boston: Reidel.

Leinfellner, W. 1986. "The Prisoner's Dilemma and its Evolutionary Iteration" Edited by Diekman, A., Mitter, P. in *Paradoxical Effects of Social Behavior.* pp. 136–148. Physica, Heidelberg.

Leinfellner, W. 1985. "Foundations of the Theory of Evolution, the Merging of Different Models to A New Theory of Evolution: Social Methods in the Biological Sciences" Edited by Weingartner, P., Dorn, G. in *Foundations of Biology* pp. 2–32. Vienna: Hoelder Picher Tempski.

Lumsden, H. and Wilson, E. 1981. *Genes, Mind, and Culture.* Cambridge: Cambridge University Press.

Lumsden, H. and Wilson, E. 1983. *Promethean Fire.* Cambridge: Cambridge University Press.

Maynard-Smith, J. 1982. *Evolution and the Theory of Games.* Oxford: Oxford University Press.

Nagel, E. 1960. "The Meaning of Reduction in the Natural Sciences." Philosophy of Science. Cleveland: The World Publishing Company.

Nickles, T. 1973. "Two Concepts of Intertheoretic Reduction." *Journal of Philosophy* 70, pp. 288–312.

Philips, D. 1976. Holistic Thought in Social Science. Stanford: Stanford University Press.

Prigogine, I., *Non equilibrium Thermodynamics,* New York, 1962.

Prigogine, I., *Vom Sein zum Werden,* Piper, München, 1982.

Radnitzky, G. 1983. "The Science of Man: Biological, Mental, and Cultural Evolution." Edited by Cappelletti, V.; Luiselli, B.; Radnitzky, G. and Urbani, E. in *Saggi Di Storia Del Pensiero Scientifico, Dedicati A Valerio Tonini.* Pp. 369–401. Roma: Soieta Editoriale Jouvence.

Skala, H. 1978. "Arrow's Impossibility Theorem: Some New Aspects." Edited by Leinfellner, W. and Gottinger, H. in *Decision Theory and Social Ethics.* Pp. 213–227. Boston: Reidel.

Sklar, L. 1967. "Types of Intertheoretic Reduction." *British Journal for Philosophy of Science* 18, pp. 109–120.

Watkins, J.W.N. 1953 "Ideal Types and Historical Explanation". Edited by Feigl, H., Brodbeck, H. in *Readings in the Philosophy of Science,* New York. Pp. 509.

5

Between Reductionism and Holism

LARRY BRISKMAN

Many scientists and philosophers of science see the programme of reductionism as the sole blueprint for scientific progress, and for a unified scientific understanding of nature. From this viewpoint, various versions of anti-reductionism (*e.g.*, emergentism) are simply so much rubbish lying in the path of science. One particularly smelly rubbish of this type is holism—the doctrine that an organised whole is not only greater than the (additive) sum of its parts (which is rather a triviality), but also that the behavior of the parts is causally determined by the transcendent whole, which follows its own *sui generis* "laws of motion" (so to speak). Committed holists, on the other hand, have often viewed reductionism as a dogmatic (or *a priori*) eliminative materialism, which is unable to see an obvious fact of existence—namely, that there are many more things between heaven and earth than are dreamt of in its philosophy. Reductionists, of course, would reply (with Nelson Goodman) that, unlike holists, their worry is that there should not be many more things dreamt of in our philosophy than there are between heaven and earth; and that it is only by following a programme of reduction that we can clear the ontological slum which holists are apt to create.

If I understand Leinfellner's paper at all—and I must admit to having had considerable difficulties in this regard—his aim is somehow to unite these two antithetical positions by modifying each of them. Each has a measure of truth-content (which needs to be preserved in a new, third, approach) and a measure of falsity-content (which needs to be renounced). The truth-content of reductionism seems to lie, for Leinfellner, in the claim that certain structural similarities can be found between higher-level "wholes" (like markets, group utilities, or living cells) and their lower-level "parts" (like psychological preferences, individual utilities, or thermodynamic systems); while reductionism's falsity-content seems to lie in its claims that the higher levels can be eliminated in favour of the lower levels, and that the laws or behaviour holding at the higher levels can be fully explained in terms of, or reduced to, those applicable at the lower levels. On the other hand, the truth-content of holism seems to reside not only in its realisation that organised wholes are more than the (additive) sum of their isolatable parts, but more importantly in its claim that the whole can causally influence the behavioural patterns of its parts; while holism's falsity-content consists in its assumption that the theories (models) required for understanding holistic systems must be totally *sui generis*, and that the laws relating to such wholes may contradict, or override, the laws governing their parts.

If I have thus got him right, Leinfellner's hope is to develop a methodological approach to explanation which is between those of traditional reductionism and traditional holism, and which incorporates the virtues of both while avoiding their pitfalls. As Leinfellner puts it: ". . . instead of reducing levels we bridge the gap between upper-level holistic systems and its (*sic*) lower-level parts (subsystems) by searching for similarities" and building up ". . . a network of theories or models". Rather than attempting to achieve a uni-directional reduction of wholes to parts (traditional reductionism) or of parts to wholes (traditional holism), our aim changes to one of achieving ". . . a 'mutual' reduction, *i.e.*, to a structural comparison between different levels, with the goal being to bridge the gap between them by showing how lower-level structures are integrated in, and correlated with higher, more complex upper-level structures." In this way we avoid, it appears, the eliminative consequences of reductionism without thereby embracing the ontological excesses of traditional holism.

What, then, is Leinfellner's new method or model of explanation?; his new way of understanding the relations between higher-level systems and their lower-level subsystems? I must admit here to being rather clearer as to what his new method or model *is not* than I am as to exactly what it is (more on this later). One thing which his model of explanation is not, is that it is not deductive. In searching for structural similarities, or even structural identities, between higher and lower-level systems, we are not attempting to explain deductively the structural properties of one in terms of the structural properties of the other—for to do this would be to land ourselves back in one of the rejected uni-directional forms of explanation. The reason for this is that, in the usual case, deductive explanation is not reversible—

one will rarely be able to turn the explanation "upside-down" and deductively explain the *explanans* in terms of the *explananda*.

But in what sense, then, is the search for, or discovery of, structural similarities or identities explanatory *at all?* What exactly does the discovery of structural similarities explain? To take a silly example: chess and checkers (or draughts) undoubtedly share certain 'structural similarities' in that both are two-person board games played by moving pieces in accordance with fixed rules. These shared properties are even, to use Leinfellner's oft used phrase, "salient and robust" aspects of each game—if, that is, it is raining outside and I wish to pass a quiet afternoon with a less than close second cousin. Yet I don't have the foggiest idea what the discovery of such 'structural similarities' by itself explains. Of course, statements of structural similarity may play a role as *part* of an explanation (for example, an explanation of why, in the circumstances described, chess and checkers may be inter-substitutable); but as part of an explanation such statements are, I maintain, part of a deductive explanation. So although Leinfellner claims that his "structural comparisons which replace fully what has been called reduction" retain "the explanatory function of the former reduction", I am less than convinced of this.

Much more intriguing, however, than the question of what Leinfellner's new method or model of explanation is not, is the question of what it is. Here again, I have had considerable difficulties understanding Leinfellner's paper; but it seems to me that his proposed method might be dubbed "the method of structural modification and comparison". The basic idea appears to be something like this: take two theories (models, sets of assertions) describing what are taken to be two "levels" of objects, processes, *etc.*, and where the domains of application of the two theories at least partially overlap (i.e., they treat of some shared referents). Then the method of structural modification and comparison consists in attempting to "match" (or, perhaps, "map") partial aspects of each theory, or model, with (or onto) the other. This will usually involve first modifying either, or both, of the initial theories so as to produce the potential for "matching". This modification process seems to be symbolised by '$\approx$' (*i.e.*, $M_1 \approx M_1^*$ seems to mean that M_1 has been modified to M_1^* either by restricting M_1 by adding certain conditions to it, or by expanding M_1 by adding some new element not previously found in it, or both). Next, having modified M_1 to M_1^*, or M_2 to M_2^*, or both, we compare them for partial structural similarity or identity (this similarity or matching relation being symbolised by '$\rightleftharpoons$'). Then if, say, $M_1^* \rightleftharpoons M_2$, then we have somehow bridged the gap, or at least partially done so, between the two "levels" described in our original theories, and shown that some "salient and robust" structural property of M_2 can be matched (mimicked?; reproduced?) at the "level" of M_1. Thus, we have brought the two "levels" into some kind of "partial structural harmony" without reducing one to the other, and have thus achieved a kind of unifying integration of the two "levels" without reduction.

Now, following Agassi, I do not mind admitting that I do not understand what I say when I say something that I do not understand. My problem with Leinfellner's viewpoint here is not so much understanding the process of modification symbolised by $\approx$ (although I do not see what constraints Leinfellner puts on it) as it is in understanding what the matching or structural similarity relation $\rightleftharpoons$ is supposed to consist in. To see my problem, consider two systems S_1 and S_2, which completely lack any structural similarities, so that presumably $S_1 \not\rightleftharpoons S_2$. It immediately follows that S_1 and S_2 share at least one rather "salient and robust" (from Leinfellner's viewpoint) structural similarity: namely, the structural similarity of bearing $\not\rightleftharpoons$ to each other! To put this point another way, any two things must be similar in some respect. For assume that they are dissimilar in all respects; then they are similar to each other in the respect of being dissimilar to each other in all respects. Complete dissimilarity is thus impossible; and so the general notion of similarity is empty.

It might be thought that this point is a mere sophism, but it isn't. As David Miller has pointed out to me, it has a clear representation in logic. For assume that two theories (which are, after all, the objects of Leinfellner's method) are totally dissimilar—that is, assume they disagree as to the truth value of every non-logical proposition (alternatively, for every substantive question Q, T_1 gives the answer "p" if, and only if, T_2 gives the answer "not-p"). Now consider, two such questions Q1 and Q2; T_1 gives the answers 'p' and 'q' (say) while T_2 gives the answers "not-p" and "not-q". Then both T_1 *and* T_2 agree that "p $\rightarrow$ q", "not-p $\rightarrow$ not-q", "p $\longleftrightarrow$ q", "not-p $\longleftrightarrow$ not-q", and so on. But this entails that they *do not* disagree as to the truth value of every non-logical proposition, or that there are questions to which both give *the same* answers, and so refutes the hypothesis that they are totally dissimilar. It follows that, as a matter of logic, no two theories can be totally dissimilar; and so it must be possible to find "Leinfellnerian structural similarities" between any two such theories.[1]

For the notion of similarity to bite, we must be supplied with some point of view, or problem, or interest from which to judge the question. For example, is ▫ similar to ⊙? If our point of view or interest is that of looking for figures with dots inside them, then they are similar; but if we are looking for circles, or for figures of the same geometrical shape, then they are not similar. There is no point in seeking "structural similarities" between theories or models describing different "levels" unless we are supplied with some problem, or point of view, or interest—for in their absence we will always be able to find *some* "structural similarities" between them and will thus be able, by Leinfellner's method, to integrate them. It follows that 'success' in employing Leinfellner's method is in itself of little interest. Much better, it seems to me, would be to investigate the question of the relation between different theories, or between different 'levels', by trying to see if a rather hard-headed, and constraining, reductive explanation can be achieved with respect to them. This attempt, whether it leads to success or failure, can at least lead to failure (unlike Leinfellner's method), and so offers us the opportunity of learning something.

These last points relate back to my previously hinted at problem with Leinfellner's process of modification $\approx$ — that is, the apparent lack of any constraints imposed on it. Some of his examples of the successful use of his method have rather the feel of a kind of hocus-pocus, in which one simply looks at (say) M_1; picks some "salient and robust" property P_1 out of it; maps some plausible M_2 analogue of P_1 into M_2 (thus getting $M_2 \approx M_2^*$); and then—*hey presto*—$M_1 \rightleftharpoons M_2^*$! But *of course* M_2^* will "integrate" with, or bear a striking structural similarity to, M_1—since it was generated just to do so. So unless some constraints are imposed on the allowable means of modification, the achievement of "Leinfellnerian integration" looks once again not only much too easy, but moreover bears a striking structural similarity to arbitrariness (*i.e.*, it looks singularly arbitrary).

Compare this with the situation that pertains when we seek a reductive explanation of one theory or 'level' in terms of another. Consider, for example, the attempt to reduce phenomenological thermodynamics to statistical mechanics. Because of the 'tightness' of reductive explanation, this attempt quickly ran into some severe difficulties—for instance, the fact that thermodynamics included irreversible phenomena, whereas the known laws of mechanics were completely reversible. How could irreversible thermodynamic phenomena be explained (deductively) from reversible mechanical laws? The answer was: they couldn't be. Rather, a completely new physical quantity—entropy—had to be introduced into the 'mechanical' premisses in order to get the explanation, and so the reduction, to go through. Because of the constraining nature of what was being at-

tempted, the introduction of entropy (and so, in effect, the modification of mechanics) was not arbitrary in the least: it seemed to be
required if the problem was to be solved.

Obviously, there are many points in Leinfellner's paper which
I cannot discuss in a brief comment such as this—for instance, some
of his particular examples are worthy of considerable discussion in
themselves. So let me end by saying that although I have here
championed the search for reductive explanation, in preference to
"Leinfellnerian integration", this should not be taken to imply that
I am a reductionist, or that I think that the programme of reduction
has any sort of privileged methodological status in science as compared
to what I have elsewhere called the programme of emergence.[2] Rather,
I champion the search for reductive explanations because a) such
searches *can* fail; b) I hope that they *will* fail, and thus allow emergentism to pass some severe tests; and c) even when they succeed,
they will generally only do so by forcing us to modify non-arbitrarily,
and so improve upon, the theoretical knowledge that was available
to us prior to the attempt. In other words, rather than aiming to
"overcome" the division between reductionism and holism, I prefer
to try to sharpen as much as possible the *debate* between reductionism
and holism—for it is only in this way that we can hope best to learn
where the truth of the matter lies.

NOTES

1. Of course, it is possible for two theories to share only tautologies as
   common consequences, so that they are maximally independent. But in
   that case one will hardly want to apply Leinfellner's method of structural
   modification and comparison to them, or to "integrate" them, since their
   domains will fail to overlap. Moreover, maximal independence will be a
   very rare occurrence indeed if what we are considering are actual scientific
   theories (such as, for example, General Relativity and the Quantity Theory
   of Money). In these cases the "relevant" or "interesting" non-logical
   consequences of the two theories will, most likely, fail to overlap; but one
   can always then construct shared disjunctive non-logical consequences, and
   from some (usually rather perverse) point of view these shared consequences
   will be "relevant" or "interesting". Incidentally, the conclusion reached
   in the text is similar to that of the "Theorem of the Ugly Duckling",
   according to which an ugly duckling and a swan are just as "similar" as
   are two swans. (See S. Watanabé, "Une Explication Mathématique du
   Classement d'Objects" in S. Dock and P. Bernays (eds), *Information and*

Prediction in Science, New York: Academic Press, 1965, pp. 39–76. I owe this reference to David Miller.)

2. See my "Three Views Concerning the Unity of Science" in G. Radnitzky (ed), *Centripetal Forces in the Sciences,* Vol. I. New York: Paragon House Publishers, 1987), pp. 105–127.

Part II

REDUCTION AND EMERGENCE IN
PHYSICS AND CHEMISTRY

6

Reduction and Emergence in the Unified Theories of Physics

BERNULF KANITSCHEIDER

METHODOLOGICAL AND METAPHYSICAL REDUCTIONISM

In his postscript to the *Logic of Scientific Discovery*, Karl Popper points out an important distinction: On the one side, there is the assertion that adjoining sciences like physics and chemistry, chemistry and biology, biology and psychology, psychology and sociology can have common methodological traits in the way they gain their knowledge, evaluate their hypotheses, and test their conjectures. On the other side, these common traits should not be interpreted in the sense that ultimately these sciences have only one ontological domain—what it means is that their reference class is a homogeneous set of objects of the same kind. This according to Karl Popper would be a metaphysical misuse of the methodological mutuality.

Common method in the Popperian sense does surely not mean, that there are no differences in the special *tactics* of the various disciplines—controlling a chemical assertion cannot be accomplished by the same procedures as the testing of a theorem in psychology. Methodological unity points only to very broad patterns. These patterns comprise the fallible states of all assertions—the preliminary way—in which science approaches its goal and the surely logically untrespassing fact that there can be no ultimate explanation—each proposed solution being open for criticisms forever.[1]

The conceptual difference between common *method* and differing *tactics* of the various sciences is a crucial one, because it mirrors the independence and ontological autonomy of the universes of discourse of the various disciplines.

Popper is anxious that the autonomy of the various ontological domains should not be lost if we transfer our knowledge-claim from methodology to metaphysics. In the following, I would like to propose how methodological communication about common procedures of different disciplines can be combined with ontological communication of different layers of reality without eliminating the crucial characteristics of the respective scientific domains. This should be managed by a balanced use of the concept of *level* and *hierarchy*. Examples from the unified theories of physics will document the fruitfulness of this explication.

REDUCTIONISM IN A STRONG AND A WEAK SENSE

There has been considerable quarrel in the foundations of biology and of the social sciences on the levels of organization—and the hierarchy of the structural layers of different complexity. In any case, this dispute revealed that the word *level* has many uses. This ambiguity can be reduced if we adopt a sharpening of the concept, which has been introduced by Mario Bunge.[2] He starts from the definition of a *level structure* L.

> *D1:* L is a level structure iff (if and only if) L is an ordered pair. L = < S,E > where S is a family of sets of individual systems and E is a binary relation in S such that the following conditions are fulfilled:
> L1 Every member of S is a set of systems that are equivalent in some respect.
> L2 E is a one-many, reflexive and transitive relation[3] in S.
> L3 E represents the emergence of qualitatively new systems in a process.
> *D2:* A set of individual systems is a *level* iff it is a member of the family S of a level structure L.
> *D3:* A level is *newer* than another level of the same structure L iff the former has emerged from the latter.

This proposal for the use of *level* characterizes the concept as a collection of systems with a typical set of properties and laws. The evolutionary line is indicated within the succession of levels only by means of the time-dependence.—A biological mechanism for descent is not necessarily included. If one level grows out of the former, it is not in any sense superior, it only came into existence at later times. Therefore, no *value concept* and no *domination relation* is involved in Bunge's reconstruction of level structure, although it could be included if it should be strengthened in the direction of the concept of a *hierarchy*. The same concerns the notion of *order:* The general concept of level structure is not bound to be partially or even totally ordered because the relation E of emergence is not in every case asymmetric. In customary analyses, too much stress has been laid on totally ordered sets of theories,[4] but it has been shown by H. Primas and W. Gans that, in general, theoretical levels are not so simply related.[5]

If we cast an eye on nature—as it is mirrored by today's best corroborated theories—we can filter out some epistemologically abstract ontological theses, which lie at the bottom of science. The universe does not seem to be a homogeneous block, but obviously it possesses a stratification, such that the different strata are ontologically and nomologically connected.

Within each sector a relative autonomy of the constituents and their mutual interaction can be observed.

A strong reductionism as a claim on the ultimate nature of reality (in the sense that in the final analysis there exists only one monistic—material or spiritual—entity) is not justified by current natural science. Whether this strong reductionist thesis can be upheld within one particular discipline, like physics, will be treated in a later chapter. On the other side, there is no vindication for an overstated emergentism in the sense that the above-mentioned strata are totally isolated realms without interactions. Emergence is real but not lawless! The stratification metaphor stems from geology. Sedimentation, the process of producing several layers, occurs surely in a lawful way and can be described by theories that make the whole edifice comprehensible. As we can understand how the marvellous structural formation of the Grand Canyon came about from the Cambrian layer of the Colorado River till the mesozoic rock formations at the south and the north rim so do we want to have an explanation how the multifarious structure of reality originated. Two possible mistakes lurk around the corner. Neglecting the level structure eliminates the explanandum, neglecting the lawful interaction between the different layers makes the understanding of the whole edifice of nature impossible, because it seems to be a miracle how the later level of higher complexity could have arisen at all.

The process of emergence that engenders new autonomous kinds of stable entities is an occurence, which surely cannot be conceived as a simple cumulative progress, since within the class of more complex entities properties and lawful connections of the simpler level may be lost. But on the other side, there is a dependence of the more complex levels on the earlier more simple constituents, which deliver the building material of the former. In order to grasp the intra-level structure of one layer of reality and the genesis of the whole construction, two kinds of laws must be taken into consideration: those laws that guarantee the morphology and *stability of one special level* and the *morphogenetic laws*, which govern the transformation of the structures into more complex ones and the decay into their elements, if the physical boundary conditions change.

Remember, if today's cosmology is to provide us with an approximately correct picture of the universe, than in each case, be it spatially closed or spatially infinite in extent, there is only a short interval of cosmic time during which structures can grow and be maintained for a while. In the case of closure, all higher structures will be broken up by the high temperatures that prevail near the final singularity (big crunch)[6]. And in the case of an open universe all complex entities will decay at very late times until only a few stable elementary particles will make up the material constituents of a thinning and ever expanding cold space.[7]

One of the decisive demands of a coherent philosophy of science consists in keeping a logically clear relation between the ontology, the epistemology, and the methodology of science. Although the fundamental nature of things cannot be grasped in an immediate theory-free way—and has to be reconstructed under the presupposition that a group of current theories is approximately true—we have to ponder Aristotle's rule that the *ordo essendi* is logically prior to the *ordo cognoscendi*. Thus, if ontology mirrors the general traits of *the way things are*, our epistemology should correspond—at most in a mediate way—to the nature of this reality.

Therefore, the assertion gets plausible that the division of science into a plurality of different sciences is not a conceptual artifact but an indicator that also within our knowledge a level structure shows up, which mirrors the diversity of peculiar natural kinds on the level of reality. If we take it for granted that neither reality is a large monolithic block nor that science can be an undivided whole, then a simple eliminative reductionism can be excluded. This in turn does not mean that research in one field of science should not care of the adjacent levels, particularly those levels in which the universe of discourse in question has its root. On the contrary, genetic questions that point to the origin of a class of systems are deeper and more difficult to answer than those that pertain to one given layer.

The investigation of the form and structure of galaxies is a live object of current research. A lot of details are known how spirals, barren-spirals, and elliptic galaxies are constructed, but far more difficult to fathom is the question of the formation of galaxies, their development from primordial fluctuations of the matter and radiation content of the universe after the era of recombination.[8]

In the physical domain, the agglomeration of matter to bulky objects represents a decisive step from homogeneity to heterogeneity in the state of the universe; and by this kind of phase transition, an entirely new type of condensed matter is created. A theory that accounts for this transition or emergence of a new level of reality and that gives reasons why galaxies are stable, enduring systems governed by a novel network of laws, can be called a *morphogenetic theory.*

Our example suggests that explanations of the origin of one level should at first be sought in the adjacent earlier existing level. If we are interested in the question why there are biological systems at all, we are well advised not to delve into the problem of galaxy formation. In this respect, we can introduce the concept of *ontological distance,* and together with it the methodological rule that explanation of levels should be contrived with minimal ontological distance. Methodology, in general, must bear in mind the ontological and epistemological hypotheses about levels. Method should be the rule-directed guide in the search for knowledge; in that endeavour it has to respect the structure of the world and our intellectual power.

In this context *methodological reductionism* has its natural place. If a strange phenomenon suddenly appears within one level of reality— seemingly disconnected from every process known so far within this realm—one is well advised to try explanations as far as possible within this level; but should it be so recalcitrant as to withstand every reduction to the constituents of this level and their interactions, one then has to be aware that possibly an *emergent phenomenon* has been discovered. No general rule can be given when to start the keen hypothesis that the phenomenon in question cannot be integrated in a specific level. When all attempts fail to construct explanations within conceptually most parsimonious intralevel solutions, it would be stubborn to stick to ontological reductionism; in this case one has to be open minded to *interlevel explanations* to catch the possible novelty of the emergent phenomenon.

In this way, a methodological reductionism can be combined with the metaphysical background conviction that the world has an ontological stratification. It is, however, a recommendable strategy of scientific method not to be too lavish of the introduction of apparent new levels.

A thoroughgoing examination of the mechanism of emergence is needed in the case of an interlevel explanation. Little is gained if we formulate just the introduction of the new layer of reality in a black box manner: "If we take for granted the unknown substance X with the emergent properties Y governed by the laws Z, phenomenon Φ can be explained." The black box by which X was introduced has to be transformed in a translucid or glass box by giving an explicit mechanism how substance X hitherto unknown within the pertinent level of explanations is related to the well-known intralevel properties. Levels cannot pop out of nothing; they have a history and therefore their genesis must be reconstructed by finding the laws of emergence. The postulate of lawless genesis of new levels is sheer obscurantism and furthers irrationalism. As we shall see in due time in connection with the mind-body problem and the methodological weight of monistic and dualistic solutions, it is the crucial point of the dualistic view to specify the mechanics of emergence of the psychic substance out of the older biological matter and to make explicit the lawful interaction among the two kinds of ontological levels.

To give just another example that belongs to physics proper: I'll remind the reader of the discussion in the 1950s of cosmology concerning the creation of matter.[9] Relativistic cosmology was at that time paralysed by the crisis of time scale. Steady State Theory (SST) offered a solution to the recalcitrant phenomenon by invoking the hitherto totally unknown process of spontaneous creation of matter. A stationary state of the universe can only be upheld if an ex nihilo process is postulated which generates the new matter replenishing that one driven away by the expansion. The SST of Fred Hoyle postulated such a creation process and gave a mathematical expression for the origin of matter, but said nothing about the kind of matter that was created, especially it was silent on the quantum details specifying the creation process.

This failure of the theory to give any hint on the nature or mode of origin of the arising matter triggered Wolfgang Pauli's famous critic: "If matter could be created, it would be very good, but you must tell me exactly how it happens."[10] Pauli laid his finger tip precisely on the weak point of the SST. If there would be a new level of physical reality that is characterized by creation processes, it had to be linked with the well known levels of nature, in order to prevent gaps in the rational description of nature. The same is valid for the age-old mind-body problem. The protagonist of the dualist solution believing in mind as an immaterial entity wherein feelings, memories, and ideas occur, must urgently pay attention that he does not dissect the spiritual minding substance from the rest of nature, because the historical process of emergence and also the actual psychophysical interaction become very difficult to understand then.[11]

The level-hypothesis should not be misused in the sense of a new dissociation of nature in nomologically unconnected parts. As we'll see in later examples it was the great success of modern science to establish a narrow interconnexity between the different domains of reality, one of the preconditions of the intelligibility of the universe. If this proviso is kept in mind ontological pluralism can be fruitfully combined with methodological reductionism.

ONTOLOGICAL UNITY AND KNOWLEDGE

The problem of the unity versus diversity of science in all three aspects of philosophical reasoning—the ontological, epistemological, and methodological one—was a matter of debate since ancient times. Geometry and astronomy belonged to the preferred topics of investigation of the Greeks. Since early times, they tried to construct rational models of the planetary motions. A famous mathematical model was developed by Eudoxos of Knidos, improved by Kallippos and further enriched and furnished with a realistic physical semantics by Aristotle.[12] It was he, who gave the decisive ontological interpretation corresponding to which there are two entirely different kinds of substances in nature, terrestrial matter (the four elements) and celestial matter (the *quinta essentia*). The bordering line between these two substances is the sphere of the moon. The sublunar realm is not only ontologically, it is also nomologically separated from the heavenly realm, namely in regard to its possible motions. The supralunar celestial "bodies" built out of the ether perform perfect circular motions in accordance with the incorruptible nature of their substance, whereas the sublunar terrestrial bodies of the four elements are by their intrinsic nature destined to perform vertical rectilinear motions. These two kinds of geometrical forms would not by themselves hamper an investigation of the heavens; the inhibitorical effect on the progress of knowledge results from the fact that no terrestrial physical law, which can be tested by earth-bound observers may be transferred to the heavenly spheres.

If we start with the preconceived opinion that beyond the orbit of the moon a realm begins, which is nomologically independent and totally different, then a genuine astrophysics is impossible. Without the minimal assumption, that the two ontological and nomological domains can lawfully interact, an empirically controlled investigation of these parts of the cosmos, which cannot be inspected by direct contact, is forever out of our reach. If the laws of nuclear physics, thermodynamics, and magnetohydrodynamics, which we control in our terrestrial laboratories, are not applicable to celestial matter, we are at a loss in astrophysics.

The assumption of the ontological unity of the universe is however not beyond control. It could be possible e.g. that the riddle of the solar neutrinos has something to do with a premature transference of local laws of nuclear physics. If taken seriously, Aristotle's dissection of the universe in two incommensurable parts would make even common sense observation of the sky incomprehensible. Historically regarded, when an optical variation of a part of the sky was observed, a meteorological explanation within the terrestrial atmosphere had to be inserted, because the location of such a variable phenomenon within the sphere of the fixed stars was forbidden by the immutability of the etherical matter.

Even before the invention of the telescope, the observation of the sky with spectacles (which was quite customary since 13th Century) must have been suspect to a genuine Aristotelian, because that would mean to apply terrestrial geometrical optics to stellar light rays. In modern terminology we would ask such an Aristotelian why at all does the etherical matter emit electromagnetical waves or photons that can affect the retina of an organism built up from terrestrial matter? Why are there not two kinds of photons: a sidereal photon beside our common terrestrial photon? If the Aristotelians would have taken their hypothesis seriously, the sky must have been unfathomable, or a miracular cosmic coincidence of unknown origin is required to take care of *some* hidden interaction in spite of the different nature of both substances. If someone objects that indeed there has been an empirical astronomy based on Aristotelian cosmology, and that an empirical refutation took place in history of science, we have to remind the reader that in this case the *unity of light* is used surreptitiously as underlying the process of observation.

The moral of this historical example is quite clear. Knowing is a kind of interaction—in one regard on a par with other kinds of interactions in physics, chemistry, and biology: Epistemological interaction means that something must be exchanged, in the same way as in physics photons, W-bosons, gluons, and gravitons mediate the interactions. To make this possible, knowing system and known system must possess some affinity, a similarity in the ground plan. So we can formulate a condition for the mutual relation between ontological unity and knowability: Ontological and nomological coherence is a precondition for the knowability of nature.

Even Karl Popper's threefold ontology can be regarded in accord with our demand of knowability, because the three layers of reality have been interacted in the past when they originated; and in principle, the process of emergence can be elucidated by rational and scientific inquiry. Furthermore, there is continuous exchange among the material, the psychic, and the ideal world, so no part of this ontology is really isolated. Excluded by our condition are such types of ontologies where different universes like two $S^3 \times R^1$ spacetimes (cylinder universes) are postulated that do not possess a common embedding and which, because of their static character, never interacted in the past nor will interact in the future. Even the splitting up of the state-vector in the many worlds interpretation of quantum mechanics, which generates causally distinct branches of the universe[13] is not eliminated by our criterion because the splitting up is an interaction in the past—ruled by the dynamical law of the quantum mechanics that is by the Schrödinger equation.

As a second historical example we'll cast a glance on renaissance astronomy. One of the splendid achievements of the Copernican model of the planetary motions was the kinematical *interconnexity* between the celestial bodies. His systematization of the members of the solar system in one concatenated whole paved the way for a dynamical treatment of astronomy and therewith prepared a decisive step for physical cosmology. In the Copernican model the crystalline sphere of the fixed stars is upheld—although there is no intrinsic necessity for this boundary of the universe. Thomas Digges and, about the same time, Giordano Bruno opened the universe towards an infinite and homogeneous space inhabited by innumerable worlds. Now the question showed up: whether this huge ensemble of star associations can be regarded in any sense as a "system." What are the lawful connections within an infinite set of bodies (worlds in Bruno's own terms) without center or edge?

If the universe is not bound in any direction, it might be that each of the individual celestial bodies "act" according to inner unphysical principles in an unpredictable way. *"Il principio di moti intrinseco (roots in) la propria natura, la propria anima, la propria intelligenza."*[14] This was indeed Bruno's conclusion. Heavenly bodies are animated beings in personal free movements, therefore an encompassing picture of the universe allowing a geometrical description is impossible. The epistemological moral is quite clear: If the systematical coherence, the lawful unity of the universe is denied—in Bruno's case by his stellar animism which defies any mathematical account—a scientific approach becomes impossible.

Today we know that the progress of the natural sciences went its way without being much impressed by Bruno's "astrobiology." Isaac Newton laid the foundations with his law of *universal* gravitation, and so he was able to treat even an actually infinite universe of stars as a lawful system. Thomas Wright of Durham, Kant, and Lambert provide the following steps for the "systematical organization of the fixed stars."[15] Without doubt it is the merit of Kant's *Natural History and Theory of the Heavens* to regard the universe as a causally connected system—the lawful patterns are knotted up so tightly that it is possible to dig out the plan of the "systematical organization."[16]

As it showed up at the end of the 19th Century, even classical cosmology, seemingly so well conceived, was burdened with conceptual paradoxes (the electromagnetical and the gravitational paradox), but here Karl Popper's thesis is validated: "even where we do not succeed as reductionists, the number of interesting and unexpected results we may acquire on the way to our failure can be of greatest value."[17]

Kant's and his follower's endeavour to reconstruct the hierarchy of the levels of reality, from the planetary system to the galactic structure, was without doubt reductionist in the sense that it was a mechanistic approach; only the laws of classical mechanics should be used for the emergence of the origin of the level structure. The strive for this reduction unveiled a bundle of new exciting problems. The solution of these problems pointed directly to the theory of relativity, which in the beginning of the 20th Century delivered the first rational treatment of the universe that was not beset by physical paradoxes.

GEOMETRIZATION, EINSTEIN, AND THE UNITY OF PHYSICS

The greatest research program ever tried in physics was the attempt to construct a monistic world picture solely based on the notion of geometry. Precursors of this idea can be found in Platon's theory of matter using the key term χώρα[18] and in the Cartesian trial to reduce everything in the physical world to *extension*. It is interesting to note that these very early approaches of a geometrization of matter deeply influenced the theorists of the 20th Century, as the following quote of Einstein shows:

> "Descartes hatte demnach nicht so unrecht, wenn er die Existenz eines leeren Raumes ausschliessen zu müssen glaubte. Die Meinung scheint zwar absurd, solange man das physikalisch Reale ausschliesslich in den ponderablen Körpern sieht. Erst die Idee des Feldes als Darsteller des Realen . . . zeigt den wahren Kern von Descartes' Idee: Es gibt keinen feldleeren 'Raum'."[19]

That means the Cartesian conception of the *plenum* got a realization within a consequent field physics, because the field is an entity continuously spread leaving no part of spacetime free. Descartes' geometrization, his reduction of the properties of matter to a static, undynamical, and unelastic space (not spacetime) was performed by a simple act of identification. It was a long way from Cartesian physical monism[20] to the modern field theories expressed in geometrical language.

An intermediate step in the evolution was Maxwell's unified theory of magnetism and electricity. The fusion of the two interacting fields $\vec{E}$ and $\vec{H}$ to an undivisible entity (relativistically described by the Faraday tensor $F_{\alpha\beta}$) played the role of a prototype of all later attempts to unify different fields of matter or radiation.

Einstein himself regarded Maxwell's theory as an archetype for his own aim—that was the unification of gravitation and electromagnetism. Classical electromagnetism has all typical traits of a strong unification, an explication of which will be given in due time. The unitary character shows up most explicitly if we write its fundamental equation in tensor notation using the above-mentioned $F_{\alpha\beta}$, which is constructed from the components of the two vectors E_x, E_y, E_z and H_x, H_y, H_z. $F_{\alpha\beta}$ is a covariant mathematical object that means that its components can be varied or transformed away, but the whole entity has meaning independent from coordinates. $F_{\alpha\beta}$ is the mathematical object that bears in this formulation the semantical reference.

This is not to say that $\vec{E}$ or $\vec{H}$ themselves have no physical meaning, but if we introduce another reference frame in which the electrical field disappears, a magnetical field pops up in a compensatory way, showing that $F_{\alpha\beta}$ points to a real entangled entity and that $\vec{E}$ and $\vec{H}$ are coupled together by a tight lawful connection. Using the Faraday tensor $F_{\alpha\beta}$, the fusion of magnetodynamics and magnetostatics can easily be verified; there exists only one Lorentz-covariant tensor law for both, and the same is true for electrostatics and electrodynamics.[21]

In any case, the unified theory is *logically* and *semantically* stronger than each partial theory; that means the nomological patterns get more tight, and a surplus meaning is generated, which cannot be grasped if separation is upheld. One of the very important, entirely new deductive results of Maxwell's electromagnetism is the explanation of the nature of light as an electromagnetic wave phenomenon.

In Maxwell's original theory, as well as in the special relativistic 4-dimensional formulations, the two fields are treated as foreign entities immersed in an immovable and undynamical spacetime. Particles and fields have their own dynamics, but spacetime itself is not involved in the interaction of particles and fields in any way, it is the mute arena of the physical events. Bernhard Riemann formulated in 1854 the heuristic idea—according to which, the structure of physical geometry might depend on the matter content of space.[22] He could not formulate a quantitative theory expressing which matter constellation produces a certain kind of space curvature, but he had a presentiment of Einstein's geometrical theory of gravitation, which in its cleanest, qualitative, one-sentence formulation can be read: "Space acts on matter, telling it how to move; and matter reacts back on space, telling it how to curve."[23] That is to say, space with its metrical property determines what can be considered the path of force-free motion. The geodesic—the trajectory of a free particle— is thereby fixed. Mass-energy in turn provides the curvature which is a metrical property of spacetime. Without doubt, general relativity is in a certain sense a reducing theory in that the older Newtonian concept of a gravitating force that acts within spacetime is foreign to Einstein's theory. His central idea was that there is no such force as gravitation, but there is a natural state of a particle, namely free fall. This is the very kernel of the principle of equivalence. Note that not space but spacetime is at stake. This is the lesson of special relativity, space and time play symmetrical roles in the transformations, which connect different inertial systems; therefore, gravitation has to be a manifestation of the curvature of spacetime, and not of space alone.

Einstein's reduction of Newtonian gravitational force by geometrization had its origin in a new perspective on what is the *natural state* of *motion* of a physical object. In distinguishing free fall as that natural state, he unified two lines of thought, which had been hitherto unconnected: Riemann's inclusion of geometry in physics and Mach's idea that the natural state of motion here in terrestrial test situations depends upon the far-away masses. Here we see how reduction and unification work together. The merging of the two great currents of thought did not only reproduce in a new language what had been known since a long time, but the new theory furnished a solution to an outstanding problem of the older theory of gravitation, namely the propagation of this force through empty space from one body to another.

Newton was quite aware of the preliminary trait of this action at a distance theory:

> That gravity should be innate, inherent, and essential to matter, so that one body may act upon another at a distance through a vacuum, without the mediation of anything else, by and through which their action and

force may be conveyed from one to another, is to me so great an absurdity that I believe no one who has in philosophical matters a competent faculty of thinking can ever fall into it.[24]

At this time, nobody had the faintest idea how the mechanism of spreading the gravity influence to far-away parts of space could be thought of. Einstein's theory is a field theory but in the early time of relativity it was not clear, whether the wave-like solutions found so far really make physical sense. Mathematical analysis of the field equations revealed that the gravitational effects of a change in the matter distributions propagate along null geodesics—that means that they have the same paths as light rays and run with the same velocity.

The physical nature of gravitational waves was shown by Bondi, Metzner, van den Burg and Sachs in 1962, in that they could prove that gravitational waves carried energy away from a bounded system in asymptotically flat space.[25] In the meantime, there is strong indirect empirical evidence for the existence of gravitational waves.[26] The existence of physical wave solutions as well as the possibility of new geometrical objects like black holes of different types revealed the intrinsic dynamic degrees of freedom within physical geometry.

There were plenty of cases to demonstrate that geometrization provides a strong unity, not just a linguistic reformulation, and therefore entailed a genuine physical surplus meaning. But there is a different aspect of the inclusion of geometry into the world of physics, which seems to point more towards an *isolation* of gravitation from the rest of physics. If it should reveal that only gravitation can be included in the structure of spacetime—but not the other matter fields and interactions—a gap would break up within physics, and the unity would be greatly jeopardized. Therefore, after the advent of general relativity the strategies of investigation divided. Quantum-field theorists were inclined to regard gravitation as a symmetrical tensor field in flat space—namely, a Lorentz covariant massless field of spin 2. Relativistic physicists tried to follow Einstein's vision of extending the approach of geometrization. The last program contains a clear cut reductionist position:

> There is nothing in the world except empty curved space. Matter, charge, electromagnetism, and other fields are only manifestations of the bending of space. (Physics is geometry).[27]

This is ontological monism with a vengence. The pathway leading to the inclusion of all classical fields into physical geometry and pursued by the defenders of Einstein's research program followed a result first discovered by Rainich (1924) and rediscovered by Ch. Misner (1957), namely the so called "Already Unified Field Theory."[28] Here source-free electromagnetism can be expressed by pure geometry without raising the number of dimensions of spacetime nor leaving its Riemannian character. Sources, electric charge and mass, can be included by taking an open degree of freedom of geometry into consideration, the connectivity of space in the large. Einstein's field equations, as well as the equations of the Already Unified Field Theory, are local relations of infinitesimally neighbouring points; they do not decide anything concerning the global properties of space. Here the possibility shows up to introduce a domain of multiply-connected space instead of points in which apparently the lines of force converge. Electricity— as an autonomous substance—is thereby eliminated if it is reconstructed as the phenomenon that occurs if lines of force are trapped in the topology of a multiply-connected space.

Here we see at work an almost universal tendency of all unification procedures: the ontological parsimony of the stronger theory has to be paid for. Unification is only possible if we retire more and more from the common-sense notions of the empirical world with its anthropomorphic elements and introduce more epistemologically abstract concepts. Multiply-connected Riemannian space allows a very simple description of charge, but which is beyond any intuitive imagination. So unification leads us in a natural way from a narrow empiristical and instrumental interpretation of physical theories to a liberal use of theoretical concepts and their ontological import. Maybe some critics watch this resurrection of metaphysics with a frown. Lawrence Sklar has expressed this metaphysical consequence of the unitary theories very succinctly:

> After several decades of retreat to meta-language, linguistic mode, talk about theory rather than talk about the world, etc., the question of unity of science has now dragged us, willy-nilly, back to the foggy realms of metaphysics. If the unity of science is to be found in the unity of theory, apparently the unity of theory must be discerned as a linguistic reflection of the unity 'in the world'."[29]

Sklars remark points in the right direction; unified theories suggest a realistic epistemology, an ontological interpretation of theoretical terms without scruples, without all these empiristical constraints hampering an unabashed interpretation of the language of science.

We cannot work out here all the details of the unification and reductionist program, which is latter covered by the catchword "Physics is Geometry."[30] But it has to be mentioned that in the last analysis, the program in its original aim failed, because it showed to be impossible the inclusion of the quantum principle into the classical mathematical machinery. There was not even a natural place for pure spin 1/2-fields like the neutrino. Even restricting to the narrow aim to encompass all classical physics, an intrinsic limit stood up because the final states of gravitational collapse could not be handled within the concept of a continuous Riemannian manifold with its Hausdorff topology. The crucial point was topology change and the growing up of singularities. The singularity theorems discovered by Hawking, Penrose, Geroch, et al. suggest strongly, that a method of theory construction has been pushed to its uppermost limits. Under very reasonable and physically very weak constraints, almost all general relativistic spacetimes develop singularities in which the principles of the theory itself break down. These mathematical theorems are especially important, because they do not depend on the full Einstein equations—but only on the property that gravitation remains always *attractive*. Thus, they would apply to any geometrical theory in which gravity is not strongly repulsive. Here we encounter the circumstantial evidence that the manifold structure presupposed by the spacetime picture has reached its limits. The breakdown presumably occurs when the radius of curvature attains the order of the Planck length (10^{-33}cm). In this domain very strange things are likely to occur. If we construct a surface around a region in which the curvature becomes extremely high, we must reckon that inside this surface a quantum description of space time would be necessary. The singularity itself might be an inexhaustible source of matter or, in the words of Hawking and Ellis:

> Matter crossing the surface could be thought of as entering or leaving the universe, and there would be no reason why that entering should balance that leaving.[31]

Unexpected events are bound to occur in the quantum domain of spacetime—on this point everyone of the great physicists agrees. But at the moment, no fully developped theory of quantum gravity exists. The crisis of the spacetime description engendered by the initial singularity of the big bang and the final singularities of collapse indicates that the borderline of a natural *level* has been reached. Common sense experience teaches similar situations. An elastic solid seems to be a continuum—on a closer look it is built out of electrons and nuclei. A selvage seems to be smooth from a distance; if we inspect it closer, it reveals to be woven out of thread. With these analogies in mind, J.A. Wheeler looks for the "pregeometry" behind the geometry of spacetime.[32] How can we grasp the hidden structure beneath the manifold spacetime picture, which gives us the impression that—approximately, and that means to an accuracy of 10^{-15}cm—our world behaves like a spacetime continuum woven out of an underlying thread? Methodologically, we can draw an intriguing conclusion from other physical situations, where deeper levels are showing up. Think of elasticity. An elastic solid—looking like a continuous substance— is really built out of electrons and nuclei; its internal structure shows upon breaking; here we see that continuity is an approximation. In this superficial tackling with elasticity, a homogeneous isotropic elastic material is described by two elastic constants. But to understand these two constants, we have to move to the forces between electrons and nuclei. Methodologically it is clear that no deductive way leads from the solid state property "elasticity" to the interaction between the constituent particles. The direction of explanation always goes from the small to the large but not the other way round.

Therefore, a pregeometric structure has to be *postulated,* which covers, in turn, the phenomena of the molar level with its spacetime properties. From this new layer perhaps it will be possible to give answers to old questions, which have always been withstanding the hardest efforts of explanation within the spacetime realm itself, *e.g.,* the problem of the dimensionality of space and of spacetime. Perhaps the deeper reason for the 3 + 1 dimension of spacetime can only be understood from the deeper level of pregeometry.[33] In this domain surely the quantum feature will play a leading rôle.

As philosophers, we can learn a decisive epistemological lesson from Einstein's research program of geometrization: even if in the narrow sense this heuristic direction is now out of date and perhaps spacetime description is not the deepest level of description, an understanding of spacetime features does not mean explaining them away. As David Armstrong put it, we should always draw the distinction "between denying that a certain entity exists and giving an account of that entity in terms of other entities . . . what is not ultimate may yet be real."[34]

FROM QUANTUM ELECTRODYNAMICS TO SUPERGRAVITY

Einstein's dream of a unitary description of all physical fields revealed as *methodologically* sound. However, this ambitious aim could only be gained with new and extended mathematical tools. It is interesting to note that the novel approach started from a principle already discovered by Hermann Weyl—when he tried to extend the Einsteinian line of reasoning to the electromagnetic field, namely the guage invariance.

Classical fields like the electromagnetic field bare the intrinsic symmetry that their potentials are not altered if the gradient of a function is added. This extra degree of freedom Weyl tried to link with a geometric description of electromagnetism. Although, as Einstein remarked, this geometrical theory revealed itself as incompatible with the observations (the existence of sharp spectra). The gauge symmetry, rediscovered for the quantum fields of particle physics by C.N. Yang and R. Mills, gained its importance, when Gerard t'Hooft in 1971 showed that even the non-Abelian fields of the unified model of electroweak interaction, proposed by Salam and Weinberg are renormalizable, that is, they are not any longer troubled by the infinities caused by the zero point fluctuations.

The unification tool in this line of reasoning is based on local symmetries. The conceptual difference between local and global symmetry is decisive. This is easy to visualize, if we regard two equal spheres whose surfaces are covered with an arbitrary net of coordinates. Global symmetry shows up if the first sphere is rotated about some axis. All points on the surface exhibit the same angular displacement. Local symmetry, in turn, is given if a part of the sphere is stretched while keeping its spherical shape. In this second case, a force has to be introduced for moving some points of the sphere independently of the others. It is important to note that Einstein's general theory of relativity and Maxwell's theory of electromagnetism are based on local symmetries. The transition from global to local symmetry is connected with the origin of the pertinent forces. As far as this local symmetry is concerned, both classical theories may be called *gauge theories*.[35] Here we see the common trait of the new unification movement towards a unitary theory of all interactions. Any theory unifying all the four forces in nature should have this local symmetry as a fundamental requirement.

It should be possible to generate each of the four known forces from the demand that the Lagrangian remains invariant under a local symmetry transformation. It is to be remembered that in this approach, general relativity has to be translated into the language of quantum-field theory where the gravitational force originates from the exchange of a mass-less spin 2 particle (the graviton).

The encompassing theoretical framework within which theorists try to unify all physical forces, bares the grandiloquent name of "supergravity." It results from the so-called supersymmetry, which connects the two hitherto disparate broad classes of elementary par-

ticles, the fermions, and the bosons. In a supersymmetrical theory a
fermion and a boson with adjacent spin can be regarded as a special
manifestation of a single underlying particle. Again we see how the
unification procedure delivers not only the old assertions of the former
isolated theories, but something more: local supersymmetry engenders
two new fields, the field of the spin 2 graviton, which expresses the
long-range gravitational force of general relativity, and a new spin
$\frac{3}{2}$ field in which spin $\frac{3}{2}$ gravitinos are exchanged exhibiting a quantum
gravity correction on microscopic scale. Needless to say, that neither
the classical graviton nor the gravitino of microscopic gravity have
been experimentally discovered, but it is of decisive importance for
judging this approach that a surplus meaning of this kind is included
in this unified theory. The most speculative content of supersymmetric
theories consists in that they give a hint to the new layer of elementary
particles beneath the level of quarks and leptons. As Bruno Zumino
expressed it: "In this picture leptons and quarks would be composite
objects, the elementary constituents (preons) being the fields of the
basic supergravity supermultiplet."[36]

Here we are possibly provided with an argument which stems
from unification—that the proliferation of elementary particles may
have an end at a deepest level of description.

UNIFICATION AS A ROAD TO HIGHER INSIGHTS IN THE
LEVEL STRUCTURE OF THE UNIVERSE

After this sketch of physical unificationary activity, it is necessary to
stress once more the epistemological upshot of this scientific task.
What cognitive advantage can be attained when scientists strive for
a strong unity of science? Strong unity is taken not only in the weak
methodological sense of common test procedures, nor in the *epistemological* sense of a prevailing nomological structure of the universe,
but in particular in an *ontological* sense according to which reality is
an interacting whole. This last interpretation of unity means that
separation of subsystems and partial forces can only have approximate
validity. Five reasons for unification in physics can be formulated in
the following way:

1. *Unification is concerned with a kind of mild* reductionism. As
represented in the case of the spacetime picture, a deeper understanding of a level, of its origin and genesis, does not eliminate the
validity and fruitfulness of one special mode of description. A structure
can be real, even if it is not basic.

2. *Unification is concerned with* coherence. In a separatistical approach, physical reality is split up in disconnected layers whose mutual relations must remain in the dark. The microworld of elementary particles (strong and weak interactions), the molar world of bulk matter (electromagnetic interaction), and the world of megaphysics (ruled by gravity) would be divided without interconnexity. The connexity of the level structure of the world is what renders nature intelligible.

3. *Unification is concerned with* surplus meaning. The physical examples show that there is a host of phenomena that would be entirely unknowable if we renounce with the stronger unified theories. The collective effort of a unified theory will be more productive than the sum of what the individual theories could accomplish working separately.

4. *Unification is concerned with* simplicity. In physics, unification also means to go up to a domain of higher energy. The gauge-theory description reveals that the world becomes much more simple at extreme energies, when symmetries—which are broken within our cold universe—are restored. Six fundamental puzzles of classical cosmology are provided with a fresh answer—if analyzed in the domain of the grand unified theories: baryon synthesis, monopole problem, flatness problem, homogeneity problem, smallness of the cosmological term, and the isotropy problem. The unifying item is, of course, the hot big bang—it makes the explanation of this different puzzles possible.

5. *Unification is concerned with* evolution. As the universe has become older, the initially very simple and symmetric universe has evolved into a hierarchy of systems with growing complexity. This chain of evolutionary steps—each link of which is ruled by very different mechanisms (*e.g.,* galaxy formation and Darwinian evolution of biosystems)—should be grasped by a particular theory that makes it especially clear why and how these different levels emerged. This is the place where morphogenetic theories like synergetics, non-linear thermodynamics, and catastrophe theory are urgently needed.

These five reasons make up, without doubt, no exhaustive role, but they suggest—against all sceptical voices—that unification is a progressive research program. Methodological unity is not enough. It was Einstein's conviction, and it is today's theorists' too, that nature itself bears a deeper unity which does not lie beyond man's possibilities of discovery. Moreover, this discovery is a necessity if our understanding of nature should not remain incomplete in a crucial way. In Einstein's own words: "In my opinion, there is *the* correct path and . . . it is in our power to find it".[37]

NOTES

1. K.R. Popper, 1981. "Scientific Reduction and the Essential Incompleteness of all Science", in: *The Open Universe*. London: Hutchinson, p. 131.

2. M. Bunge, 1973. "The Metaphysics, Epistemology and Methodology of Levels", in: *Model, Matter and Method*, Dordrecht: Reidel, p. 160.

3. The formal reconstruction of the relation of emergence E is surely a matter of debate. Cf. Prof. Jammer's arguments in this volume that the "one-many" restriction is too narrow and may possibly be dropped.

4. P. Oppenheim and H. Putnam, "Unity of Science as a working hypothesis," in: *Minn. Stud. Phil. Sci.* II. Minneapolis 1958 pp. 3–36.

5. H. Primas and W. Gans, 1979. "Quantenmechanik, Biologie und Theorienreduktion", in: B. Kanitscheider (ed.): *Materie—Leben—Geist*. Berlin: Duncker & Humblot, pp. 15–42.

6. M.J. Rees, "The Collapse of the Universe: An Eschatological Study." *The Observatory* 89 (1969) pp. 193–198.

7. J.D. Barrow and F.J. Tipler, 1978. "Eternity is unstable". *Nature* 276 p. 453–459.

8. cf. J. Silk, 1980. *The Big Bang*. San Francisco: Freeman.

9. For a broader analysis cf. B. Kanitscheider, *Kosmologie. Geschichte und Systematik in Philosophischer Perspektive*. Stuttgart: Reclam, 1984.

10. F. Hoyle, 1980. *Steady-State Cosmology Re-visited*. Cardiff: University College Press, p. 9.

11. M. Bunge, 1980. *The Mind-Body Problem*. Oxford: Pergamon.

12. N.R. Hanson, 1973. *Constellations and Conjectures*. Dordrecht: Reidel, p. 61.

13. H. Everett III, 1957. "Relative State Formulation of Quantum Mechanics". *Rev. Mod. Phys.* 29 pp. 454–462.

14. G. Bruno, 1955. *La cena de le ceneri* (ed. G. Aquilecchia) Torino, p. 208.

15. "Die systematische Verfassung der Fixsterne". Cf. I. Kant, *Allgemeine Naturgeschichte und Theorie des Himmels oder Versuch von der Verfassung und dem mechanischen Ursprung des ganzen Weltgebäudes nach Newtonschen Grundsätzen abgehandelt*. Akademie Ausgabe Band 1, Berlin 1910, p. 246.

16. "Wir sehen die ersten Glieder eines fortschreitenden Verhältnisses von Welten und Systemen und der erste Teil dieser unendlichen Progression gibt schon zu erkennen, was man von dem ganzen vermuten soll" (I. Kant, *loc. cit.* p. 256).

17. K.R. Popper, *The Open Universe:* a.a.O., p. 134.

18. Platon, *Timaios* 49a For a more complete treatment cf. B. Kanitscheider, *Vom absoluten Raum zur dynamischen Geometrie*. Mannheim: Bibliographisches Institut, 1976.

19. A. Einstein, 1969. *Über spezielle und allgemeine Relativitätstheorie.* Braunschweig: Vieweg 21th ed., p. 125.

20. In his entire ontology Descartes was of course a dualist, but the 'res cogitans' is irrelevant in our physical context.

21. Ch. Misner et al., 1973. *Gravitation.* San Francisco: Freeman, p. 80.

22. B. Riemann, 1959. *Über die Hypothesen, welche der Geometrie zugrunde liegen.* Darmstadt: Wissenschaftliche Buchgesellschaft.

23. J.A. Wheeler, 1980. "Physics as Geometry." *Epistemologia* III Special Issue, p. 59–93.

24. I. Newton, 1957. "Third letter to Richard Bentley", in: M.K. Munitz (ed.) *Theories of the Universe,* New York: Free Press, p. 217.

25. H. Bondi, F.R. Sachs, M.G.I. Van den Burg, and A.W.K. Metzner, *Gravitational Waves in General Relativity. Proc. Roy. Soc. London* Ser. A 269 (1962) p. 21–48.

26. The most natural explanation of the loss of energy of two compact stars, whose orbit about each other is shrinking, seems to be the emission of gravitational waves. (I.H. Taylor, L.A. Fowler and P.M. McCulloch, "Measurements of General Relativity Effects in the Binary Pulsar PSR 1913 + 1916", *Nature* 277 (1979) p. 437–440).

27. J.A. Wheeler, *loc. cit.* p. 89.

28. Ch. W. Misner in J.A. Wheeler, "Classical physics as geometry. Gravitation, electromagnetism, unquantized charge and mass as properties of curved empty space." Reprinted in *Geometrodynamics.* New York/London: Academic Press, 1962, p. 225.

29. L. Sklar, 1974. "The Evolution of the Problem of the Unity of Science", in R.J. Seeger, R.S. Cohen: *Philosophical Foundations of Science.* Dordrecht: Reidel, p. 541/42.

30. Cf. B. Kanitscheider, 1976. *Vom absoluten Raum zur dynamischen Geometrie.* Mannheim: Bibliographisches Institut.

31. S.W. Hawking, and J.F.R. Ellis, 1973. *The Large Scale Structure of Spacetime.* Cambridge: Cambridge University Press, p. 363.

32. J.A. Wheeler, "Physics as Geometry". a.a.O. p. 87.

33. J.A. Wheeler, 1980. "Pregeometry: Motivation and Prospects", in *Quantum Theory and Gravitation.* A.R. Marlow (ed.) New York: Academic Press, pp. 1–12.

34. D.M. Armstrong, 1977. "Naturalism, Materialism and First Philosophy", in D. Henrich, ed. *Ist systematische Philosophy möglich?* Stuttgarter Hegelkongress 1975, Hegel-Studien Beiheft 17, Bonn, p. 412.

35. Special relativity is however a theory with the global space time symmetry of the Poincaré invariance.

36. B. Zumino, "Supersymmetry—a way to the unitary field theory," in H. Nelkowski et al. ed., *Einstein Symposium Berlin Lecture Notes in Physics*, Vol. 100, Berlin: Springer 1979, p. 123.

37. A. Einstein, *On the method of theoretical physics.* New York: Oxford University Press 1933.

7

Comments on Kanitscheider's Essay

MAX JAMMER

It has become quite popular to view the history of science, and of physics in particular, as a recurrent sequence of alternating phases of "normal science" and "revolutions." The history of physical sciences may perhaps equally well be viewed as a sequence of alternate periods of fractionations and unifications of science. These two points of view are not necessarily antithetic to each other. On the contrary, there are good reasons to maintain that all great "revolutions" in science were coupled with sweeping conceptual unifications, and all phases of "normal science" were coupled with processes of diversifications.

The Newtonian "revolution" originated from a fusion of terrestrial and planetary motions into a unified theory of mechanics; the Maxwellian "revolution", or more precisely, the emergence of field theories in the second half of the 19th century, involved a unified treatment of electricity, magnetism and light; special relativity produced the unified notion of spacetime ("the only kind of union [of space and time] that preserves an independent reality," as Hermann Minkowski phrased it in his famous lecture of 1908). The central idea of Einstein's general relativity, which unified inertial motion and gravitational acceleration (equivalence principle) and quantum mechanics, may be viewed as a formalism of unifying the corpuscular and undulatory aspects of physical reality.

Many physicists believe that future historians of science will regard the present period as being again an important, if not the most important, phase of unification, and this because of its stunning—though for the time being only partial—success in the quest toward a complete, consistent, and unified theory of all known physical interactions. Of course, one has to be cautious about making predic-

111

tions—"especially about the future", as Niels Bohr would have added. History offers numerous examples of similar prognostications that subsequently turned out to be false prophesies.[1] But the present research in unified theory differs, I believe, fundamentally from all preceding argumentations for the completeness and unification of physics, and this not only in its theoretical approach but also in its methodological aspects: the intimate interplay between ingenious mathematical constructs and sophisticated experimental techniques elevates the epistemological status of modern unified theory above that of all previous speculations about the unity of physics. And yet, the epistemological and methodological foundations of these unified theories are still an almost completely unexplored territory in the philosophy of science[2]—the reason being, of course, the complexity and uncompleteness of the subject. It is, therefore, most meritorious that Prof. Kanitscheider, whose previous work on this theme is well know to all of us, has chosen this subject again, and this time in the context of his proposal of how to combine a methodological analysis of common procedures in different scientific branches with an ontological study of different levels of reality without ignoring the specific characteristics of the respective disciplines.

I shall confine my comments, which are more explanatory than critical, to the early and final sections of this paper. It is not so much Kanitscheider's own deliberations but rather his point of departure, namely Bunge's allegedly rigorous definition of "level" or "level structure" that I would like to enlarge upon.

In 1950 L. von Bertalanffy, one of the pioneers in the development of General System Theory, wrote that ". . . reality, in the modern conception, appears as a tremendous hierarchical order of organized entities, leading, in a superposition of many levels, from physical and chemical to biological and sociological systems. Unity of science is granted, not by an utopian reduction of all sciences to physics and chemistry, but by the structural uniformities of the different levels of reality."[3] Eight years later, Paul Oppenheim and Hilary Putnam, adopting this categorization of reality, presented their method of derivational reductionism by proposing a system of reductive levels that were so chosen that a class of objects of a given level could serve as a potential reducer of any class of objects of the next higher level, if there is one, as e.g. in the categorization: elementary particles, atoms, molecules, cells, multicellular organisms, social groups. To each class of objects of a given level, it was claimed, corresponds a scientific discipline which, with the exception of physics, should be derivable from the laws of science belonging to the next lower level, together with bridge principles, which identify the nature of objects at the level to be reduced with particular structures of the objects of the reducing level, that is, the next lower level.

It soon became apparent that the Oppenheim-Putnam scheme of levels is not only greatly oversimplified but that also its linear, hierarchical order does not hold in concrete applications. Thus, to mention a more recently discussed example,[4] any ecological system, such as that of bacteria, combines in its structure at least three levels: molecules, single cells, and multicellular organisms. Moreover, it became clear that the very notion of "level" was highly ambiguous.

To remove this ambiguousness, Mario Bunge proposed in 1960 a semantical classification of "levels," which in his view could clear the ground for ontological speculations. In his classification Bunge listed nine different meanings of "level," the first of which ($Level_1$) explicates "level" as synonymous with "degree" in a purely quantitative sense (like "height") and the last of which ($Level_9$), described by Bunge as being the "most important for the building up of scientifically oriented ontologies", is used if one speaks of levels of reality.[5] As it seems, Bunge himself was not satisfied with his analysis, for thirteen years later he proposed[6] what he regarded to be a more rigorous definition of "level", and which has been adopted by Kanitscheider in his present paper.

Bunge also argued for the elimination of the order relation (which had been postulated by von Bertalanffy as well as by Oppenheim and Putnam) and in its stead introduced the emergence relation E to express the appearance of qualitative novelties. Thus, just as in differential geometry, where the definition of a "differential structure" precedes that of a "differential manifold", Bunge defined first a *level structure* as an ordered pair $<S, E>$ and then a *level* as "a set of individual systems if it is a member of the family S of a level structure. The binary relation E is "a one-many, reflexive, and transitive relation in S." Since the relation E plays an important role also in Kanitscheider's conception of "emergence," it is not out of place to look at it more closely. As just mentioned, this relation E is postulated to be "one-many" as well as "transitive." Now, the "many" in "one-many" is already implied by the transitivity and hence redundant; the requirement under discussion is therefore confined to only demanding that cases like $\Sigma_1 \ E\Sigma$ and $\Sigma_2 \ E\Sigma$ are not admitted, where Σ_1, Σ_2 and Σ are elements of S.

True, E not being an asymmetric relation, a level structure is certainly not a partially or totally ordered set, although it is nevertheless a set of "chains" (in the sense as used in lattice theory). I am not sure whether the above-mentioned "one-many" restriction was really intended and whether it is essential. In any case, it seems to me that Bunge himself did not adhere to it in some of his illustrations[7] and applications.[8]

Let me now turn to the substance-matter of Kanitscheider's paper proper. The argumentation for the inadequacy of a simple eliminative reductionism, in contrast to his plea for a methodological reductionism, involving interlevel explanations, are quite convincing. The notion of "ontological distance," as introduced in his paper, seems to be very fruitful not only with respect to his insistence that "explanation of levels should be contrived with minimal ontological distance." But is this kind of "distance" accessible of metrization?

Prof. Kanitscheider's historical remarks about the problem concerning the unity versus plurality of science, in its ontological, epistemological, and methodological aspects (from Copernicus to Wheeler) are very instructive, and I fully accept his conclusion concerning the need of ontological and epistemological coherence as a precondition for the knowability of nature.

Let me now turn to the final sections of Prof. Kanitscheider's essay and comment on the problem raised there: whether the recent development of unified theories in physics can be regarded as supporting the claim of the strong reductionist that physical reality will ultimately reveal itself as being only one ontological entity. Reviewing the development of modern physics with the progressive and cumulative unification of its diverse branches, one gets the impression that the answer is positive. It is worthwhile to recall some of the critical steps in this development.

Classical physics and even the quantum theory—as far as it was developed until 1928—were ontologically based on the dichotomy of physical reality into particles on the one hand, and fields (or waves) on the other. The conceptual breakthrough toward the unification of these two seemingly disparate categories was achieved in 1928 when Wigner and Jordan were able to show that "die Existenz materieller Teilchen [wird] in ähnlicher Weise [erklärt], wi durch die Quantelung der elektromagnetischen Wellen die Existenz von Lichtquanten . . . erklärt wird."[9] By showing that material particles can be regarded as quanta of fields, Wigner and Jordan paved the way toward a unified field-theoretic conception in which the status of particles was reduced to that of merely an epiphenomenon. The emerging quantum field theory, which so successfully accounted for the creation and annihilation of particles, was soon faced, however, with a serious difficulty. Only two years later when Robert Oppenheimer tried to calculate the energy shift produced by the interaction of an atomic electron with the quantum electromagnetic field, he found that the result diverges to an infinity. Soon similar infinities were found in other contexts such as electron scattering or the polarization of the vacuum by applied electric fields. To overcome these difficulties the renormalization method was developed (Weisskopf), a method that eliminates infinities simply by absorbing them into a redefinition of physical parameters such as mass or charge. Yet in spite of its brilliant predictions of the Lamb-Retherford shift (Bethe) and of the anomalous magnetic moment of the electron (Schwinger), quantum field theory lost much of its credibility after it was shown in 1949 (Dyson) that only a small class of quantum field theories were renormalizable. In particular, the phenomena of weak interaction—responsible for beta-decay or neutron-decay—could not be accounted for by a renormalizable field theory. Nor was it possible—though for different reasons, as we know today—to construct for strong interactions a renormalizable field theory that yields quantitative predictions in agreement with experience.

The resolution of this difficulty was found only after an idea was revived that had been proposed already in 1919 by Hermann Weyl in his abortive attempt to unify Einstein's general relativistic theory of gravitation with Maxwell's theory of the electromagnetic field: the idea of gauge invariance (a classic example of how good ideas are often discovered long before their time). Because of the paramount importance of this notion—all modern physical theories are gauge field theories—I shall discuss it in more detail. Instead of explaining how Weyl introduced this idea by enriching the affine connection of Riemannian geometry—through an additional rule that determines whether two vectors at neighboring points are of equal length and interpreting this extra affine structure as the electromagnetic potential—I shall give an example, which is simpler and also more congenial with its revival, for field theory by C.N. Yang and Robert Mills in 1954.

As is well known from classical particle physics, any invariance or symmetry of the Lagrangian entails the existence of a conserved quantity. This theorem (Noether 1918), or its generalization for Lagrangian densities, remains valid also in quantum field theory. For example, the Lagragian (which via the Euler-Lagrange variational process leads to the non-relativistic Schrödinger equation) is invariant under a phase transformation of the wave function $\psi(x)$:

$$\psi(x) \rightarrow \psi'(x) = e^{ia} \psi(x)$$

If a is a constant, this transformation is called a *global* gauge transformation (for the phase is being fixed "globally", that is, at every spacetime point to the same extent); if however a is itself a function of x, the transformation is a *local* gauge transformation. We speak of a local gauge invariance if the Lagrangian remains invariant under a local gauge transformation—which in our example happens if the electromagnetic four-potential is subjected to the classical (electromagnetic) gauge transformation. It should be clear that although the term "local" has the connotation of something more restricted than that suggested by the term "global", the requirement of a local symmetry imposes far more stringent constraints upon the construction of a theory than the requirement of a global symmetry. In fact, to preserve the invariance under a local transformation a new factor has to be added, a force (or equivalently a particle that transmits this force) so as to compensate for the variations at different spacetime localities. Any direct or indirect experimental demonstration of the existence of such a force (or particle) would of course constitute a corroboration of the theory. This also explains why Prof. Kanitscheider could justifiably declare that "there is a host of phenomena that would be entirely unknowable, if we renounce . . . unified theories" and that "unification is concerned with surplus meaning."

This brings me back to the introductory considerations of the paper, namely Bunge's conception of level structure, etc. For I claim that "would be entirely unknowable", or more precisely, the emerging knowability does not necessarily imply an innovation *de facto* and in a temporal sense. According to Bunge, any innovation, even in an epistemological sense, is always chronologically later—"just 'later' in the game", as he put it.[10] But consider a static distribution of electric charges. Charge conjugation (i.e., exchanging every positive charge by an equal negative charge and *vice versa*), or increasing the potential of the whole distribution system by a constant amount, are clearly global gauge transformations: no change of the electric field will be observed. If however, some of the charges are in motion, producing thereby a magnetic field, the global symmetry is broken. It is precisely the effect of the (emerging) magnetic field that reinstitutes local symmetry. But, as is well known, man's knowledge of magnetism (loadstone) is older than his knowledge of electricity, although in this example the level of magnetism "emerged" from that of electricity. However, with "electricity" or rather "electric charges" the situation is not much different. When Steve Weinberg (1967) and Abdus Salam (1968) proposed their unified gauge theory of the electromagnetic and weak interactions—ignoring the renormalizability problem, which eventually was solved only in 1971 (G. t'Hooft)—it transpired that (due to the W boson gauge field) the classical electric charge e of the electron (measured by Robert A. Millikan in 1906 on the assumption of being described by Coulomb's law) actually contains contributions from the new weak interaction.

Such consequences of the Weinberg-Salam unified gauge theory are essentially reinterpretations of well-established results, and as such can hardly be regarded as verifications of the theory—in contrast, say, to the recent discoveries of the $W^{\pm}$ bosons and the Z^0 neutral currents.

But let us point out that there are a number of other predictions of the unified theories—the methodological status of which with respect to their verificational power remains even more problematic. To provide the spontaneous symmetry-breaking mechanism in the Weinberg-Salam model, Higgs bosons had to be introduced—whose existence is subject to verification but not to falsification since their masses can be given arbitrarily high values. In the "grand unified theory" (GUT), which tries to unify the weak, electromagnetic, and strong interactions, the respective coupling constants merge only at energies of the order of 10^{15} GeV, an amount which may be unattainable. The most promising model of the supergravity theory, which attempts to unify these three interactions with that of gravitation, is based on the assumption of $N = 8$ particles or preons (Zumino)—whose experimental detection seems likewise to be beyond human possibilities. From the methodological as well as epistemological point of view these facts raise problems rarely, if at all, encountered in the past. It seems as if knowledge progresses not only at the expense of intuitive understanding but also by a mortgage on the future.

NOTES

1. Cf., e.g., L. Badash, 1972. "The Completeness of Nineteenth Century Science," *Isis* 63, pp. 48–58.

2. Among the few exceptions we mention the papers written by J. Cushing, M. Redhead, M. Melvin and K. Shrader-Frechette.

3. L. von Bertalanffy, 1950. "An Outline of General System Theory," *The British Journal for the Philosophy of Science 1* pp. 134–165.

4. J. Dupré, 1983. "The Disunity of Science," *Mind* 92, pp. 321–346.

5. M. Bunge, 1960. "Levels: a Semantical Preliminary," *Review of Metaphysics* 18 pp. 396–406.

6. M. Bunge, 1973. "The Metaphysics, Epistemology and Methodology of Levels," in *Method, Model and Matter* (Dordrecht: Reidel), pp. 160–168.

7. M. Bunge, *op. cit.* (Ref. 6), p. 162.

8. M. Bunge, 1982. "Is Chemistry a Branch of Physics?," *Zeitschrift für allgemeine Wissenschaftstheorie* 13, pp. 209–223, where even the notion "hierarchy of sciences" precisely in the context of level structures is made use of (p. 210).

9. P. Jordan and E. Wigner, 1928. "Über das Paulische Äquivalenzverbot," *Zeitschrift für Physik* 47, pp. 631–651.

10. M. Bunge, *op. cit.* (Ref. 6), p. 161.

8

Can We Reduce Chemistry to Physics?

HANS PRIMAS

CRITICAL REMARKS

Reductionism, if accepted, is usually accepted on faith and without logical evidence or sound reasons. Overblown claims in the philosophical literature[1] for the reducibility of chemistry to physics are not justified by present scientific knowledge. Most theoretical concepts of chemistry have not yet been successfully reduced to quantum mechanics and it is an open question whether such a reduction can always be achieved.

Very vaguely, reductionism claims that all the laws of higher levels can be explained by those of the lowest level so that nothing intrinsically new enters at the higher levels. Such assertions are obscure if they are not supplemented by a delineation of what is meant by "explaining." Every scientific craft has its rules of thumb and many analogies that are heuristically important have no explanatory power.

For example, the concept of valency is of great importance to chemistry, but to this day there is no theory of valency. (Proof: for every statement of any kind of valence model one easily can find a counterexample.) Hence it makes no sense to say, for example, that "the theory of valency by Heitler and London has reduced the concept of valency to quantum mechanics." Models, analogies, and rules of thumb have an intuitive appeal—they are helpful and important—but they should not be confused with theories, and they should not be accepted as reductions.

In order to avoid muddled arguments, I restrict my discussion to *theory reductions* and to well-defined theories that are logically consistent and empirically reliable. Furthermore, it should be recalled that derivations of limiting theories without the use of mathematically proper limit procedures are usually fallacious.

Practicing scientists are eminently interested in any intertheoretical relations, and in chemistry reductionistic ideas have been quite successful. However, it turns out that the intertheoretical relationships as they manifest themselves in the mathematical structure of the current theories in exact sciences do not fulfill the relations postulated by the philosophers of science[2]. The moral of this affair is that abstractions should come after detailed investigations of concrete examples, not before.

The traditional discussions of reductionism rest on much too simple a view of the structure of scientific theories. Nearly all of the philosophical studies of theory reduction have their origins in an analysis of classical physics and reflect the dogmas and limitations of this approach. Experiments involving molecular phenomena made it clear that Newtonian physics and classical statistical mechanics do not suffice for a fundamental theory of matter. Because the logical and conceptual structure of classical physics fails as a foundation for a theory of molecular matter, it also fails as a foundation of chemistry, molecular biology, and biology. If one wants to discuss the hypothesis that there is a global theory for the behavior of matter, one has to define the concept of theory reduction in accordance with the conceptual and logical basis of quantum physics, which is utterly different from that of classical physics.

The traditional concept of theory reduction assumes that a reducing theory can explain everything that can be accounted for by a reduced theory, and that a reduced theory cannot provide a more complete description than the reducing theory (Sneed, 1971, pp. 218–219). That is, traditional theory reduction presupposes that subtheories can always be totally ordered. This is indeed true for classical theories, but wrong for quantum theories. The subtheories of a non-Boolean theory (like quantum mechanics) may be incomparable and form a directed set which cannot be totally ordered (Primas, 1977).

The underlying logic of the theories of classical physics is Boolean, as in the predicate logic of Frege and Russell. Many philosophers of science failed to notice that quantum mechanics has a radically different logical structure than classical physics, and that this fact has crucial consequences for theory reduction.

In non-classical theories with a non-Boolean propositional calculus a *restriction* of the domain of discourse can lead to the emergence of novel properties and the appearance of qualitatively new phenomena (Primas, 1977, 1981). This feature of theory reduction in the framework of non-Boolean theories refutes some profound objections against reductionism. It is no longer necessary that "the vocabulary of the reducing theory must be at least as rich as the vocabulary of the reduced theory" (as required by Sneed, 1971, p. 220), but higher level concepts (like temperature, entropy, shape, adaptive behavior, function, purpose, which have no meaning with respect to elementary particles), can emerge by a restriction of the universe of discourse. Accordingly, the ideas of emergence and holism are not *a priori* in conflict with the idea of the reducibility of complex chemical or biological phenomena to physics.

CAN MACROPHYSICS BE REDUCED TO MICROPHYSICS?

On the one hand, chemistry deals with the composition and the properties of substances and with the transformations they undergo. On the other hand, chemistry studies the properties and the behavior of atoms and molecules. Both the macrostructure and the microstructure of matter is therefore of importance to chemistry.

Chemical systems are typically partly quantal and partly classical so they do not share the simplicity of purely quantal or purely classical systems. In one and the same object, quantal and classical subsystems coexist and interact with each other. A naive application of traditional quantum mechanics[3] to such systems gives no reasonable description. In fact, contemporary quantum chemistry uses additional *ad hoc* rules to describe molecules. For example, the all-important concept of molecular structure is a classical idea, foreign to traditional quantum mechanics. In a consistent theoretical description it comes into being by the breaking of some logical symmetries; but usually it is smuggled into quantum chemistry via the so-called Born-Oppenheimer approximation.

A presumed reduction of chemistry to traditional quantum mechanics implies an explanation of the properties and the behavior of substances in terms of electrons and nuclei, hence also a successful reduction of macrophysics. Such a reduction would be a triumph indeed; it would, for example, include the resolution of the notorious "measurement problem of quantum mechanics," which is known to have no solution within the mathematical and conceptual framework of traditional quantum mechanics.

In order to understand measurements, macrophysics, and chemistry from a quantum theoretical viewpoint, we must first understand the existence of classical subsystems in a quantum world. That is the main problem and a tough one.

If we would adopt the popular view that the reducing theory has a broader scope than the reduced theory, then macrophysics could definitely not be reduced to microphysics. The shape of a macroscopic piece of matter and its temperature are example of concepts of macrophysics, which are not definable in terms of traditional quantum mechanics.

The nonreducibility of the phenomenological concepts of thermodynamics to mechanics compelled hardboiled reductionists to say that temperature is not a true physical quantity but only a parameter for the estimation of the energy distribution, or that "strictly speaking" the second law of thermodynamics is false. The reason for this muddle is a widespread category mistake: taking the concept of substances as being on equal footing with molecules. Substances are either gaseous, liquid, or solid—molecules are not. Substances can have a temperature—molecules cannot. Thermodynamics is not the same as statistical mechanics; chemical kinetics is not the same as collision theory. These theories refer to different levels of description in the sense of Russell's notion of type. Their intertheoretical relationships are of great interest to chemistry, but much more complicated than our popular texts say.

Thermodynamical and mechanical descriptions of one and the same object are sometimes possible, but these two descriptions are mutually exclusive (Bohr, 1932). None of them is more authentic than the other, none can replace the other, both are necessary, none is sufficient. We say that thermodynamical features of macroscopic matter stand in a *complementary relationship* to the underlying molecular structure.[4]

Complementarity cropped up as a fundamental trait in the discussion of quantum phenomena. The gist of quantum mechanics lies in comprising all the possible complementary description within a single logically consistent theory. We can interpret the formal logical structure of quantum mechanics (also called "quantum logic") as a logic of complementarity.

QUANTUM MECHANICS IS A HOLISTIC THEORY

A basic premise of classical science is the tacit assumption that we have not to consider the whole universe at once but that in a useful approximation we can go ahead by compartmentalization. That is, classical science concentrates its attention to small parts of the world and examines them as well-isolated objects. This isolation procedure is then counteracted by the introduction of "interactions," which connect the otherwise isolated parts in such a manner that the resulting behavior depends only on the states of the isolated objects and the interaction between them. Accordingly, classical physics (and also the so-called "general system theory") assumes that reality can be divided into individual objects having independent ontological status.

This preconception is reflected in the logical structure of classical physical theories and system theories. It is in fact a mathematical property of classical mechanics and of classical electrodynamics that for *every* decomposition of a system into subsystems the states of the subsystem already determine the state of the entire system.[5] This property is called *separability*. If a system does not possess this property, we call it *nonseparable*. If there exists *no* nontrivial decomposition of a system into subsystems such that the states of the subsystems determine the state of the entire system, we call it maximally nonseparable or *holistic*.

Quantum theories are nonseparable and exhibit holistic effects. In particular, traditional quantum mechanics is the first mathematically formalized holistic theory. The essential difference between classical theories (including all variants of systems theories) and quantum theories is not the occurence of Planck's constant of action (classical systems may very well depend on Planck's constant) but the fact that quantum systems are entangled by the holistic Einstein-Podolsky-Rosen correlations. The existence of such holistic correlations (which have nothing to do with interactions) is a compelling consequence of quantum mechanics and is experimentally well confirmed.

The universal existence of Einstein-Podolsky-Rosen correlations implies that the concept of a "system" cannot be used without explanations. Quantum mechanics describes the world as an undivided whole and any analysis of it into parts requires an abstraction from some factually existing holistic correlations. The fact that the world exhibits itself in well articulated parts reflects the action of our pattern recognition devices, which work only in virtue of the associated abstractions of irrelevant details. What is considered as relevant and what is irrelevant is, of course, not determined by quantum mechanics.

The world cannot be described by a single compartmentalization but has to be viewed from a number of mutually exclusive perspectives. Different perspectives imply different abstractions that yield different nonisomorphic decompositions of the world into parts. In a quantum-theoretical description, the corresponding abstractions are made by dismissing some of the Einstein-Podolsky-Rosen correlations. The possibility of mutually incompatible viewpoints is related to the existence of incompatible properties in quantum systems. Maximally incompatible properties are called complementary. In exactly the same sense (which easily can be formalized), maximally incompatible viewpoints of subtheories are also called *complementary*.

EMBEDDING OF COMPLEMENTARY DESCRIPTIONS INTO A GLOBAL THEORY

Any compartmentalization separates things from their natural embedding. If we want a theoretical description of how the world is, the unavoidable compartmentalization has to be balanced by an attempt to grasp things in their interrelations, their conflicts and contradictions—that is, by some kind of dialectical thinking. Of course, there are no contradictions in nature, but conflicts may arise by tacitly using different frames of references.

In spite of the importance of dialectical thinking in informal discussions of human experience, it has contributed little to a formal unification of the compartmentalized domains of scientific knowledge. At least within the domain of molecular phenomena, we have nowadays a more powerful method: the embedding of the *local* descriptions given by a Boolean frame of reference[6] into a comprehensive *global* description, called *quantum logic*. Since there exists incompatible frames of reference, quantum logic is in general non-Boolean. Boolean frames of reference give only a *partial description*, nevertheless they play a distinguished role in quantum logic. The different frames of reference necessary for a full description of nature can be pasted together into structured families of Boolean algebras, called *Boolean atlases*, which can be used to represent non-Boolean quantum logic. This framework is the conceptual basis of the theory of the so-called W*-systems—a form of generalized quantum theory that covers traditional quantum mechanics, classical mechanics, electrodynamics, and dissipative dynamical systems.

The possibility of embedding the formal structure of complementary descriptions of one and the same object into a single global theory opens the possibility for a fruitful discussion of their intertheoretical relationships. Given the formalism of a theory, we are within certain limits free to choose its interpretation. If the interpretative rules and the regulative principles of different theories are not the same, these theories have no common vocabulary, and a comparison makes not much sense. That is, if we would like to discuss the reducibility of chemistry to quantum mechanics, then the interpretations of chemical theories and of quantum mechanics cannot be chosen independently.

It is part of every chemist's creed that he is studying the properties of real things like flowers, cells, crystals, or molecules. Accordingly, chemical theories are always about individual things in objective reality and not about our knowledge. In everyday life, nobody is prepared to abandon realism—so if we discuss a quartz crystal as an object of chemical investigations, we hardly can avoid the view that such a crystal exists objectively in nature. Quartz crystals of enormous size can be found in the Alps; they exist in two enantiomorphic forms called "right-handed" and "left-handed," which are mirror images of each other and rotate the plane of polarized light in opposite directions. Accordingly, the handedness of quartz is considered by everybody as a real objective property. For a chemist, there is no difference in principle between the handedness of a macroscopic quartz crystal and the handedness of a single molecule of alanine; intermediate molecular systems of any size can be provided easily. Hence, if in everyday life we attribute a real objective existence to quartz crystals, then we have to attribute a real objective existence to molecules of any kind, hence also to atoms and to electrons. If the chirality of a quartz crystal is accepted as a real objective property (independent of our knowledge or measurements) then we also have to accept the chirality of a single molecule of alanine as a real objective property. If this reasoning is accepted, one is forced to adopt an individual and ontic interpretation of all theories involved in a reduction of chemical theories.

Many physicists and philosophers have claimed that a consistent ontic interpretation of quantum mechanics is impossible. This view is wrong. An individual and ontic interpretation is consistent with the formalism of quantum mechanics if and only if we adopt a *non-Boolean* propositional system.

We take the notion of a *property* as a primitive concept. Quantum logic is defined as the propositional calculus of the propositions about the properties.[7] Characteristic for nonseparable systems (like quantum systems) is the existence of incompatible propositions so that the set of all propositions of a nonseparable system cannot be a Boolean lattice (as it is in all classical theories). In a nonseparable system not all propositions of the system can be truth-definite (*i.e.*, either true or false) at the same instant. The ontic interpretations posits that propositions that are true at a certain time t correspond to properties the system *has* at time t. Propositions that are not truth-definite correspond to potential properties not actualized. Hence, only the actualized properties are identified with elements of reality; the set of all truth-definite propositions characterizes the ontic state of the system.[8]

EXAMPLES OF SUCCESSFUL THEORY REDUCTIONS

A large number of physical and chemical theories can be formulated as dynamical W*-systems and therewith embedded in a common structural and interpretative framework. In this way, it becomes possible to study their intertheoretical relations in a rigorous way. In this structure, quantum mechanics can be regarded as the basic theory so that our main interest lies in the reducibility of the W*-theories of macrophysics and of chemistry to quantum mechanics.

Quantum mechanics describes an unbroken wholeness. How do we come to recognize objects in a holistic world? Apart from the unbroken wholeness there are no absolute objects or patterns. An indispensable prerequisite of every description of nature is a splitting of the world into essential and accidental parts. What is essential is not given by quantum mechanics but depends on the particular viewpoint adopted. Since the quantum world is nonseparable, there is no such thing as a perfect testable description of nature. A good description always is a good caricature, exaggerating some aspects by deliberate simplification and by permitting extravagance. *Every testable description of nature is a caricature involving deliberate drastic simplifications.* The nonseparability of nature implies the existence of incompatible aspects, that is, of aspects that cannot be put in evidence in one and the same description. To ask whether one caricatural description is "better" than another cannot be answered without considering "better for what purpose." A caricature is neither a replica of something nor does it rely on pre-existing forms. In art, a caricature is a true creation by the artist—a creation that enables us to see reality from a new perspective.

In order to derive chemical facts from quantum mechanics, we have to know what a chemist is considering as relevant and what as irrelevant. The main reason why only a tiny part of chemistry has been reduced to molecular quantum mechanics is that most chemical concepts are not (or, maybe, not yet) defined in a language that can be translated into quantum mechanics. For example, keto groups play an important role in chemical taxonomy, but this concept has no natural place in the framework of traditional quantum mechanics. Accordingly, the main stumbling block for reducing chemistry to quantum mechanics is to characterize the caricatures chemists use tacitly.

The basic tools for creating caricatures are abstraction and emphasis. In exact science, the only way known to create theoretically consistent caricatures are singular limiting procedures—like asymptotic expansions. Different limiting processes represent different viewpoints and create different patterns, which may be appropriate for different aims. Inevitably, a price has to be paid for making asymptotic caricatures: we may say things about nature that are not strictly true. Since chemistry can be derived from quantum mechanics only if one destroys some of the holistic correlations of a full quantum mechanical description, it would be unwise to object that we look at nature through half-shut eyes.

In recent years considerable progress has been made in establishing precise links between microscopic dynamical laws and the dynamics of higher level systems.[9] In the thermodynamic description of irreversible processes one encounters many situations where some of the variables vary on a much slower time scale than others. A rigorous asymptotic description of such systems is possible by rescaling some of the variables. In this way one can suppress in a consistent way some of the holistic Einstein-Podolsky-Rosen correlations so that holistic systems may factorize asymptotically into uncorrelated systems. The asymptotically induced new patterns give often an excellent caricature of the observed systems.

The recent impressive progress in algebraic statistical mechanics has fulfilled the long-standing desideratum of reduction of thermodynamics to quantum mechanics at least to some extent. This reduction has been achieved with the aid of new and very sophisticated mathematical tools, showing that the elucidation of a theoretical pluralism is not sheer routine. A full clarification of the theoretical relations between chemical substances and molecules is still out of sight,[10] but at least we know that thermodynamic systems have an algebra of observables of type III. Since the notions of temperature and chemical substances are intertwined, we can state an important result of algebraic quantum theory in the following form: molecules are described by quantum theories of type I, while chemical substances are described by theories of type III. These two descriptions refer to different levels of the same reality: they are mutually exclusive but both indispensable for chemistry.

The molecular theories of type I are in the main a mathematically precise formulation of the methods of quantum chemistry, but they are not identical with traditional quantum mechanics. The intertheoretical relations are well understood. They throw considerable light on the problem of emergence of new qualities on a higher level description.

The basic technical tool for the description of *emergent quantities* in the framework of quantum theories is the concept of classical observables. Properties that are truth-definite in every ontic state of the system are called classical. Correspondingly, observables that have a sharp value in every ontic state of the system are called *classical observables*. Traditional quantum mechanics has no classical observables—classical mechanics has only classical observables. Chemically relevant molecular systems always have both quantal *and* classical properties: they are described by the type I theories in which some but not all observables are classical.[11]

In this scheme the reduction of a higher level description to quantum mechanics is identical with the problem of emergence of new qualities: how can classical observables be derived from quantum mechanics? Since the coming into being of new classical observables is the same as the coming into being of new superselection rules, the answer is: by discharging some of the Einstein-Podolsky-Rosen correlations. Although this recipe is general and in principle straightforward, a rigorous mathematical discussion is (in every example) somewhat different and always exceedingly subtle. Successful reductions in this sense are related with the emergence of the classical observables mass, chirality, molecular shape, temperature and chemical potential, which arise by appropriate singular limits from traditional quantum mechanics.

As a first example, consider the concept of mass in the sense of Lomonossow's and Lavoisier's phenomenological law of conservation of mass in chemical reactions. This law follows directly from the Galilei group. The so-called "nonrelativistic" quantum mechanics is Galilei-relativistic and has the mass as a classical observable (which is in the traditional formulation treated as a parameter of the theory). In Einstein-relativistic quantum theories the mass is an observable but not a classical observable. The contraction of the Lorentz group to the Galilei group is a singular limit, which is difficult to discuss but which can be worked out rigorously. This limit creates a novel classical property: the mass in the sense of Lomonossow and Lavoisier.

As a second example, we consider the chemist's notion of a molecule with its special structure. The shape of a molecule is an all-important concept in chemistry and in molecular biology. It is a classical concept, which has no place in traditional quantum mechanics. In spite of the contrary claims in many of our textbooks, this concept cannot be derived by purely logical arguments from traditional quantum mechanics. However, it can be retrieved from this theory by the singular Born-Oppenheimer limit $m/M \to 0$, where m is the electron mass and M is a typical nuclear mass. In quantum chemistry this singular limit is hidden under the innocent name "Born-Oppenheimer approximation" or "adiabatic approximation". However, it is conceptually important that quantum chemistry is not the same theory as traditional quantum mechanics. Quantum chemistry possess a family of new classical observables, which describe the molecular structure and the molecular shape. It is the theory that originates by an asymptotic expansion of traditional quantum mechanics around the singular point $m/M = 0$, which corresponds to the viewpoint of the chemists. As any particular viewpoint, it is not "true," but in general it is the only description that is useful for chemists.

ON THE EMERGENCE OF HIERARCHICAL PATTERN

The preceding discussion of the Born-Oppenheimer limit is just a simple example of a hierarchical system generated by an asymptotic expansion about a singular point. A complex system is called *hierarchical* if it can be decomposed into an ascending family of successively more encompassing subsystems such that every lower level system is subordinated by an authority relation to the next higher level where the higher level in the hierarchy has always a much longer reaction time than a level classified as lower.

Most systems of interest to chemistry and biology have a marked hierarchical pattern with grossly differing reaction times. For example, in molecular spectroscopy one classifies spectra according to the ratio $\varepsilon^2 = m/M$ of the electronic mass m and a mean nuclear mass M. If the so-called electronic spectra (visible and ultraviolet light) are discussed in the original time scale $\tau_0 = \varepsilon^0 t$, then the so-called vibration spectra (in the infrared region) are governed by the time scale $\tau_1 = \varepsilon t$, while the rotation spectra (including spin resonances, in the radiofrequency region) have to be discussed in the time scale $\tau_2 = \varepsilon^2 t$. In the biological domain, it is more difficult to give precise scaling parameters, nevertheless phenomenologically many hierarchical levels are clearly indicated, for example:

A. the biochemical scale (a fraction of a second or less),
B. the metabolic scale (in order of a minute),
C. the epigenetic scale (several hours),
D. the development scale (days or years),
E. the evolutionary scale (thousands to millions of years).

Scientists and philosophers claiming that there is only *one* correct explanation of natural phenomena should ponder over the enormous simplification in description one can get if a language adapted to the hierarchical level is used. It is true that a description of a hierarchical system with a language belonging to a low level is possible but it may be very complex and almost incomprehensible.

How can we find a language adapted to a hierarchically higher level? It may be expected that the singular limit $\varepsilon \to 0$ with properly rescaled observables creates new classical observables and therewith new algebras of observables. The new language adapted to the hierarchical structure of the original system is given by the language of the W*-system created by the singular limit $\varepsilon \to 0$. An asymptotic expansion around this singular point accounts for the differences between the original system and its caricature.

CONCLUDING REMARKS

In its quantum-mechanical description the world appears very differently structured from what the Cartesian-Newtonian view understands by the "empirical world." In quantum mechanics there are no isolated systems unless *we* isolate them by neglecting Einstein-Podolsky-Rosen correlations between the investigated object and its environment. Without abstractions there is no science. There is no such thing as a perfect description of nature: every testable description of nature describes only certain aspects and neglects other aspects. Inevitably, such a description is true only within the adopted partition of the world, that is, within the chosen context. It would be very narrow-minded to use only one context: we have to learn to be able imaging different points of view.

Classical physics has believed in a universal frame of reference— a universal context that permits independent variations of its elements. This doctrine has encouraged the search of basic building blocks of matter through which one hoped to understand nature. Such an approach has the flavor of a purely empirical undertaking in which discoveries play the basic role. However, quantum mechanics taught us that the hunt for a universal context is in vain.

While classical science encourages discoveries within a single given context, modern quantum theories encourage the invention of new contexts, complementary to those already known. A theoretician has the creative freedom to find new viewpoints. Presently, the most effective strategy is to begin at some rather fundamental level and to work upwards to hierarchically higher levels. But we should not be dogmatic and leave the door to alternative approaches open. The "top-down" is at present technically rather difficult and certainly not fashionable, but it may be a sensible alternative for the future.

The idea of reductionism has been very much oriented on classical science, which presupposes that the world can be understood by understanding its parts. If we take quantum mechanics seriously, it refers to the undivided wholeness of nature. Wholes are not explicable in terms of their parts because wholes have no parts.

Holism is often considered as the opposite of reductionism, but this view must be rejected as naive. Quantum logic is a well-defined holistic theory, and non-Boolean theory reduction represents a sophisticated variant of reductionism. As examples from chemistry show, in this framework reductionism is in harmony with holism, and the emergence of essential novelty in a higher-level description is a compelling consequence of the theory.

NOTES

1. Compare, for example, Russell (1948), Kemeny and Oppenheim (1956), Oppenheim and Putnam (1958).

2. Compare, for example, Kemeny and Oppenheim (1956), Oppenheim and Putnam (1958), Nagel (1961), Sneed (1971), Stegmüller (1973).

3. By traditional quantum mechanics I mean the theory as discussed in the texts by Dirac (1930) and von Neumann (1932). In the modern terminology, traditional quantum mechanics is the theory of reversible dynamical W*-systems whose algebra of observables is a factor of type I and whose kinematical group is the Galilei group.

4. It is difficult to find the works of Bohr a really satisfying characterization of the notion of complementarity. The best formulation I know is due to Klaus Michael Meyer-Abich (1965): "Komplementarität heisst die Zusammengehörigkeit verschiedener Möglichkeiten, dasselbe Objekt als Verschiedenes zu erfahren. Komplementäre Erkenntnisse gehören zusammen, insofern sie Erkenntnis desselben Objekts sind; sie schliessen einander jedoch insofern aus, als sie nicht zugleich und für denselben Zeitpunkt erfolgen können. Die Struktur des Objekts, die darin zum Ausdruck kommt, dass es komplementär erfahren und beschrieben wird, kann mit Bohr als Individualität oder Ganzheit bezeichnet werden." For a precise mathematical definition of complementary properties and complementary theories in the context of the theory of W*-systems, compare Primas (1981, 1982).

5. Here and in the following "state" always is understood as *ontic state, i.e.,* as the maximal partial truth function on the lattice of temporal propositions of the system considered. This ontic state at a fixed time refers to those potential temporal properties which are actualized at this instant and which are supposed to have reality beyond the observing mind and independent of it. In algebraic quantum mechanics ontic states are (cum

grano salis) represented by *pure* normalized positive linear functionals on the algebra of observables (for details, compare Primas 1980, 1981).

6. A point of view relative to which a *classical* partial description of the world can be given will be called a *context*. More precisely, a context is defined as a part of the world that is singled out by a well-defined set of prior conceptions whose ontological structure is amenable to the application of classical two-valued logic. As a consequence, a context is a *Boolean frame of reference* so that within one and the same context all properties are compatible and all experimental questions are simultaneously decidable. (compare also Primas, 1980, 1981).

7. Note that quantum logic is a logic of properties, not a deductive logic. The metalanguage of quantum logic corresponds still to the usual two-valued Boolean logic.

8. For more details on the ontic interpretation of general W*-systems compare Raggio (1981) and Primas (1980, 1981).

9. Examples: The van Hove limit for the rigorous derivation of Markovian master equations for open quantum systems, the Boltzmann-Grad limit for transport equations in the kinetic theory of dilute gases, the Brownian-motion limit for the Markov process of a Brownian particle, the Hartree limit in the limit of infinitely many particles. For a review of these asymptotic limits, compare *e.g.*, Spohn (1980).

10. For example, we do not know how to characterize chemically pure substances in the sense of chemical thermodynamics. Furthermore, we have no reasonable idea how to reduce the notion of chemical purity to molecular concepts. For example, liquid water is supposed to be a pure chemical substance but to this day nobody has been able to advance a sound molecular argument in support of this claim. Note that from a molecular point of view we not even know how to characterize a liquid.

11. In algebraic quantum mechanics observables are represented by elements of an algebra and classical observables by elements of the center of the algebra of observables. The center of an algebra is defined as the set of all elements of the algebra that commute with every element of the algebra. The algebra of observables of traditional quantum mechanics is a factor of type I, hence an algebra with a trivial center. The algebra of observables of every theory of classical physics is commutative, hence identical with its center. The algebra of observables of a generic type I theory is a non-commutative W*-algebra of type I having a nontrivial center.

REFERENCES

Bohr, N. 1932. "Chemistry and the quantum theory of atomic constitution." *Journal of the Chemical Society* 134, pp. 349–384.

Dirac, P. 1930. *The Principles of Quantum Mechanics*. First Edition. Oxford: Clarendon Press.

Kemeny, J. and Oppenheim, P. 1956. "On reduction." *Philosophical Studies* 7 pp. 6–19.

Meyer-Abich, K. 1965. *Korrespondenz, Individualitat und Komplementarität. Eine Studie zur Geistesgeschichte der Quantentheorie in den Beiträgen Niels Bohrs*. Wiesbaden: Franz Steiner Verlag.

Nagel, E. 1961. *The Structure of Science*. New York: Harcourt, Brace and World.

Neumann, J. 1932. *Mathematische Grundlagen der Quantenmechanik*. Berlin: Springer. (English translation: *Mathematical foundation of quantum mechanics*. Princeton: Princeton University Press, 1955).

Oppenheim, P. and Putnam, H. 1958. "Unity of science as a working hypothesis." Edited by H. Feigl, G. Maxwell, and M. Scriven, in *Concepts, Theories, and the Mind-Body Problem. Minnesota Studies in the Philosophy of Science*, Volume II, pp. 3–36. Minneapolis: University of Minnesota Press.

Primas, H. 1977. "Theory reduction and non-Boolean theories." *Journal of Mathematical Biology* 4, pp. 281–301.

Primas, H. 1980. "Foundations of theoretical chemistry." Edited by R. Woolley, in *Quantum Dynamics of Molecules: The New Experimental Challenge to Theorists*. NATO Advanced Study Institutes Series, Volume 57, pp. 39–113. New York: Plenum.

Primas, H. 1981. *Chemistry, Quantum Mechanics and Reductionism*. Second Edition. Berlin: Springer.

Primas, H. 1982. "Chemistry and complementarity." *Chimia* 36, pp. 293–300.

Raggio, G. 1981. "States and composite systems in W*-algebraic quantum mechanics." (Thesis). Zurich: ETH Zürich.

Russell, B. 1948. *Human Knowledge: Its Scope and Limits*. London: Allen and Unwin.

Sneed, J. 1971. *The Logical Structure of Mathematical Physics*. Dordrecht: Reidel.

Spohn, H. 1980. "Kinetic equations from Hamiltonian dynamics: Markovian limits." *Review of Modern Physics* 53, pp. 569–615.

Stegmüller, W. 1973. *Theorie und Erfahrung. Theorienstrukturen und Theoriendynamik*. Berlin: Springer.

9

Comments on Primas' Essay with a Rebuttal by Primas

MARCELO ALONSO

I consider the paper by H. Primas on the relation between Chemistry and Physics very interesting and thought provoking, but I also find it very difficult to accept his main line of thought, although his espistemological analysis of quantum theory is well taken.

In his opening paragraph Primas equates the reduction of Chemistry to Physics to the reduction of Chemistry to Quantum Mechanics. This is not correct since it is neither correct to say that Quantum Mechanics is Physics or that Physics is Quantum Mechanics. The fact is that Quantum Mechanics is simply a formalism, or theoretical construct, to analyze—very successfully, indeed—the basic properties of matter and energy. Thus it does not make sense to talk of the "reduction" of Chemistry to Quantum Mechanics.

It also does not make much sense to talk any more about the reduction of Chemistry to Physics. Rather, what we may say is that the two sciences are closely related or perhaps complementary. They use the same basic principles (such as energy conservation) and deal with processes involving matter (assumed composed of operational structures designated as particles, nuclei, atoms, molecules, *etc.*) and energy exchanges (such as radiation). They assume the same set of interactions (particularly electromagnetic and nuclear), and utilize the same formalism (quantum mechanics). In fact, what has occurred in the last 50 years or so is the development of a coherent or unified theory of matter and radiation, which serves as the common basis for the "traditional" sciences of Physics and Chemistry, each one dealing with particular types of phenomena but with strong overlaps.

The best proof of this last fact is that Primas is Professor of "Physical-Chemistry." This is why I do not understand how Primas can say that "the concept of molecular structure is a classical idea foreign to traditional quantum mechanics." Again, Quantum Mechanics is simply a formalism used to analyze atomic and molecular structure, i.e. the properties of matter and radiation.

A quite different question is whether Quantum Mechanics is the "perfect" or "ultimate" theory to describe the behaviour of matter and energy. Nobody can be so arrogant as to assume so, but so far it is a quite "satisfactory" formalism. On the other hand, we all recognize certain theoretical and philosophical problems associated with Quantum Theory. Two of these difficulties are Bohr's complementarity and the Einstein, Podolsky, Rosen analysis of objective reality and separability, both analyzed by Primas. But it would be difficult to deal with them in detail in this short note. However, neither of these concepts has much to do with "traditional" Chemistry. I will say only that I believe it is very difficult to renounce a certain degree of objective reality at the fundamental level and that we must not confuse objective reality with the way we find out about it through the process of measurement. Also, the relation between the concept of separability and the holistic approach implicit in Quantum Mechanics is a matter that requires a good deal of additional analysis and thought, but is essentially a philosophical question, rather than pertaining to the realm of Chemistry—or even to Physics.

I refer now to some specific points related to Chemistry discussed by Primas. The first is the concept of valency and the affirmation that "to this day there is no theory of valency," and that "it makes no sense to say, for example, that the theory of valence by Heitler and London has reduced the concept of valency to quantum mechanics." I am very surprised at such statements by Primas. The initial concept of valency, as introduced in the early 20th century, has become obsolete and has *evolved* into a broader and generally satisfactory understanding of chemical bonds. Once we recognize that atoms are composed of electrically charged particles, obeying the rules of quantum mechanics, it is relatively simple to explain the stable polyatomic systems (ions, molecules, solids) *using* the properties of electromagnetic interactions and the formalism of Quantum Mechanics. But of course, that does not mean reducing valency to Quantum Mechanics, and nobody has ever made such a claim, which obviously is conceptually incorrect.

Primas affirms that "chemical systems are typically partly quantal and partly classical." Although the same could be applied to some physical systems (such as gases or solids or the motion of electrons in a TV tube), the statement itself is not correct. Whether we use a quantal or a classical analysis of a system depends on the nature of the system (one particle, few particles, many particles), the kind of properties being considered (pressure, dielectric permitivity, emission or absorption of radiation, etc.) and the degree of approximation needed. This is why I do not understand statements such as that "keto groups play an important role in chemical taxonomy, but this concept has no natural place in the framework of traditional quantum mechanics." In this statement Primas is again mixing apples and oranges. Besides, using elementary quantum mechanics, it is relatively simple to explain keto-enol tautomerism. Similarly, I am amazed by the statement that while "the shape of molecules is an all-important concept in Chemistry and in Molecular Biology, it is a classical concept that has no place in traditional Quantum Mechanics." I find it hard to believe that Primas has never heard how by using Quantum Mechanics one can explain that CO_2 is a linear molecule, H_2O is bent with an angle a bit larger than $90°$, NH_3 is pyramidal, C_6H_6 is a plane hexagon, and so on.

Another topic dealt with by Primas and with which I do not agree is the relation between thermodynamics and statistical mechanics. There is no doubt that classical Thermodynamics is a monumental theory, developed in the second half of the 19th Century by intellectual giants such as Joule, Mayer, Helmholtz, Boltzmann, Kelvin, Maxwell, and Gibbs, at a time when the structure of matter was not well understood. Although "classical" Thermodynamics is a very successful, elegant, and formal discipline, it is essentially empirical and macroscopic, developed to describe the behavior of matter in bulk. As time evolved and the structure of matter became gradually better understood, it was clearly recognized by Boltzmann, Maxwell, Gibbs, and many others that it was necessary to relate the classical thermodynamical concepts with the molecular structure and properties of the systems involved. Thus emerged what is called statistical mechanics or statistical thermodynamics—or perhaps even better "molecular thermodynamics."

Certainly, "thermodynamics is not the same as statistical mechanics." Rather, both stand at opposite extremes in the description of the behavior of complex many-particles systems: the micro-and the macro-descriptions, with statistical mechanics providing the molecular basis for explaining classical thermodynamics concepts (pressure, temperature, internal energy, entropy, heat capacity, *etc.*) incorporating, whenever required, the methods of Quantum Theory. They are two methods for analyzing processes occurring in matter. Rather than being mutually exclusive, they are complementary; and each science is valid in its own domain.

There are other aspects in Primas' essay that deserve comments. But the above discussion is sufficient to indicate a fundamental disagreement with the way the author uses the term "quantum mechanics" and his interpretation of its applicability to explain "chemical phenomena."

REBUTTAL BY PRIMAS

Physics vs. Quantum Mechanics

Alonso says that I have identified physics with quantum mechanics. That is not correct. On the contrary, I stressed that neither physics nor chemistry are axiomatic systems, they are not even well-defined fields. There are, of course, no sensible boundaries between physics and chemistry. Solid state chemistry, for example, is the same field of inquiry as solid state physics.

The claim that all natural science, in particular biology and chemistry, can be reduced to physics has been discussed seriously for over 300 years, and the meaning of this claim can be understood only in the historical context. The assertion that chemistry can be reduced to physics means that the behavior of all manifestations of matter on the molecular and the macroscopic level can be explained completely in terms of a few fundamental first principles. Nowadays, it is reasonable to ask whether these first principles are nothing but the first principles of quantum mechanics.

What Is Quantum Mechanics?

I do not understand what Alonso means when he says, "Quantum mechanics is simply a formalism." But I essentially agree with Richard Feynman that "Quantum mechanics is the description of the behavior of matter and light in all its details and, in particular, of the happenings on an atomic scale."[1] More precisely, I mean by *quantum mechanics* the most fundamental physical theory currently available, defined as a triple consisting of *quantum logics* (*e.g.*, the orthomodular logic of a W-algebra together with an ontic interpretation), an appropriate representation of the *space-time structure* (*e.g.*, given by an automorphic representation of the Galilei or the Lorentz group), and the appropriate *interactions* (for molecular problems the electromagnetic interaction is the only one of the four known fundamental interactions we have to consider). *Traditional quantum mechanics* uses as logic the lattice of closed subspaces of some separable Hilbert space and a Galilei-relativistic space-time-structure. The so-called *elementary* systems (like electrons or nuclei) are given by irreducible representations of the Galilei group. The physically important observables mass, energy, position, linear momentum, angular momentum (including spin) and their conservation laws are consequences of the presupposed Galilei group.

Reduction of Chemistry to Quantum Mechanics

Alonso thinks that talking of the reduction of chemistry to quantum mechanics does not make sense. One of the greatest physicists, Paul Adrian Dirac, thought otherwise. In his review of the newly developed quantum mechanics he wrote in 1929: "The underlying physical laws necessary for the mathematical theory of . . . the whole of chemistry are thus completely known."[2] This statement is in fact the basic motivation of modern numerical *ab initio quantum* chemistry, which tries to reduce all chemical phenomena to molecular phenomena—and to reduce them to the first principles of quantum mechanics. Personally, I have serious reservations against such a program, not because quantum mechanics is an insufficient basic theory, but because most people use the phrase "reduction" in a rather ill-defined or heuristic way.

Strong and Weak Reductions

The widely accepted traditional concept of reduction of theories says that a theory T_2 has been reduced to a theory T_1 if one can infer T_2 from T_1. If no additional assumptions are necessary, one speaks of a reduction in the *strong sense*, otherwise of a reduction in the *weak sense*.[3] I do not know of any really interesting case of a reduction of one traditional field of inquiry to another in the strong sense. A reduction in the strong sense can be considered as a special case of deductive-nomological explanation where the explanandum T_2 is the logical consequence of the explanans T_1.

The weak form of reductionism requires only that the laws of the theory T_2 do not violate the laws of the reducing theory T_1. It allows for constraints that do not belong to the reducing theory but, nevertheless, are compatible with it. The weak form of reductionism is difficult to discuss because it is not *a priori* clear which class of assumptions is admissible. In all successful reductions I know, the additional assumptions refer to the context of an *asymptotic limit*. In this asymptotic weak sense geometric optics can be reduced to Maxwell's electrodynamics, and quantum chemistry can be reduced to traditional quantum mechanics.

Reductionism cannot be discussed by plausibility arguments. Each assertion of a successful reduction requires a *proof*. As a rule, intertheoretical relations are mediated by singular asymptotic limits which are mathematically delicate and require hard mathematical analysis. For example, to the present nobody has been able to deduce Ohm's law for a real substance rigorously in the asymptotic weak sense from the first principles of quantum mechanics and electromagnetism. The standard for a serious discussion of asymptotic descriptions has been set by Friedrichs[4] in his analysis of the relations between geometrical optics and electrodynamics. Heuristic arguments without a rigorous proof can be extremely misleading.

Theory reductions should not be confused with reductionism as a heuristic tool as a motivation for research. For a working scientist anything that inspires him is allowed—it does not have to be logical nor consistent, not even reasonable. If a chemist thinks he can get a good idea from physical considerations, that's fine; but it has nothing to do with theory reduction. Unfortunately, it seems not to be easy for nonexperts to distinguish between speculative analogies and well-established and intrinsically consistent interrelations between different branches of sciences since again and again mere analogies are quoted as successful reductions.

Classical and Quantal Properties

Alonso says my statement that "chemical systems are typically partly quantal and partly classical" is not correct, but he does not care to ask what these concepts mean in modern theoretical science. In the last 25 years, extensive work has been done in generalizations and axiomatics of quantum mechanics and more general physical theories. In the algebraic way of speaking, the generally adopted terminology is as follows: A system is called *classical* if its algebra of observables is commutative. A system is called *purely quantal*, if its algebra of observables is noncommutative and has only a trivial center. A system is called partly quantal and partly classical if its algebra of observables is noncommutative and has a nontrivial center. A nontrivial observable is called *classical* if it belongs to the center of the algebra of observables, otherwise it is called *quantal*. Examples for classical observables are the electric charge, in Galilei-relativistic systems the mass, in molecular systems the chirality, in thermodynamic systems the temperature and the chemical potential. A single molecule of L-ascorbic acid is an example for a chemically relevant system that is partly quantal and partly classical.

Molecules Have a Shape

In the framework of generalized quantum mechanics (which allows that the algebra of observables has a nontrivial center) the shape of a molecule and the molecular structure are described by *classical* observables. My statement "the concept of molecular structure is a classical idea foreign to traditional quantum mechanics" means, in more precise terms, that the shape of a molecule is described by a classical observable and that traditional quantum mechanics does not know the concept of a classical observable since its algebra of observables has only a trivial center.

As a professional theoretical chemist I have, indeed, heard that by using quantum mechanics one can explain that in the *electronic ground state* CO_2 is a linear molecule and C_6H_6 a planar hexagon. I even know how to derive such results in a *rigorous* way and that this procedure is a typical example for an asymptotic *weak* reduction. It is simply not true that one can derive these results from the first principles of traditional quantum mechanics alone. The fact that the molecular structure and the shape of molecules cannot be reduced in the strong sense to traditional quantum mechanics has been discussed extensively in the literature (i.e., see notes 5 and 6).

In order to receive the concept of the shape of a molecule from traditional quantum mechanics, one has to break a particular logical symmetry of quantum mechanics, namely, one has to neglect the factually existing Einstein-Podolsky-Rosen-correlations between the nuclei and the electrons of a molecule. In older discussions this symmetry breaking is hidden in the so-called Born-Oppenheimer approximation. The mathematically rigorous treatment is based on an asymptotic expansion around the singular point $m/M = 0$, where m is the electron mass and M a mean nuclear mass. This limit is singular and changes *qualitatively* the description; the algebra of observables changes from a noncommutative algebra with trivial center to a noncommutative algebra with a nontrivial center. It can be proved that observables describing molecular shape and structure are elements of the center—hence classical properties. The asymptotic expansion around the singular point $m/M = 0$ leads to a new theory, qualitatively different from traditional quantum mechanics. It is the mathematically rigorous formulation of the so-called *ab-initio* quantum chemistry, which, therefore, can be reduced in the asymptotic weak sense to the first principles of traditional quantum mechanics.

Complementary and Einstein-Podolsky-Rosen-Correlations

Alonso thinks that Bohr's concepts of complementarity and the Einstein-Podolsky-Rosen-correlations have not much to do with traditional chemistry. Maybe modern chemistry is different from traditional chemistry. Many contemporary chemists have learnt again that chemistry is not only the science of molecules but also the science of substances. For them, Bohr's remark that the molecular and the substantial description are in a complementary relationship is the guideline for the development of a modern theory of substances.

The importance of a careful discussion of the Einstein-Podolsky-Rosen-correlations should be evident from the given sketch of a rigorous derivation of a Born-Oppenheimer-type description of molecules. Moreover, the relationship between the microworld and the macroworld is a central theme of chemistry. There is, of course, an almost continuous transition between the typical microworld and the typical macroworld. Assumed that quantum mechanics is the correct theory of the microworld, it is difficult to see why this theory should break down somewhere in between the micro- and the macroworld. According to Schrödinger[7] the existence of Einstein-Podolsky-Rosen-correlation is *the* typical characteristic of the microworld. Hence, we have to explain why in the macroworld the Einstein-Podolsky-Rosen-correlations seem to be irrelevant. That is not a philosophical question but one of the most urgent problems of theoretical chemistry.

Alonso thinks the concept of separability is essentially a philosophical question rather than pertaining to the realm of chemistry or even to physics. I strongly disagree. Most importantly, there are no genuine philosophical problems of quantum mechanics which do not have a genuine scientific interest. Again, the question of separability is one of the most important topics of modern theoretical chemistry. For example, up today, nobody has been able to reduce molecular thermodynamics to quantum mechanics in the asymptotic weak sense. The main stumbling block is the zeroth law of thermodynamics (which defines the concept of temperature), which presupposes a separability very difficult to achieve within the holistic structure of quantum mechanics.

There is no Theory of Valence

If I say there is no theory of valence, then I speak of the concept of *valence* and not of the concept of molecular stability or molecular shape. Of course present-day numerical *ab-initio* quantum chemistry is an extremely successful theory, it is able to make precise and empirically correct predictions about the existence of stable molecules, its dissociation energies, its shapes, its spectroscopic properties and so on. But these results have nothing to do with the concept of valence. Valence does not refer to the geometry of a molecule but to the interconnectedness of its nuclei. Ab-initio quantum chemistry *can* explain why the electronic ground state of benzene has the symmetry D_{6h}, but *not* that in the six-membered structural formula of C_6H_6 only the nearest neighbours are connected by a bond.

Heitler and London have the credit of having shown in 1927 that quantum mechanics can explain the existence of the H_2-molecule. In this sense, they are the fathers of the highly successful ab-initio quantum chemistry. But it is a different story that between 1928 and 1932, Heitler and London, together with Rumer, Hermann Weyl and Eduard Teller, seriously tried to develop a genuine theory of directed valence. This attempt failed completely. Even nowadays we have only semiempirical considerations inspired by valence-bond and molecular orbital methods. They are of great heuristic value but in spite of really great efforts these rules of thumb could not advance to a logically consistent theory.

To say the concept of valence has become obsolete is certainly a logically possible way out: *reduction by elimination*. No practical chemist, however, will accept such a solution since the symbolism of valence formulas is an indispensable tool for modern chemists. The task of theoretical chemistry is to sharpen and to explain chemical concepts and not to reject a whole area of inquiry.

NOTES

1. R. Feynman, R. Leighton, and M. Sands. 1965. *The Feynman Lectures on Physics.* Volume III, *Quantum Mechanics.* Reading: Addison-Wesley.

2. P. Dirac, 1929. "Quantum Mechanics of Many-Electron Systems." *Proceedings of the Royal Society.* London A 123, pp. 713–733.

3. N. Rashevsky, 1973. "A Unified Approach to Physics, Biology and Sociology." Edited by Rosen, R. in *Foundations of Mathematical Biology*, Volume III, pp. 177–180. *Supercellular Systems.* New York: Academic Press.

4. K. Friedrichs, 1955. "Asymptotic Phenomena in Mathematical Physics." *Bulletin of the American Mathematical Society* 61, pp. 485–804.

5. S. Weininger, 1984. "The Molecular Structure Conundrum: Can Classical Chemistry Be Reduced to Quantum Chemistry?" *Journal of Chemical Education* 61, pp. 939–944.

6. P. Claverie, and S. Diner, 1980. "The Concept of Molecular Structure in Quantum Theory: Interpretation Problems." *Israel Journal of Chemistry* 19, pp. 54–81.

7. E. Schrödinger, 1935. "Discussion of Probability Relations between Separated Systems." *Proceedings of the Cambridge Philosophical Society* 31, pp. 555–563.

10

Order and Chaos

ROMAN SEXL

THE MECHANISTIC WORLD VIEW

When Isaac Newton derived Keplers laws of planetary motion and the laws of terrestrial mechanics from his system of axioms, he achieved a historical unification of the realms of the world. The physics of the aetherial heavens and the physics of the terrestrial elements earth, water, air and fire, which had been strictly separated since the times of Aristotle, were subsumed under one system of mechanics by which God seemed to govern the universe.

A few problems remained unsolved, however. In order to prevent the planets from falling into the sun, it was necessary for them to have initial angular velocities. Where did these initial velocities come from? For Newton the answer was obvious as he wrote in his fourth letter to Bishop Bentley:

> In my former (letter) I represented that the diurnal rotations of the Planets could not be derived from gravity, but required a divine arm to impress them. And though Gravity might give the Planets a motion of descent towards the sun, either directly or with some little obliquity, yet the transverse motions by which they revolve in their several orbs, required the divine arm to impress them according to the tangents of their orbs.[1]

GOD AS A COSMIC GUEST WORKER

While the laws might be "laws of nature," the initial conditions had to come from somewhere else, from a "first mover" who started it

all. But even beyond this first initial push, God was needed continuously to keep the system going, as Newton's pupil, Clarke, discussed
in his famous exchange of letters with Leibniz. In these letters he
argued that the solar system would become disorganized periodically
by the mutual attractions of the planets and that God would have to
intervene personally about once in 10,000 years to rearrange the
system and to keep everything in shape. It was mainly the "great
anomaly of Saturn and Jupiter" that led to this conclusion—the fact
that these planets seemed to deviate more and more from their initial
orbits designed for them in the creation of the universe.

It was only 100 years later that Laplace was able to provide a
satisfactory answer to this great challenge. He argued that the mutual
perturbation of Jupiter and Saturn was a resonance phenomenon that
would lead the planets away from and back to their original orbits
quite automatically every 1000 years. God had lost his role of a
"cosmic guest worker," and an entirely mechanical conception of the
world and the heavens began to predominate.

The most famous presentation of this mechanical world view is
"Laplace's demon," who, given the initial positions and velocities of
all molecules, could calculate the past history and future fate of the
universe in all detail.

THE DEMON BECOMES ENTANGLED IN PAPER WORK

It is easy to show how absurd this conception of a omniscient demon—
who would achieve the perfect reduction of all sciences to mechanics
without any further effort—really is. In order to calculate the future
of the universe, the demon would have to know the initial conditions
of all molecules *exactly—i.e.,* to to infinitely many decimal places. To
write these initial conditions down or to store them into a computer
would exceed the capacity of the universe for storing information.

On the other hand, it is easy to show that *limited accuracy* is
insufficient to achieve the desired capacity for prediction or retrod-
iction. One can show *e.g.,* that a set of billiard balls arranged on a
table at an average distance of about 1 m and hit by an additional
ball becomes indeterministic due to quantum effects after only 8
collisions—*i.e.,* even if the balls are arranged and fixed in whatever
manner the player chooses, he cannot be certain whether he will hit
or miss the ninth ball.

LAPLACES DEMON IS A LOUSY HISTORIAN

The example of the billiard balls shows that even macroscopic systems
become indeterministic due to quantum effects. The situation is even

worse if we consider microscopic systems such as molecules in a gas. In this case quantum indeterminacies prevent one from predicting whether a given molecule will hit or miss the very first target molecule at the mean free path length typical for gases under standard conditions. One might argue that the individual fate of a molecule is of no particular interest, and averages are all that will be needed. That this is not quite true can be shown by considering the famous library of Alexandria, which was burned destroying many of the most famous Greek manuscripts. Couldn't one reconstruct this library from the smoke that should still be around? In this case it is obviously insufficient to find the *average* position of the letters—more details will be needed.

PHYSICS AND TECHNOLOGY LIMIT YOUR VISION

Frogs have a very selective vision of the world. They see moving objects only, since these are the "socially relevant" phenomena from their point of view. In the same manner human vision and the human perception of the world works very selectively. Not motion is the criterion here, but the regular, the repeatable event. Human vision tends to see patterns and regularities even if there are none. As with the frog, questions of survival and orientation in this world lie at the origin of this selective vision.

Physics and technology enhance this evolutionary pattern. The codification of the regular, the repeatable is the task of physics. The use of reliable structures with foreseeable reactions lies at the heart of technology.

Physics education is in part an education for adaption to the system of knowledge created during the course of several centuries. It is a school of seeing—a school of selective vision. The paradigmatic examples provided by textbooks have to be studied by every student. The world as a planetary system, the world as a harmonic oscillator—this is the vision of the world for which he is trained. It is a regular, predictable, causal (and boring) world, dominated by Laplace's demon.

ROULETTE AND DIE—THE EXCEPTIONS TO THE RULE

A few exceptions disturb and perturb this universal world view of Newtonian mechanics. Roulette and casting the die are examples for these exceptions. In these cases, unpredictability is not only accepted, but demanded by society (and people capable of predictions in these cases are usually separated from the rest of mankind by police).

These exceptions do not appear to be very serious at first. One might hope that better control of the variables involved might help. But there are other systems that come to mind where such a better control of the dynamical patterns have been tried for decades— without too much success. The weather forecast is but one example (economical forecasts might be another). These are examples of systems in which slight deviations from the initial conditions, slight changes in the starting positions and velocities of the atoms, molecules, clouds . . . involved lead to drastic consequences.

CAUSALITY IS AT STAKE—AND SOME SYSTEMS ARE NO SYSTEMS

"Similar causes have similar consequences"—this is the principle of causality as formulated by David Hume. This principle does not hold for the systems mentioned above. Similar causes, a similar start of the ball in a game of roulette, a similar cast of the die—they can have drastically different consequences. These systems are indeed so sensitive to small changes in the initial conditions that even a fly jumping around on Sirius or some other star might change the behaviour of the system appreciably.

In this case the very notion of a "physical system" breaks down. These systems are supposed to be isolated parts of the universe that can be studied on their own—without taking into account what happens in the rest of the world. The super-sensitive "chaotic systems" are no physical systems for which such an isolation and separation from the rest of the world would be possible. The unity of the whole universe has to be taken into account when detailed predictions about the behaviour of these systems are needed. The example of the library of Alexandria has shown that such predictions are indeed needed in some, and probably in many cases. It is only our tacit knowledge about the impossibility of such predictions that prevents us from asking such "stupid questions."

THE EXCEPTION BECOMES THE RULE AND THE RULE IS THE EXCEPTION

Roulette and die seem to be rather exceptional cases at first. The rule seems to be the regular and predictable planetary system or the harmonic oscillator. These are the canonical examples contained in all textbooks and generations of students have learned their view of the world from these books.

Theorems proved by Siegel in 1941 and 1954 have shaken this mechanically stable universe.[2] His results have shown that among the class of all possible physical (Hamiltonian) systems the regular and predictable ones are the exceptions (form a class of measure zero) and the unpredictable, chaotic ones are the rule (generic case). "All-most all" mechanical systems defy the physicists attempt to calculate and predict their behavior since even the smallest cosmic perturbation is sufficient to throw these systems out of their calculated path.

This result is not quite as bad for physics as it might seem. There are many important systems that do show regular behavior and even the chaotic ones are regular for large regions of initial coordinates and velocities. Hydrodynamics is an example, where a regular "lam-inary" part of phase space exists, while the system becomes turbulent and thus chaotic for other ranges of velocities.

ORDER BEHIND THE CHAOS

Unpredictability is the rule and regularity is the exception. This is the lesson that the recent history of physics has taught us. Chaos everywhere—a rather negative outlook at least at a first glance.

But behind the chaos there is order again. It is a new type of order—spontaneous order, soft order, very different from the rigid order of Laplaces demon or the "rigor mortis" of the crystalline world of mineralogy. It is the "soft order" of snowflakes—a type of order characterised by a delicate balance of regularity and individuality. Each snowflake has its own characteristic individuality and no two snowflakes are exactly alike. At the same time they are all snowflakes—all of them are characteristic members of a easily recognizable family of objects. Only due to this regularity can we assign a common name to this set of natural objects.

How can order be found behind the chaos? Is this not in contradiction with the second law of thermodynamics? Is this not a violation of the universal "heat death" of all matter? How can the regular pattern of a snowflake emerge from the chaos of a cloud? It is here that a new discipline sets in. It has been called "synergetics" by Hermann Haken, one of its main proponents, who has written several excellent expositions of this new science.

PRIGOGINES ROAD TO ORDER

There have been several independent paths towards the understanding of spontaneous order emerging from chaos. One of the main ideas

is due to Ilya Prigogine and his school.[3] His idea is that thermodynamics far from equilibrium is the key to structure.

Ordinary thermodynamics is really thermostatics. It deals with
equilibrium states with simple and definite properties that can be
related to one another with the help of thermodynamic arguments
(making use mainly of the interchangability of second derivatives) or
can be calculated from the microscopic structure of matter with the
help of statistical mechanics.

"Thermodynamics" can deal with dynamical processes such as
the flow of a gas from a container only by relating the static initial
and final configurations. Slightly better is the standard "nonequilibrium thermodynamics." It enables one to calculate transport coefficients such as electrical or thermal conductivities, diffusion coefficients,
etc. In its "classical form" it deals with slight deviations from equilibrium, *e.g.*, with small temperature differences where the distributions
of the coordinates and momenta of the particles do not deviate
appreciably from their equilibrium values.

What happens when the deviations from equilibrium are no
longer small? This is the problem underlying the "thermodynamics
far from equilibrium," which forms the center of Prigogines work.
The canonical example for the surprising effects that can be expected
in this case are the "Benard cells." When a liquid is heated from
below its thermodynamic equilibrium is disturbed. When the heat
current streaming through the liquid is small, no very exciting effects
are observed. Here, we are in the range of the classical nonequilibrium
thermodynamics, which describes the heat current through the liquid
by a thermal conductivity.

When the temperature difference across the liquid exceeds a
critical value, a completely new phenomenon sets in. The molecules
rise no longer in small irregular patches, transporting the heat from
the bottom to the top of the liquid but in regular convection cells.
This phenomenon can not be described by classical equilibrium or
nonequilibrium thermodynamics. It is due to a "phase transition far
from equilibrium." Such phase transitions are observed when (heat,
electric, *etc.*) currents through a system exceed a certain critical value.

THE CRITICAL ENERGY CURRENT

The general idea behind this and other spontaneous transitions from
disorder to order, from irregular individual molecular motions to
highly regular collective motions, is that these transitions are possible
only when the energy flow through a system exceeds a certain value
characteristic for the individual system considered. In this case the

transition from disorder to order—from a state of high entropy to a state with low entropy—does not contradict the second law of thermodynamics. The reason for this is that the incoming energy E1 carries only a small amount of entropy S1, while the outgoing energy E2 (which will usually be equal to E1) carries very high entropy S2. The total entropy S of system plus energy flow can increase due to the increased entropy contained in the energy, while the entropy of the system can even decrease at the same time due to the spontaneous creation of order within the system.

It is the flow of solar energy through our ecosphere that provides the explanation for the possibility of evolution, *i.e.*, of the creation of order on earth. The earth receives solar energy in the form of highly ordered radiation at a temperature of 6000 K and re-radiates this energy in the form of infrared radiation at a temperature of 300 K. The entropy of the outgoing radiation is more than 20 times higher than the incoming entropy! The difference explains how "the French Academy of Science could form spontaneously from a sea of tadpoles."

Thermodynamics, far from equilibrium, is one of the key concepts for the understanding of the emergence of new properties and of spontaneous order. Prigogine has tried to build a completely general theory of thermodynamic processes far from equilibrium. This attempt was, however, only partially successful. The phenomena are too rich, too complicated, and too interesting to fit into a thermodynamic theory based on a few general principles. In order to deal with relevant problems, it was soon necessary to use more specific dynamical considerations—*i.e.*, reaction kinetics. This leads to the approach pioneered by Eigen and Schuster.

THE EIGEN-SCHUSTER ROAD TO ORDER

It has often been argued that the origin of life is an extremely improbable event. Arranging the atoms of a single biomolecule correctly by chance would require incredibly many universes filled completely with matter. Is there some principle unknown to physics and chemistry at work to create the order of the living organism? In a fascinating series of papers Eigen and Schuster have shown that such conclusions are unwarranted.[4] Order can spontaneously originate from chaos when non-equilibrium conditions are prevalent, as the ideas of Prigogine have shown. Rather than trying to formulate this into a general thermodynamic theory Eigen and Schuster wrote down the specific equations for the reaction kinetics of autocatalytic processes.

This became the basis for a theory of evolution, in which concepts like "survival of the fittest" and "selection" could be formulated quantitatively (although only in rather restricted models).

The dynamical equations of Eigen and Schuster are non-linear equations, since the probability for the collision of molecules—leading to the formation of new molecules—is proportional to the numers A and B of molecules already present:

Probability for formation of A+B = const.* A * B

This lead to rather general studies of such nonlinear equations, *i.e.*, to the theory of dynamical systems, which has become one of the most fascinating research topics of the past decade. Here we find also the connection to the approach to order studied mainly by Hermann Haken.

HAKENS ROAD TO ORDER

For Haken the laser was the prototype of a spontaneous transition to oder.[5] When the atoms within a laser are excited by a weak flow of energy, the radiation is emitted individually by each atom and the usual "natural light" results. It is incoherent, *i.e.*, uncoordinated. When the energy flow through the laser exceeds a critical value, the behavior of the system is changed drastically. Photons emitted by one atom induce transitions in other atoms, and a single, intense light wave is emitted. The connection with Prigogines ideas is obvious here.

The formulation of the dynamical equations of this system is rather easy. The number n of photons within the laser changes due to:

induced emission of photons   a * N * n
loss at the endface of the laser   − b * n.

Here a and b are constants and N is the number of excited atoms in the laser. This number N is given by:

Number of excited atoms   N = Nx − c * n,

where Nx is the number of atoms excited by the external energy source while the term − c * n takes into account that some of these atoms have returned to the ground state after emitting photons. The dynamical equation of the laser is thus given by:

dn/dt = A * n − B * n * n.

This is a non-linear differential equation containing two constants A = a * Nx − b and B = − a * c. The behavior of its solutions depends strongly on the sign of the constant A. When Nx, the number of the externally excited atoms, is small, A is negative. In this case any photons that were initially present are quickly radiated away and no laser action takes place.

When the energy flow through the system, and thus Nx is sufficiently large to make A positive, a completely new behavior is observed. In this case a new equilibrium value n = A/B is obtained besides n = 0. The laser begins to work, and the atoms that had been radiating independently start their coherent actions. Order has emerged from disorder.

HAKENS SWIMMING POOL

Before we study the mathematics of this system any further, it is useful to describe a simple analogy to this transition to atomic order. Consider a swimming pool where a number of people swim in a random, uncoordinated manner. Frequent collisions will take place, and the "mean free-path length" of the swimmers will be rather small. When some of the people begin to swim in a circular pattern by chance, they will soon be joined by others since this regular pattern diminishes the number of collisions and eases the motion. Order has emerged from chaos.

The order that has emerged is the soft order of the snowflake. While the circular pattern might proceed to the right on one day it could proceed to the left the next morning. On some other day two "convection cells" could form—one for the girls and one for the boys. That order will emerge is a necessity when the equations of the systems are suitable. Which type of order will emerge can not be predicted from the basic equations. "Chance and necessity" form a perfect union in this example. Individual and regular features of the system are in harmony.

INSTABILITY AND BROKEN SYMMETRY

Hakens swimming pool is an example of a broken symmetry. The initial arrangement of swimmers prefers no sense of direction—neither to the left nor to the right. When one of the circular patterns emerges the left–right symmetry is broken. When the double pattern is observed, it is the up–down symmetry that has been violated. A new feature of the system has thus emerged spontaneously that had not been observed before. This new property of the system is either handedness or a prefered direction.

Which property will emerge in an individual case can not be predicted. Each such property is consistent with the basic dynamical equations, but which one will be realized in an individual event can only be determined afterwards. This fact is due to the basic dynamic instability of the system. Even small perturbations will suffice to induce either the rotation to the left or the one to the right. Before the order emerges it is impossible to predict which one it will be.

NEW PROPERTIES EMERGE

Let us emphasize this central point again. It is not only undetermined what the specific numerical value of the newly emerging property will be. Such a numerical value might be +1 when the swimmers rotate to the right and −1 when a rotation to the left sets in. The emergence of new properties means much more than this: It is undetermined whether the system will develop the property "handedness" or the property "prefered direction". *Not only the numerical value but the very type of property that will emerge is undetermined. It is in this very strong sense that genuinely new properties emerge.*

Here we begin to see the connections to the instabilities and to the chaotic properties of systems that we discussed before. "Soft order" and individuality can emerge only when instabilities are present—otherwise everything would be rigidly determined. It is the order *behind* the chaos, which we observe, and only systems that are linked to all of the Universe due to their sensible reactions to external perturbations are capable of displaying new and unpredictable properties.

BACK TO THE LASER

Let us return now to the example of the laser. In this case it is the linear term in the basic equation

$$dn/dt = A * n - B * n * n$$

that causes the instable behavior and thus the transition to the new and ordered state. If this A-term were the only one present, n would increase exponentially and the system would "explode." Such systems were usually ignored by the pre-computer world of physics, since their exponential and instable character made them appear to be rather unsuitable models of the real world.

It is only the non-linear term that stabilizes the system. This term lets the number of photons level off when the equilibrium value n = A/B has been reached. But non-linear systems were hard to deal with in the pre-computer age of physics. Therefore, they were usually ignored and nonlinearities were linearized (or discussed) away. It was only with the availability of computers that the importance of non-linear dynamical systems was recognized and their properties were investigated in detail. The computer has turned out to be a genuine research instrument of great heuristic value in this case.

Non-linear dynamical systems are also the principle uniting the approaches of Prigogine, of Eigen and Schuster, and of Haken. They have been arrived at with different methods, different motivations, different backgrounds, and different interpretations. They have turned out to be some of the most important innovations in mathematicals physics or even in "natural philosophy", if we may use this old fashioned term.

SYNERGETICS AND THE REDUCTION PROBLEM

Let us turn now to the reduction problem. Can chemistry be reduced to physics? Has this been achieved already in quantum mechanics? Can biology be reduced to chemistry? Has this already been achieved by molecular biology? Can psychology be reduced to biology? Has this already been achieved by . . .?

Problems of central importance to philosophy of science are raised by these questions. What can synergetics contribute to answering these questions?

What we have learned is that instable dynamical systems (systems that are stabilized by nonlinearities only) possess completely new properties. These properties emerge in systems far from equilibrium and lead to new types of order. The decisive point is that not only the specific values of these properties can not be foreseen, but also that the type of property that emerges can not be predicted.

This fact is of relevance for all disciplines in which structures and processes do have a strong historical component, i.e., are not determined almost exclusively by differential equations but mainly by initial conditions. Examples for such disciplines are geology; the origin of the solar system; and biology. In this respect the question of the reduction of biology to chemistry is analogous to the reduction of e.g., geology to physics (and not to the reduction of chemistry to physics).

HAS CHEMISTRY BEEN REDUCED TO PHYSICS?

The electron distribution in many molecules has already been calculated from first principles on the basis of quantum mechanics. The results are in excellent agreement with experiment, and it is only a question of time and money to extend these calculations to larger and larger molecules. Has chemistry been reduced to physics?

1. We can argue that axioms—such as the axioms of quantum mechanics—do not specify which theorems (or numerical results) can be derived. The motivation and the idea for such derivations has to come from outside. Furthermore, the axioms provide no algorithm for the derivation of the theorems.

To use a specific example: The axioms of number theory do not contain any motivation for the proof of the great Fermat theorem nor do they provide an algorithm for the automated proof of this or any other theorem. In this sense the axioms are necessarily incomplete, and any highly formalistic point of view concerning the nature of scientific proofs provides no answers to these questions. Motivation, skill, experience, and luck are elements that play an important role even in the most theoretical science.

In a similar manner the axioms of quantum mechanics contain no instruction to calculate *e.g.*, the structure of the water molecules and no hints how to do it.

2. The calculation of molecular structures is an important task of theoretical chemistry. But this is not all of chemistry. While the theoretical language of chemistry—or at least a major part of it— may actually have been reduced to physics, there is still the empirical language. This language contains words like ion exchanger, catalyst, solvents, spectrographs, *etc.* These expressions belong to the specific idiom of chemistry and have not been reduced to physics. According to Bohrs version of the Kopenhagen interpretation of quantum mechanics there is no chance to reduce these terms to the theoretical terms of quantum mechanics since these classical expressions precede quantum mechanics logically and are presupposed there.

3. Even theoretical and empirical language taken together are not equivalent to the complete structure of a scientific discipline. Another part of a science that must not be underestimated is its canonical set of problems and textbooks. These books do not start with powerful and general axioms and proceed from there to the elementary problems of introductory laboratories. The specific method by which a

field is being learned and taught is as much part of a scientific discipline as its empirical and theoretical terms. This part of chemistry has never been reduced to physics. It is probably due to the highly formalistic conception of science prevalent in early philosophy of science that these important parts of the conception and tradition of science have been ignored.

4. There is one more argument for the fact that the reduction of chemistry to physics is only a formal one. It is the old problem of what is meant by "understanding" in a field of science. Let us start with a specific problem again.

It is well known that charged particles spiral around magnetic field lines. An example for this are the electrons in the van Allen belts. What is the influence of the earth's gravitational field on these particles? A naive argument might suggest that they will fall in this field in a downward spiral. The calculation shows that this is incorrect. The particles will spiral horizontally across the field lines and not downward! This is the result of the calculation. But has one understood the strange behavior of these electrons? Can one transfer this answer to other, similar situations? A very different approach is needed to reach this level of understanding. Only *qualitative reasoning* about the behavior of the electrons in velocity space will be useful to achieve this.

Such qualitative reasoning is characteristic and specific for each science. It is the tool needed for a wide ranging insight and indispensable for problem solving as educational research has shown.

NOTES

1. I. Cohen, ed. 1978. *Isaac Newton's Papers and Letters on Natural Philosophy.* Cambridge, MA: Harvard University Press.
2. C.L. Siegel and J.K. Moser, 1971. *Lectures on Celestial Dynamics.* Berlin: Springer.
3. I. Prigogne and P. Glansdorff, 1971. *Thermodynamic Theory of Structure, Stability and Fluctuation.* New York: Wiley.
4. M. Eigen and P. Shuster. 1978. *Naturwissenschaften* 65.
5. H. Haken, 1976. *Synergetics.* Berlin: Springer.

11

The Evolution of Physics: Comments on Roman Sexl

ERWIN SCHOPPER

Roman Sexl's paper is written in the author's humorous style and with his well-known didactic skill. In my opinion, its subject is one of the central topics in a conference on the unity of the sciences, because the insights gained from studies in the new field of synergetics and dissipative nonlinear (chaotic) systems will have far-reaching consequences for our understanding of nature throughout *all* scientific disciplines. It constitutes the third revolution in the development of physics in our century, besides the theory of relativity and quantum theory. While relativity theory and quantum theory have marked out the limits of classical physics with respect to the very large (the geometry of space) and with respect to the very small (the submicroscopic world), the concept of chaotic systems dominates various domains of classical physics and at the same time leads far beyond its realm. Processes that hitherto seemed to be explicable as random events only, can now be interpreted as *deterministic chaos;* and traditional concepts of chance and of necessity have to be revised. *Spontaneous order* (soft order) *emerges from chaos.*

It is the meritorious concern of Sexl's paper to bring out the essential difference between the rigid order of classical systems—regularity (which, in Sexl's view, is an exceptional phenomenon)—and the soft order occurring in chaotic systems. Sexl strongly emphasizes the dominance of the irregular in nature. Without intending to weaken Sexl's conclusions I think he may have overstated his case and I would like to restore the balance in some passages of his interesting paper.

1. IN DEFENSE OF THE REGULAR IN PHYSICS

The introductory section of Sexl's paper outlines the world of Newton and Laplace, the area of classical mechanics, of physics based on persistant causality and determinacy and of practically unlimited predictability under the presupposition of certain idealizations, *viz.* infinite accuracy and completeness of the knowledge of the initial conditions of the motion of idealized bodies. In this rigid model deviations from predictions are due to incomplete knowledge.

What if the Laplacian demon were less pretentious and would not attempt to predict the course of the whole universe, but were only asked to solve the problem of the billiard balls? In order to keep him from evasion, Sexl adduces the indeterminacy arising from quantum effects at the impact of the balls. With human experimentalists, less wise than a demon, incomplete knowledge of the initial conditions would by itself be sufficient to preclude the prediction of the ninth impact of the billiard ball: it is well known that the inaccuracy of the initial state of a variable of a classical system at a time t_0 may increase with time and render it undetermined at a time t_1 when, for instance, the inaccuracy of an angular variable becomes larger than 2π. I would prefer to regard the billiard ball puzzle as an example of a "multicausal" process: we have incomplete knowledge of additional minor causes arising, e.g., from the uneveness of the balls and of the billiard desk. We are, however, able to take this into account and to make use of "regularity" when we limit the range of the prediction, which in quantum mechanics would in principle be impossible.

We should not forget that, when physics changed into a quantitative science with Galileo and his contemporaries, it was one of its essential methodological features and the reason for its success that it searched for the regular *behind* the observed phenomena. On the other hand, Laplace himself was very much aware of the difficulty of finding the solution of three- and many-body systems in classical mechanics. The stability of our planetary system, questionable because of the mutual perturbation of the planets, had been occupying famous mathematicians: besides Laplace, e.g., Lagrange, Poisson and Poincaré. The latter won the award offered for the answer to this problem by King Oscar of Sweden in 1889: Poincaré's answer was not a definitive one, even unfavorable, but not alarming. In his paper he offered a new qualitative approach to the mathematical treatment of many-body problems. Definite solutions to these problems have not yet been found, even after two young mathematicians, I. Moser of Göttingen and V.I. Arnold of Moscow (the latter proving a conjecture by A.N. Kolmogrov), had made important contributions around 1960. However, Voyager I and II are proceeding on their course, passing Jupiter and Saturn, and thereby will demonstrate the reliability of the predictions and calculations within the realm of the regular.

Reduced (statistical) regularity

Sexl makes the demon fail again because of quantum effects when he lets him predict the position of single molecules of a gas. As a wise demon he will chose the same approach as L. Boltzmann in his theory of heat, and he will find predictions for thermodynamic variables of state of his gas, like temperature, pressure, entropy, at least near equilibrium. In my opinion, this class of phenomena belongs to the regular ones: engineers are making reliable use of them, and the success of our technologies would not be possible without them. A wise demon would not either attempt to reconstruct the library of Alexandria from its smoke. He would know about entropy and the loss of information by the fire. He would hint at the pages of Sexl's paper, where we read about snowflakes emerging from water vapor as an example of the creation of order from chaos. And he would remember the fact that the library of Alexandria had been written and constructed by self-organizing systems, which are able to distribute incoming energy in such a way that order and information are created in certain regions of decreased entropy, while the overall entropy of the system increases. This is, I think, what happened when the library was created; and this is, admittedly, fundamentally different from the Laplacian picture. Such a complex process is contingent and irreversible; hence we cannot be sure that the attempt at identical reconstruction would be successful at all. We are beyond the regular.

2. CHAOS AND SPONTANEOUS ORDER

Sexl elucidates the phenomena that are the subject matter of this large new field of physics and the different ways of approaching them, like the synergetics of H. Haken, the thermodynamics far from equilibrium developed by I. Prigogine, the Schuster-Eigen conception, systems with basic dynamic instabilities, and so forth. It would mean "carrying owls to Athens" if I tried to add more examples. Hence, this section of my comments does not need elaborating and is in full agreement with Sexl. However, I would like, to make a few comments on some of the more general remarks in Sexl's paper.

3. COMMENTS ON SOME OF SEXL'S GENERAL REMARKS

3.1. *Causality at stake*

Sexl mentions systems which are extremely sensitive to small changes of the initial conditions. The ball of a roulette game serves as example. This example is similar to that of the billiard balls: insufficient knowledge of all contributing (and of minor) causes. The behavior of the system is causal in the small but stochastic in the macroscopic scale, and hence the resulting process is contingent and irreversible.

We can find instances of an even more surprising behavior in some macroscopic systems—classical ones like the bipendulum as well as quantum-mechanical systems with macroscopic equations of motion like He II or superconductors. In spite of being describable by deterministic differential equations and in spite of stationary external conditions they exhibit irregular quasi-stochastic behavior. It is "deterministic chaos", a dynamical quality *sui generis:* the process is again causal in the short run, but becomes unpredictable in the long run, contingent. These systems are extremely interesting. Contingency in general can be regarded as a consequence of crossing or coupled causal chains. Konrad Lorenz analyzing the concept of chance in biology in this context speaks of "causal felt." If it can be disentangled, we are dealing with apparent causality.

3.2. *Aristotle's "Everything happens with everything."*

Following the usual definition, physical systems (an ensemble of interacting objects) are supposed to be isolated parts of the universe, "closed" systems without exchange of matter and energy with the outside; they can be studied *per se* without taking into account what happens in the rest of the world. In this context Sexl points out that the systems discussed in the foregoing section do not constitute systems in the above-mentioned notation; in its phases of instability the bipendulum, for instance, strongly depends on the smallest influences from its environment.

However, the concept of closed systems is one of the established idealizations of classical physics. Newton, when deriving the law of the gravitational force between two masses, had to suppose that interaction with other (distant) masses could be neglected.

When, 300 years ago, physics began to develop into a measuring, quantitative science, it was extremely fortunate and, in my opinion, a determining factor for its evolution, that the scientists of that period investigated separate mechanisms in closed systems. The tremendous

success of the natural sciences is a consequence of the principle of
dissecare naturam, articulated by natural philosophers of that period:
disentangling the tissue of nature into small comprehensible parts
that admit the explanation of their behavior as linear causal chains
which are governed by regularity. This principle—I would call it the
Grand Simplification—has been successful for 300 years and nobody
would deny its decisive influence in the history of science. No wonder
that other scientific disciplines, even those dealing with extreme complexity like biology or the social sciences, were inclined to adopt this
principle as a methodological approach to their subject matter. Often
these efforts lead to an inadequate physicalism.

What would have become of physics, if "natural philosophers"
and scientists had followed Aristotle's very pretentious principle? Physics would have remained for a long time the type of a descriptive
discipline that botany or geography have been.

We have to pay for the success of our analytical way of studying
nature: natural scientists had neglected the fact that for a complete,
or simply a sufficient, understanding of nature we not only must be
able to dissect it, but we must also view it as a whole, as a network
which is more than the sum of its parts. Science has learnt "to read
the notes of the symphony of nature" and also to make "one-finger
play" of certain passages. Our curiosity has been raised and we are
now beginning to understand the full score. Without giving up well-
tested methods of studying nature, we have to progress from causal
chains to the complexity of networks, from a purely analytic understanding of nature to a synthetic one, in Aristotle's sense. This is a
change of revolutionary dimensions, the third in physics in this century. It is supported by strong new incentives from different disciplines:
biology, chemistry and physics since about 1960, together with an
improved instrumentation, including computers.

3.3. *Do physics and technology really limit our vision?*

What Sexl does in his contribution is, in my opinion, to throw away
the baby with the bath water. Human perception, of course, can grasp
aspects of reality only with the help of patterns and regularities.
Repeatability (regularity) and causality are preconditions of the possibility of experience. Hence, teaching and learning have to begin
with the regular and lawful, irrespective of the dominance of the
irregular. Understanding the irregular presupposes an understanding
of the regular. The teaching of astronomy has to begin with Newton's
law of gravitation rather than with the calendar of the Mayas and
its complicated calculations. Trying to abandon the analytic way of

teaching has turned out to be an unpardonable mistake (e.g., legas-
theny as a consequence of the wrong method of teaching how to
read: beginning with full words instead of letters). The impressive
success of technology has, admittedly, enhanced the tendency of the
way of vision criticized by Sexl. We are now turning towards a synthetic
understanding of physics and other disciplines. This new understanding will find its adequate outcome in textbooks.

3.4. *Synergetics and the problem of reduction*

Reduction is one of the central themes in the discussion of the unity
of science, and it leads to a wide range of controversial arguments.

Sexl does not make it sufficiently clear what he regards as the
goal of reduction. So far as I can understand him, he wishes to
discourage hopes for a *methodological* reduction (unification). In this
respect I agree with him; each scientific discipline has by itself developed an adequate approach to the phenomena it studies, irrespective of the fact that the phenomena in these different fields obey the
same fundamental laws. On the other hand, investigating the behavior
of synergetic physical systems can provide useful clues for the investigation and the understanding of the behavior of biological systems
and even of social systems. Here I am much more optimistic than
Sexl. Our aim should be to recognize the *ontological* unity of the
universe and, hence, of the sciences describing it.

Part III

REDUCTION AND EXPLANATION IN BIOLOGY, THE SOCIAL SCIENCES, AND HISTORY

12

Mind and Brain—Reduction or Correlation?

PERCY LÖWENHARD

INTRODUCTION: DEMARCATION OF THE TOPIC

The meaning and implications of "reduction" in relation to a unity of science has, from different points of view, been the topic of several contributions to this volume. The presentation included methodological, ontological, epistemological, terminological, and conceptual points of view as well as specific problems, relating to different sciences.

The present paper deals with a question that represents a special case and a very general one at the same time: the question is whether "psychology" can be reduced to "biology." (The terms here are intentionally used in a broad sense.) Initially some of the general aspects of the question may be given as an illustration:

1. Since the brain and nervous system are part of a biological organism, their psychological manifestations (behavior and experiences) may be treated within a biological context. In this sense "psychology," at least partially, may be viewed as a biological discipline.

2. All human activities, including scientific and cultural ones, have their origin in activities of the brain. This fact is self-evident to a degree that we are not always aware of its importance. The implications of this fact, however, lead to questions about the nature and meaning of knowledge and thus to epistemology and ontology.

3. More specifically, a study of the relationship between mental ("psychological") and neurophysiological ("biological") events in a

165

broader sense, inevitably touches upon the body-mind problem
and thus again upon ontology.

While the above-mentioned questions will be dealt with as part of a
necessary frame of reference, the emphasis will be on the meaning
and implications of consciousness as a phenomenon that characterizes
certain modes of information processing and which, as far as we know
it, seems to be restricted to a class of living organisms, which utilize
a nervous system. The model, which is given below, is characterized
by the following features and assumptions:

• The intrinsic relationship between "life" and "consciousness"
will be stressed, since consciousness, as we know it, seems to presuppose
the existence of life.

• The meaning of both phenomena, *i.e.*, the connotations of the
terms "life" and "consciousness", seem to change with respect to
scope and quality as a function of critical system properties of the
organism to which they are related. Properties of this type are the
complexity level of the organism or functional features of its information processing system, *etc.* This means that both phylogenetic and
ontogenetic aspects of evolution are reflected in this way.

Now, with respect to the main topic of this paper, the question
can be dealt with from at least two different points of view, one
leading to a partial reduction, the other to a correlation:

• Reduction in a proper sense here has two aspects, which can
be phrased as follows:

a) Given a complex system, is it then possible to explain its functions
   solely in terms of properties of its subsystems or elements?
b) Given a set of simpler systems, is it then possible to predict the
   result of their integration into a supersystem, to predict the functional
   properties of the latter? This amounts to a predictability of "emerging" system properties.

One may view an organism as a very complex, hierarchically organized
system in the above mentioned sense. An application of the task of
reduction to such a system would at least demand sufficient knowledge
about the relationships between its neurophysiological, biochemical,
physico-chemical and quantumphysical levels of function.

But would this knowledge be sufficient? Are there principal or
perhaps only technical limitations with respect to our ability to understand such systems? Are these limitations due to unavailability of the
necessary information or to an inadequacy of our theoretical concepts?

• The second view leads to a line of approach that makes it
necessary to state an ontological position, which will then determine
the interpretation of what is said below.

The problem of "classical" psychophysics is related to an attempt to establish a metric relationship between physical stimuli and their subjective correlates (subjective experiences). Within any experimental context, this means a correlation. An interpretation of these correlations in terms of a Cartesian ontology would nevertheless imply a causal relationship, which underlies the body-mind interaction.

In terms of a monistic ontology (body-mind identity), however, the interpretation of a psychophysical relationship as a correlation would be preserved at a more basic level. One should not be confused by the fact, that "psychophysical functions" are expressed in terms of mathematical equations which imply a "direction" in that they make use of dependent and independent variables. While the psychophysical model works satisfactorily with respect to intensity scales, it breaks down, if it is applied to other metric aspects of stimuli such as the frequency of light or soundwaves. The reason is that the latter *aspects* of stimuli have a different type of internal representation: *quantitative* differences between stimuli are transformed into *qualitative* differences between corresponding experiences. The latter may be illustrated by pitch, timbre or colours. A closer analysis shows, that the models of classical psychophysics are too simple. One has to introduce multi-stage information processing models. While stimuli may be mediated by a single external channel, they usually convey complex information. At the receptor level this information may be split up and distributed into several internal channels. The receptor processes may trigger a sequence of partly competing neural processes, which ultimately determine a state of the brain. This brain state may then be the neurophysiological correlate of a mental state, i.e. a state of awareness about an external stimulus.

The process, which is touched upon here reveals a complex relationship between external stimuli and their internal representation: while "simple" features of the stimulus can be described by single parameters, this is not possible for the resulting states of the brain. The mechanisms behind the sensory processes are adapted to complex *patterns* of stimuli, which explains their features. Messages from the outer world are based on *selected* information, which remains invariant during all stages of information processing, while the code and mode of representation may vary between different steps of the process.

• The external world can in this way be "mapped" in terms of cognitive constructs, which may be called "mental objects".

• Entropy should finally be mentioned as a key concept, which in a sense links together the different phenomena, mentioned above.

Entropy and order show an inverse relationship. The main direction of all physical processes in our universe is defined by an increase of entropy, which then may be said to characterize the "arrow of time." In contrast to this, living organisms tend to increase their order during ontogenetic development, which means a decrease of entropy. Furthermore, *negentropic flexibility* may be said to characterize the efficiency of the process of adaptation, which fits the organism to its environment.

The transfer of information, finally, means the transfer of organizing principles, which increase the degree of order within the receiving organism (system). The storage of processed information then means a growth of knowledge, which not only implies an increased *amount* of order, but also the stepwise emergence of more efficient ways to *organize* information into comprehensive patterns: general concepts and theories, simpler descriptions, more efficient models which discriminate essential from occasional elements or features of our world. An example is Newton's important distinction between "Laws of Nature" and "Boundary Conditions." Knowledge (both at the individual level and in the sense of cultural heritage) has features in common with entropy. Both grow as a function of time, but increased knowledge means a growth of order, while increased entropy means an increase of disorder.

LIFE

"Life" and "consciousness" are phenomena, which like "energy", "matter", "space," and "time" seem to be *basic attributes* of our universe. Physical theory has ultimately led to a description of nature in terms of particles and interaction between them. But life and consciousness represent different levels of existence. They are intrinsically dependent on matter, energy and negentropy in that they *presuppose* the existence of complex systems of organized matter. Nevertheless, they may be said to exist as a *potential* of our universe, although their *emergence* as manifest phenomena is bound to restricted conditions. Of course, I am only speaking of "life" and "consciousness" as we know them on earth.

This may be the place to make some remarks on energy: Energy is a *quantitative attribute* of both matter and (electromagnetic) radiation, but it is not known if energy exists independent of them. The well known mass-energy relationship

$$E = mc_0^2$$

just means that a *quantity* of matter (mass, m in kg) is equivalent to a *quantity* of energy (E in Joule, J), related to radiation. (c_0 = velocity of light in vacuum $= 2.997 \cdot 10^8$ m/s; c_0^2 then is a constant of proportionality, the "exchange rate" between mass and energy.) E here means the total energy, including the initial kinetic energy $(E_v = \frac{1}{2} mv^2)$ of a moving mass. If an elementary particle of mass m is annihilated, the relationship

$$E = mc_0^2 = h \cdot f$$

gives the frequency (f) of the radiation (or the energy $h \cdot f$ of its photons; h = Planck's constant $= 6.625 \cdot 10^{-34}$ Js).

While the different "types" of energy (such as chemical, electrical, heat or mechanical energy) are well known, there is still no generally accepted definition of this "something" we call energy. Hence, the term ἐυέργαια (which at the time of Aristotle meant activity, force, power or "action" as the cause of movement) still held some of this meaning in common language.[1]

The definition of energy as "the ability to perform work" is only partly true, since it applies solely to that part of energy that is actually available for work. At the beginning of the 1950s, Z. Rant proposed the name *exergy* for this part of energy. Exergy is formally defined as the product of negentropy and environmental temperature (T). Negentropy here means the difference between the actual entropy of a system and its maximum entropy (Nordling, 1982). While energy, according to The First Law of Thermodynamics neither can be created nor destroyed, exergy can be lost. It should be noted here, that the term "negentropy" will be used later on in a slightly different way.

While the exact nature of energy may still be the object of discussion, it is without doubt a necessary condition for life. "Life" is the label for an intuitively well-known phenomenon, which nevertheless until about 30 years ago eluded attempts to define it strictly. This has several reasons:

• Life is bound to very complex chemical systems in certain states.

• Life is not a uniform concept; it has different ranges of connotation in different connections. The term applies to a large number of different systems, which vary greatly with respect not only to complexity, but also with respect to features. Life, hence, means partly the same and partly different things in different cases.

• There are aspects of life, which could not be grasped and understood by the models of classical science.

These difficulties promoted the emergence of vitalistic theories and supported their existence up until today. Vitalistic theories try to relate the existence and function of living organisms to the effects of a non-physical "life force." Additional difficulties arose from the connection of these questions with the problem of life's origin in relation to devine or other metaphysical influences, but also from the connection with teleological speculations about the "purpose" and "meaning" of life within the great scheme of our universe. A good survey on these aspects has been given by Wuketits (1982). It is important to remind oneself of the influence which the "Zeitgeist" or certain ideas may have on the promotion or impediment of scientific progress. At the time of Lavoisier (late 18th Century), "organic" compounds were thought to be dependent on living organisms for their existence (the notion "organic" for carbon compounds has its origin here). It was then a discovery of importance, not only for chemistry, when Friedrich Wöhler (a pupil of Justus Liebig) in 1828 synthesized urea from ammonium cyanate:

$$NH_4\ CNO \longrightarrow \begin{matrix} NH_2 \\ \\ NH_2 \end{matrix} \diagdown\!\!\diagup CO$$

ammoniumcyanate   *urea = carbamide*

Urea is a typical metabolite from animals, and ammonium cyanate is an "inorganic" compound, which under certain conditions, can be synthesized directly from its elements.

This illustrates nicely how our opinions about which questions principally can be answered (in this case "reduction" of organic matter to inorganic) is dependent on the actual level of knowledge.

During the 19th Century, biology gradually became a science in a modern sense (with hypotheses, experimental tests, and predictive theories). Some main steps in this direction were the development of genetics, cellular theory, the biochemistry of metabolism, the theory of evolution, and the application of concepts from physics to living organisms. We know today, that organisms are very complex, hierarchically organized systems, which are structured in minor detail. There is, furthermore, a predetermined functional interaction between all levels of the system. The genetically determined high degree of coupling between the elements of living systems is also the main reason that makes any comparison between organisms and societies (other than superficially analogies) misleading or nonsensical.

All living systems are characterized by a set of properties, some of which are common to all organisms, while others are specific to certain types of them. The following four characteristics are presently viewed as sufficient conditions for life:

1. Metabolism
2. Reproduction
3. Mutability
4. Interaction between functional elements (such as proteins) and carriers of information (DNA and RNA), which seems to be a precondition for evolution. Furthermore there are additional characteristics such as activity, reactivity, homeostasis and self-regulation, exchange of energy with the environment, maintenance of flow equilibria, self-mend and maintenance of structure, program controlled growth (ontogenesis), exchange of information with the environment, behavioural modifications by learning, consciousness, *etc.*

These characteristics are found in most, but not all living systems. A more detailed treatise of the subject is given by Kaplan (1978). The above mentioned characteristics, however, can only express themselves under certain conditions, since they are critically dependent on the *total state* of the system. The functional characteristics, which are necessary to sustain the existence of a living organism may be called its life functions. If some of these functions are disturbed or blocked to a certain critical extent, the entity ceases to exist at the level of the organism. The organism, *e.g.*, a dog, dies. Meanwhile, after the clinical death of the animal has occurred, its heart may be surgically disconnected, placed into a Lindbergh-pump and submerged into a suitably oxygenated solution of nutrients, which is then circulated. As already shown by Alexis Carrel fifty years ago, the life functions of the heart may thus be preserved a long time after the death of the organism to which it once belonged (Carrel & Lindbergh, 1938).

Undoubtedly an organ may be desribed as a living subsystem of an organism. This subsystem shows a range of life functions, pertinent to the functional role of the organ. Since the life functions of the organ can be destroyed, one may speak of "life" at the level of the organ. While some people want to restrict the use of the term "life" to organisms, there undoubtedly is a distinct holistic difference between *any* system in a "living" and a "dead" state.

Now, the heart may be dissected and thus be destroyed as an organ, but it is still possible to keep its subunits, the single heart cells, functionally intact and they may, under certain conditions, be stimulated to grow and to devide. This means that there still exist typical life functions at the cellular level. But there the limits of living systems seem to be reached. If the cell is damaged physically, it dies. But still some elementary life functions persist: the contractile properties of the actino-myosin molecules, which are responsible for the cell's ability to contract. This property of actino-myosin (two types of specifically interacting proteins, which are found in muscles), remains intact even outside the cell body if the molecules are dispersed in a suitable solution of nutrients. As in the living cell, contraction may be triggered by ATP (adenosine triphosphoric acid) a molecule able to deliver energy, (see Fulton, 1956). This illustrates clearly, that the term "life" means partly the same, partly different things at different levels of complexity. It furthermore implies several *aspects:* a set of *system properties*, which partially *change* during ontogenesis, a *state* of the system (living or dead) and a *process*, limited to a *time-span* between "birth" and "death".

Living organisms are in a sense highly improbable to such an extent that a cynic once defined life as a peculiar disease of matter. Since living organisms show a very complex structure, the probability of their occurrence by chance is infinitesimally small. During growth and development the complexity of the organism increases steadily. This means that growth implies the occurrence of consecutive states with steadily decreasing probabilities. In order to maintain its structure and life functions intact, the organism has to rely on well-established and stable principles of self-organization, homeostasis and self-mend. In a certain sense, mechanisms of defence and the ability to change the environment so as to fit the needs of the organism may be looked upon as an extension of homeostatic functions outside the physical boundaries of the organism. Their task is to prevent any disruption of the organism's life functions and integrity.

A key concept regarding living organisms (systems) is *entropy*. The concept entropy was introduced into thermodynamics by Rudolf Clausius as a principle which could characterize the direction of *possible* processes within isolated systems of constant energy content (no energy exchange with the environment). In terms of this principle, The Second Law of Thermodynamics can be phrased as follows: "In any closed system, the entropy of the system either increases or remains constant":

$$dS \geq 0 \ (dS = \text{change of entropy})$$

This is supposed to be one of the most general laws of nature and probably valid for the universe as a whole (if the universe is closed and has a finite mass). It also gives a mathematical formulation of the extent to which a given quantity of energy (originally formulated for heat) can be used to perform mechanical work (see Sears, 1953; Fermi, 1956). This quantity has earlier been mentioned as exergy. Different forms of energy can be transformed into each other. Energy cannot be destroyed, but for each transformation a part of the given quantity of energy is "lost" in the sense that it is no longer available for useful work. The entropy of an amount of energy increases as its ability to perform an equivalent amount of work decreases. Now, entropy has an aspect that is related to the degree of order (or randomness) of elements. Energy states of high entropy have high probability. So have states of systems with a high degree of randomness (lack of order). This is the reason why the concept of entropy is used within the Mathematical Theory of Communication to denote the degree of order for elements of a message (Shannon & Weaver, 1959). The information content (amount of information) of these elements is described in terms of information theoretical entropy. The thermodynamical entropy (S) of a physical system (of molecules) is according to Boltzmann a logarithmic function of its thermodynamic probability (P) of its occurrence:[2]

$$S = k \cdot \ln P$$

(k = Boltzmann's constant = $1.38^{\cdot-23}$ J/deg.)
The information content (H) of a message (information theoretical entropy) on the other hand, is a negative logarithmic function of the probability of its elements:

$$H(A) = - \Sigma \, P_a \, {}^2\log P_a$$

(a are the elements of an ensemble A (a message)).

Thus both types of entropy and the concept of information are related to the probability of the state of a system. The main formal difference is the minus sign. The relationship between the concepts has been interpreted so, that information theoretical entropy (information content) can be looked upon as a negative function of thermodynamical entropy, which means that H increases as S decreases. This fact gave rise to Brillouins and Wieners characterization of information as negative entropy or negentropy (Wiener, 1961; Brillouin, 1962). The deeper implications of this relationship have, however, been the object of slightly different interpretations.

The transfer of information means the transfer of structural or organisational principles. Living organisms receive their vast store of basic instructions through genetic information, which is stored and encoded as sequences of nucleotides within the DNA of genes. Later on the organism receives information through sensory processes and stores it in different types memories.

The living organism, during its life, maintains a high level of negentropy. This is made possible by the use of energy-rich com-

ponents, which are extracted from the environment by the expenditure
of an excess of energy. Thus, living systems have to be open systems
whose negentropy is maintained by a corresponding increase of entropy (disorder) in their environment. This resolves the apparent
contradiction between their functional principles and The Second
Law of Thermodynamics. It is also the basic issue behind the energy
problem of mankind: the need for low-entropic energy. The energy
crisis of mankind seems really to be an *exergy* crisis. The role of living
organisms in this context has been nicely formulated by Sayre: "Life
thus is a catalyst, working to increase disorder within its hosts environment, acting more effectively in life forms that are more complex"
(Sayre, 1976, p. 93).

A short note concerning *information* and *negentropy* should be
added. One has to be careful how to use the terms. The transfer of
information proper in the sense of Shannons Theory is formulated
for energetically *closed* systems. The theory presupposes the existence
of established channels, transmitters and receivers. No net energy is
transferred to the receiving system, only the structuring impulse
(information). Meanwhile, all living systems are thermodynamically
open systems, exchanging energy and matter. The apparent contradiction may be solved by assuming that information is gained by
different processes at different stages of ontogenetic development and
by different processes at different levels of the hierarchy:
1. Flow systems (living systems belong to this category) tend to decrease their entropy when moving from an arbitrary initial state
   to a final stationary state (equifinality in dissipative systems; Prigogine, 1967).
2. The increasing order (negentropy) of organisms during ontogenetic
   growth is due to the effect of genetically transferred instructions
   (order through order).
3. Transfer of information (in the sense of Shannons theory) starts
   in connection with learning and feedback processes when underlying mechanisms have been developed. This type of information
   transfer is restricted to certain structures which at the *given hierachical level* of the system behave as partially closed subsystems.
   Hence, this presupposes the existence of established networks (subsystems) that encode transferred information in a way which con-
   fines it to the boundaries of this subsystem. It also implies that
   the internally coded information is comparatively stable to the
   influence of metabolic processes, which always bring about a change
   of thermodynamical entropy.

The survival of vitalistic theories up to the present day may
primarily depend on the fact that the concept of "life" could not be

grasped by the models of classical science. The theory of dissipative systems as developed by Prigogine and other scholars shows that complex structures could emerge outside the range of thermodynamic equilibria by dissipation of energy and matter and that local information could be gained by processes which selectively filter away noise. An example is the spontaneous emergence of dissipative structures in thermodynamically unstable systems by a principle denoted "order through fluctuation" (restructuring of the system in order to gain stability with respect to fluctuations). This implies the possibility of self-organizing systems from a thermodynamical point of view. A general evolution criterion has also been derived by Glansdorf and Prigogine (Prigogine, 1967). Thus the creation of artificial life seems to be a technological and economical question rather than a principal one (Eigen & Winkler, 1975).

This may essentially also be the answer to questions about the relationship between "biology" and "chemistry." Biology here favours a reductionistic view, since biological systems *are very complex chemical systems*. An excellent treatment of the subject, both comprehensive and extensive, is given by James Greer Miller (1978). The difficulty then is to describe such systems, since the problem of reduction leads to the task of handling complexities. What one normally does is to apply the principle of Pandora's boxes (small boxes within larger boxes within still larger boxes) to this kind of problem. It means the stepwise compression of detailed information into more general and formally simpler concepts and symbols. The different levels of description then reflect the hierarchical levels of the system to which they relate. This may easily be illustrated by figure 12.1.

A scientific description of our world makes use of its redundancy to describe it simply (Vollmer, 1983). In living systems, however, one mostly finds common mechanisms and principles mixed with unique ones. The same hormone may affect different receptor sites of similar response characteristic all over the organism, but each single receptor may then trigger quite different functional subsystems. Nevertheless, these subsystems then may be part of a higher order regulatory system, which serves the stability of the organism as a whole. In this way organisms, and particularly their nervous system, may be described as highly cooperative systems or synergistic structures.

PHYLOGENETIC ASPECTS ON LIFE

It has already been mentioned that living organisms are highly improbable from a stochastic point of view. Nevertheless, they exist,

Figure 12-1: Molecular Arrangment of DNA (Figure from Lindahl et al. 1967).

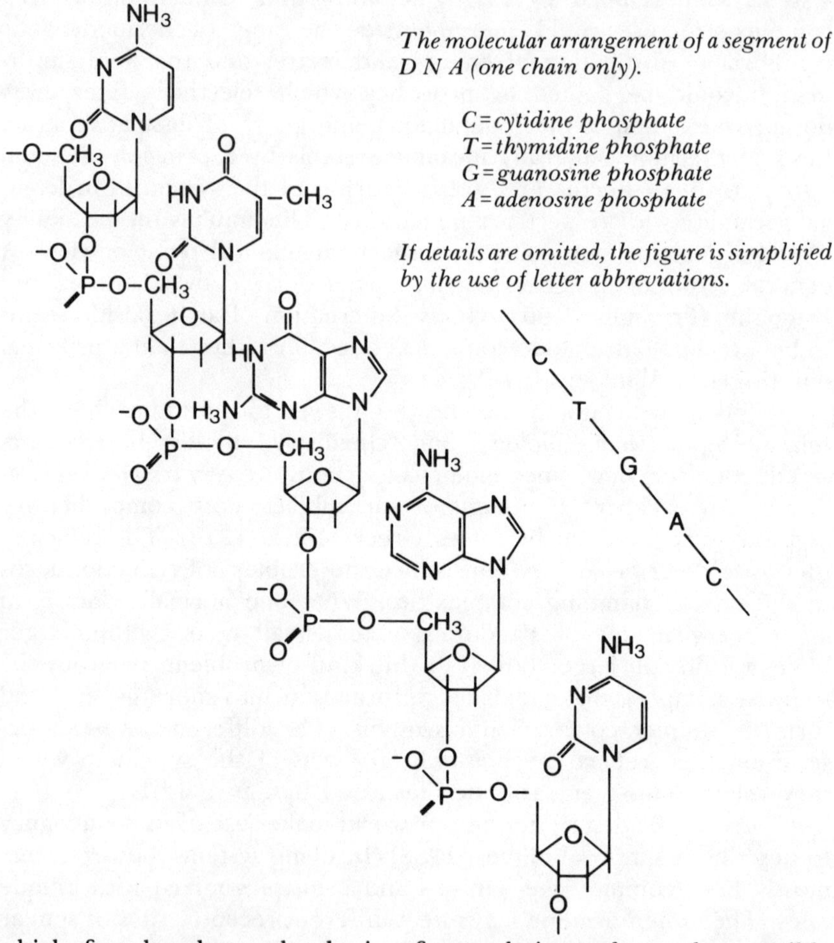

The molecular arrangement of a segment of D N A (one chain only).

C = cytidine phosphate
T = thymidine phosphate
G = guanosine phosphate
A = adenosine phosphate

If details are omitted, the figure is simplified by the use of letter abbreviations.

which fact has been the basis of speculations about the possible existence of living organisms elsewhere in the universe. This idea is not new, which is known from the tragic fate of Giordano Bruno, who was burnt as a heretic in 1600. While our knowledge in this respect is still fragmentary, it is coherent enough to allow for educated guesses (Ball, 1983; Mustelin, 1983). As to direct evidence, only the existence of simple carbon compounds outside our earth have been reported. Recently a report from China states the discovery of an amino acid in a meteorite. Nevertheless, the fact that there exists at least one species of observers, *homo sapiens*, gave birth to the Anthropic Principle, which is said to "explain" a quite improbable chain of events and conditions: initial conditions during the BIG BANG determined the formation of heavier elements; furthermore a suitable planetary mass, critical distance from a sun of suitable spectral class, planetary rotation, the tilt of the axis of rotation with respect to the ecliptica, the "abnormal" properties of water, the homeopolar bound of carbon atoms (ensuring the formation of larger carbon chains), and so forth are a few of the conditions that had to be met in order to make life possible on earth (Breuer, 1981; Gale, 1981).Our knowledge about the origin of life on earth is to a large extent based on conjecture, even if some details are known with a reasonable degree of certainty (detailed references are given by Löwenhard, 1981). The age of our earth is estimated to about 4,600 million years. The first signs of life seem to have appeared some 3,200 to 3,900 million years ago (Halstead, 1975; Sagan, 1978). The timepoint somewhat depends on where (at which level of complexity) the limit for forms of life is set. With a high degree of certainty, only simple carbon compounds (chains of 2 to 3 atoms) existed 4,500 million years ago, while 3,000 to 4,000 million years later highly differentiated life forms had emerged (Ehrensvärd, 1961). The oldest known microfossils date back to about 3,500 million years, while the first "modern" unicellular organisms seem to have appeared about 1,500 million years ago (Mustelin, 1983). Microscopic fossils, identified as remnants of the earliest eukaryotes (originally called acritarchs = of uncertain origin), have been shown to be unicellular planktons, about 1,400 million years old (Vidal, 1984). Recently it was mentioned (Lagerkvist, 1983) that prokaryotes and eukaryotes might have a common origin in archaebacteriae.

The mergence of early forms of life and their development into the existing forms, reflect a complex interaction with and interdependence on that environment, which gave birth to them. According to Haldane and Oparin, the early predominantly reducing atmosphere (anoxygenic atmosphere) of earth was supposed to promote the origination of a chemical background from which the earliest protoforms of living systems could emerge (Dickerson, 1978; Mayr, 1978).[3]

During some billion years one-celled, mainly anaerobic organisms were the only forms of life. However, these early primitive microorganisms gave rise to biochemical systems and the oxygen-enriched atmosphere on which modern life depends (Schopf, 1978). It also seems that these changes created the necessary conditions for a more rapid diversification of life forms and the emergence of multicellular organisms with steadily increasing efficiency.

After the first stable forms of life had been established, further evolution was mainly governed by two mechanisms: genetic variation and selection. Genetic variation is accomplished by mutations, *i.e.*, rearrangements of molecular sequences in DNA and RNA. Another mechanism depends on the exchange of corresponding chromosomal segments between homologous chromosomes by formation of chiasms and crossing over. This means rearrangement of genetic information at the chromosomal level. Gene drift and jumping genes are mechanisms proposed more recently.

Genetic variation is a necessary precondition for evolution. Modern molecular genetics have also shown that variations within a species are much larger than Darwin once postulated (Ayala, 1978). The present view is confirmed by studies about protective color adaptation for different kinds of insects in relation to a changing environment. While random mutations safeguard continued variation and recombination for the development of new capacities to deal with environment, the test of survival accomplishes the natural selection of organisms that are best adapted to existing conditions.

What then could be said about the probability of occurrence of living organisms? To illustrate this, suppose that a simple organism without redundancy could be built on the basis of 1,000 bits of information. The selection of this organism from alternates of possible atomic arrangements would mean a single choice from 2^{1000} possible ones. This gives a random probability of about 10^{-301}. If one considers the low magnitude of these probabilities, the question arises if the time period of earth existence is sufficient to allow for the development of such complex organisms as the mammals of today? To quote Laszlo: "The unqualified random shuffling hypothesis runs into difficulties at this point, since the probability of achieving systems of the order of complexity of living beings far exceeds the order of the time-span indicated by astronomical and geological evidence. However, when we take systems as ordered wholes, adapting to environment in order to compensate for changes, and realize that atoms and molecules are systems of this kind, we get a more conservative time estimate. Using Simon's hypothesis, according to which the time required for the evolution of complex from simple systems depends critically on the number and distribution of potential intermediate stable forms, organic evolution fits into the physically available time period. It becomes evident that nature can build complex structures relatively rapidly by using existing systems as building blocks and combining them into stable associations under favorable conditions (Laszlo, 1973, p. 95).

Cybernetic self regulation is a universal system property. While homeostasis may be defined as *adaptive self-stabilization, adaptive self-organization* characterizes selective progression towards the emergence of better adapted species, capable of handling increasing amounts of environmental changes:

Figure 12-2.

According to Ashby, adaptive self-organization inevitably leads to known biological systems. "In the isolated system, life and intelligence develop." (Ashby, 1962, p. 272.)

The importance of "system theoretical" aspects in relation to phylogenetic evolution may be summarized in the words of Dobzhansky: "Adaptation and emergence of new genotypes is a feedback process within a reproductive group, natural selection is homeostasis within a relatively isolated biotic system. The results of these two processes operating together is the evolution of established species." (Dobzhansky, 1955, p. 131.)

A mark of success of an organic form in evolution is the ability of its members to achieve stability within their environment. This amounts to persisting ability on the part of the organism to feed upon the negentropy of its immediate environment (Schrödinger, 1951). Sayre coins, in this connection, the term negentropic flexibility: "In speaking of flexibility in the assimilation of negentropy, I refer to the capacity of an organism to establish efficient couplings with its environment, under a range of different conditions, through which negentropy can be obtained to support growth and metabolism and to control its response to environmental contingencies. Let us name this capacity *negentropic flexibility*. Mobility supports the development of negentropic flexibility. Individuals with superior mobility will tend to replace others within their reproductive group, thereby strengthening the genetic factor that makes mobility possible. Among such factors, however, is perceptual sensitivity, which contributes directly to the organism's capacity to acquire negentropy in form of information." (Sayre, 1976, p. 117.)

If one looks for the results of evolution, reflected in life forms of today, one finds a large variety of interdependent living organisms, where complex multicellular organisms coexist with unicellular ones and with protoforms of life. It is interesting, and a lucky circumstance from the standpoint of the scientist, to find a reflection of phylogenetic evolution in the existence of a whole scale of organisms with varying degree of complexity. All life forms together, fauna and flora, constitute the large ecological system of life on earth. This does not imply that simple life forms such as bacteria of today are identical with their early ancestors. Their total amount of information may approximately be unchanged, but the "quality" of their genetic information, expressed in terms of the organism's biochemical efficiency, is probably higher in organisms of today.

One can arrange systems in order of increasing complexity. The given scale should be interpreted as an ordinal scale, since no estimates of the real magnitude of complexity can be given.

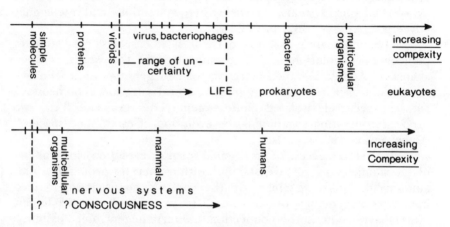

Figure 12-3: The Complexity Scale of Living Organisms.

This presentation does not, of course, consider qualitative differences between life forms on approximately the same level of complexity, which would imply a comparison between plants and animals. The increase of complexity reflects the emergence of additional life functions. Proteins and nucleic acids show some of the basic properties which are the foundation of life functions proper.

Aggregates of complex molecules show an increasing versatility in their reactions with the chemical environment. With increasing complexity the systems gain independence from their environment. This means that their demands on the environment with respect to certain premanufactured components decreases. At the same time, more regulative functions are incorporated within the boundaries of the system. An important mark of progress is the emergence of closed cells, protected from environment by membranes, which facilitate the selective absorption of nutrients and the excretion of metabolites. The earliest types of cells, prokaryotes, lack nuclei. They are represented by bacteria and cyanobacteria. The next essential step is the development of eukaryotes, cellular organisms with distinct nuclei. All higher plants, animals and fungi are based on this type of cell. The main differences between prokaryotes and eukaryotes are summarized by Schopf (1978).

A final illustration will conclude this section: reduction in relation to the complexity of a system. While a given system may be analyzed in principle (if not always in a strict quantitative manner), this may for economical reasons not always be possible in detail. The structure and genetic layout of some simple virus, such as the bacterial virus ΦX 174 (Fiddes, 1977; Sanger et al., 1977) or the Tobacco Mosaic Virus (TM) (Butler & Klug, 1978), are known in detail. The genome of the ΦX 174 contains 9 genes of different length and shows a remarkable economy by partial overlapping of genes. The genetic information is stored in a single circular DNA molecule of 1.8 μm length, comprising 5,375 nucleotides. A print-out of this genetic array (using letter abbreviations) would demand one A 4 page. A corresponding description of our intestinal bacterium, *Escherichia coli*, would probably demand a space corresponding to several volumes of *Encyclopaedia Britannica*. Also there is the question of *implicit* genetic information. A gene not only specifies a protein, it specifies implicitly the secondary or tertiary structure of the protein and, hence, its chemical behavior and biological enzyme function. The description of these functions would demand further knowledge about this specific protein and about each amino acid component. The given picture thus speaks in favour of a partial, but not radical reductionism.

The purpose of this section has been to show that "life" from a phylogenetic point of view is no unitary concept. Rather the meaning of the term and its range of connotation changes with the increase of complexity of the systems (organisms) to which it is applied. There seems to be no definite demarcation that allows an exclusive classification into so-called living and non-living systems. Rather there is a continuous transition from non-living matter, which nevertheless may show typical basic life functions, via an extended range of uncertainty to definite "living" systems. The transitory types of systems show the gradual incorporation of an increasing number of homeostatic life functions and metabolic processes into their boundaries. Thus it has been shown that "life" is a label, used to denote the totality of life-functions, which are necessary to sustain the continuous existence of the system (organism) as a whole. It is also evident that the exact connotation of the term "life" is a function of the set of life functions which define the organism in question.

THE INFORMATION SYSTEM

The above-given sections on living systems had several purposes.

1. The brain is a very specialized subsystem of an organism. Its functions are more easily understood against the given background.[4]

2. Psychology deals with manifestations of living organisms (behavior and experiences), which, in fact, are consequences of brain functions or acitities of the nervous system.

3. The specific problem is, of course, related to conscious experience. The model of "consciousness", which is given below, follows the "system-theoretical" approach, since consciousness here is viewed as a consequence of system properties of the brain.

There are, however, differences. The principle of reduction applies to physiological (biological) systems, while the phenomenon of consciousness is more easily treated as a correlate of physiological processes.

The brain and nervous system are essentially information systems of an organism. The following picture may summarize the essence of it:

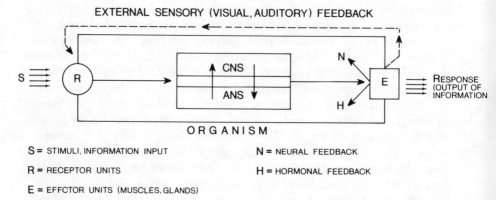

Figure 12-4: EEG as a Function of Flicker Frequency.

Both the nervous system and the endocrine system are information systems. The endocrine system, however, conveys solely internal information, using hormones as signal molecules, which are distributed by the blood stream and affect specific receptors all over the organism. The nervous system and endocrine system interact at the synapses.

Essentially, the brain may be viewed as an autoanalytic instrument, which is able to detect, recognize, and record its own states. This implies the availability of internal information about the brain itself and, hence, an access to different sources of information: external and internal ones. Since the processing of information often (but not always) is based on conscious processes, this gives rise to the so-called psychophysical problem, which may be illustrated by the following picture:

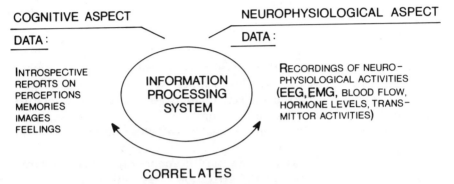

Figure 12-5: Cognitive and Neurophysiological Aspects of the Organism.

A simple example may illustrate the meaning of correlation in this case. If the eyes are stimulated by a slowly flashing light, each flash is perceived separately. If the EEG (electroencephalogram) is recorded simultaneously from the occipital lobes of the cerebral cortex (area striata, the site of visual information processing), one gets a sequence of evoked potentials as a response to the repetitive light stimuli: (arrow indicates flash; f = 5 Hz).

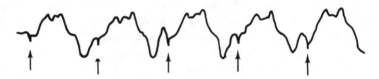

Figure 12-6: EEG Pattern.

However, when the flicker frequency reaches a certain critical value, the light is perceived as a steady one. This makes it possible to use alternating current (AC, 50–60 Hz) for illumination purposes. The critical value is called CFF (critical flicker fusion frequency) and changes as a logarithmic function of the light intensity (I):

$$CFF = a + b \cdot \log I$$

(a and b are constants). Now, when this limit is reached, the separate EEG-responses disappear and the (mainly) spontaneous EEG-activity is restored. The very close correspondence of subjective experiences and EEG responses as a function of the CFF value makes them correlates.

CONSCIOUSNESS

This section will start with a clarification of the terminology used:

Consciousness is used as the technical term to denote the phenomenon behind what, in subjective language, is described as awareness, subjective experience and so on.

Awareness is used as an equivalent of consciousness from the standpoint of the subject.

Sensation is used as a general term to denote the effects in terms of subjective experience of the activation of receptors.

A clear distinction is made between the phenomenon of consciousness as such and the content of subjective experience (mental objects, symbols, images, *etc.*).

Feelings (Gefühle) is the most ambiguous of the terms. In everyday language it means both sensations, moods, emotions, and unspecified qualities of awareness, not related to mental objects. In the words of Jaspers the concept may be restricted according to the following definition: "Gewöhnlich nennt man Gefühl alles Seelische, das weder deutlich zu den Phänomenen des Gegenstands-bewusstseins (awareness concerning objects; my note) noch zu Triebregungen und Willensakten zu stellen ist. Alle unentwickelten, unklaren psychischen Gebilde heissen Gefühl, mit einem Wort, alles was man sonst nicht zu nennen weiss." (Jaspers, 1984; *c.fr.* Zethraeus, 1962, p. 146.)

Self-consciousness is not used as identical with consciousness. The distinction is treated later on. Consciousness has a larger connotation.

Mind is used as a label to denote the non-physical "universe of mental phenomena" (world 2 in the terminology of Karl Popper), a conceptual framework, which is related to all phenomena of conscious experience. The use of the term here does not imply any connotation of a homunculus.

The following postulates should be regarded as speculative hypotheses, or, in some cases as descriptions of observable phenomena. They should serve as starting points for discussion and model building.

POSTULATES

1. Consciousness, as we know it, seems to be restricted to a certain class of living organisms, utilizing nervous systems.

2. Consciousness may be described as a phenomenon that accompanies certain modes of information processing, characterized by a direction of attention onto the information content of the ongoing process. This amounts to an ability of the participating nerve net to sense its own states. Consciousness is one of the principles that enables the brain to work as an autoanalytical instrument. It should be noted, however, that the subjective nature of "immediate knowledge," which characterizes conscious information processing, does not seem to be a necessary condition for a system to "sense" changes in its own states or to analyze its own functions. This would only demand a suitable hierarchy of analyzing agents. Also a distinction should be made between the phenomenon of "being aware" (*i.e.*, the participation in an immediate act of experience) and knowledge about the principles which underly the emergence of this awareness.

3. The human brain and probably that of other animals (which show periodic phases of sleep) seem to utilize both "conscious" and "non-conscious" modes of information processing.

4. Consciousness may arise as a consequence of system properties, which a computer lacks. The critical system parameters are, as yet, not known, which does not mean that they are inaccessible. Consciousness is, hence, probably not solely a consequence of a systems complexity as such, but reflects an inherent principle, which gives rise to the phenomenon. This principle may be related to the cellular level, the subcellular level or both. A tentative guess may be that the phenomenon arises as a consequence of basic properties of the neuron, but manifests itself only clearly in sufficiently complex systems. Such a basic property may be an extrapolation of the excitability of complex aggregates of protein molecules. At the cellular level, a complex interaction of large aggregates of cells creates a spatio-temporal pattern of slow potentials and discrete pulses (bioelectric fields) which fulfil certain conditions (though not in detail known) regarding structure and temporal continuity ("world lines"). It is furthermore empirically known, that a number of necessary conditions must be fulfilled in order to let consciousness occur. Such conditions are the activation of the brain by the thalamo-reticular system and an ongoing electrophysiological activity in the cerebral cortex.

5. Consciousness as a phenomenon seems to change with respect to both quantitative and qualitative aspects as a function of the complexity of the system to which it is related. Thus, the concept of "consciousness" is, in analogy to "life", no unitary concept. In a phylogenetic sense "consciousness" seems to develop alongside of

new system properties of living organisms. "Consciousness" here means a phenomenon that increases in quality and scope from primitive awareness at lower phylogenetic levels to abstract thinking in humans alongside an increasing complexity of the corresponding brain structures.

6. Conscious information processing is supposed to represent a principle that combines a high efficiency regarding sensory discriminative power with economy regarding the necessary amount of neural elements.

7. Subjectively we speak of different states of consciousness, corresponding to different neurophysiological states. It is well known, that conscious experience is influenced by biochemical changes within the brain. However, there have to be physiological states of the brain or nervous system, which do not correspond to any conscious experience.

8. There is a distinction between consciousness (awareness) as a phenomenon and the content of mental experience. Very broadly one may speak of two classes of mental experience: mental objects, which are related to sensory information from the external world and feelings, emotions or motivational states, representing changes of internal physiological states. Both types of experience are, of course, interrelated. Mental objects (symbols) may be said to represent an "internal mapping" of external objects and relationships between them. They generally reflect essential features of the external world with high degree of fidelity. There are, however, other symbols, such as abstract concepts, imaginations or hallicinatory experiences which do not primarily reflect the presence of external equivalents.

9. Consciousness as a phenomenon is dependent upon the perpetuation of all life functions that are necessary to support the normal functions of the information processing system (organism) to which it is bound.

10. The essential genetic instructions, necessary to develop the system properties that underly the emergence of consciousness, have to be encoded into the genome as part of the explicit and implicit genetic information.

CONSCIOUSNESS FROM A PHYLOGENETIC
POINT OF VIEW

The study of consciousness is limited by its very nature as a "private phenomenon", *i.e.* due to the lack of direct access. Since the phenomenon as yet cannot be analyzed directly in humans, the same is true to a still higher degree for animals, since not even the communication of introspective reports by means of language is available. The study of this area is, hence, restricted to indirect assessment.

According to postulate (5), consciousness develops slowly together with other system properties of living organisms. This means that with increasing capacity of the organisms' information processing system, the extent and quality of the accompanying phenomenon of consciousness is supposed to increase in proportion hereto. Furthermore, consciousness is supposed to develop in all species that are equipped with sensory organs and associated information processing circuits. This also implies, that consciousness at a lower phylogenetic level does not mean exactly the same thing as at a higher level. In analogy to what has been shown regarding "life", there are probably protoforms of consciousness since the system property, which underlies the emergence of consciousness is the result of a continuous development.

One may ask why consciousness did arise at all? A suggestion is, that consciousness represents a principle of economy that makes information processing more efficient and reduces the amount of elements, necessary to perform this task (postulate 6). A hypothesis of this import was already expressed by Culbertson (1963, p. 79 and chapter 7). But the existence of such a principle would mean a strengthening of the organisms "negentropic flexibility" and thus would have survival value for the organism. A similar view is held by Sayre: "Human consciousness, like learning, is the product of evolutionary bias towards life forms with superior negentropic flexibility, for conscious organisms excel in their ability to receive information and to apply it under a wide variety of living conditions. Like learning, also consciousness is a form of adaptation parallel to the evolutionary process in its feedback characteristics." (Sayre, 1976, p. 139.)

To be more specific: any organism that is confronted with the problem of coping with its adaptation to a very complex environment not only has to integrate a large amount of different information, but this integration also has to be done in a way that makes it possible to optimize a holistic response. Such a task includes, for example, the probability matching of different sensory messages in space and time in order to reveal their possible causal relationship.

The performance of an appropriate behavior within the given context has to be based on a processing of information that includes an internal representation of the organism itself together with elements of its environment. An animal that successfully wants to jump over a cliff, has to judge its own trajectory in relation to distance and initial acceleration. Hence both information about the environment and the organism itself has to be integrated into an internal "model" or program which determines complex actions. It is probable, that "conscious" modes of information processing have developed as being superior in relation to this type of task, which demands the simultaneous integration of large amounts of information into a single pattern. A detailed discussion of this topic from a phylogenetic point of view is given by Jerison (1978).

It is, at present, not possible to prove the above mentioned principles conclusively, but there are several indications, which all point into the same direction. If one compares different species of living organisms, let us say frogs, rats, dogs, monkeys, and humans, one finds striking similarities in the way these organisms react to different classes of stimuli: painful stimuli, light stimuli, sound stimuli, and so on. This is, of course no proof of the existence of consciousness in the above stated sense. It may, in the terminology of Ryle (1949, 1967) be described as a propensity or disposition to react. To this, Blakemore comments: "If this kind of unmasking of consciousness destroys its special qualities, must we conclude that consciousness does not exist at all? To call "knowing" a disposition to act may bring consciousness within the professional realm of brain research (and this is an essential step), but it does not mean that there is nothing to explain. Ryle has exorcised the Ghost from the Machine, but he has left a machine of much greater complexity." (Blakemore, 1977, pp. 35–36.)

As mentioned above (postulates 2 and 4) the phenomenon of consciousness reflects the existence of a system property, which seems to be common to organisms that are equipped with subsystems, able to process sensory information. This implies that the principles behind the emergence of conscious modes of information processing somehow have to be encoded in the genome of the organism. But this reflects an essential fact: the instructions that are necessary to develop the system properties in question have to be part of the explicit and implicit genetic information. This means that the principles that underlie the functions behind "consciousness" can be expressed in terms of a material code.

A principle that represents superior qualities is likely to be preserved in phylogenetic evolution and will probably, at a very early stage, be "adopted" by all organisms that can make use of it. Concerning conscious experience, this implies that we probably share the basic features with our ancestors from earlier stages of evolution. There are strong reasons to believe the existence in most animals of sensory awareness as well as certain types of cognitive abilities, related to sensory analysis and memory functions. Elementary mental functions have been shown to exist in very simple systems of neurons and isolated neurons (Kandel 1979 · Sokolov 1981).

It is well known that animals show behavioural signs to recognize objects and other animals *both* as individuals and members of a species or a class. Also there are several reports that indicate dream activity in animals (Sagan, 1978). However, a cat is not a dog and a chimpanzee is not a human. One should be careful not to project *human* concepts or modes of experience into other animals. This is part of the relevant criticism, which early behaviorists made against the animal psychology of the 19th Century.

An adequate action of an organism demands access to appropriate environmental information. This gives reason to assume a general adequacy of its receptor mechanisms. But this also gives reason to believe that the perception of the external world shows speciesbound variations. Von Uexküll had already stated in 1928: "It would be a very naive sort of dogmatism to assume that there exists an absolute reality of things that are the same for all living beings. Reality is not a homogeneous thing, having as many different schemes and patterns as there are different organisms."

A last question shall be raised: Does a distinct borderline exist between "conscious" systems and protoforms of them? Has, for instance, the bee awareness? Nobody can answer this question today, but the *possibility* that the bee is aware, cannot be denied, even if awareness here would mean a very rudimantary form. From what has been said earlier it is probably not possible to state the existence of a definite borderline. Rather in analogy to "life" it seems probable that there is a transition from "unconscious" life forms via a range of uncertainty to definitely "conscious" ones.

Due to lack of space, further details have to be omitted. A more extensive treatment of the model is given by Löwenhard (1981). From a much broader point of view, the evolution of the human mind and its cultural products has been the object of a rapidly developing section of philosophy: evolutionary epistemology. Since the field has been the object of an earlier ICUS session, only a few references will be given (ICUS proceedings, 1982, vol.2., pp. 783–910; Lorenz & Wuketits, 1983; Radnitzky, 1983, Riedl, 1979, Vollmer, 1981).

Returning to the question of reduction vs. correlation, the answer within the framework of an evolutionary model will be: both principles coexist in a complementary manner. The classical "reduction" of biology to chemistry seems to be a matter of terminology (or more precise the conceptual level of it) in relation to system complexity.

The "reduction" of psychology to neurophysiology is split up into two main problems. One deals with the control of behavior, viewed as a high-level manifestation of integrated systems. Partially, this also applies to advanced computer technology and robotics. One may think of the difference between low-level (binary) and high-level computer language. This problem is essentially similar to the above mentioned about biology.

The other problem regards consciousness. Here the ontological position is essential for an interpretation of facts. If consciousness is viewed as a function of the nervous system (or a phenomenon, related to certain properties of the CNS), then the correlation model applies strictly. This also means that the manifestation, which we call consciousness, shows a covariation with the properties of the neurological system to which it relates. In a deeper sense, however, consciousness may reflect a very basic integrative potential of matter to achieve the reflexive property of awareness, if the necessary preconditions are given.

MIND AND BRAIN

The final section will deal with the correlational aspect of the body-mind problem. As known from the history of philosophy, the classical treatment of the body-mind problem is part of ontology. For reference see, *e.g.*, Leahey, (1980) or Vollmer (1980). The well-known clock analogy, which normally is used to illustrate Leibniz' principle of pre-established harmony, may serve this purpose for other monistic and dualistic ontologies as well.

Initially, the general ontological notion of a "substance" can be excluded from the present context. The problem then is reduced to the relationship between "brain and mind". Nevertheless, the classical psychophysical problem was born out of a (monistic or dualistic) concept of parallelism. While G.T. Fechner (1801–1887) tried to give mathematical proof to the identity hypothesis of Spinoza, E.H. Weber (1795–1878) tried to describe variations in human experience against a background of Leibniz' theory of monads. The results were well-known psychophysical laws, such as the Weber ratio

$$\frac{\Delta S}{S} = \Delta R = k$$

(ΔS = just noticeable difference in stimulus intensity; "law" here means an empirical generalization). The term ΔR was supposed to represent the constant "unit" of a subjective intensity scale. If ΔS

Table 12-1: Dualism and Monism (Table from Vollmer 1980).

DUALISM
(two substances)

Parallelism: Brain and mind are independent from each other, but work synchronous. How is this correspondence achieved?

Autonomism: By chance.

Occasionalism: Continuous supervision by God.

(1)

Pre-established harmony: Established by God forever during the act of creation ("programming")

(2)

Dualistic epiphenomenalism: The brain controls the mind without feedback.

Animism: The mind animates all matter (also controls the brain).

(3)

Interactionalism: Brain and mind interact actively.

(4)

MONISM
(one substance)

Neutral monism: Mind and matter are only different aspects of one single (unknown) substance.

(5)

Spiritualism: Everything is mind. Matter does not exist independently from mind.

(6)

Strict materialism: Everything is matter. There is no mind.

(7)

Behaviorism: (eliminative materialism) Mind is a short, but mostly misleading name for certain behavioral dispositions. As our knowledge grows, mantalistic terms will be substituted by neurophysiological ones.

(8)

Monistic epiphenomenalism: Mind is only an accompanying phenomenon (epiphenomenon, shadow, picture).

(9)

Hylemorphism: Matter and mind correspond to each other as substance and form *(anima forma corporis)*. They constitute a conceptual unity, but may dissolve after death.

(10)

Identity theory: Mind is a function of the brain, which only manifests itself at a sufficient level of complexity. Mental or conscious states are states of neural aggregates of the CNS.
(one clockwork—two faces)

(11)

(1) Geulincx, Malebranche (2) Leibniz (3) Plato, Plotinus, Augustine (4) Descartes, Penfield, Popper, Eccles, V. Dithfurth (5) Heraclitus: Logos; Spinoza: God; Ostwald: Energy Etc.
(6) Berkeley, Hegel, Fichte, Mach, Schopenhauer, Whitehead. (7) Hobbes, Vogt, Lamettrie, Holbach. (8) Watson, Skinner, Ryle, Rorty, Feyerabend. (9) Epicurus, Lucretius, E. Von Hartmann, Nietzsche, L. Büchner, Th. Huxley. (10) Aristotle, Thomas Ab Aquino. (11) Bunge, Lorenz, Riel, Steinbüch, Riedl.

and ΔR are viewed as approximations of differentials (dS and dR), then an integration gives the Fechner Law:

$$pR = k \cdot \log S$$

(k = a constant, S = stimulus intensity, R = response intensity). It has, however, been doubted, that the assumptions behind Fechner's reasoning (ΔR = constant and adding up to a linear scale of sensation) are valid. S.S. Stevens (1906–1973) hence proposed a power law, based on comparative judgements:

$$R = k \ (S - S_0)^n$$

S_0 = a threshold correction. A logarithmic transformation of this law then gives a linear relationship, which makes it easy to compare different stimulus modalities.

For a sound of 1000 Hz, the relationship between subjective loudness (in sone units) and physical intensity (in dB units) is

$$R = k \cdot S^{0.3}$$

The equation says, that an increase of the intensity S by a factor 10 gives an increase by a factor 2 in loudness (both scales are logarithmic ones).

Now, a *generalized* psychophysical problem mainly is identical with the brain-mind problem. Behind this, however, lies all the complexity of the brain. It is not possible to consider the wealth of relevant facts, concepts, and hypotheses within the limited space of this paper. The following summary just gives a hint of it.

1. In accordance with what has been said above, "consciousness" seems to exist separately for each nerve structure that is capable to produce it. This is indicated by observations on split-brain patients (with surgically dissected corpus callosum = the great cerebral commissure) or in connection with cerebral angiography (X-ray mapping of the cerebral arterial network), where sometimes *one half* of the brain is put into narcosis by unilateral injection of amytal (ethyl-isoamyl-barbiturate). This drug has a hypnotic effect of short duration and induces sleep in the injected hemisphere of the brain.

The corpus callosum provides the facility for a mutual exchange of highly specified neural codes, which allows for a balanced availability of information for both hemispheres. This is a necessary precondition for an integrated mind (Gazzaniga & LeDoux, 1978).

2. It seems probable, that different modes of consciousness are related to different stages of information processing. This includes reactivation of the memory content, images etc. A model of this import has been proposed by Aurell (1979).

It is well-known that the vivid intensity of sensory awareness is different from the pale reproductions of past experiences. Nevertheless, there exist conditions during which images may reach some of the qualities of actual sensations: hallucinatory states, which may be induced by hypnosis, intoxications, infections, or mental diseases.

3. The brain uses both conscious and non-conscious modes of information processing. Strictly, one has to make a distinction between *unconscious processes* (information not retrievable except by inference), *subconscious processes* (information only retrievable under appropriate circumstances) and *non-conscious processes* (information not stored in memory) (Hilgard, 1980).

4. Our conscious experience can be characterized with respect to *content, mode* and *state of consciousness.* These distinctions are, however, not always quite clear, since several modes of experience may exist simultaneously (*e.g.*, "seeing", "hearing", "feeling a touch" etc.) and *transitory states* can make it difficult to define the category of a momentary state. The *modes* of conscious experience (awareness) are most easily demonstrated by reference to sense modalities. It is a different sensation to hear or to see. The implication of the concept sense modality is clear from the fact that sense modalities represent *distinct* internal sensations, which means that a given modality cannot be transformed to another. It is normally not possible to image "what a sound looks like" or "how a colour smells" (notwithstanding hallucinatory experiences of synesthetic nature, *e.g.*, a sound stimulus that evokes color experience).

As to the *states* of consciousness, one generally makes a difference between normal states of consciousness (NSC) and altered states of consciousness (ASC). NSC varies with respect to vigilance (effects of arousal and reticular activation), attention (selective cortical activation) or changes in alertness due to circadian rhythms. ASC occurs naturally during sleep and its different phases, during transitory states, such as the hypnagogic state (= transition from NSC to sleep) or as an effect of psychotropic drugs or toxins.

5. As to the *content* of conscious experience, our mental objects are no simple projections of corresponding external objects, but *sophisticated constructs* based on a *selective flow* of information from the external world. One has to remind oneself, that only a fraction of

existing information is available for our senses. Also there is an integration of *temporal sequences* of information into a single "momentary sensation". Perception is defined as the interpretation of an actual sensory message in terms of earlier experiences. But this includes a process of reconstruction, where lost or otherwise missing sensory information may be "regained" in a hypothetical way. This demands the existence of earlier stored knowledge. Actual perceptions, experience and science share a common feature in that they are related to knowledge in the sense of "insight" (Erkenntnis). There are, however differences. The internal *reconstruction* of mental objects in connection with *perception* is generally *unconscious, uncritical* and *non-revisable*, but instead *perspicuous. Experience*, which includes language, logic and conceptualizations makes use of conscious, but still *uncritical* reconstructions. In science, where mathematical models and highly abstract concepts are used, reconstruction is *critical*, but very often no longer perspicuous (Vollmer, 1982).

6. The activities of the brain are highly integrated, which means that subjective experience generally comprises both cognitive (symbolic) and emotional elements. This implies that all brain structures, including subcortical structures such as the hypothalamus, limbic system, *etc.* in specific ways contribute to the total experience. Mental constructs are superimposed by moods, emotions and motivational states. This does not only mean a coexistence of cognitive and emotional elements, but motivational states exert control functions on sensory filter mechanisms (direction of attention), which selectively influence the flow of information.

7. The necessity for an organism to make a distinction between itself and the environment may have been the origin of *self-consciousness*. Higher organisms then probably have developed the ability to create an internal cognitive representation of themselves.

At least humans have an awareness about being aware. This seems to be the essence of Descarte's "cogito, ergo sum". Humans perceive themselves as feeling and sensing entities of continuous existence. In this connection the use of terms such as the "ego" or the "self", makes it easy to slip into the fallacy of an internal homunculus" ("the little man in the outer man") (Crick, 1979).

8. The way we perceive our world is to a high degree determined by the innate functions of our brain and receptors. Some examples may be given:

a) The brain is self-programming in a way, which (in the language of computer technology) makes any distinction between "software" and "hardware" rather subtle. The brain runs without anyone telling it how to run, and its efficiency develops further during this process.

b) The brain is genetically preprogrammed to react to specific stimulus patterns. If these evoke a predetermined response, we speak of *instinctive behavior*. The organism here mainly makes use of receptors in connection with filters and trigger mechanisms. The brain seems, for example, to show innate expectations regarding the solidity of three-dimensional objects (Bower, 1971). There are specific forms of learning, which are bound to critical stages of development. Imprinting in birds may illustrate this issue. A key stimulus, which fulfils certain minimum conditions, may trigger an innate behavior: to keep close to the stimulus object. The conditions regarding this stimulus-object may be that its retinal image covers a certain percentage of the retina and that it moves within roughly specified limits of velocity. This rough genetic specification then is substituted by the detailed picture of the key stimulus object.

c) Hubel and Wiesel have analyzed the hierarchical organization and functional architecture of the visual cortex. This has revealed a mechanism, which analyzes the composition of our visual world in terms of figural elements: contrast and dots at the lowest level, bars and edges at a higher level. Essentially, the visual cortex is composed of columns ("chips") which work as orientation detectors with respect to linear elements (Hubel, 1963; Hubel & Wiesel, 1979). Later on, however, it has been suggested, that these "bar detectors" really might be viewed as spatial frequency filters, which perform a spatial Fourier analysis across a strip of the visual world (De Valois & De Valois, 1980).

d) A randomly moving group of dots is perceived as independent dots. An example would be the depiction of Brownian motion of microscopic particles. If, however, some dots show a *common* motion, they are perceived as forming a group. This means the spontaneous formation of a visual pattern. If some of these dots show a systematic movement in relation to others within the same group, this is perceived as the movement of a subgroup within a larger group. An example would be the movement of legs and arms in relation to a walking person. Essentially, the visual system performs a vector analysis with respect to the degree of coupling between the velocity vectors in space for each single dot. The mechanism works equally well for lines. The phenomena, which in psychology are called *size constancy* and *shape constancy* may be explained in terms of this mechanism. It makes us perceive the shape and seize of an object as constant (*i.e.*, the object is always perceived as identical with itself), despite a changing shape and size of the retinal image. In terms of this analysis the set of changing retinal images may be said to form a geometrical transformation group. Size constancy then corresponds to the group of equiform transforms and shape constancy to the group of projective transforms (Johansson, 1964, 1975).

The mechanism is able to perform several modes of analysis simultaneously.

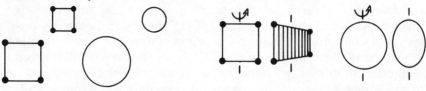

Size Constancy	*Shape Constancy*
A continuously changing size of a retinal image is perceived as a linear motion in depth of the corresponding object.	*A continuously changing shape of a retinal image in perceived as a rotation in space of the corresponding object.*

Figure 12-7   The pictures illustrate "samples" of the continuously changing retinal images (due to the movement of external objects) at different points of time.

Figure 12-7: Examples of a Size Constancy and a Shape Constancy.

Corresponding mechanisms exist for brightness constancy, colors and contrast.

How does this complexity affect the correlation between "brain and mind?" The simple stimulus-response models of psychophysics are inappropriate outside the range of pure intensity scales, irrespective of the usefulness of moderns varieties such as the Signal Detection Theory (Swets, 1964), were the detection of signals is described in terms of binary events (yes-no). Instead, one now has to approach the problem of quality. In order to illustrate the issue, one may initially compare the eye and the ear. Primarily, the eye mediates spatial information (secondarily temporal information, which is implicit in motion), while the opposite is true for the ear. Written language, for example, is based on spatial sequences of graphic symbols, while spoken language is based on temporal sequences of phonetic symbols. The eye integrates complex stimuli (such as a mixture of light rays with different wave lengths) into a single colour perception. A mixture of monochromatic "red" and "green" light of equal intensity is perceived as "yellow".[5] A composite sound stimulus, however, is mostly (but not always) analyzed in terms of its components. This phenomenon is called "Ohm's Acoustic Law" (Georg Simon Ohm, known from the theory of electricity). This makes it possible for us to hear the timbre of a sound or polyphonic music. The perception of pitch quality is essential in this connection. If the frequency of a simple sound is doubled, *e.g.*, from 440 Hz to 880 Hz, we perceive this jump in musical terms as an octave. This gives a linear relationship between frequency and perceived pitch, the "musical scale." This scale, however, is partially the result of learning, related to the "well tempered clavichord" (J.S. Bach). Thorough laboratory measurements give a more complex picture. Up to a frequency of 500 Hz, there exists a linear relationship between pitch (in "mel" units) and frequency (in Hz). Above 500 Hz, the relationship is logarithmic:

$$z \text{ (mel)} = 500 + 1{,}300 \log \frac{f}{500}$$

But the picture becomes still more complex, if we regard color perception. Colors may be described in terms of hue, brightness, and saturation. It is, however, not possible to arrange perceived colors within an orthogonal euclidean space. This implies that the dimensions of description are not independent. The arrangement of colors within a three dimensional color space can, however, be described in terms of a non-euclidean geometry, in this case a Riemann geometry (Born, 1963; Schrödinger, 1920; spherical geometry is an example of non-euclidean geometry).

Figure 12-8: Spectral Cone
(Figure from Schrödinger 1920).

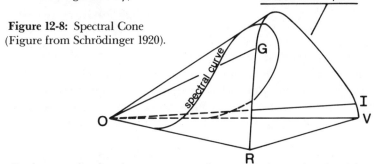

Each perceived color corresponds to a finite point in this space.

It has been known for centuries that colors are not properties of external objects, but rather reflect properties of our perceptual mechanisms. Light is basically electromagnetic radiation. Monochromatic light is defined by its wavelength or alternatively by the energy of its photons, *i.e.*, quantitative measures. But what are the quantitative values of different colors?

physical scale   *subjective scale*

λ_1 . . . . red

λ_2 . . . . orange

λ_3 . . . . yellow

λ_n . . . . blue

Obviously, there are no such measures. It is evident that *quantitative* differences in wavelength (or energy) are transformed into *qualitative* differences in colour perception. The discriminative power of this principle is evident from the fact that the normal eye is able to discriminate about 7.10^6 different shades in direct comparison. This result is obtained by stepwise information processing. The eye contains three types of spectral sensitive receptor elements (cones). Their spectral sensitivity characteristics have maxima at about 445 nm, 535 nm and 570 nm respectively. The elements may be described as equivalents to band-pass filters within the range of visual light and with partially overlapping characteristics. Edwin Land pointed out that color perception demands a contrast situation, *i.e.*, a comparison of signals from different receptors within the same receptive field (Crick, 1979). Hence, color perception is based on competing processes within nerve nets. The nature of these processes, in turn, is determined by the relative intensity of signals from the three wavelength-discriminating receptor elements (cones); (for reference see Biernson, 1968). The balanced interaction of these signal inflows (both excitatory and inhibitory) determines a very large number of different states of the nerve net and, hence, corresponding states of conscious experience. Meanwhile, how the latter comes about is part of the mystery of conscious experience.

The given examples show, that basic conscious experience is due to *intrinsic* properties of the brain, while it is the role of receptors to establish a transfer function, which gives the necessary coupling to external patterns of stimuli.

It is quite clear, that any description of very complex phenomena, such as color perception, is outside the range of simple correlations. Living organisms furthermore show an intrinsic true variability (not due to error variance of measurements) as one of their characteristics. Any state of the brain is determined by a multitude of interacting factors. In psychology it is common to account for this by the use of multivariate statistical methods (multiple correlations, eigenvalues, principal factors *etc.*). These methods are mainly based on linear algebra (which does not mean that they are simple). The description of brain states (including *e.g.*, feedback or "autocatalytic" processes) may demand the introduction of non-linear models, which adds to the technical difficulties.

The brain is a marvelous instrument. The understanding of its most salient manifestation, the mind, is still outside the range of contemporary science. Nevertheless, each really new discovery will change our understanding—sometimes in quite unexpected ways. As yet, we don't even know if we ever will get the whole picture, but it would be an unjustified overestimation of our present state of knowledge, to give a decisive answer in either direction.

NOTES

1. The term energy was introduced in 1807 by T. Young to denote half the amount of "vis viva" = "living force" = mv"^{2}. In a broader sense the term was first used by W. Rankine in 1854.

2. Strictly speaking, P is not a probability in a statistical sense, but a large number, denoting the amount of possible microstates of a system that correspond to a given macrostate. However, the thermodynamical probability is proportional to the statistical.

3. Recently F. Crick and E. Orgel made the suggestion that life perhaps did not arise on earth at all but may have been deliberately seeded by highly intelligent beings from outer space. This venturesome hypothesis, which is a modern variety of Arrhenius' theory of panspermia, tries to explain why many key enzymes are dependent upon very scarce elements such as molybdenum (Dickerson, 1978).

4. In a more strict language, one should make a distinction between anatomical structures such as the brain or nerve subsrate and functional systems such as the CNS or RAS (reticular activation system).

5. "Red," "green," and "yellow" are used here according to common language as labels to denote dominant wavelengths. In a more strict language the wavelength numbers should be given.

REFERENCES

Ashby, R. 1962. "Principles of Self Organising Systems." Edited by Foerster and Zopf in *Principles of Self Organization*. New York: Pergamon.

Aurell, C. 1979. "Perception: A Model Comprising Two Modes of Consciousness." *Perceptual and Motor Skills* 49, pp. 341–444.

Ayala, F. 1978. "The Mechanisms of Evolution." *Scientific American* 239 (3), pp. 38–61.

Ball, J. 1980. "Extraterrestrial Intelligence: Where Is Everybody?" *American Scientist* 68, pp. 656–663.

Biernson, G. 1968. "A Review of Models of Vision." Edited by Levine, S. in *Advances in Biomedical Engineering and Medical Physics*, 2. New York: Interscience Publishers, Wiley & Sons.

Blakemore, C. 1977. *The Mechanics of the Mind.* London: Cambridge University Press.

Born, M. 1963. "Betrachtungen zur Farbenlehre." *Jenaer Rundschau* 8 (6), pp. 235–248.

Bower, T. 1971. "The Object in the World of the Infant." *Scientific American* 225 (4), pp. 30–38.

Breuer, R. 1981. *Das anthropische Prinzip.* Wien/Müchen: Meyster.

Brillouin, L. 1962. *Science and Information Theory.* New York: Academic Press.

Butler, P. and Klug, A. 1978. "The Assembly of a Virus." *Scientific American* 239 (5) pp. 52–59.

Carrel, A. and Lindbergh, C. 1938. *The Culture of Organs.* London: Harper and Harper Broth.

Crick, F. 1979. "Thinking about the Brain." *Scientific American* 241 (3), pp. 181–188.

Culbertson, J. 1963. *The Minds of Robots.* Urbana: University of Illinois Press.

DeValois, R. and De Valois, K. 1980. "Spatial Vision." *Annual Review of Psychology* 31, pp. 309–341.

Dickerson, R. 1978. "Chemical Evolution and the Origin of Life." *Scientific American* 239 (3) pp. 62–78.

Dobzhansky, T. 1955. *Evolution, Genetics and Man.* New York: Wiley.

Ehrensvärd, G. 1961. *Liv, ursprung och utformning.* Stockholm: Aldus.

Eigen, M. and Winkler, R. 1975. *Das Spiel.* München/Zürich: R. Piper.

Fermi, E. 1956. *Thermodynamics.* New York: Dover Publications.

Fiddes, J. 1977. "The Nucelotide Sequence in a Viral DNA (φX 174)." *Scientific American* 237 (6), pp. 54–67.

Fulton, J. 1956. *A Textbook of Physiology.* Philadelphia/London: W.B. Sounders.

Gale, G. 1981. "The Anthropic Principle." *Scientific American* 245 (6), pp. 114–122.

Gazzaniga, M. and LeDoux, J. 1978. *The Integrated Mind.* New York/London: Plenum Press.

Halstead, L. 1975. *The Evolution and Ecology of the Dinosaurs.* London: Peter Lowe, Eurobook Limited.

Hilgard, E. 1980. "Consciousness in Contemporary Psychology." *Annual Review of Psychology* 31, pp. 1–26.

Hubel, D. 1963. "The Visual Cortex of the Brain." *Scientific American* 209 (5), pp. 54–62.

Hubel, D. and Wiesel, T. 1979. "Brain Mechanisms of Vision." *Scientific American* 241 (3), pp. 150–162.

Jerison, H. 1978. "The Evolution of Consciousness." *Proceedings of the Seventh International Conference on the Unity of the Sciences*, Boston. Pp. 711–723.

Johansson, G. 1964. "Perception of Motion and Changing Forms." *Scandinavian Journal of Psychology* 5, pp. 181–298.

Johansson, G. 1975. "Visual Motion Perception." *Scientific American* 232 (3), pp. 76–88.

Kandel, E. 1979. "Small System of Neurons." *Scientific American* 241 (3), pp. 66–76.

Kaplan, R. 1978. *Der Ursprung des Lebens*. Stuttgart: G. Thieme.

Lagerkvist, U. 1983. *Gene Technology*. Lecture given at The Institute of Physics, Chalmers University of Technology, Göteborg.

Laszlo, E. 1973. *Introduction to Systems Philosophy*. New York: Harper and Row.

Leahey, T. 1980. *A History of Psychology*. Englewood Cliffs: Prentice Hall.

Lindahl, P.; Kihlström, J.; Kiessling, K. and Sundell, L. 1967. *Zoofysiologi*. Stockholm: Almkvist & Wiksell.

Löwenhard, P. 1981. "Consciousness—A biological view." *Göteborg Psychological Reports* 12, p. 10.

Lorenz, K. and Wuketits, F., editors 1983. *Die Evolution des Denkens*. München/Zürich: Piper & Company.

Mayr, E. 1978. "Evolution." *Scientific American* 239 (3) pp. 38–47.

Miller, J. 1978. *Living Systems*. New York: McGraw Hill.

Mustelin, N. 1983. "Livets utbredning i universum." *Kosmos* 60, pp. 213–233.

Nordling, C. 1982. "Energi—en introduktion." *Kosmos* 59, pp. 19–34. Stockholm: Forskningsradens Förlagstjänst.

Prigogine, I. 1967. *Thermodynamics of Irreversible Processes*. London/New York: Interscience (Wiley).

Radnitzky, G. 1983. "The Science of Man—Biological, Mental and Cultural Evolution." Edited by Cappelletti, V., Luiselli, B., Radnitsky, G., and Urbane, E. in *Saggi Di Storia des Pensiero Scientifico dedicati a Valerio Tonini*. Rome: Societa Editoriale Jouvence.

Riedl, R. 1979. *Biologie der Erkenntnis*. Berlin/Hamburg: Paul Parey.

Ryle, G. 1967. *The Concept of Mind*. London: Hutchinson.

Sagan, C. 1978. *Die Drachen von Eden (Das Wunder der menschlichen Intelligenz)*. Translated by vom Scheidt, F. Müchen/Zürich: Droemer-Knaur. Original title: *The Dragons of Eden: Speculations on the Evolution of Human Intelligence*. New York: Random House, 1977.

Sanger, F.; Air, G., Barrell, B.; Brown, N.; Coulson, A.; Fiddes, J.; Hutchison, C.; Slocombe, P. and Smith, M. 1977. "Nucleotide Sequence of Bacteriophage φX 174 DNA." *Nature* 265, pp. 687–695.

Sayre, K. 1976. *Cybernetics and the Philosophy of Mind.* London: Routledge & Kegan Paul.

Schopf, J. 1978. "The Evolution of the Earliest Cells." *Scientific American* 239 (3) pp. 85–102.

Schrödinger, E. 1920. "Grundlinien einer Theorie der Farbenmetrik im Tagessehen." *Annalen der Pyysik* 63 pp. 397–520.

Schrödinger, E. 1951. *Was ist Leben?* Translated by Mazurczak, H. Bern: A Franche.

Sears, F. 1953. *Thermodynamics.* Reading: Addison-Wesley.

Shannon, C. and Weaver, W. 1959. *The Mathematical Theory of Communication.* Urbana: University of Illinois Press.

Sokolov, E. 1981. "Introduction to Learning in Isolated Neural Structures (Intracellular Mechanisms of the Associated Learning)." Edited by Adam, G.; Meszaros, I. and Bangai, E. in *Advanced Physiological Science, 17, Brain and Behaviour.* Budapest: Pergamon Press/Akademiai Kaido.

Swets, J., editor 1964. *Signal Detection and Recognition by Human Observers.* New York: Wiley.

Uexkull, J. 1928. *Theoretische Biologie.* Berlin: Springer.

Vidal, G. 1984. "The Oldest Eukaryotic Cells." *Scientific American* 250 (2), pp. 32–41.

Vollmer, G. 1980. "Evolutionäre Erkenntnistheorie und Leib-Seele-Problem." Edited by Böhme, W. in *Wie entsteht der Geist? Herrenalter Texte 23,* pp. 11–40.

Vollmer, G. 1981. *Evolutionäre Erkenntnistheorie.* Stuttgart: Hirzel.

Vollmer, G. 1982. *Das alte Gehirn und die neuen Probleme.* Aspekte und Folgerungen einer evolutionären "Erkenntnistheorie. Contributor to Darwin Symposium über "Das Phänomen Evolution." Wien: University of Technology.

Vollmer, G. 1983. "The unity of science in an evolutionary perspective." Communication to the Twelfth International Conference on the Unity of the Sciences. Chicago: International Cultural Foundation Press.

Wiener, N. 1961. *Cybernetics or Control and Communication in the Animal and the Machine.* Second Edition. New York: MIT Press and John Wiley, Incorporated.

Wuketits, F. 1982. "Das Phänomen der Zweckmässigkeit im Bereich der lebenden Systeme." *Biologie in unserer Zeit,* 12 (5), pp. 139–144.

Zethraeus, S. 1962. *Känslan.* Stockholm: Natur & Kultur.

13

Comments on Löwenhard's Essay

FRANZ M. WUKETITS

The essay by Dr. Löwenhard is an interesting and important contribution to an old and venerable problem: the mind-body problem. In particular, it examines the questions of whether *mind* can be reduced to *brain* and whether psychological phenomena, in general, are explainable in terms of biology. Recently the mind-body problem has stimulated discussions among neurobiologists, and *psychobiology* results from pursuing the biological view."[1]

Löwenhard argues from the viewpoint of a neurobiologist, too, and—as in some of his earlier publications[2]—he comes to the conclusion that the phenomena of mind and consciousness are related to human brain functions. Such a conclusion, I think, is widely acceted among biologists these days. However, Löwenhard does not support an ontological reductionism; he rather shows that the brain is a complex system and that it represents an integral part of the information system of higher organisms. His paper brings together current interdisciplinary research that adds up to the *emergentist* view of man.

I am quite in accordance with Löwenhard's conclusions, however, I hope that my following remarks, made from the standpoint of a philosopher of biology, are apt to stimulate the debate in the "interface" between biology and psychology.

My own view of the problem in question is that of evolutionary biology and *evolutionary epistemology*. Evolutionary epistemology bases upon the fact that man is an outcome of evolution by natural selection; furthermore, it implies the assumption that mental activities are bound to specific biological conditions. To put it more precisely: *"All psychic phenomena in the subhuman world as well as mental abilities proper to human systems . . . are based on biological structures and functions; biological*

evolution has been the precondition to psychological and spiritual evolution."[3]
That is to say that spiritual evolution, although it transgresses the
boundaries of evolution by natural selection (!), cannot be sufficiently
explained without reference to biological evolution and development.

In this context it is again worthwhile to mention that already
Charles Darwin in his *The Descent of Man* (1871) and *The Expression
of Emotions in Man and Animals* (1872) adopted the view of evolutionary
psychology and, therefore, anticipated some of the most important
assertions of evolutionary epistemology. Evolutionary psychology and
epistemology coincide with a host of empirical results in the fields of
neurobiology, sensory physiology, ethology, and evolutionary research—but they do not coincide with any dualistic view of the mind-
body problem. (Remember for example Descartes' interactionism or
Leibniz' preestablished harmony.) Actually, " . . . a consistent evo-
lutionist . . . need not postulate immaterial minds and will postulate
instead that mental functions, no matter how exquisite, are neurophysiological activities."[4]

Well, if mind is an activity of the (human) brain, why should
we not, then, reduce all mental phenomena to biological structures?
And why should psychology not be reduced to biology? Löwenhard
in his paper states that, after all, "since the brain and nervous system
are part of a biological organism, their psychological manifestations
may be treated within a biological context. In this sense 'psychology',
at least partially, may be viewed as a biological discipline."

Nevertheless, one cannot simply state that brain and mind are
one and the same and that psychology is *nothing else* but biology. We
rather must admit that *mind is a special function or manifestation of brain
processes.* To do so means to avoid the old "category—mistake," which
is described by Gilbert Ryle in his excellent *The Concept of Mind.* Let
me give here a brief quotation:

> A foreigner visiting Oxford or Cambridge for the first time is shown
> a number of colleges, libraries, . . ., scientific departments and admin-
> istrative offices. He then asks 'But where is the University? I have seen
> where the members of the Colleges live, where the Registrar works,
> where the scientists experiment . . . But I have not yet seen the
> University in which reside and work the members of your University.'
> It has then to be explained to him that the University is just the way
> in which all that he has already seen is organized. When they are seen
> and when their coordination is understood, the University has been
> seen.[5]

Now, in this example the foreigner has made a category-mistake: He
expected that "University" is just a thing to be seen; but a University,
as we all know, is rather the outcome of specific human activities.

Likewise the terms "mind" and "consciousness" do not describe ontological categories, but certain states and/or activities of the brain and the central nervous system. In a previous paper Löwenhard already stated that "consciousness . . . seems to be restricted to a certain class of living organisms, utilizing nervous systems" and that it ". . . may be described as a phenomenon which accompanies certain modes of information processing."[6] In addition, we can lay down the thesis that all conscious activities have emerged in the course of evolution of living systems. Moreover, evolution itself can be described as a process of emerging systems. Emergence, *e.g.*, in Mario Bunge's terminology, means "the appearance of a new quality or of a thing possessing qualitatively new traits. In particular, the emergent properties of a system are those possessed by the system *as a whole* and lacking in every component of it."[7] So it would be absurd to say that a single nerve cell possesses mind or consciousness; it is the whole system of the brain and the nervous system that show mental activities.

Many positions on the mind-body problem suffer from the false questions, for example "In which way mind and brain are interacting?"—they do not interact, because the one (mind) is a *systems property* of the other (brain). In order to come to a consistent theory of the mind-body problem we must, therefore, first of all abandon some of the many old-fashioned approaches to the problem; above all, this means to give up the dualistic world view, which has bewitched up to now many philosophers. Evolutionary epistemology seems to be a viable proposition to handle the question, how does mind (and/or consciousness) come into existence as systems property of the brain.

I think that Löwenhard is on the right track when he postulates:

• Psychic and mental phenomena are specific manifestations of very complexly organized and structured biological systems; and that

• according to his model, consciousness may be viewed as a phenomenon, which emerges due to intrinsic properties of the (central) nervous system.

Furthermore, in order to understand brain processes and their specific manifestations, we have to replace the models of classical psychophysics by *multi-staged interactive models of information processing.* Here again Löwenhard's postulates coincide with basic postulates of evolutionary epistemology, which boils down to a model of life as an information processing system.[8]

Yet we cannot say that we are able to understand all aspects of our brain and its manifestations. Löwenhard concludes that ". . . the brain is a marvellous instrument. The understanding of its most salient manifestation, the mind, is still outside the range of contemporary science." Unfortunately, up to now many of the theories and speculations on brain and mind have been chapters of a "brain-mythology" or something like that. So how could this be improved?

Perhaps we have reason to be more optimistic, like Charles J. Lumsden and Edward O. Wilson: "If and when we are able to characterize the organization of these various processes (brain processes) and identify their physical basis in some detail, it will be possible to define in a declarative and unambiguous manner the urgent but still elusive phenomenon of mind, as well as self and consciousness. The evolutionary reconstruction of the mind should be pressed to the limit of this understanding."[9]

In any case, it is important to bring together interdisciplinary research, from paleobiology to molecular biology, and to try to fit the results of this research into a conceptual scheme. However, for the time being it seems to be clear that the mind-body problem neither has been solved by dualistic world conceptions, nor by mechanistic approaches to life and mind. It is of greatest importance to adopt a much broader view. Such a view is indicated in Löwenhard's paper as an evolutionary, emergentist view, showing that both principles, *reduction* and *correlation*, coexist in a complementary manner. What is still lacking, however, is a comprehensive model demonstrating *how* these principles coexist. Löwenhard's reflections are a decisive step in this direction, but there is still much work to be done.

In my opinion, it would be necessary that disciplines like neurobiology and psychology take into consideration the "evolutionary dimensions" of brain and brain activities. This was suggested by Darwin's program of an evolutionary psychology, but such a program has not yet been completed.

NOTES

1. See, e.g., M. Bunge, *The Mind-Body Problem—A Psychobiological Approach.* Oxford/New York/Toronto: Pergamon Press, 1980; R.M. Restak, *The Brain—The last Frontier.* New York: Doubleday, 1979.

2. See, e.g., P. Löwenhard, "Consciousness—A Biological View", in *Göteborg Psychological Reports* 11 (10), 1981, pp. 1–88; "Knowledge, Belief and Human Behaviour", *Göteborg Psychological Reports* 12 (11), 1982, pp. 1–71.

3. F.M. Wuketits, "Evolutionary Epistemology—A Challenge to Science and Philosophy", in F.M. Wuketits (ed.), *Concepts and Approaches in Evolutionary Epistemology,* Dordrecht/Boston/Lancester: Reidel, 1984, p. 8; see also F.M. Wuketits, "Evolutionary Epistemology, Objective Knowledge, and

Rationality", in *Proceedings of the Eleventh International Conference on the Unity of the Sciences*, New York: The International Cultural Foundation Press, 1984, pp. 881–899.

4. M. Bunge, *op.cit.*, p. 18.

5. G. Ryle, *The Concept of Mind*, Harmondsworth/New York: Penguin Books, 1976, pp. 17–18.

6. P. Löwenhard, "Consciousness . . .", *op.cit.*, p. 23.

7. M. Bunge, *op.cit.*, p. 224 (my italics).—Note, by the way that Konrad Lorenz prefers to use the term "fulguration" instead of emergence; cf. K. Lorenz, *Behind the Mirror*, New York: Harcourt, Brace, Jovanovich, 1977.

8. See on this especially K. Lorenz, *op.cit.*

9. Ch.J. Lumsden and E.O. Wilson, *Promethean Fire—Reflections on the Origin of Mind*. Cambridge, MA: Harvard University Press, 1983, p. 3.

14

The Individualistic Research Program in Sociology

KARL-DIETER OPP

Sociology's explanatory problems refer to social aggregates or, as we shall also say, collectives. These may be simple aggregates of individuals (such as voters, criminals, employees) or groups in a broad sense (such as cities, families, societies). Typical questions exemplifying sociology's universe of discourse are: Why does the suicide rate vary between countries? Why are all societies stratified? Under what conditions do social movements emerge?

In answering these questions two different theoretical orientations are possible. The one—we call it the *collectivistic research program*—posits that properties of collectives (like the suicide rate of countries) and even the existence of collectives can be explained only by applying propositions whose universe of discourse is collectives, *i.e.* by *collectivistic theories.*

The other theoretical tradition—the *individualistic research program (IRP)* in sociology—claims that properties of collectives as well as the existence of collectives can be explained by applying theories about the behavior of individual actors, *i.e., individualistic theories (ITs)*. Adherents to this program also postulate that individualistic theories *should* be utilized in explaining collective phenomena.

This rough characterization of the two conflicting research programs raises two questions: 1) What are the claims of the two programs? They can be discussed only if we know what adherents to the programs assert and postulate. 2) What are the arguments in favour of and against both programs?

Both questions are posed in this paper. In section I, some material on both programs will be presented, proceeding from special schools in sociology. In section II, an explication of the programs will be given, and in section III some of the most frequently raised objections against the individualistic research program will be discussed. In the final section, a short critical outline of the present state of the IRP will be given.

I. CONFLICTING RESEARCH PROGRAMS IN SOCIOLOGY

The two purely collectivistic theoretical orientations in sociology are sociological functionalism and marxist sociology. *Functionalist sociology*[1] is concerned with social systems. Its aim is to explain the stability ("equilibrium") or change of these systems. The fundamental orienting theoretical postulate is that social systems exhibit certain functional requirements (or functional prerequisites), which are met by particular mechanisms (such as social control or economic institutions). If the realization of the functional requirements is threatened, these mechanisms will develop forces that reestablish the equilibrium (or stable state) of the system, within certain limits. This simplified outline of functionalism indicates that individuals have no place in explanatory arguments, at least not explicitly.

In evaluating functionalism, it must be said that its failure lies in its not having generated a precise testable theory with explanatory power.[2]

On the surface, marxism seems to be explicitly concerned with individuals: the working class and the bourgeoisie consist of individual human beings with conflicting interests. The working class and the bourgeoisie, however, are social aggregates and marxist theory deals with "objective" relations between these aggregates: conflicts of interest are not subjectively experienced divergent goals, but objective relations, whatever this is supposed to mean. Furthermore, collective properties such as relations of production (Produktionsverhältnisse) and productive forces (Produktivkräfte) are important collective properties that marxist theory is concerned with. Such properties are the explananda (*e.g.*, "death" of the capitalist system) and the explanatory variables (*e.g.*, "contradictions" between relations of production and productive forces).

Marxists have also failed to develop a general, testable theory with high explanatory power. Single propositions that have been tested could not be confirmed.[3]

Why have these research programs failed? Adherents to the IRP may suggest that functionalism and marxism have failed because individuals are completely disregarded in their explanations. For example, one might argue that workers and employers behave according to their subjectively held aims (preferences), taking into account their opportunities for various actions. As the preferences and opportunities of individuals may differ to a great extent, it might be expected that given certain distributions of preferences and constraints there would be no revolution and no overthrow of the capitalist system. Thus, from the perspective of the IRP marxist hypotheses only hold under certain conditions.

Such individualistic claims have obviously to be tested. Explanatory arguments whose consequents are collectivistic hypotheses must be stated rigorously and must be subjected to empirical tests.[4]

The antipode of the two collectivistic research programs is the attempt to realize the individualistic research program in sociology. Its theoretical tradition is called *behavioral sociology* or *exchange theory*.[5] As George C. Homans is the founding father of this theoretical tradition in contemporary sociology and its most prominent advocate, a short outline of his position will be given. The following three of his theses appear to be of central importance:

1. The most general propositions of all social sciences are those of behavioral psychology (1967, pp. 38–39).

The term *behavioral psychology* first of all denotes propositions from learning theory. The rational choice model (or utility theory) is, however, also subsumed under this term. This model "coincides in part with the body of propositions of behavioral psychology" (1967, p. 38); ". . . it is not an alternative to behavioral psychology; the two are in fact largely the same" (1967, p. 39). In what sense are these propositions "psychological"? Homans' answer is: "First, they are usually stated and empirically tested by persons who call themselves psychologists. Though they are, as we shall see, used in explanation by all the social sciences, the field of research in which they lie is the special concern of only one of these sciences, psychology. Second, they are propositions about the behavior of individual human beings, rather than propositions about groups or societies as such; and the behavior of men, as men, is generally considered the province of psychology." (1967, pp. 39–40).

2. Sociology has failed to develop propositions about aggregates that are of great generality and explanatory power and which are well confirmed (1967, p. 83, p. 85).

What can sociologists do to improve their explanations?

3. In order to solve sociology's explanatory problems, psychological theories should be applied. More specifically: "We need psychology to explain both why social propositions hold good, and why they do not, when they do not" (1969, p. 17).

Homans' position is often called *psychological reductionism* in the sense that he aims at reducing sociological propositions to psychological ones. Homans argues, however, that there are no sociological propositions to be reduced (1967, pp. 85–86).

Homans did not only put forward an individualistic research program, but also made original contributions to substantive sociological problems (see particularly 1974) and critical analyses of alternative theoretical orientations (see, *e.g.*, 1964).

II. AN EXPLICATION OF THE INDIVIDUALISTIC RESEARCH PROGRAM OF SOCIOLOGY

In this section we want to restate the individualistic research program. Our explication is not in conflict with Homans' position, as will be recognized by the reader on comparison of the following theses with our outline of Homans' research program in the preceding section. Our aim is to make those postulates more explicit which are, so to say, the core of the IRP.[6]

A research program—similar to the program of a political party—should not contain terms that evoke misunderstandings about the content of the program. Unfortunately, the terms *psychological theory* and *reductionism* have connotations that grossly misrepresent what adherents to the individualistic program actually mean. Those terms, however, can be easily avoided and be substituted by more appropriate terms.

The basic propositions of the IRP are general theories specifying how individuals behave in their social context. We call these theories *individualistic theories* (ITs) as opposed to *psychological theories.* Due to space restrictions we shall not attempt a general characterization of these theories. In this essay we will focus on the *rational choice model* (or utility theory), also taking hypotheses from learning theory into consideration when referring to ITs. The reason is that these ITs are mainly used by social scientists working within the framework of the IRP. A *collectivistic theory* is given if, and only if, a theory completely restricts itself to collectives as its universe of discourse.

The term *reduction* will be substituted by the term *explanation* in the sense of "explanation of singular events" (or, more precisely, of statements describing such events) or "explanation of—more or less—general propositions." The term "explanation" describes what the IRP is really aiming at, and this is expressed in the following theses:

1. ITs can be used to derive (*i.e.*, explain) singular and general collectivistic propositions.

2. If attempts are made to derive existing singular and general collectivistic propositions by using ITs, the collectivistic propositions can be derived in their original or in a corrected version.

Thesis 1 states that if you want to explain a collectivistic phenomenon (like the increasing crime rate in a particular city) or if you want to propose a collectivistic theory (*e.g.*, about conditions for the emergence of democracies), you can accomplish this by using ITs.

Thesis 2 refers to the situation where there is an attempt to confront *existing* collectivistic statements with ITs. The result will be a deductive argument, where the conclusion is the collectivistic proposition in its original or—from the point of view of the IT applied— in a corrected form. For example, it may turn out that a collectivistic statement is only valid under certain conditions.

Theses 1 and 2 claim, in short, that it is possible to explain sociologically relevant collectivistic propositions by applying ITs. Both theses are called the *explanation theses* of the IRP.

Individualists accepting postulates 1 and 2 also accept a third thesis. Let us assume, for example, that an IT is to explain why different societies develop a division of labor to a varying degree. On the one hand, the explanandum refers to collectives (societies) and to a collective variable (division of labor). On the other hand, the respective IT refers only to individuals and their properties (*e.g.*, preferences and constraints). In order to explain the collective phenomenon by an IT, it must be specified how the collectivistic concepts can be "translated" into the individualistic concepts of the IT. In other words, there must be some "bridge assumptions" specifying what "society" and "division of labor" mean in terms of the applied IT. If we use the rational choice model and if a meaning analysis indicates that "society" designates a set of individuals (with particular relational and non-relational properties) and that "division of labor" refers to a particular distribution of activities among the "members" of the "society", then the rational choice model can be applied.

This example illustrates that ITs can only be applied to explain singular or general collectivistic statements if the collectivistic concepts can be reconstructed in terms of the concepts of the IT applied.[7] In general, adherents to the IRP claim:

3. Concepts designating aggregates or their properties (*i.e.*, collectivistic concepts) in fact refer to individuals or their (relational or non-relational) properties, as is always revealed by a meaning analysis of the collectivistic concepts.

This third thesis is often expressed in the following manner: collectivistic concepts can be defined by individualistic concepts. "Defining" a term means introducing it by stipulating a convention. Thesis 3, however, does not mean that conventions are introduced specifying that collectivistic concepts are equivalent to concepts designating individuals or their properties. Thesis 3 claims that an analysis of the meaning of collectivistic terms will bear the result that the referents of collectivistic terms are individuals or their properties. We suggest calling thesis 3 *reconstruction thesis* because the meaning of the collectivistic terms is often so vague that a reconstruction (*i.e.*, an explication) is necessary.

Let us assume for a moment that the preceding theses hold true. A social scientist adhering to a collectivistic research program may find them interesting—and continues to work as he did before. There is nothing objectionable about this reaction as our three theses do not make any normative claim but simply assert that collectivistic propositions *can* be explained by ITs without expecting that anything *should* be done.

Of course, the IRP comprises a postulate (in the normative sense) as was apparent in our discussion of Homans' position. This normative claim—which we term *explanation postulate*—may be stated in the following manner:

4. ITs should be applied to explain singular and general collectivistic propositions.

Thus, if a social scientist wants to explain singular collective events, or if he wants to state new collectivistic theories (see thesis 1), he should proceed from ITs (see thesis 4). Furthermore, if a social scientist deals with existing collectivistic propositions (see thesis 2), he should confront them with ITs (see thesis 4).

It is important to separate the factual and normative parts of the IRP as different arguments may be invoked for each part. Consequently, one may accept the factual statements (theses 1 through 3), but may not agree with the normative thesis 4. However, acceptance of the factual theses 1 to 3 is a necessary precondition for accepting the normative thesis 4, as nothing will be claimed that cannot be realized.

Why should individualistic theories be applied? As we mentioned already in outlining Homans' position, the answer to this question is:

ITs have a relatively high explanatory power and the explanations they provide are more valid than those offered by collectivistic propositions. This is also expressed in thesis 2, according to which ITs may provide corrected versions of existing collectivistic propositions. To put it briefly, ITs achieve deeper explanations (to use a term by K.R. Popper) than collectivistic propositions.

This outline of the IRP leaves several questions open. For example: What is the relationship between the individualistic and collectivistic concepts? How do individualistic theories correct collectivistic propositions? How can the IRP be evaluated, *i.e.* can it be refuted?

Although some of these questions are dealt with in the literature, it must be conceded that there is still a great deal of work to be done. But even if some questions remain unanswered, the IRP, as it is explicated in this essay, can and actually does serve as a *regulative idea* or, in other words, as a *positive heuristic:* it advises the social scientist to apply ITs in order to solve his specific explanatory problems.

The focus of our explication was the individualistic research program. What does the *collectivistic* research program entail? We are not acquainted with any explicit statement of this program. The criticism evoked by the IRP suggests that an advocate of the collectivistic research program refutes each of the foregoing theses. Thus, the collectivistic research program is a strict antipode of the IRP.

The four theses have been proposed as the IRP of sociology. We suggest, however, that our explication is the IRP for the social sciences in general. Presumably economists, anthropologists, historians, *etc.*, advocating an IRP subscribe to the four theses.

III. THE INDIVIDUALISTIC RESEARCH PROGRAM UNDER ATTACK: PROBLEMS, MISUNDERSTANDINGS, AND "BAD SHOTS"

Similar to other aspects of the social sciences, the IRP in general and, particularly, in sociology has brought forth wide criticism and counter-arguments. In sociology a debate on "reductionism" was provoked by the work of George C. Homans, mainly in the sixties. Philosophers like Karl R. Popper and J.W.N. Watkins (see O'Neill 1973) have been involved in a similar debate labelled "methodological individualism." Both debates hardly had any influence on each other.

The arguments for and against the IRP in general, and particularly in sociology, are so manifold and often vague, that it is not possible in this paper to give an exhaustive account and an evaluation of them. Instead, we shall confine our attention to four *objections* that seem to be raised most frequently and which we deem most important and most plausible.[8]

1. *Concepts denoting social aggregates do not refer to individuals and their properties.*

The reconstruction thesis is one of the most widely discussed theses of the IRP (see, for example, O'Neill 1973, see also Opp 1979). The rejection of the reconstruction thesis as stated in the preceding section is at least partially due to different authors attacking or defending different theses. It is, therefore, more advisable to first discuss why we stated the thesis as we did, before discussing the thesis itself.

Existing ITs can explain relational properties of individuals.[9] These may be relations between individuals (such as interacting, communicating, being more powerful than) or relations between individuals and things (such as individual a owns thing b or individual a exchanges good b with individual c).

Even a superficial look at collectivistic concepts in the social sciences suggests that they refer, perhaps not exclusively, to relations between individuals or between individuals and things. The power structure of a group, for example, denotes a distribution of power relations existing between individuals. Consequently, collectivistic concepts can only be reconstructed by concepts designating individuals and/or their relational or nonrelational properties. This is what our reconstruction thesis asserts.

Other reconstruction theses may be wrong. This holds, *e.g.*, for the assertion that collectivistic concepts can be reconstructed by individualistic concepts denoting purposes of individuals (Wisdom 1970). Such theses are irrelevant for the IRP and will be left out of account.

How can the reconstruction thesis be criticized? The only way is to carry out meaning analyses of collectivistic concepts and to examine whether these concepts actually refer to individuals and their relational or nonrelational properties. Primarily, concepts should be selected that can most probably be expected to falsify the reconstruction thesis.

Such an analysis has been provided by Hummell and Opp (1971) and Opp (1979, pp. 127–132). The result was unequivocal. Each collectivistic concept under analysis could clearly be reconstructed individualistically.

Two other facts can be adduced in support of the reconstruction thesis. First of all, the meaning analyses mentioned in the preceding paragraph may have flaws. However, up till now no scholar has pointed out any shortcomings of these analyses. So we conclude for the time being that these analyses are sound.

Secondly, there is no thorough meaning analysis of a collectivistic concept showing that no individualistic reconstruction is possible.

Thus, at present there is no reason to doubt that the reconstruction thesis is correct.

2. *The unintended consequences of individual actions cannot be explained by individualistic theories.*

An action of a single individual or of a group of individuals may be of two kinds: Firstly, the behavioral consequences may be intended or unintended and, secondly, they may be desirable or undesirable for one or more other individuals. For example, an accident caused by the driver of a car is an unintended consequence of his driving and undesirable for him and often for others too. Perhaps the most famous example of an unintended consequence of individual actions is Adam Smith's analysis of the consequences of self-interested actions in the market. Such egoistic actions in fact lead to the promotion of the welfare of society (see Adam Smith's *The Wealth of Nations*, book 4, chapter 2), which is unintended and simultaneously desirable for the members of society.

The explanation of the unintended consequences of actions is often considered to be the most important task of the social sciences. Even if one does not accept this, every social scientist will agree that a fruitful theoretical approach must successfully cope with the explanation of the unintended consequences of individual actions.

It is sometimes claimed that an individualistic research program is unable to handle this problem successfully. One may argue that preferences (*i.e.*, among other things, intentions) are regarded as a relevant set of conditions in the theories under consideration (like utility theory) and, accordingly, only intentional behavior can be explained.

The charge that unintended consequences of individual actions cannot be explained by ITs can be met in two ways. First of all, it may be pointed out that numerous analyses exist showing in detail by applying ITs how unintended consequences of social actions emerge. The most striking example are *prisoner's dilemma* situations (see, *e.g.*, Luce and Raiffa 1957, pp. 94–97, Barry and Hardin 1982). This is a situation where each individual chooses the behavioral alternative that yields the highest payoff to himself. However, all individuals involved would be better off, if they had chosen otherwise. Unintended consequences of individual actions are also dealt with under headings like paradox (or perverse) effects and social traps.[10]

The second way of coping with the criticism that the IRP is unable to adequately deal with unintended consequences of individual actions is to analyse the ITs themselves: Do the ITs imply that unintended consequences of individual actions are possible?

Let us look at the rational-choice model. One set of conditions relevant for the explanation of actions are the preferences of individuals. These preferences may be termed intentions. Thus, people may want more material goods of a particular kind, they may prefer more social support to less social support, they may want to increase the welfare of their families and so on. In deciding how to achieve these goals individuals take into account the constraints they perceive. In other words, they will consider to what extent certain behavioral alternatives lead to the achievement of their goals. They choose the action that yields the highest net utility to them. It is important to note that among the constraints are the actions of other people or of groups (police, organizations, *etc.*).

Does this theory imply that individuals will always achieve their goals or, in other words, can the theory only explain those actions which accord with the individuals' goals? The answer is clearly "no." The theory does not exclude that individuals totally misperceive the consequences of their actions, *i.e.*, subjective and objective constraints may diverge. Furthermore, an individual may even realize that an action not chosen by him would make him better off, if others behaved in a certain way (see the prisoner's dilemma). Thus, it can be maintained in case that individuals deliberately choose even those actions, the consequences of which being neither intended (but predicted) nor desired. Finally, individuals often have no control over desired consequences of their behavior so that they cannot attain their goals.

The criticism under consideration is indeed very strange in view of the fact that the most extensive literature on unintended consequences of individual actions has been provided by the advocates of the IRP, as the preceding references indicate.

3. Groups have emergent properties (properties which cannot be assigned to individuals). Therefore individualistic theories cannot be applied to explain properties of groups.

This objection has two parts. The first is the assertion that groups have emergent properties in the above sense. The second is that the existence of these properties prevents their explanation by means of ITs.

Are there emergent properties? Take the property "age." An individual and a group may have a certain age (or, to take another example, they may be more or less authoritarian). Do these examples falsify the assertion under discussion?

Although the terms used to designate the properties of the individual and the collective are the same, their meaning is different. With regard to an individual "age" means the time elapsed from his physical birth up to a certain point in time; if we speak of the "age" of a group, however, we mean the time period from its foundation up to a certain point in time. (To measure "authoritarianism" for an individual, we may present him items of a questionnaire and compute his test score. If the "authoritarianism" for a group is to be ascertained, we first have to measure the authoritarian attitudes of the group members and then aggregate the scores of the individual attitudes.) Thus, even in cases where the terms used to designate properties of individuals and aggregates are the same, the meaning of these terms is always different.

For other properties it is apparent even at first sight that they can be assigned only to groups and not to individuals or *vice versa*. For example, variables like bureaucratization, hierarchy, division of labor, crime rate, mean age, cohesion, and homogeneity can be ascribed only to groups, but not to individuals.

These examples clearly confirm the claim that there are emergent properties in the above sense. Thus, an advocate of the IRP will accept the first part of the above assertion.

Does this assertion imply or at least support the second part of the above criticism, namely that ITs are unable to explain these properties? Firstly, the existence of emergent properties would make their explanation by ITs impossible if the terms, designating these properties, could not be reconstructed by the terms of the ITs applied (see thesis 3 in section II). However, as was demonstrated, the reconstruction thesis has so far not been falsified. A meaning analysis of the preceding examples ("age", "authoritarianism", "bureaucratization" of groups etc.) also indicates that these are aggregations of (relational or nonrelational) properties of individuals. "Hierarchy," for example, is a particular distribution of power between individual actors. "Power" refers to certain relations between individuals (individual a is more powerful than individual b).

Even if it is conceded that the emergent properties can be reconstructed individualistically, it may be argued that the ITs are unable to explain relationships between individuals or between individuals and things. This argument seems to assume that ITs can only explain the actions of isolated individuals. But actions may be of a relational character. For example, individuals may decide to communicate with each other, to appropriate or to exchange things, to bargain etc. Such relational actions may lead to certain outcomes in an aggregate of individuals. These aggregate outcomes may be denoted by collectivistic terms (power structure, communication structure, *etc.*).

These intuitive considerations suggest that the existence of emergent properties is no obstacle to their explanation. This is not only endorsed by the intuitive considerations of the preceding paragraph, but also by investigations of individualistic social scientists, examples being the economic theory of crime or works on exchange.

4. *Individualistic theories do not take into account the social (and particularly the institutional) context in explaining individual behavior. Thus, these theories are wrong and not appropriate as a basis for a research program.*

One of the objections most often raised against the IRP is that the ITs applied explain individual behavior by the motives or drives of the individual actors. This reproach is often called *psychologism.* Accordingly, a theory is called "psychological" if behavior is explained by the motives of the actors. Thus, "individualistic" and "psychological" (in the above sense) are used as equivalent terms.[11]

Every scholar is, of course, free to assign any meaning to a term. But it seems that the use of the term "psychological" is not intended as a nominal definition, but as a description of how members of a scientific community, namely psychologists, explain behavior. The assertion that psychologists explain behavior by recourse to motives is plainly false. Even a superficial look at a psychological (and particularly social psychological) textbook shows the falsehood of this claim.

With respect to the currently most-often used IT, namely, the rational choice model, it is again clearly false that the social or institutional context is neglected. According to this model preferences (*i.e.,* motives, wants) and restrictions (or opportunities) are determinants of behavior. The social and institutional context pertains to the restrictions. For example, enforced rights limit the behavioral opportunities of actors. This also holds for various reactions of the social environment such as social support, negative sanctions or social approval.

Thus, the predominant IT avoids *psychologism* in the above sense. But it posits that motives or preferences are one class of relevant variables. The rational choice model also avoids *sociologism* in the sense that only the social environment or, to be more explicit, only social structures are explanatory variables. The rational choice model, however, posits that the social environment is one class of relevant variables. In view of these features, the IRP should perhaps be called *structural-individualistic research program* in order to express that preferences *and* constraints (including social structures) are determinants of social behavior.

IV. ON THE PRESENT STATE OF THE INDIVIDUALISTIC RESEARCH PROGRAM IN THE SOCIAL SCIENCES

The best way to evaluate the success or failure of the IRP is to look at the research of those social scientists working in the individualistic tradition. In this context the following six features of this research are important for an evaluation of the IRP.

Feature 1: The IT applied by the overwhelming majority of individualistic social scientists is the rational choice model. Apart from the success of this model there seems to be a tendency towards dogmatization in several respects. First of all, those problems are neglected that the rational choice model is unable to solve. This holds particularly for the explanation of preferences and expectancies. Secondly, research findings of social psychology that could lead to new applications of the rational choice model are neglected. For example, according to cognitive consistency theories (*e.g.,* dissonance theory, balance theory) certain combinations of cognitions (opinions, attitudes) are dissonant (or unbalanced), *i.e.,* unpleasant to an individual. To illustrate this with one of Festinger's (1957) examples: a heavy smoker who is at the same time aware that smoking is unhealthy, feels dissonance. In terms of the rational choice model, the simultaneous existence of certain cognitive elements is more or less *costly.* This example suggests that taking cognitive consistency theories into account could draw the attention to new kinds of costs, which may be termed *cognitive costs,* and to new types of behavior to be explained (such as selective reading of newspapers which may be a strategy to avoid cognitive costs).

Feature 2: The actual research of social scientists accepting the IRP can be quoted for specific theses of the IRP and against specific criticism of the IRP. This has already been done several times in section III. Three points will be added here:

a) Postulate 4 of the IRP (collectivistic propositions should be explained by ITs) is fully realised. Individualistic social scientists are usually concerned with macro-phenomena, in any case with social aggregates, and not with single individuals.

b) The foregoing point implies that the reconstruction thesis is confirmed by each piece of research produced by the respective social scientist. It is possible, however, that explananda the individualistic reconstruction of which led to difficulties have been excluded from research. This is merely a possibility but no cases of this sort are known to us.

c) Point **a** implies that emergent properties (see section III, point 3) are not an obstacle to explanations by means of ITs.

Feature 3: There is wide consensus in the philosophy of science that the most effective way of criticizing a theory is to confront it with competing theories. Consequently, one would have expected that one of the preoccupations of individualistic social scientists is to design crucial empirical investigations where deductions from ITs and existing competing propositions are tested. Such empirical confrontations are rare. If one of the main arguments for applying ITs is that they are able to correct competing propositions, this should be demonstrated more extensively.

It is true, as Homans emphasizes (see section II), that sociological hypotheses are of a low explanatory power and, it may be added, are often not put forward in such a form that they can be criticized at all. Even if sociological propositions have a low empirical content (like hypotheses on suicide or on the formation of protest groups), they are of interest to many social scientists—and practitioners—and should be confronted with the pertinent deductions from ITs. If sociological propositions are not testable, the first step should be to explicate them so that they can be criticized. This, however, should only be attempted for those hypotheses whose meaning is not totally obscure.

Feature 4: The individualistic tradition in sociology conforms more than other sociological schools to the standards of an empirical-theoretical science. Its procedure—*model building*—consists of stating explicit deductive arguments. Among the premises of a model are the IT applied and other assumptions referring, among other things, to distributions of initial conditions in a social aggregate or to semantic stipulations about the meaning of collectivistic concepts in terms of the IT applied. Thus, the IRP may be a paradigm for an exact social science.

Feature 5: The main criterion for evaluating a research program is to what extent substantive theorizing and research has been brought about by those adhering to the IRP. In applying this criterion, it turns out that the IRP was extremely prolific in suggesting new solutions to a great many quite different problems. To get an impression about this diverse range of problems a look at the books by G. Becker (1976), Boudon (1981), Hechter (1983), and McKenzie and Tullock (1978) is informative, although many topics of relevance to individualistic social scientists (like property rights or political processes) are only superficially touched upon.

Original theoretical propositions and explanations of specific events (like historical processes) are not only proposed; there is also ample empirical research testing these propositions.

It is not possible for a single social scientist to have an overview of all the propositions and empirical investigations provided by individualistic social scientists. To our knowledge the overwhelming number of investigations could not falsify the propositions tested.

Thus, in evaluating the IRP according to the extent to which new theoretical insights have been provided and empirically confirmed, it cannot be denied that the IRP has so far been successful.

Feature 6: One implication of what was previously said should be noted: A new unity of the social sciences has developed: Firstly, a single theory—the rational choice model—is applied by scientists of different disciplines. Secondly, there are many identical research questions that are of interest to scientists of different disciplines. Thus, for various topics the borders of the disciplines break down: there is no longer a division of labor with respect to the kinds of problems dealt with, and there is no longer a division in the disciplines with respect to the kinds of theoretical propositions accepted.

NOTES

1. A good exposition of this tradition is provided by Turner and Maryansky (1979); see also the anthology of Demerath and Peterson (1967).

2. See the detailed criticisms, particularly by George C. Homans (see, *e.g.*, 1962, 1964, 1967); Hempel 1965; Nagel 1956, 1961 (pp. 401–28, pp. 520–35).

3. For criticisms of marxist theory see particularly Helberger 1974, Popper 1966, Schumpeter 1942.

4. For an excellent criticism of functionalism and marxism from the perspective of the IRP see Vanberg 1975.

5. The latter term should be avoided because it suggests that only exchange processes are under scrutiny which does not hold true.

6. Some of the following arguments are elaborated in Opp 1979.

7. Accordingly, collectivistic propositions cannot be derived solely from an IT. In addition at least one "bridge assumption" must be specified.

8. For a more extensive discussion see Opp 1979. See, furthermore, Raub and Voss 1981. Also in the writings of George C. Homans many objections are dealt with.

9. ITs can also explain nonrelational properties like "being a thief." Perhaps these properties can also be formalized as two-place predicates (like "individual a steals thing b"). Then we may say that all explananda of ITs are relational properties of individuals. Whether this is so, will be left open in this paper.

10. For a thorough analysis of many examples of unintended consequences of individual actions see, with further references, Wippler 1978, 1980. See also Boudon 1982.

11. See, *e.g.*, Gellner 1956, pp. 261–62. The term "psychological" is used in the above sense by Popper (1966, p. 90) and apparently also by Goldstein (1956, p. 269) and Lenk (1977).

REFERENCES

Barry, B. and Hardin, R., editors 1982. *Rational Man and Irrational Society.* Beverly Hills: Sage.

Becker, G. 1976. *The Economic Approach to Human Behavior.* Chicago and London: University of Chicago Press.

Boudon, R. 1981. *The Logic of Social Action.* London: Routledge and Kegan Paul.

Boudon, R. 1982. *The Unintended Consequences of Social Action.* London and Basingdale: Macmillan.

Demerath, N. and Peterson, R., editors 1967. *System, Change and Conflict.* New York and London: Free Press.

Festinger, L. 1957. *A Theory of Cognitive Dissonance.* Stanford: Stanford University Press.

Goldstein, L. 1973. "The Inadequacy of the Principle of Methodological Individualism (1956)." Edited by O'Neill, J. in *Modes of Individualism and Collectivism*, pp. 264–276. London: Heinemann.

Hempel, C. 1965. "The Logic of Functional Analysis." *Aspects of Scientific Explanation.* New York: Free Press.

Helberger, C. 1974. *Marxismus als Methode.* Frankfurt: Athenaeum.

Homans, G. 1962. *Sentiments and Activities: Essays in Social Science.* Glencoe: Free Press.

Homans, G. 1964. "Contemporary Theory in Sociology." Edited by Faris, R. in *Handbook of Modern Sociology*, pp. 951–977. Chicago: Rand McNally.

Homans, G. 1967. *The Nature of Social Science.* New York: Harcourt.

Homans, G. 1969. "The Sociological Relevance of Behaviorism." Edited by Burgess, R. and Bushell, D. in *Behavioral Sociology. The Experimental Analysis of Social Process*, p. 1–26. New York and London: Columbia University Press.

Homans, G. 1974. *Social Behavior. Its Elementary Forms*, Second Edition. New York: Harcourt.

Hummell, H. and Opp, K.D. 1971. *Die Reduzierbarkeit von Soziologie auf Psychologie. Eine These, ihr Test und ihre theoretische Bedeutung*, Braunschweig: Vieweg.

Lenk, H. 1977. "Strukturund Verhaltensaspekte in Theorien sozialen Handelns." Edited by Lenk, H. in *Handlungstheorien interdisziplinaer*, Volume IV, pp. 157–175. Muenchen: Fink.

Luce, R. and Raiffa, H. 1957. *Games and Decisions*. New York: Wiley.

McKenzie, R. and Tullock, G. 1978. *The New World of Economics*. Homewood: Irwin.

Nagel, E. 1961. *The Structure of Science*. London: Routledge and Kegan Paul.

O'Neill, J., editor 1973. *Modes of Individualism and Collectivism*. London: Heinemann.

Opp, K.D. 1979. *Individualistische Sozialwissenschaft. Arbeitsweise und Probleme individualistisch und kollektivistisch orientierter Sozialwissenschaften*. Stuttgart: Enke.

Popper, K. 1966. *The Open Society and Its Enemies. Hegel and Marx*, Volume II, Fifth Edition. London: Routledge and Kegan Paul.

Schumpeter, J. 1942. *Capitalism, Socialism and Democracy*. New York: Harper.

Turner, J. and Maryanski, A. 1979. *Functionalism*. Menlo Park: Benjamin/ Cummings.

Vanberg, V. 1975. *Die zwei Soziologien*. Tuebingen: Mohr-Siebeck.

Wippler, R. 1978. "Nicht-intendierte soziale Folgen individueller Handlungen." *Soziale Welt*, Volume XXIX, pp. 155–179.

Wippler, R. 1980. "Erklaerung unbeabsichtigter Handlungsfolgen: Ziel oder Meilenstein soziologischer Theoriebildung." Edited by Matthes, J. *Lebenswelt und soziale Probleme. Verhandlungen des 20. Deutschen Soziologentages*, pp. 246–261. Frankfurt and New York: Campus.

Wisdom, J. 1970. "Situational Individualism and the Emergent Group Properties." Edited by Borger, R. and Cioffi, F. in *Explanation in the Behavioral Sciences*, pp. 271–296. Cambridge: Cambridge University Press.

15

Comments on Opp's Essay

ANGELO M. PETRONI

Professor Opp's paper has many excellent qualities. First of all, it succeeds very well in giving a clear statement of the most important features of the theses about the individualistic perspective in the social sciences. Secondly, the paper gives a very good rational reconstruction of the individualistic research program. Last but not least, it makes the crucial but often neglected distinction between factual and normative aspects of such a research program. These qualities alone would be enough to justify the great attention that the paper deserves.

Professor Opp summarizes his reformulation of the positive aspect of the individualistic research program in three theses:

a) "IT_s (individualistic theories) can be used to derive (or explain) singular and general collectivistic propositions";

b) "If attempts are made to derive existing singular and general collectivistic propositions by using IT_s, the collectivistic propositions are derivable in their original or in a corrected version."

c) "Concepts designating aggregates or their properties (*i.e.*, collectivistic concepts) in fact refer to individuals or their (relational or non-relational) properties, as a meaning analysis of the collectivistic concepts always reveal."

The normative claim is in turn expressed by the following fourth thesis:

d) "IT_s should be applied in explaining singular and general collectivistic propositions."

Professor Opp remarks that acceptance of the positive theses does not imply acceptance of the normative claim; but acceptance of the positive theses is a necessary condition for acceptance of the normative claim, given that "one will not claim anything, if this cannot be realised" *(ibidem).*

However, we prefer to start our analysis from the normative claim. Well, why one should attempt to reduce general collectivistic propositions to IT_s? Professor Opp's answer is that "IT_s have a relatively high explanatory power, and the explanations they deliver are more valid than those offered by collectivistic propositions" *(ibidem).* Unfortunately, in the paper there is no valid demonstration of this thesis. References to the failures of functionalist or "marxist" explanations are merely a *de facto,* not a *de jure* (i.e. logical or methodological) argument.

Let us focus on the first part of the above quoted statement. What Professor Opp seems to have in mind is that IT_s will constitute a *theoretical explanation* in Hempel's sense[1]: that is to say, IT_s will explain collectivistic theories exactly as particular facts are explained by general laws. If some IT_s explain some collectivistic theories, then it trivially follows that IT_s have an explanatory power higher than these collectivistic theories. But the crucial point is precisely whether IT_s with such explanatory power exist.

First of all, we have to point out that the problem at issue is completely different from that of the above quoted reconstruction thesis c. The individualistic reduction statement (or reconstruction statement, as Professor Opp prefers to say) of a collectivistic concept will be constituted by a conjunction of statements "describing" the behavior of an individual (or, if one prefers, containing the description of properties appertaining to individuals). Even on the supposition that this conjunction will be complete—i.e., that it will cover the whole descriptive range covered by the collectivistic concept—it follows that there is no reason at all why the testability or the logical strength of the conjunction should be higher than that of the collectivistic concept. Each statement that refutes the conjunction refutes also the collectivistic concept; and no additional information is contained in the individualistic reduction statement.

Professor Opp affirms that "throughout this paper we have in mind particularly the rational choice model (RCM, or utility theory)." The assumption of RCM, which should be supplemented by "hypotheses from learning theory," is justified by Professor Opp on the reason that these IT_s "are mainly used by social scientists working in the frame" of the individualistic research program (IRP). But, as it is obvious, the fact that RCM is widely used does not help at all in solving the logical problem that we are facing.

It is probable that lack of space prevented Professor Opp from giving further specifications about RCM itself. But such specifications would be extremely useful for our purposes. We can conjecture that what Professor Opp has in mind is the expected utility theory (as it has been classically formulated in slightly different ways by von Neumann and Morgenstern, Friedman and Savage, or more recently, by John Harsanyi. It is well known that the original EUT is confronted with many difficulties and that some reformulations have been produced—especially in order to take into account the discrepancies between *observed choice behavior* under uncertainty and EUT axioms.

Of course, it is not our concern to consider these reformulations and their validity. What we have to examine is whether EUT in any of its versions can succeed in "covering" Professor Opp's theses a and b. Given that general collectivistic propositions are intended to be explained by IT_s, EUT will have to be of a higher content than that of the collectivistic theories. If one accepts the widely held position that higher content means higher testability, it follows that EUT will have to be more testable than any general collectivistic proposition (*e.g.*, that the suicide rate in all industrialised countries has increased, or that division of labor has increased). However, in our opinion, this is plainly false. One of the main features of EUT is exactly its adaptability to any observed behaviour. If discrepancies arise, they will be eliminated by a suitable change in the structure of the utility functions held by the agents. This is not merely an *ad hoc* procedure, but is *de facto* the very hard core of EUT.[2]

Let us just take the example of one of the most important reformulations of EUT put forward in recent times, *i.e.*, Loomes and Sudgen's "regret theory." This theory has been conceived in order to take into account the well-known empirical evidence first pointed out by Maurice Allais in 1953, and systematically analysed in recent years by several researchers.[3] The following quotation summarizes very clearly the aims and the results of regret theory:

> "We do not claim that acting according to our theory is the only rational way to behave. Nor do we suggest that all individuals who act according to our theory must violate the conventional axioms. Some individuals may experience no regret or rejoicing at all, while some others may have linear Q (.) functions: in these special cases of our theory, we could predict that the individual's behaviour would conform with all the conventional axioms. On the other hand, individuals with non-linear Q (.) functions of the kind described in this paper may consistently and knowingly violate the axioms of transitivity and equivalence without ever accepting, even after the most careful reflection, that they have made a mistake."[4]

Facing this situation, one could be tempted to say that the utility theory presupposed by Professor Opp's IRP is not one of the family of EUTs in the technical sense. What IRP presupposes is just an unformalized and "broad" utility theory. However, this is an unsatisfactory move. If we reduce the formalization and the precision of the utility theory involved, its explanatory power will be weakened.

As we learn from examples, such as the explanation of the laws of thermodynamics by the laws of mechanical statistics, theoretical explanation cannot be just a matter of linguistical sussumption.[5] Therefore, in any case we cannot accept the thesis that EUT can explain any general collectivistic proposition because this can be expressed in EUT terms.

We have to stress that the point at issue is not whether EUT is an empirical or an analytical/normative theory. (Of course, if it would be an analytical/normative theory, our thesis would be fully demonstrated.) Even if we allow that EUT has an empirical character, and hence that it is empirically refutable, this would not be sufficient to demonstrate that its empirical content is sufficiently high as to explain all the possible collectivistic concepts (regularities). For example, if one should demonstrate that EUT, in one of its versions, explains people's gambling behavior, this could not be considered as a demonstration that EUT's axioms can explain (in the nomological sense) any human behavior described by collectivistic propositions. We can extend this consideration to any rational-choice model, which could be used in economics: even if one of them could be able to explain (and to predict) people's observed economic behavior, we are not allowed to extend this explicative power beyond its given boundaries.

If we consider the seminal works by Gary Becker on the economic approach to human behavior, we can easily recognize that their importance is due to the fact that they find "economic causes" of some previously "unexplained" social phenomena (*e.g.*, why rich people marry younger and divorce less frequently).[6] In such fields we are ready to accept that the economic causes postulated by the models have to be considered as the cause (or, at least, the determinant cause) of the behavior under analysis (*e.g.*, crime behavior). But can we accept that economic reasons (or economic-like reasons) *and* a cost-benefit analysis (or a utility calculus) are responsible for the behavior of Khomeini or Hirohito's kamikazes? Of course, one could even say that, if the collectivistic proposition "Many Muslims in the eighty's accepted to die for their faith" is true, it is because the utility functions they held are such as to produce the verified effect.

The first problem that such a thesis poses is that it is almost impossible to conceive an empirical test that should demonstrate that the utility functions involved are such as to produce, under specified conditions, the observed behavior. After all, the fact that the utility function of a kamikaze is such as to make him prefer death to say, *e.g.* dishonor, can be ascertained "only" by his acting as a kamikaze! However, this is not the main point. Independent from this difficulty, one should question if any significant progress in knowledge has been made when the collectivistic concept has been "explained" by some sort of UT. For example, from our *explanans* can we deduce additional empirical descriptions that cannot be drawn from the *explanandum?* And—*more important*—can we consider the deductions from the *explanandum*—for example, predictions—as having a higher reliability with respect to those coming from the *explanans?* Even under the hypothesis that the behaviors of the agents included in the domain of the collectivistic proposition are determined by economic-like causes,[7] this could happen only if we had effected a complete recognition of the utility functions of all the agents (and, as far as predictions are concerned, if we had been assured that these utility are stable). But it is obvious that this is *de facto* impossible. Therefore, in practice, for non-trivial sociological concepts, we never have methodological reasons in favour of the *explanans.*

As one can easily see, the problems here involved go beyond the purely methodological problems of empirical content, testability, *etc.* Our example of kamikazes' behavior is not at all unique. The same situation happens when we consider all those behaviors that are strongly determined by traditions that give to the individuals the patterns they have to follow—and which they actually follow. There is an enormous difference between choosing between two prospects in a lottery from one side, and choosing between different traditions, or also between different options within a given tradition, from the other side. This explains why the choice of a kamikaze is something very different from the choice of a gambler, and therefore it also explains why there is no reason for assuming (as does Professor Opp's normative claim) that the best we can do for knowing the behavior of a kamikaze (to "explain" it, if one prefers) is to try to reduce it to the model of a gambler's or investor's behavior. The demand that all sociological (collectivistic) concepts must be deduced from some UT (plus some given initial conditions) has the unavoidable effect of making superfluous what constitutes the empirical aspect of sociology. But then, what role will be *de jure* assigned to sociology? Why should we search for sociological laws or, more generally, for general concepts, if they must be explained by some UT? The unintended and unpleasant consequence of conceiving sociology as a kind of "general economics" is that sociology would become *de jure* (and perhaps *de facto*) undistinguishable from history.[8] As a matter of fact, the essential task of sociology would be to establish the "initial conditions" that are part of the *explanans* of any human action.

It is obvious that I do not claim any originality for the theses just exposed. One can find quite identical positions in the history of sociological theory.

I think that it is worth while to raise here a question, which is also a very old one, but which assumes a new and greater importance after the rising of sociobiology. If all sociological propositions have to be explained by a UT, how could those human behaviors that are biologically determined—or at least, biologically conditionated—be taken into account? How could one legitimately replace empirical causes, or, if one prefers, empirical laws, by teleological causes, or teleological laws? (All RCM_s or UT_s are teleological!)

As far as I know, no viable solution to this problem has been proposed. The famous thesis of Max Weber, according to which the work of the sociologist begins at the point where "psychological" or "physical" ("physiological") aimless laws "finish"[9]—that is to say, at the point where the "Sinn-haftes handen" take place—is a way of stating the problem, not a solution of it. Why should we assume that there is a point at which a biologically or psychologically determined action becomes a "Sinn-haftes handen"? And if these actions obey biological laws, how could one affirm that these very same actions are determined by a "Sinn-haftes handen" or by a "Zweckrationalität"? To assume a kind of "complementarity principle"—*i.e.*, that the very same action is considered under two different but complementary points of view—is not at all a satisfactory solution. It is no more satisfactory than to assume that the falling of a stone can be considered under the complementary points of view of Newtonian mechanics and of Aristotle's teleological theory of natural places.

It is important to remark that these considerations hold under the general supposition that man's behaviors obey empirical laws of *any* kind (as psychological laws), and are by no means confined to the hypothesis that they obey biological laws.

As it is obvious, these same problems do not arise if we assume that sociology has the task of searching empirical regularities (general concepts), not that of explaining them on the basis of some theory of rationality. As a matter of fact, the mere finding of empirical regularities does not contrast with the assumption that some, or even all of them are *e.g.*, biologically grounded.

If our analysis is correct, it follows that Professor Opp's "explanatory program" is untenable. Of course, this does not means that any "explanatory program" is impossible (*e.g.*, our arguments do not

concern at all the problem whether collectivistic general concepts can
be explained by psychological laws). We have also to emphasize that
the fortune of IRP is in no way unavoidably linked to the "explanatory" program. If we are right, Professor Opp wishes to substitute
reductionism with explanation. But, in our opinion, IRP *cum* utility
theory may eventually be a viable program if one gives up the
"explanatory" program, and considers IRP as a case of microreduction
in the sense of Oppenheim and Putnam.[10]

The situation for IRP is very well described by Hempel when
he points out that microtheories are normally required in science in
order to ensure the full understanding of the phenomena.[11] Professor
Opp seems to have quite a different opinion:

> It is true, as Homann emphasizes, that sociological hypotheses are of
> a low explanatory power and, it may be added, are often put in such
> form that they cannot be criticized at all. Even if sociological propositions
> have a low empirical content (like hypotheses on suicide or on the
> formation of protest groups), they are of interest to many social sci-
> entists—and practitioners—and should be confronted with the pertinent
> deductions from IT_s.

We have already expressed our opinion about the theoretical
invalidity of this claim;[12] but it could also be questioned whether such
deductions in IRP are *de facto* intended to explain the sociological
propositions, or rather they have to give a microtheoric foundation
(reduction). Of course, this is a matter of empirical enquiry. Personally,
I am unable to answer the question. However, we would like to point
out the example of the important works of Raymond Boudon in the
field of sociology of education.[13] In our opinion, the models produced
by Boudon are much more similar to a microreduction than to an
explanation of some well-known collectivistic general concepts (regularities)—*e.g.*, the correlation between social status and educational
level. It seems to us that the importance of Boudon's works is not
to be attributed to their underlying IT_s, but to the models they put
forward.[14]

Hempel has very well indicated the ontological roots of the
scientific reductionism. We think that this ontological dimension "explains" also the importance of microreduction in Hempel and Oppenheim's sense.[15] Many years ago, as is well known, Leo J. Goldstein
explicitly put forward the distinction between ontological and methodological individualism.[16] Ontological individualism is "that doctrine
which denies the existence of certain alleged entities."[17] As successive
debates showed, acceptance of ontological individualism does not imply

acceptance of methodological individualism. If our theses are correct, it is only on the basis of the ontological claim that individualistic microreductions can be justified. Microreduction cannot be justified from the point of view of progress in explanation. If we adopt a Popperian methodology (in the broad sense of this term) we do not need to offer a microreduction of general collectivistic statements. We only have to test these hypotheses. A sociology composed only of general collectivistic statements could fit very well the basic Popperian criteria. Therefore, even if Popper is an advocate of methodological individualism, in our opinion methodological individualism *cum* utility theory has no justification within his own theory of method.[18]

Finally there is the problem of the so-called "rationality principle." Any utility theory presupposes this principle in one of its versions, and therefore, also methodological individualism (as it has been presented by Professor Opp) needs it. Popper put forward a version of the rationality principle, and some criticisms of it have been produced.[19] However, in our opinion the crucial point is not the formal adequacy of Popper's definition. The point at issue is whether sociology can be grounded on a purely syntactical principle without at the same time losing its empirical character (that is to say, without being reduced to a "pure logic of choice"). In this case, sociology would be distinguished from pure economics only in reason of its object—"sociological" phenomena).

We repeat that these remarks are not concerned at all with the explanation (or reduction) of sociological hypotheses by psychological laws, in any empirical sense of "psychological." Of course, this program has in turn many well-known difficulties, and it does not seem to be too popular. But we have also to point out that EUT is not the only existing theory of rational choice, and that IRP is not to be bound by any of its variants. In our opinion, Herbert Simon's theory of rationality is a more adequate research program and a more promising foundation for IRP. As a matter of fact, it is possible to argue that, as a more empirical and wider theory, the range of social phenomena that it covers is greater than that of the EUT models. Of course, this does not mean that all the objections that stand against the explanation of any collectivistic sociological regularities *via* a UT are removed.[20]

NOTES

1. C.G. Hempel, *Aspects of Scientific Explanation and Other Essays in the Philosophy of Science*, New York, Free Press, 1965. See also E. Nagel, *The*

Structure of Science, London, Routledge and Kegan Paul, 1961; and K. R. Popper, *The Poverty of Historicism,* London, Routledge and Kegan Paul, 1961[3], section 28.

2. See the criticism of this strategy by H. Simon, *Rationality as Process and as Product of Thought,* "American Economic Review," LVIII (1978), pp. 1–16. Dr. Enrico Colombatto has very clearly resumed the situation: "Research on utilitarianism in general, and on expected utility in particular, is based, one way or another, on the assumption that individuals behave rationally. If a 'rational' model yelds predictions which differ from the observed individual's behavior, then it follows that the model is not well specified, and that some important variables or relations have been forgotten. However, if we agree to take into consideration all the important variables and relations, we end up by making rational all sorts of behavior; by defining within sufficiently wide boundaries the very concept of utility, all actions become—by definition—utility maximizing. For instance, while we may have problems in justifying altruism in the framework of an individual 'short-term utility function,' it becomes perfectly logical and acceptable within 'long-term utility function,' since altruism can be looked upon as some sort of investment. By the same principle, the utilitarian principle has no difficulty in explaining all sorts of subjective behaviour, provided all utility functions are properly estimated" (*Teoria della decisione e razionalità: commento su Harsanyi,* in A.M. Petroni and R. Viale (eds.), *Individuale-Collettivo. Il problema della razionalità in filosofia, politica ed economia,* Torino, La Rosa, forthcoming).

3. M. Allais, *Le comportement de l'homme rationnel devant le risque; critique des postulats et axiomes de l'école américaine,* "Econometrica," XXI (1953), pp. 503–546 (see also the volume by M. Allais and O. Hagen (eds.), *Expected Utility Hypothesis and the Allais Paradox,* Dordrecht, D. Reidel Publishing Co., 1979). The widest empirical evidence against EUT axioms has been produced by P. Sclovic and A. Tversky, *Who Accepts Savage's Axioms?,* "Behavioural Science," XIX (1974), pp. 368–373; and A. Tversky and D. Kahneman, *The Framing of Decisions and the Psychology of Choice,* "Science," CCXI (1981), pp. 453–458. For a philosophical interpretation of the so-called Allais paradox see J.W.N. Watkins, *Contro la massimizzazione dell'utilità attesa,* in A. M. Petroni and R. Viale (eds.), *op.cit.* (see also the discussion of Watkins' paper by Harsanyi and Watkins' rejoinder).

4. G. Loomes and R. Sugden, *Regret Theory: an Alternative Theory of Rational Choice under Uncertainty,* "The Economic Journal," xCII (1982), pp. 805–824; p. 820. The $Q(.)$ function is such that for all $\theta, Q(\theta) = \theta + R(\theta) - R(-\theta)$. R is the regret-rejoice function such that if m_{ij}^k is the modified utility, $m_{ij}^k = c_{ij} + R(c_{ij} - c_{ij})$; that is to say, R assigns a real-valued index to every possible increment or decrement of choiceless utility.

5. See G. Bergmann, *Philosophy of Science,* Madison, University of Wisconsin Press, 1957, pp. 131–144. For a good exposition and analysis of the most important epistemological aspects of reductionism see R. Egidi, *Il lin-*

guaggio delle teorie scientifiche, Napoli, Guida, 1979 (in particular the fourth chapter). I am much indebted to this book.

6. G.S. Becker, *The Economic Approach to Human Behaviour,* Chicago, Chicago University Press, 1976; and *Economic Analysis and Human Behaviour,* in L. Lévy-Garboua (ed.), *Sociological Economics,* London, Sage, 1979.

7. Of course, we have also to assume that the laws to which economic-like behavior obeys are of a level of universality higher than that of the collectivistic laws (or collectivistic concepts) from which the behavior of the agents is described.

8. In the sense of Popper/Hempel's theory of history. As is well-known, Popper holds two completely different positions on the nature of history as a science. On this point see pp. 76–78 of our *Introduzione,* in A.M. Petroni (ed.), *Karl R. Popper:il pensiero politico,* Quaderni di "Biblioteca della liberta," Florence, 1981.

9. M. Weber, *Ueber einige Kategorien der verstehenden Soziologie* (1913), in M. Weber, *Gesammelte Aufsätze zur Wissenschaftslehre,* Tübingen, 1922; cfr. p. 407.

10. P. Oppenheim and H. Putnam, *Unity of the Sciences as a Working Hypothesis,* in H. Feigl and G. Maxwell (eds.), *Concepts, Theories, and the Mind-Body Problem,* "Minnesota Studies in the Philosophy of Science, 2," Minneapolis, University of Minnesota Press, 1958, pp. 3–36.

11. C.G. Hempel and P. Oppenheim, *The Logic of Explanation,* "Philosophy of Science," XV (1948), pp. 135–175.

12. Of course, under the condition that involved IT, are utility theories.

13. R. Boudon, *L'inégalité des chances,* Paris, Colin, 1973; *Institutions scolaires et effets pervers-2/L'enseignement supérieur court,* in *Effets pervers et ordre social,* Paris, P.U.F., 1977 (See also the model of "relative deprivation" in *La logique de la frustration relative,* ivi.)

14. Boudon's models presuppose some general concepts of utility theory. However, Boudon himself has pointed out that sociology cannot use only a single model of men. Cfr. R. Boudon, *La place du désordre,* Paris, P.U.F., 1984, p.55.

15. C.G. Hempel, *Reduction. Ontological and Linguistical Facets,* in S. Morgenbesser, P. Suppes, M. White (eds.), *Philosophy, Science and Method. Essays in Honour of J. Ernst Nagel,* New York, Macmillan Press, 1969, pp. 179–199.

16. L.J. Goldstein, *The Two Theses of Methodological Individualism,* "British Journal for the Philosophy of Science," IX (1958), pp. 1–10. In the note 38 of the Eleventh chapter of *The Open Society* Popper affirms to share a methodological nominalism, but not a methaphysical nominalism. However, after his epistemology of World 3, it seems very unprobable that Popper can be called a methodological nominalist.

17. L.J. Goldstein, *Methodological Individualism,* p. 3.

18. This is an important fact, given that Popper explicitly rejects the reduction of sociology to psychology. Popper acknowledges his debt to von Hayek as for the principle of methodological individualsim. However, as K.J. Scott has shown, "Hayek's principle is synthetic, Popper's analytical; Hayek says that the social sciences do not deal with 'given' wholes but their task is to *constitute* these wholes by constructing models from the familiar elements; Popper says that 'institutions (and traditions) must be *analysed* in individualistic terms' " ("British Journal for the Philosophy of Science", X (1959–1960), p. 332). Anyone who is acquainted not only with von Hayek's works, but also with "Austrian Economics" in general— especially with Carl Menger and von Mises—can easily understand the important consequences implied by this difference between Popper's and von Hayek's principles as far as the conception of the nature and role of economics is concerned.

19. On this point see the section 7 of our *Introduzione*, cit. (in particular pp. 66–76), as well as our review-article of Boudon's *La place du désordre*, cit. ("L'Année Sociologique," LX (1985)). Popper's various formulations of the rationality principle are often contradictory *inter se*. Noretta Koertge has given an interesting reformulation of Popper's principle, but in our opinion her proposal is still unsatisfactory (see *The Methodological Status of Popper's Rationality Principle*, "Theory and Decision", X(1979), pp. 83–95, and the discussion at pp. 67–68 of our *Introduzione*).

20. On the comparison of EUT and Simon's theory see the good article by P. Mongin *Modèle rationnel ou modèle économique de la rationalité?* "Revue économique," XXV (1984), pp. 9–63.

16

Explanation, Interpretation, and Understanding in the Social Sciences

RAYMOND BOUDON

The notions of *explanation* and *interpretation* have several meanings in the social sciences. The word *interpretation* evokes the idea, if not of arbitrariness, at least of the interference of the subjectivity of the analyst. And it is commonly accepted that some interpretations of a given object can be incompatible with others, very different ones. In other words, various interpretations of the same object or phenomenon can coexist. An interpretation has not the ambition of telling *the* truth, but of containing *some* truth.

The idea of *explanation* implies, by contrast, an ambition to reach the truth about its object. And if different explanations are proposed of this object, they arouse the feeling that an urgent task is to determine which is best, and, if they are contradictory, to determine which is false.

Beyond the various definitions and conceptions that can be proposed of the two concepts—at the root of these definitions, so to say—one can detect, I think, such contrasted feelings: some analyses give the feeling that they are more objective and others that they are more subjective, but still interesting and valid. We tend to call the first ones explanations and the second ones interpretations. The points that I would like to make are:

1. That interpretations play an important role in actual researches and analyses

2. That they can have a heuristic value and are intelligibility function

3. But that they are very often taken or presented as explanations, though for understandable reasons

4. So that an important task of the philosophy of the social sciences is to try to make the distinction as clear as possible

5. That, while recognizing the importance of interpretations in actual research processes, the final objective is always explanation.

THE NATURE OF EXPLANATION IN THE SOCIAL SCIENCES

As I said earlier, there are several definitions of the notion of explanation. There is, for instance, the Hempelian nomological conception,[1] according to which, to explain a phenomenon M means subsuming this phenomenon under a "covering law." If M is observed in a society, if A is also observed, and if I have at my disposal a "covering law" of which I would be convinced such as "if A, then M," M would be explained by this covering law.

I will not discuss this theory of explanation which, it seems to me, does not capture the nature of explanation in the social sciences. A much more general and useful definition is the following one, which I would qualify as neo-Weberian : Weberian, because it is clearly inspired by Weber's methodological writings and neo (Weberian) because Weber never presented it, to my opinion, in the analytical fashion in which I present it myself. This theory of explanation can also be qualified as "individualistic" since it considers any social phenomenon as the product of individual actions, behaviors, or attitudes and that understanding why the actors had such behaviors or attitudes is a crucial moment in the analysis.[2]

This neo-Weberian conception of explanation can be summarized in the following way. Suppose we want to explain a given phenomenon, say M. To explain M means :

1. Making the phenomenon M the aggregate outcome of a number of individual actions m, *i.e.*, showing that M is produced by the behaviors or attitudes of a number of individual actors; in mathematical symbols: $M = f(m)$.

2. Showing that the action or attitudes of the actors can be understood given the social environment S of the actors; this is the famous Weberian notion of Verstehen : $m = g(S)$.

3. Eventually showing that the situation S or the social environment of the actors, or rather that such and such characteristics

of this environment are the effect of such and such factors, say P, located at the level of the system: $S = h(P)$.

In order to illustrate this theory of explanation, I will consider two examples borrowed from sociology. The first is taken from Tocqueville's *Old Regime*, a piece of comparative sociology, since a large part of it can be held as an attempt to explain a list of differences between the French and the British societies in the 18th Century.

One of these differences is the underdevelopment of the French agricultural system at a time where the British agriculture becomes modern. This is puzzling since the Physiocrats have a great influence among the French political elites at that time.

Tocqueville's explanation of the difference follows the typical individualistic theory of explanation, which I have described above. Because of the high degree of "administrative centralization" (P), the French landlords are not in the same situation (S) as the British ones. As a consequence of P, the public offices are more numerous in France. Also, because of the centralization, every civil servant may consider himself a part of the central power. Consequently, power, prestige, and influence are attached to the public offices to a larger extent in France than in Britain. And, as the public offices are sold by the Crown and represent for the latter an important source of income, an inflationary spiral is created: both the supply and the demand of offices increases. On the whole, the landlords are strongly incited to buy public offices (they have the resources to do so); public offices are available; and rewards are associated to them; so, as an outcome of the structure of the environment (S), they buy public offices, they leave their land and get settled in the next city, while tenants take care of the land. As the landlords are not motivated to increase the productivity of their land, and as the tenants have not the capacity of doing so, as an aggregate outcome $f(m)$, the agricultural system remains underdeveloped in comparison to the British one.

Another macroscopic factor, say P, reinforces these effects: in the long historical process during which the Crown reinforced its power over the society, the cities had long been centers of resistance. For this reason, they had been able to keep a number of privileges, such as tax privileges. There was no income tax in the cities in the 18th Century. This circumstance reinforced the other factors generating landlord absenteeism.

Thus, Tocqueville explains the macroscopic feature represented by the differential development of agriculture in Britain and France as the aggregate outcome of the behavior of the landlords. And he makes this behavior understandable, in the Weberian sense, by relating it to what I called the structure of their situation, while the structure of the situation is explained by such macroscopic factors as the tax privileges of the cities or the administrative centralization.

I will consider briefly the Tocquevillian analysis of another difference between Britain and France in the 18th Century in order to suggest that the above formula, $M = f\{g[h(P)]\}$ summarizes adequately not only one but most of the *explanations* developed by Tocqueville.

This difference deals with the style of the French political philosophy as compared to the British one. The question is important since a great deal of the intellectual production at that time takes the form of political philosophy. Now, while the British political philosophy, says Tocqueville, is more concrete, pragmatic, and reformist, the French one tends to be abstract, utopian, and radical. While the former insists on the spontaneous mechanisms of social control, which develop within the society, the latter tends to locate this control almost exclusively at the level of the State. Why is that so?

Tocqueville's explanation takes here the same form as above—because of the higher degree of administrative centralization in France, the French political philosophers have the impression that everything in the society is dependent on the State. Moreover, as the State is centralized, the real power is perceived as located in the last instance at the central level. The visibility of the State has the consequence that it is perceived by the French political philosophers as the main, if not as the only, collective actor endowed with power.

Of course, the structure of what we would call their role as they perceived it incited the political philosophers to present their ideas in a universal fashion, without any reference to any concrete society. But, suggests Tocqueville, while they wrote about the state or about the society in general, they had in mind the singular society within which they lived. Moreover, they could expect to draw an influence from their theories to the extent where these theories, although dealing with the eternal and universal problems of political philosophy, were perceived by their audience as related to the singular social and political context characteristic of this audience. Moreover, by deriving their proposals of political change from universal theories, they could expect to give them a greater strength and influence.

To these circumstances, Tocqueville adds the fact—which is more controversial—that the French philosophers had, in general, less often than the British, a direct experience of the public affairs, since the real decision centers were limited to the narrow political circles surrounding the King. At any rate, all these circumstances incited the French philosophers to describe and conceive the society as regulated and dominated by the state, and to promote the radical view of an equal participation of all to the power of the state.

Again, in this piece of analysis—belonging to what we could call the sociology of knowledge—Tocqueville explains a macroscopic difference by making it the outcome of actions (in this case, these actions take the form of the production of political theories). And these actions are interpreted as *understandable* given the social and political context surrounding the actors, given also the structure of their role, and the perception that they had "naturally", so to say, of the relationships between the state and the society, etc.

In sum, what we have here in Tocqueville's *Old Regime* is a good example of the "individualistic" theory of explanation: various macroscopic features are explained as the outcome of actions. These actions of the ideal-typical actors (*e.g.*, the landlords, the philosophers) are considered as *understandable* given the context, and in that sense as *rational*.

Let us now turn to our second example: Weber's article on *the protestant sects in America*.[3] Already the topic of this short but brilliant paper is worth consideration. Those sociologists committed to a nomological theory of explanation, Comte and Durkheim for instance, had claimed that with the increase in the division of labor, the traditional religions would loose their power of attraction: industrialization (modernization) would produce a laicization effect. In general, very skeptical about the validity of nomological statements in the social sciences, Weber was possibly attracted by the case of the U.S. partly because they were a live refutation of the commonsense law-like statement on the effects of modernization on laicization: in this highly modern industrialized society, protestantism appeared as lively as ever.

The explanation of the vitality of protestantism in America takes the form of a model following the individualistic theory of explanation. To begin with, Weber lists in a very sketchy and abstract fashion some major macroscopic differences between the American society and the two European societies, which he implicitly (and in many incidental remarks explicitly) compares to the latter throughout, *i.e.*, the German and the French societies. In the U.S., social and geographic mobility are greater, ethnic heterogeneity is greater, the stratification system is less rigid, and the stratification symbols are less visible and less marked than in France or Germany. The French have their *légion d'honneur* and the Germans make great use of their academic titles, for instance. As far as the religious system is concerned, while *churches* prevail in France or Germany, the American protestantism takes the form of *sects*, for reasons historically easy to explain.

In my symbols, this list of factors describe the explanatory macroscopic factors P. While the U.S. is P with respect to these factors, Germany or France are, say, P.'

The next stage in the analysis, as I reconstruct it here, is to show that P and P' will respectively create distinct situations, say S(P) and S'(P') for the categories of actors relevant with regard to the objective of the analysis.

These categories are two in Weber's analysis: those in charge of the protestant sects, and those willing to make business with one another.

As far as the latter are concerned, the factors P make that in the U.S. it is more difficult for two persons (say A and B, who wish to make business with one another) to know whether they can have confidence in their potential partner. Firstly, because of the greater mobility in the U.S., they are less likely to know one another: previous familiarity is less likely to provide indicators of the degree of trustworthiness of the partner. Secondly, because of the weaker visibility of status symbols, the latter will not be as easily usable as in France or Germany. In other words, P creates a demand for symbols, for signals whereby A and B would know whether they can have a sufficient degree of confidence toward one another before embarking in a business relationship which, given the complexity of the economic system, will in many cases include effects delayed over time. Such a demand exists also in the European societies, but the factors P' make sure that it is more likely satisfied, either by previous knowledge or by the use of stratification symbols.

This demand will now be naturally met on the supply side by the protestant sects. Firstly, because the elites of the country are much more than proportionally protestant, so that "being protestant" can easily in many occasions work as a positive *label* (this word is not Weber's). Secondly, the competition among sects is a favorable factor. By imposing high-entry costs, those in charge of a given sect can 1) increase the resources of the sect, 2) test the economic liability of their members, 3) hope to increase the value of the certificate of honorability they grant to their members and also, by the same token, 4) increase the influence of the sect. In other words, the general conditions P reinforce the competition between the protestant sects: the more influential are those that are able to deliver their certificates of honorability to a high cost. With amusement, Weber notes that if the costs of entry in the Lutheran church had been as high in Germany as in America, there would be possibly no Lutherans in Germany any more.

Thus, P creates a situation h(P), which generates a demand g(S) from the part of those who want to enter into a business relationship with one another. This demand is met by a supply provided by actors who, given the conditions P, can be considered as natural suppliers, those in charge of the protestant sects. On the whole, P generates the macroscopic phenomenon, which constitutes the object of the analysis, *i.e.* the vitality of protestantism in the U.S.

The two above examples illustrate to my opinion the theory of explanation, which I called earlier the individualistic or the neo-Weberian theory of explanation. It can be useful to summarize its main features, starting from our two examples.

1. In this theory, explaining any phenomenon, say M, amounts to showing that it is the outcome of actions, that these actions can be made understandable given the social environment of the actors, *i.e.*, the structure of the situation within which they move. As to the structure of the situation, it has to be explained as the product of some variables defined at the level of the system.

2. The explanation takes the form of a *model, i.e.*, of a deductive system resting upon highly simplifying assumptions. Relevant categories of actors are defined—in small number generally, and these actors are provided with simple motivations. In the same way, the structure of the situation of action is characterized by a few features.

3. The social actors are supposed to be rational—given the context within which they move. But this is only another way of saying that in principle any observer who would know the situation of the actor could conclude, "I could have easily done the same thing as he did, if I had been in the same situation." Rationality here is entirely coextensive to Weber's notion of *Verstehen*, which can be reworded by the notion of situation-bound rationality.

4. Among the objections raised against the individualistic paradigm, one is very frequent: that it cannot easily be used with macroscopic analysis. The examples show that this is not the case, since both Tocqueville and Weber were concerned in these examples with macroscopic questions. The individualistic approach becomes compatible with macroscopic analysis as soon as it is perceived that it uses highly simplifying assumptions built up into a model. The three main pieces of Weber's methodology, models (ideal-types), rationality of action *(Verstehen)*, and individualism are organically related to one another.

5. Because of these simplifying assumptions, the question is raised as to the validity of the model. This question is implicitly solved in the individualistic definition of explanation in a fashion, which I would (anachronistically) qualify as Popperian: a model is considered as valid if it succeeds in explaining a number of observational data. Tocqueville's analyses in the *Old Regime* are still considered important and valid possibly because, starting from the simple notion of "administrative centralization," he was able to explain a number of differences between France and Britain in a parsimonious fashion, and because his microsociological assumptions meet the Weberian *Verstehen* criterion. Thus, the assumptions on the motivations of the landlords or of the *philosophes* can be easily considered as understandable. In summary, a model is valid if it meets the Weberian *verstehen*-criterion and the Popperian criteria.

6. The individualistic theory of explanation is general: it can be applied, as already mentioned, to phenomena located at all scales—small groups, organizations, and also, say, national societies. Moreover, as the two examples sufficiently suggest, it can be applied to any kind of phenomena. By some of its aspects Tocqueville's analysis belong to the sociology of knowledge, by others to economic sociology. And it can be applied to any kind of society.

This latter point is important, since it is often contended that the individualistic theory of explanation can be used in the case of "individualistic" modern societies, but not in the case of "traditional" societies. This criticism rests on a confusion, however—a confusion between the methodological and the sociological-ethical meaning of the word "individualism." In a traditional society, in a *Gemeinschaft* in the sense of Tönnies, the individuals are generally more closely interdependent on one another than in a *Gesellschaft*. In this sense, the autonomy of the individuals is weaker. But this does not say in any fashion that the phenomena, which occur in such social systems, should not be analyzed as the outcome of individual behaviors.

To sum up:

1. A good *explanation* in the social sciences (I have taken my examples from sociology but I could have taken them from other disciplines as well) is a theory of the type $M = \{g[h(P)]\}$.

2. Where all the statements m(S) are *understandable*, that is, where all the statements on the reasons as to why the actors behaved as they behaved, thought as they thought, *etc.*, can be (at least in principle) easily accepted by any analyst.

3. And where the number of data that the theory brings together is so important that it evokes the impression that it would be very

hard to find an alternative theory, which would explain the same set
of data. In that sense, the theory arouses the feeling that it is "true,"
although it can rest, here as in any *model*, on very simplifying and
rough assumptions.

The two examples are good explanation in the sense that both
use easily testable microscopic statements. And both succeed in *bringing*
together numerous data. Tocqueville's theory explains why French
philosophers were more abstract and radical, why they gave more
importance to the State, why French agriculture was underdeveloped,
and also (I did not develop this point) why the distribution of the
French cities was different from the distribution of the British cities.
In the same way, Weber brings together a number of differential
data on stratification, mobility, the organization of religious life, and
its vitality.

INTERPRETATION AS WEAK EXPLANATION

Very often the interpretation proposed for such and such phenomenon
M can be called a *weak explanation* in the sense that: 1) it corresponds
to the above definition of the structure of explanation: in other words
the form of the analysis is $M = f \{g[h(P)]\}$; 2) but the explanation is
weak because, either the microscopic statements m(S) are weakly credible or seem to be introduced precisely to explain M, in an *ad hoc*
or *post factum* fashion; 3) or because the theory f{ } connects a small
number of facts or features, so that it does not arouse the feeling
that it would be difficult to find an alternative theory.

This tentative definition actually characterizes many theories in
the social sciences, to my opinion at least. As in the case of explanation,
it may be useful to illustrate the definition by some examples. Curiously
enough, the success of a theory in the social sciences is sometimes
due less to its degree of validity, *i.e.*, less to the fact that it is a theory
stricto sensu or an explanation in the strong sense rather than a weak
explanation, than to many other factors. The case of Weber is interesting. The example drawn from Weber, which I have presented
above, is little known and it is seldom considered as one of Weber's
major works, although it is an explanation in the strong sense. By
contrast, the *Protestant Ethic* is a very well-known work, although it
is rather an interpretation or an explanation in the weak sense.[4]

Weber's thesis in the *Protestant Ethic* is well-known. It can be
summarized very briefly and roughly in the following way: As the
protestants (or rather the Calvinists) believe in the predestination
doctrine, they are incited to look for this-worldly signs of their eventual

other-worldly election; so they will value achievement and success in their this-worldly activities—for this success will likely be interpreted as a sign of election; they will invest rather than consume; they will be obsessed by the desire of success and achievement.

Weber's theory is presented in a more subtle way than I present it here. He stresses the fact that he does not propose a theory of the development of capitalism, but of the congeniality between the spirit of capitalism and the spirit of Calvinism-Puritanism. He devised the theory to explain why the Calvinists seemed to have played an eminent role in the development of capitalism by the 16th Century and after. And the congeniality between Calvinism and capitalism is the answer: because of their *need for achievement*—this need being itself the product or the effect of the belief in the predestination dogma—the Calvinists and Puritans were more interested than others in undertaking, investing, and taking risks.

Even during Weber's time, many objections were raised against this theory. Thus, Sombart noticed that many capitalist entrepreneurs of the 16th Century were Jews or Catholics. Others noticed that capitalist entrepreneurs had been numerous by 15th Century, before Calvinism was born. But above all, the connection that Weber saw between the belief in the predestination dogma and the need for achievement appeared to many people—and is still widely perceived—as unconvincing:[5] why should this-worldly achievements be necessarily interpreted as a sign of election? In other words, why should my anxiety with regard to my other-worldly destiny incite me to make business or to look for this-worldly success?

So, Weber's theory is weak with regard to the microscopic statements it incorporates. Paradoxically enough, it does not really meet the *Verstehen* criterion, which Weber himself considered as fundamental: the psychological reconstruction of the states of mind of the Calvinist is unconvincing and has a flavor or arbitrariness. In other words, it is hard to conclude by projection: "If I had believed in the predestination dogma, I would certainly—or likely—have felt a need for achievement and for this-worldly success more strongly that if I had not believed in the dogma."

But the same theory is weak also because the facts, which it brings into relationship with one another, are very few and rather vague. The theory explains only why the Calvinists played a particularly important role in the development of capitalism.

I think Weber's celebrated theory on the protestant ethic is an excellent example of what I call a weak explanation or an interpretation. As any good interpretation, it gives the feeling both that the interpretation is *interesting*, that it contains (eventually) some truth, but also that it contains a part of arbitrariness, that it reveals the subjectivity of its author, and that alternative interpretations could be offered.

Weber's work on the protestant ethic is probably one of the best-known pieces of research in the social sciences, and one of the most influential. Why is that so, given that this theory is a weak explanation or an interpretation rather than a strong explanation?

The first reason is that it raised a question, which had not been raised before. All kinds of theories had been developed before Weber on the birth and expansion of capitalism. But none of these available theories gave the weakest hint as to the causes of the overrepresentation of Calvinists among the capitalist entrepreneurs. And the question itself was interesting, since it suggested that economic processes could be placed under the control of religious attitudes and values, provided at least the answer—as this is actually the case in Weber's theory—suggested that the overrepresentation of Calvinists indicated the existence of a causal relationship between calvinism and capitalism.

So, what we have here is an important theory. It is important for both scientific and epistemological or even metaphysical reasons. It raised questions, which existing theories on the development of capitalism were all unable to answer: why the overrepresentation of Calvinists among capitalists? Why the economic success of the countries under strong Calvinist influence? Moreover, these questions were not mere questions of curiosity. It suggested that economic processes could not be exclusively explained in the usual "materialistic" fashion, where values are treated as dependent variables.

This classical example shows that weak explanations (interpretations) can play a very important role in the development of research—even though they are weak explanations.

In fact, Weber's weak explanation raised an important and new question: it opened and enlarged the dominant materialistic paradigm predominantly used in the analysis of economic processes, and it gave birth to important currents of research: 1) researchers trying to show the role of values in social development in such and such context; 2) researchers trying to complement, to refute, or to make more precise the original theory of Max Weber.

I will try to clarify the second point. As a matter of fact, the discussion of Weber's weak explanation or interpretation led after some time to a *strong explanation*. This process is rather typical: it shows that interpretations are often a preliminary form of a scientifically more acceptable or valid explanation. In other words, the process from weak explanations or interpretations to strong explanations shows one of the function of interpretation: they are often essential in starting a rational discussion, which eventually will produce a strong explanation.

I will illustrate this point by comparing very briefly Weber's original theory with Trevor Roper's *explanation* (which probably would never have existed without Weber's interpretation).[6]

The initial question is, again, why were the capitalist entrepreneurs of the 16th and 17th Century so often Calvinists? Weber's theory does not explain why many others were Jews (in Cologne for instance); it does not explain why there were many Catholic entrepreneurs in the 15th Century already. To meet this difficulty, Weber treated them as *adventurers,* but this is of course a purely verbal solution. It does not explain—and is even contradictory to the fact— that capitalism in the 16th Century was more developed in England than in Scotland; that 17th-Century Milan, where the Calvinist influence had been strong, declined economically, while Venice, which had remained Catholic, became more and more prosperous; it does not explain why the Calvinist entrepreneurs active in Geneva were never born in Geneva; and why the same was true of the main Calvinist areas: Calvinist entrepreneurs active in the Netherlands, in German Palatinate were practically never born there.

The Trevor Roper theory is simply the following: in the early 16th Century the business circles were very enthusiastic about Erasmus von Rotterdam. It is not hard to *understand* (in the Weberian sense) why. Erasmus' message was that, according to the Gospel, doing one's business in this world with seriousness, with the will of success and achievement, was a way of serving the glory of God. In a society where the Catholic ideology claimed that prayer was the only way of honoring God, and where the businessmen were considered second-class citizens (useful but without dignity) the message of Erasmus was well accepted by the economic elite. So, many businessmen became Erasmian. Later, the Calvinist message took much from Erasmus. Of course, while Erasmus had been only a "humanist" (an "intellectual" in our words)—though an incredibly influential one—Calvin founded a militant church and a State. Thus, when the Counter Reformation came, the older Erasmian entrepreneurs and businessmen (themselves or their followers) became Calvinists. In a time of tension the militant character of the Calvinist Church was very useful.

Now, under the pressure of the Counter Reformation, many businessmen emigrated toward warmer waters: the Calvinists from Antwerp went to Amsterdam, others went to Geneva, or to the Scandinavian-Lutheran kingdoms. This explains why the bankers in Sweden and Denmark are Calvinists and not Lutherans—they were immigrants. And the entrepreneurs from Flanders who had remained

Catholic emigrated also—from Liege to Cologne for instance. As regards the entrepreneurs who remained in the countries that were exposed to the pressure of the Counter Reformation, they urged their children to turn to the professions, which were highly valued in the Counter Reformation society or to become civil servants of officers rather than to keep the old business. For this reason Milan declined in spite of the strong Calvinist influence, since Milan was strongly exposed to the Counter Reformation.

This theory of Trevor Roper is to me a *strong explanation* in the sense that not only the relationships between Calvinism and business, but also an impressive number of data unexplained by Weber's theory or even contradictory with it is explained by this theory. Thus, with Trevor Roper's explanation it is no longer necessary to assume that the 15th-Century entrepreneurs were more adventurers. This undesirable idea was introduced by Weber to reinforce his main causal assumptions: that Calvinism had created a new type of man oriented toward asceticism, achievement, and search of this-worldly success. On the whole, the Trevor Roper theory explains an important number of observational data (among others the fact that businessmen were often Calvinists) with the help of a set of easily acceptable microscopic statements: it is easily understandable, for instance, that the 16th-Century businessmen were attracted by Erasmus and then by Calvin; and it is also easily understandable that many of them tried to move when the Counter Reformation came; and that when they did not emigrate, they adapted their ambitions and activities to the values of the Counter-Reformation societies, contributing by so doing to the decline of business in these societies.

I spent some time on this example because: 1) It illustrates well the contrast (hard to clarify completely at an analytical level) between strong and weak explanations or between interpretation and explanation. 2) It shows that weak explanation is often (and maybe in most cases) the modality in which important new questions are dealt with. 3) If the weak explanation is interesting for one reason or another (and this example shows that these reasons can be metaphysical as well as scientific), it can lead along a more-or-less linear process to a strong explanation. 4) The example also shows the contrast a) between a theory that uses difficultly acceptable microscopic statements and a theory that meets in this respect the *Verstehen* criterion; and b) between a theory that relates only a few facts with one another to a theory that relates the facts of an important set of observational data to one another.

Modern examples, similar in their structure to Weber's theories could easily be found. Thus, Lipset[7] in a famous comparative study noted that social mobility appeared as very similar in most European countries, in North America, and in Japan. This finding attracted a great deal of attention since it was expected that mobility would appear as greater in the U.S. or in the Scandinavian countries, say, than in France or Germany, because of historical, sociological, or political factors. As in the case of Weber, Lipset starts from a fact that appears puzzling since it seems to as contradict most impressions. At any rate, current theories on mobility were unable to explain it.

To solve this puzzle, Lipset proposed a theory, which is typically an interpretation or a weak explanation:[8] in countries where stratification is less marked, the possibilities of climbing the social ladder are greater, but the motivation to do so is smaller, since the symbolic rewards of being higher on the scale are smaller. Thus, less stratification would produce two effects of opposite sign. This would explain why in countries where stratification is less visible and less important socially, mobility is not greater.

This is typically an explanation: a macroscopic variable P/P' (rigidity and visibility of the stratification system) creates different types of situations $h(P)/h(P')$. But the assumption can be made that $h(P)$ and $h'(P')$ create different amounts of motivations toward mobility $m(S)/m'(S')$, with the result that the differences in motivations and in objective opportunities can compensate one another. But the explanation is also a *weak* explanation or an interpretation. Firstly because the microscopic statements, though plausible, are not more plausible than statements that would be contradictory with them. Thus, Tocqueville has suggested[9] that when the social distances between classes tend to dwindle, envy and the motivation to climb is enhanced. Secondly, because the microscopic statements appear as *ad hoc*—as devised exclusively to explain the puzzle. Thirdly, because, while differential mobility is certainly affected by an important number of factors, the theory takes into account and relates exclusively two features (rigidity of stratification and rates of mobility). Finally, because a rate of mobility is certainly not only the result of the will of the individuals to move.

As in the case of Weber's theory, Lipset's interpretation has produced a continuous flow of researches: empirical researches, theories, and methodological works—with the result that today strong explanations can be mentioned in this area of research.[10]

Another example of *interpretations* would be the analyses proposed by many sociologists of the student movement in the sixties. Thus, according to one theory, the student would have seen that, given the importance of information and communication in modern societies, college graduates would become the most vital production force in these societies. But, because of their number, they would have no access to social power and influence. In other words, they would have the knowledge, but not the power. Hence a feeling of frustration, a temptation to reject "the society" and a kind of Saint-Simonian conviction that power and influence are illegitimately retained by those "who do not know." This type of theory, which is very typical of the structure of many theories proposed by the social sciences, is well an explanation of structure $M = f\{g[h(P)]\}$ but the explanation is weak because of the *ad hoc* and only plausible character of the microstatements it uses, and because the facts and features related to one another are both vague and scarce.

Very often it is asserted that interpretations in the sense I give this expression here are more typical of the soft social sciences like sociology and less typical of the harder ones like economics. The view that economics would be harder is often founded on the facts that mathematical models are more numerous in economics than in sociology. But mathematics in no way guarantees that we are closer to explanation than to interpretation. A good mathematical model can correspond to a weak explanation, as well as a good verbal theory can represent a strong explanation. Let us recall Tocqueville and Weber's examples on the protestant sects.

In fact, weak explanations are very often produced by the hasty application of a model to a complex reality. Let us consider an example. In West Bengal—as in many other places—in spite of the efforts made by the Indian administration to convince the peasants to increase their productivity, the peasants stubbornly refuse to adopt the innovations proposed. The economist Bhaduri proposed a sophisticated and interesting model to *explain* this resistance.[11] The rejection of the innovation would be the consequence of the production relationships in this society. These relationships are "semi-feudal" in the sense that:

1. They are not feudal *stricto sensu* since the tenants sell their labor force to the landlord freely on the labor market;

2. They are, however, feudal since the tenant's income being below the subsistence level, they have to borrow money to survive. Because of their poverty, they have no access to the banks, and so they borrow money from the landlord, and are consequently in a state of permanent indebtedness towards him.

Given these conditions, will the landlord accept an innovation to the effect of augmenting his productivity? To answer the question, Bhaduri builds the following model:

(1) $Z_t = aX_t + (1+i)(C_{t-1} - Y_{t-1})$

This first equation says that the income 3t of the landlord at time t, has two components: he gets a part a of the value X_t of the crop at time t, this part a being fixed by his contract with the tenant. But he also gets the interest of the sum he has lent to his tenant the previous year. This sum is $C_{t-1} - Y_{t-1}$ the difference between the consumption $(_{t-1})$ of the tenant the previous year and his income $(_{t-1})$ also the previous year. And at the beginning of year, t, the landlord, also gets back the money he has lent the previous year.

(2) $Y_t = (1-a)X_t - (1+i) (C_{t-1}) - Y_{t-1})$

This second equation gives the income of the tenant at the beginning of of year t: he gets his part $(1-a)X_t$ of the value of the crop, but has to refund the capital borrowed the previous year plus the interest.

Suppose the system is in an equilibrium or reproduction state; so that, if no element were changed, neither in the system itself, nor in its environment,

(3) $Y_{t-1} = Y_{t\,=\,Yt+1} = \ldots = Y^*$

$Z_{t-1} = Z_t = Z_{t+1} = \ldots = Z^*$

the adoption of the innovation proposed by the administration would have the effect of increasing the value of the crop from X to X $+\Delta X$. Of course, this increase would destroy the equilibrium (3). But, interestingly enough, for large sets of values of the parameters (and even if the tenant's marginal propensity to consume is high) the new equilibrium will be less favorable to the landlord than the original one: Even if the effect of the innovation on the productivity level is low (and also, of course, if it is high), and even if the marginal propensity of the tenant to consume his additional income is high, the increase in the tenant's income can reduce his indebtedness in such a way that, at the new equilibrium, the landlord will loose the benefit of the increase in the value of the crop. This effect is likely to appear for large areas of the parametric space, as the mathematical analysis of the model shows. Now, the landlord does not know at which point of the parametric space the *game* is actually located (since he ignores notably the value of the tenant's marginal propensity to consume, which would only be revealed if the innovation were adopted). Consequently he will hesitate before adopting the innovation: as a matter of fact, he could possibly be worse off than better off if he adopted the innovation. So, why adopt it?

This brilliant explanation is a weak explanation, however. The microscopic statements included in the model are acceptable and do not appear as far-fetched nor as *ad hoc*. So, the weakness is not located at this level, but rather at the level of the set of empirical data included in the theory. This set, as in most weak explanation, is very poor. In fact only two pieces of information are taken into account: 1) the semi-feudal organization of the production relationships, 2) the rejection of innovation.

The model "shows" that (1) tends to generate (2). If it were interpreted without caution, one could derive from it a conditional law: if (1), then (2). And this "covering law" would explain why (2) is observed when (1) is also present. This is exactly what Bhaduri does here: his model leads to the "covering law:" if (1), then (2). Now (2) is observed in West Bengal, as well as (1). Hence, (2) has to be explained by (1).

A difficulty comes however from the fact that in many systems with semi-feudal relationships, as many historical data show, innovations have been adopted. In other words, the theory would be convincing if we had much more information on the situation under examination. The model assumes implicitly that the landlord has the exclusive power of deciding whether the innovation should be adopted or not. This is, of course, not so, and obviously more likely for some innovations than for others. The landlord is more likely to have the monopoly of the decision power if the innovation implies an investment in capital than if it bears on the organization of the workers teams or on the working methods. The model also assumes that the landlords are not in competition with one another. It assumes that none of them considers deriving an advantage from the fact that, if he would adopt the proposed innovation, he could sell his rice at a lower price on the market and, by so doing, derive from the sale a larger income. Nor do the landlords fear that the others adopt the innovation and by so doing threaten their part of the market. All these assumptions are, of course, not *necessary*. In other words, the model assumes a huge number of implicit assumptions, which are neither justified nor explained. If these assumptions were dropped, the model would not no longer be valid, and the conclusion as to the rejection of innovation could not be maintained.

The model brings us into an ideal, abstract world where the landlords have the total power of decision, where they do not compete with one another, where the administration (although it has an interest in fighting poverty) never thinks of giving the tenants an access to the banking system, *etc.* Why is that so? The model does not explain it at all. It contains only two points of the reality, which it wants to explain: 1) the rejection of the proposed innovations, and 2) the semi-feudal structure of the production relationships.

So that we do not know to what extent the abstract world portrayed by the model can be considered as an adequate picture of the real one, it has the ambition to explain. Consequently, although the model is interesting, we do not have the feeling that it would be difficult to devise another very different explanation which would explain the same data as well. In fact, it is hard to see why the simple idea that it is sometimes very difficult to bring peasants to abandon practices which they have used for generations would not be as well a candidate to the explanation of the rejection of the innovation. The idea is obviously less sophisticated. But this does not say that it is less true.

The situation illustrated by the previous example is very frequent in the social sciences, in economics as well as in sociology, political science or olemography. The process of explanation is the following:

1. A model M is devised or used. This model says, for instance, that when P appears, Q should also appear.

2. Although the model includes all kinds of implicit assumptions founding its validity, these assumptions are often ill-perceived, not perceived at all, neglected, or forgotten.

3. If the model is original, or sophisticated, or convincing as far as the abstract world designed by the implicit assumptions is concerned, it will have a strong conviction power: it will tend to be perceived as generally true or valid independent of the assumptions under which it is valid.

4. Because of these psychological processes—in a real world where both P and Q are present—M will likely be considered a valid and convincing explanation of Q.

5. M will only be a *weak* explanation (or an interpretation), however, since P and Q will be the only points of contact between the model and the real world under examination.

Many other examples can be given of this typical process. Very briefly, I will consider some examples taken from the economic theory of development.

In the fifties and sixties, a certain model was very popular and it has been politically very influential: Nurkse's theory of the vicious circle of proverty.[12] This theory says that if a country is poor, it will likely remain poor for the following reasons:

1. Poverty implies weak saving capacities.

2. Without savings no investments are possible.

3. In the absence of investments, productivity remains stagnant.

4. If productivity does not increase, the standard of living remains stagnant.

5. Hence, poverty reproduces itself.

This theory (law or rather model) attracted much attention. It is easy to understand why: each of its statements is a quasi-analytical one: true, the saving capacities in a poor country are low; true, investment is impossible in the absence of savings, *etc.* Thus, the model has an intrinsic strength of conviction. Moreover, it can be connected to the real world though in a very loose fashion.

But a little reflection shows that this model, in spite of its apparently analytical character, implies an important set of assumptions, which have to be satisfied in order for the model to be valid. Thus, a country can be poor and still include in its population an elite of people with saving capacities. If this is the case, the model does not apply, unless additional assumptions are introduced. The model implies also a closed economic system without international exchanges. Otherwise, the country could take benefit, say, from the increases in productivity outside. Also, productivity can increase without investments in physical capital. This eventuality of crucial importance is tacitly excluded from the model. Thus, when the theory of the vicious circle is applied to any real society, it has always the character of a weak explanation, of an interpretation. Without further information and analysis, it is difficult to give the theory a high credibility.

Because of its strong intrinsic conviction power, the theory has nevertheless been viewed as a convincing explanation of the stagnation, not only of such and such society in particular, but of the reproduction of underdevelopment in general.

The case of the *theory of dependency* is in many respects similar and in others different.[13] The theory of dependency says that the relationship of interdependency between the "peripheral" countries and the countries of the "center" turns always into a relationship of dependency to the disadvantage of the "periphery" and to the advantage of the "center." This theory does not have the logic nor the same strength of conviction as the theory of the vicious circle. It could not be put, as in the case of the latter theory, into a mathematical model. But it has a strong force. The lightest historical observation shows, however, that interdependency can turn as well to the advantage as to the disadvantage of the central as well as of the peripherical partner. The dependency model is also a model resting on an important set of implicit assumptions. When it is applied to any society in particular, it will always represent a weak explanation.

Or take the theory of the size of the markets—also a popular theory in the field of the economics of development. When the markets are fragmented and small, the entrepreneurs will not be incited to increase their productivity and notably to invest in physical capital since they see that they will not be able to sell many additional units of their product. Here again the model is almost analytical, and as such, produces a high level of conviction. Consequently, the contitional law to which it leads (i.e. with fragmented markets, no development), has a chance to be perceived as a law of universal validity, characterized by the same degree of inexorability as the natural laws. So that if a country is characterized both by 1) economic stagnation and 2) fragmented markets, the "covering law" drawn from the pseudo-analytical model will tend to be considered as a sufficient explanation. It will be a weak explanation, however, since the model rests as all models of this type on a high number of implicit assumptions, and is analytical only in the appearance.

FINAL REMARKS

First of all, it should be clear that the word interpretation (as explanation) has many meanings. If it describes operations of research and analysis, which I have qualified here as weak explanations, it also describes operations of a different nature.

Let us take an example: in his *Kultur der Renaissance in Italien,* Burckhardt is struck, as are many historians, by the new world that was born in Italy in the 15th Century. In his book he tries to qualify this new world, to find a label, a concept characterizing the extraordinary originality of the culture of the Renaissance. And he tries to show that the common feature that would best characterize this culture is "individualism." This operation, which consists in covering a huge number of facts and features by a label or by a concept, is typical of the social sciences. To characterize it, Weber used the notion of ideal-type (in one of the two senses where he uses this notion, since he uses it also in the sense of our modern concept of model), since the conceptualization process does not follow the customary inductive process classically described by the logicians. This procedure which consists in building ideal-types or, as Lazarsfeld said,[14] "matrix formulas" can also be called an operation of interpretation.

When Ruth Benedict speaks of the *Appolonian* and the *Dionysian* cultures, she also proposes an interpretation, and here the interpretation consists in building matrix formulas. The same could be said of Tönnies' distinction between *Gemeinschaft* and *Gesellschaft,* of Durkheim's *anomie,* of Marx's alienation, *etc.* In other words, one form of interpretation, crucial in the development of all social sciences, is this concept and type-building process, which these examples illustrate. This sense of the notion of interpretation would be worth a long discussion, which I cannot undertake here.

In this essay, I have essentially tried to suggest that the distinction between explanation and interpretation also corresponds to the dis-

tinction between strong and weak explanation. Explaining a phenomenon M, in the social sciences, is always to my opinion making M a
function M {g=[h(P)]}. In some cases, one has the impression 1) that
the microscopic statements m(S) are convincing and acceptable, and
2) that the theory M { } incorporates so many observational data,
making them hold together, that the feeling is occurs that it would
be difficult to find an alternative different theory that would explain
as well the same body of data or a larger one.

When these two conditions are satisfied, we have what I propose
to call a strong explanation. Other theories have the same structure.
But, 1) either the microscopic statements m(S) appear as farfetched,
unconvincing or ad hoc; 2) of the theory M { } incorporated exclusively
a scarce set of data, eventually rough data.

In response to the above set of conditions, I propose to talk
about weak explanation or interpretation.

It is very important to distinguish at least *conceptually*—but *practically* this may be more difficult—between explanation and interpretation in that sense. One of the reasons why it is crucial to make this
distinction is that explanations in the weak sense often constitute the
core of ideologies. In other words, ideologies are often weak explanations perceived as strong explanations. I have suggested some examples of this process above: the theory of the vicious circle of poverty
or the theory of dependency have often been perceived—not as what
they actually are (as interesting models valid under a number of
assumptions)—but as theories realistically explaining the phenomenon
under examination, in that case underdevelopment.

Thus, weak explanations are often dangerous. If a theory of this
type meets either the expectations or the passions or the interests of
such and such category of social actors, it will likely be taken as a
strong explanation, as a theory proper and will lead to false prophecies,
false analyses, and/or ill-oriented collective actions.

On the other hand, as some previous examples suggest, weak
explanations often have a heuristic value and a clarification function.
They can bear important intellectual innovations and throw new light
on problems important to the progress of knowledge. Eventually they
can also be true, *i.e.*, constitute the core of a strong explanation,
which will not be contradictory to the original weak explanation.

Many confusions in the social sciences result—in my opinion—
from the fact that the distinctions I have sketchily discussed here are
not clearly perceived. The reasons why they are not would be worth
more analysis. One of these reasons is that social theories (by contrast
with natural theories) arouse passions and emotions and can serve the
interests of categories of social actors. Thus, rational criticism is more

difficultly practiced and institutionalized in the case of the social theories. On the other hand, it must be recognized that a clear distinction is not always made and accepted between such notions as *theory* and *model*. And the implicit assumptions, which restrict the validity of any model, are often not even perceived by their authors, who, evidently, can be reluctant to spend much time on a detailed reflection and account for the conditions that restrict the validity of their models.

Finally, while most of my examples deal with economics or sociology, I think the discussion introduced here is relevant to all social sciences, from history to economics. In all these sciences, the distinction between interpretation and explanation is a crucial one. In all of them, there is a tendency to treat weak explanations as though they were strong explanations. And this shift in the epistemological status of the theories produced by these sciences is a main source of confusion and of misunderstanding. Most cases of *Methodenstreit* in the social sciences, directly or indirectly, rest on the disregard of this distinction.

NOTES

1. C. Hempel, *Aspects of Scientific Explanation and Other Essays in the Philosophy of Science*, New York: The Free Press, 1965. R. Boudon, "On the underlying assumptions of some sociological theories and on their scientific consequences," *Synthese*, 24, 1972, pp. 410–430. "The three basic paradigms of macrosociology: functionalism, neo-marxism and action analysis," *Theory and Decision*, 6, 1976, pp. 381–406. G. von Wright, *Explanation and Interpretation*, London: Routledge and Kegan Paul, 1971.

2. I have discussed the importance of the neo-Weberian paradigm in the analysis of social change and development in my *La place du desordre*, Paris, Presses universitaires de France, 1984. See also "Individual action and social change," *The British Journal of Sociology*, 34, 1, 1983, pp. 1–18; "Why the theories of social change fail," *The Public Opinion Quarterly*, 57, 1983, pp. 143–160.

3. M. Weber, "The Protestant Sects and the Spirit of Capitalism," edited by H. Gerth and C. Mills in *From Max Weber*, New York: Oxford University Press, 1958, pp. 302–322.

4. M. Weber, *The Protestant Ethic and the Spirit of Capitalism*, New York and London: Allen & Unwin, 1950.

5. See notably the very hard judgment of Schumpeter on the Protestant ethic in his *Business Cycles*, New York and London: McGraw Hill, 1939.

6. H. Trevor-Roper, *Religion, the Reformation and Social Change, and Other Essays*, London: Macmillan, 1972.

7. S. Lipset and R. Bendix, *Social Mobility in Industrial Societies*, Berkeley and Los Angeles: University of California Press, 1959.

8. S. Lipset and H. Zetterberg, "A theory of social mobility," in *Transactions of the Social Third World Congress of Sociology*, Londres, 1956, pp. 155–177.

9. Notably his *Democracy in America* but also in his *Old Regime*.

10. See for this discussion R. Boudon, *Education, Inequality and Social Opportunity*, New York: Wiley, 1974.

11. A. Bhaduri, "A study of agricultural backwardness under semi-feudalism," *Economic Journal*, 83, 1976, pp. 120–137.

12. R. Nurske, *Problems of Capital Formation in Underdeveloped Countries*, Oxford: Blackwell, 1953.

13. R. Boudon, "Deux études de cas," chapter 9 *in* R. Boudon, *L'idéologie*, Paris: Fayard, 1986, pp. 247–272.14. A. Barton and P. Lazarsfeld, "Some functions of qualitative analysis in social research," edited by S. Lipset and N. Smelser in *Sociology, the Progress of a Decade*, Englewood Cliffs: Prentice Hall, 1961, pp. 95–122.

17

Comments on Boudon's Essay

ALAIN BOYER

The individualistic program of research as advocated by Raymond Boudon seems to me to be well-founded, even if it is not without difficulties. I agree with Boudon that situational analysis of unintended consequences constitutes the fundamental aim as well as the best method of the social and historical sciences. He shows that mathematical exactness is neither a necessity nor a sufficient condition of the adequacy of an explanation. One must try to explain social global effects as complex results of "rational" actions, *i.e.,* actions adapted to certain more or less demanding situations.

I nevertheless think that "understanding" can be an almost trivial matter, when one has carefully reconstructed a complex situation. Boudon seems to think that the operation called "Verstehen" is not only a heuristic device (as Hempel would say), but may be a kind of *a posteriori* check of the accuracy of the hypotheses. Every explanation is understandable if "all the statements on the reasons as to why the actors behaved as they behaved can be easily accepted by any analyst." This subjective process provides an objective test, as it were—but notice that Boudon makes it clear that this process has to be inter-subjectively checked. Yet, could we not say that this very process can be simulated by deduction of the behavior from a set of premises, including the dispositions and goals of the acting individual? True, the difficulty of "re-enacting in one's mind the process of thought" of an actor, as Collingwood would have had it, *may* nevertheless be a negative sign of the "weakness" of an explanation.

Boudon's third requirement, that an explanation endowed with great explanatory power must give "the impression that it would be very hard to find an alternative theory that would explain the same data," appears somewhat too subjective for me. Popper once said, "Whenever a theory appears to you as the only possible one, take this as a sign that you have neither understood the theory nor the problem which it was intended to solve."[1] This may sound far-fetched, but it seems to me that Popper's advice could be a regulatory principle, which is more helpful for critical discussion than Boudon's maxim. As John Watkins said *à propos* of the so-called "double-confirmation" in the social sciences, "the same conclusion can, of course, be deduced from different sets of premises, and we cannot be certain that one set of psychological assumptions is the correct set."[2] The distinction that Boudon has made amounts to identifying interpretation with "weak explanation." That is, interpretation is not an alternative to explanation, because adequate explanation in the social sciences is not nomological, but "interpretative" in the traditional sense. Boudon wishes to describe interpretations as insufficient singular explanations. His distinction is not a logical, but an epistemological value judgement.[3]

In my opinion, Boudon makes a good case in suggesting that searching for *universal* social laws only (even if they are conditionally stated) is likely to be misleading. This is because of the intrinsic difficulty of formulating laws that are both simple and true: concrete analysis of a concrete situation, as Lenin once put it, seems to be a much more realistic aim for the social science.[4] Following Boudon, sociology (properly understood) is nothing but conceptual history, as opposed to narrative history. This position undermines the traditional idea of sociology as a "nomothetic" (as opposed to an "idiographic"), science.[5] The so-called laws are nothing but statements of possibility.[6] Most of the putative laws are refuted, or valid only with the proviso of a *ceteris paribus* clause, which is hardly ever realistic and which endangers the testability of the laws. If the so-called law incorporates all the conditions of its validity, then it is likely to be tantamount to a singular model of the very situation which was to be subsumed under it. (This point had been made by W. Dray against Hempel.) The danger of interpretations is that they suggest that a general law has been discovered: in fact the *explanans* is weak precisely because it fails to explain the singularity of the case. The difference between weak and strong explanations is more a difference in degree than a difference in nature. The weak one has for Boudon some of the functions Popper attributes to a "metaphysical program of research": to raise new problems, to challenge a received view, to make it possible to re-interpret data, to promote new kinds of hypotheses. This heuristic dimension can perhaps be used as a (soft) criterion of demarcation between pseudo-explanation and weak explanation.[7] The nomological model, which is often called "the Popper-Hempel model"—even if the former doesn't consider it as a very relevant feature of historical explanations,[8] requires that every complete explanation incorporate two ingredients: universal laws, where no mention is made of any singular object, and initial conditions, stating the occurrence of certain events at certain times and places.[9] In the physical sciences, there are very informative universal laws, which "cover" the entire field of physical events. The scientistic illusion in the moral sciences, as criticized by Weber and especially by Hayek, was to wish to exhibit a set of universal statements analogous to Newtonian laws: informative rather than trivial, covering all human history, and deterministic in character. According to Popper at least, most if not all social "laws" are trivial.

Social informative laws, describing unintended recurrent effects, if there are any, must be explained away according to the principle of individualistic reconstruction. Regularities are not so much explanatory hypotheses as phenomena to be explained.

But Boudon seems not to be content with suggesting that every putative law is an oversimplification—a claim which is true but harmless. He appears also to make the stronger claim that every such law is too poor to be connected with the relevant initial conditions of any singular situation.[10] The only way of keeping up with scientific method in the social sciences and of backing a claim to truth is to concentrate on *singular* situational analysis by building one single model for every single historical question. This is his idea of sociology as an analysis of singular facts.[11] Boudon doesn't claim that finding sociological conditional laws is utterly impossible,[12] but he proposes to give up the utopian idea of a systematized theoretico-empirical sociology, in the same way as Popper proposed to renounce the utopia of a theoretical history. Yet, is it really impossible to make use of some part of one singular model to construct another one? It is not clear to me whether Boudon has conclusively shown that the logic of the situation always varies from one model to another to such a degree that nothing is left in common. If this is not the case, social sciences can be more than simply historical sciences. They have among their objects the quasi-logical sequences of events which follow, although not necessarily deterministically, from a given typical situation. Do we have to suppose that men are so different that every such sequence is a unique one? Are we committed to so strong a nominalism?

Popper somewhat vaguely speaks of the possible discovery of conditional macro-laws,[13] describing social propensities, or "the resistance of the social material to our attempts to transform it." The social engineer needs not only a lot of singular informations, but also general "technological laws" such as: it is almost impossible to have a situation of type X without making probable consequences of type Y (eventually bad ones). In his latest book, Boudon argues, rightly, that the Popperian distinction between historicist law and scientific conditional law is not clear enough to get rid of historicism.[14] He proposes to abandon the idea of a societal law,[15] with its deterministic and naturalistic flavors, on behalf of the notion of a "local model."[16]

Yet, is this distinction more effective? Are conditional laws nothing but red herrings?

As a matter of fact, in his paper first published in French,[17] Popper argued that we need no other completely universal statement in historical or sociological explanations than a minimal theory of rationality,[18] which constitutes the only common "hard core" of the social sciences, from psychopathology to anthropology (nothing is said about linguistics). The other part of the *explanans* consists of an oversimplifying *model* of the situation, including the analysis of their situation made by the agents themselves. If this model is singular, we have a historical explanation. If it is a typical one with typical initial conditions, we have a sociological model of a given degree of generality,[19] and the conclusion is a typical situational "law", which, of course, can state that in a certain condition a rational agent may take *more than one* course of action. As Max Weber saw, the more general the model, the less precise it is likely to be. In the natural sciences the opposite is the case. But does Boudon think that social scientists cannot hope to produce "semi-general" models, which would be more than heuristically fruitful instruments? If a model is refuted, its overall generality is refuted. But is it therefore impossible to explain its failure by producing a more powerful model? In other words, is the methodological "principle of correspondence" unfeasible in the social sciences? I am, of course, unable to answer these questions; yet, if one is satisfied with general models, the crucial issue seems to be the question of whether one can interpret them realistically or only as instrumental devices. Boudon is entitled to have a pragmatic answer: *çà dépend.* For instance, the game-theoretical structure called "the Prisoner's Dilemma" is used by him (not as a universal conditional law) but as an instrument, which makes it easier to understand a host of concrete situations. Yet, one can sometimes adhere to a more realistic, although not essentialist, view. As J. W. N. Watkins puts it, "The economic principles displayed by economists' models apply only to these situations that correspond with their models; but a single model may very well correspond with a very large number of historical situations widely separated in space and time."[20]

NOTES

1. K.R. Popper, 1972, *Objective Knowledge,* London: Oxford University Press, p. 266.

2. "I deal types and historical explanation" in O'Neill, ed., *Modes of Individualism and Collectivism,* London: Heinemann, p. 157.

3. One could compare this distinction with Aron's and Popper's views; according to the latter, historical interpretations are principles of selection which are metaphysical but unavoidable; cf. R. Aron, *Introduction à la philosophie de l'histoire,* Tel, Appendice III; K. Popper, *The Open Society,* II, ch. 25, London, R.K.P.

4. Cf. L. Althusser, *Contradiction et surdétermination,* in *Pour Marx,* Paris-Maspéro; the latter concept is nevertheless a rather holistic and deterministic one.

5. This is Windelband's phrase. Popper has endorsed it: cf. his paper *"The Logic of the Social Sciences,"* in *The Positivist Dispute in German Sociology,* 1976, ed. T. Adorno *et al.,* London: Heinemann, pp. 87–104.

6. R. Boudon, 1979, *La logique du social,* Paris: Gallimard.

7. This may also correspond reasonably well to the hempelian notion of an "explanation sketch" in history.

8. Cf. K.R. Popper, 1976, *Unended Quest,* London: Fontana, ch. 24.

9. Hempel, 1965, *Aspects of Scientific Explanation,* N.Y. passim.

10. Hempel would claim that a *conjunction* of laws is actually needed.

11. *La logique du social,* ch. II; English trans., *The Logic of Social Action,* London: R.K.P., 1981.

12. Cf. his last book *La place du désordre,* Paris: P.U.F., 1984.

13. Cf. e.g. K.R. Popper, 1962, *Conjectures and Refutations,* London: R.K.P., ch. 16.

14. Cf. Donagan's paper in *The Philosophy of K. Popper,* II, Schilpp. ed., La Salle, IL: Open Court.

15. This term is used by Parsons and Mandelbaum.

16. *La place du désordre,* P.U.F., 1984, ch. 3.

17. "La Rationalité et le statut du principe de rationalité" in *Hommage à Rueff,* Paris; Payot, 1967; now available in English in David Miller's *Pocket Popper,* London: Fontana, 1983.

18. The nature of which is intriguing; J. Watkins "Imperfect Rationality" in *Explanation in the Behavioural Sciences,* Borger and Cioffi eds.,; and Ph. Mongin, "Modèle Rationnel ou modèle économique de la rationalité," in *Revue Economique,* Vol. 35, 1984; N. Koertge, (1979): "The method-

ological status of Popper's rationality principle," in *Theory and Decision*, 10.

19. Cf. Hayek's "Degrees of explanation," in *Studies of Philosophy, Politics and Economics*, R.K.P.; Hayek's charge against laws seems to be valid only against a positivistic and simplistic concept of them; cf. his "Theory of complex Phenomena," *Postcript, ibid.*

20. "Historical Explanations in the Social Sciences," in O'Neill, *op.cit.*

18

Explanation in History

PETER MUNZ

THE HISTORIAN AS A SPECIALIST IN TIME-RELATED CHANGES HAS A PRIVILEGED PLACE IN THE UNITY OF SCIENCE

As specialists in time-related changes, historians have a proprietary interest in explanation, for (in an important sense) all explanations are historical explanations. If we want to know why somebody is angry or why a wire conducts a certain charge of electricity, the explanation has to take a historical form. There has to be an antecedent condition and a subsequent consequence—*i.e.*, a statement about how one thing leads to another. And this, though not always an exhaustive explanation, is the minimum requirement for a historical narrative.

Thus the historian, when it comes to explanations, is in a privileged position. Whether one is doing physics or psychology, sociology or history proper, cosmology or neurology, a great deal is explained when one can point to a short historical sequence of events, which stand in an explanatory relationship to one another. In this way a historical explanation is a good explanation, and when one can show a historical sequence in physics or sociology, one has explained something. The historian's privilege consists in the fact that such a recourse to history is built into the notion of explanation. The physicist and the psychologist, the sociologist or the cosmologist has no comparable privilege. If he wants to argue that a psychological event is explained by recourse or reduction to physics, or a biological event by reduction to chemistry, he has to do a lot of special theorizing to make his claim good. The historian needs no special theorizing. All he needs to do is to show that an explanation is a historical explanation in order to have physicists and cosmologists, psychologists and biologists eating out of his hand. This privileged position does not depend on reduction but on the mere presence of the time factor. To quote Arthur C. Danto: ". . . there is no intrinsic difference between historical and causal explanations, and . . . causal explanations do in fact all have the form of stories . . . Narrative is a *form* of explanation . . . We can reconstruct a 'scientific explanation' as a narrative . . . and . . . an account in narrative form will not lose any of the explanatory force of the original."[1] This is not to say that historical explanations are simple temporal sequences. On the contrary, as we shall see, a historico-causal sequence is mercifully quite distinct from temporal succession.

WHAT COUNTS AS AN EXPLANATION IN HISTORY?

Having said this, we have not solved anything but merely opened up a problem. What, indeed, is a historical explanation? When we are doing history—and we are doing history when we are discussing physics or psychology—what counts as an explanation and what form ought an explanation in history take?

An explanation in history is not to be confused with an explanation of the past. An explanation in history presupposes that somebody has transformed the totality of past events *(res gestae)* into one or more narratives of the sequence of select events *(historia rerum gestarum)*. An explanation in history is therefore always an explanation within a narrative and should never be confused with an explanation of history. History as a totality of all events of the past is something we cannot conceive and are not aware of and a non-entity which is not in need of an explanation.

THE SIX PRIME REQUIREMENTS OF AN EXPLANATION

I would like to suggest that we must make the following requirements of an explanation in history:

1. Any explanation offered must be criticizable.
2. The explanation must remain within the context of the matter to be explained, unless a special theory is offered why a reduction to a different context is helpful.

3. The explanation must make one see that what happened *had* to happen; or, at least, contingency has to be played down.

4. The quality of an explanation depends on its width, *i.e.*, on the range of its explanatory power. Hence, we must in all cases give preference to a model of explanation that can be applied to cases in which human beings are involved as well as to cases in which non-human entities or phenomena are involved.

5. Any ontological committment must be minimal. An explanation that requires a strong ontology preempts the explanation.

6. In history an explanation that explains change or that implies change is preferable to one which does not.

I do not claim that these six requirements are exhaustive. They merely represent a minimum list, and even so, it is conceivable that an explanation model is useful or acceptable if it fulfills only two or three of these requirements.

EXPLANATORY STRATEGIES IN HISTORY

It is impossible within the scope of a single paper to present and evaluate all arguments about explanation in history. I will therefore present the outlines of the problems in the form of summary assertions—something like *Thesen* in German—and refer for full discussion and argument to support my conclusions to my *The Shapes of Time.*[2] The present paper should be taken as a *Referat* rather than as a contribution to the subject.

Let us begin with a list of explanation models that are either used or advocated for employment in history:

1. *Reductionism*—which states that in order to explain, we must reduce the phenomenon to be explained to a different level of phenomena. For example, it is claimed that a given form of government is explained when it is shown that it is consequent upon certain climatic conditions and that changes in forms of government can be explained as changes in the climate.

2. *Historicism*—which states that there are developmental laws, which govern the succession of all events and that one can explain a phenomenon by locating it in the series of events governed by a developmental law. For having located it, it becomes immediately obvious that it had to succeed what went before and had to be followed by what came after.

3. *Colligation*—which states that all phenomena are colligated or linked in temporal sequences and that if one can plot one's way from

one event A to the next event B by minimizing the temporal gap between them, one goes a long way towards explaining B. It is often admitted by advocates of this model that such an explanation is not exhaustive and that in plotting forward in this manner one can only hope to "abate the mystery," as one of its famous propounders put it.[3] According to this strategy, one explains as one plots the course of events; or, history is its own explanation.

4. *Empathy*—which states that one can explain an action or a performance if one can enter into the mind of the author or agent and re-live the state of mind that existed when the performance was made.

5. *Unmasking*—which states that explanation consists in showing that a phenomenon is not what it purports to be or what its author professed but that, since its author always had something to hide, it is something else. Explanation is an exposing of the *real* condition the professed condition was designed to veil or disguise.

6. *Historism*—which states that every constellation is a unique individuality. (I am using the word "historism" to label this position because it was so labelled first by some of its upholders. Unfortunately through a series of literary accidents and confusions the German word *Historismus* is often rendered in English as "historicism," a word that should be reserved for a different position, that is, for the view that there are developmental laws that govern temporal processes.) Historism is based on a famous maxim by Goethe: *individuum est ineffabile.* This maxim was taken up by a whole school of historians and led to the formation of the view that there is a special kind of science called *Geisteswissenschaft* to deal with individual constellations, which cannot be classified and which show no regularities in their behaviour. Eventually special, mostly dubious, methods were devised in order to achieve a special *geisteswissenschaftliches* understanding. The maxim asserts that there can be no science of individuals and therefore no explanations. The position to which this maxim has given rise is diametrically opposed to all notion of the unity of science. The maxim itself, though based on an important truth, which among other things also forms a corner stone of Darwin's theory of evolution, obscures an all-important fact about the nature of individuality. Every individual, consciously or unconsciously or non-conciously is capable of making abstractions so that in spite of the undeniable reality of individual differences, it is always possible to make abstractions, which enable one to observe regularities and to classify so that individuals, without ceasing to be individuals, can arrive at explanations about themselves or about each other which are based on generalizations. As a historical curiosity, it is interesting to note that the influential school of *geis-*

teswissenschaftlicher non-explanation derives from such a misconception of individuality and not from any argument about the fact that history deals with human beings who have minds or mental contents which are as such not accessible to outside observers. The hard core of *Geisteswissenschaften* with their ineradicable bias against explanation consists in a misconception of individuality, not in the appreciation of the privacy of mental contents. This is high-lighted by the fact that in *Geisteswissenschaft* one purports to do idiography and steer clear of nomothetical pursuits.

7. *Employment of a covering law*—which states that an event is explained when it is shown to follow from another event with the help of a general law. In the terminology of Karl Popper, the first explicit proponent of this model of explanation, an event is explained when it appears as a prognosis deduced from an initial condition with the help of a general law. The general law establishes the initial condition as the cause and the prognosis, as the effect. This model of explanation can be used for events with human beings and without human beings; it covers nature and society; conscious and non-conscious performances; planned and non-planned events, and is applicable to events that are caused as well as to events that happen because people willed them. It can be applied in the natural sciences as well as in the social sciences. Explanations by covering laws are always nomological and deductive.[4]

The list of strategies may not be exhaustive, and the strategies listed are not necessarily exclusive of each other. Colligation and historism are often used together; unmasking and reduction often go hand in hand; and the covering law model is tacitly used in colligation and historicism. But for the sake of discussion I have listed them separately.

EXAMINATION OF THE MERITS OF THE SEVEN STRATEGIES

To start with, it is helpful to state how Napoleon's invasion of Russia would be explained by the seven strategies.

1. *Reduction*—Tolstoi in *War and Peace* reduced the invasion to an episode in the flux of population from west to east and east to west.

2. *Historicism*—There is a developmental law that states that empires expand until they burst. Napoleon's invasion of Russia was an event that had to take place just before the final bursting.

3. *Colligation*—The mystery of Napoleon's invasion of Russia is abated if one can locate it temporally immediately after the next preceding event and that event, immediately after its predecessor, and so on.

4. *Empathy*—Napoleon's invasion is explained if one can locate by empathy what went on in Napoleon's mind as he was giving orders for the preparation of the invasion.

5. *Unmasking*—The invasion is explained if one can show that it was nothing but a diversionary maneuver to distract attention from a domestic political or economic crisis in France.

6. *Historism*—There is nothing to be understood. Napoleon and his armies are a unique historical constellation following an inner law of their own.

7. *Covering Law Model*—Depending on the macrocity or microcity of the narrative, one will find covering laws that state that dictators will lash out when cornered; or that men seek glory by conquest; or "when a system of continental economy against England is in force, statesmen will seek to make it more perfect," *etc.*

The next task is to evaluate the seven strategies:

1. The *reductionist model* is obviously of very questionable value because it operates always by taking us into a different context. This is not necessarily wrong. A great deal of chemistry can be explained in a reductionist way by recourse to physics and a lot of biology can be explained by recourse to chemistry. But in all these fruitful cases, the reduction is not in itself the explanation. In these cases, the reduction is only explanatory because the validity of the knowledge to which the phenomenon to be explained is reduced is established independently. When it comes to attempts to employ this model in human history and where it is suggested that forms of government can be reduced to climatic conditions, we are on very shaky ground for our knowledge of climate says nothing that could be linked to forms of government. We are in this case simply invited to accept a reduction as an explanation without a possibility of seeing whether there is something in climate that would make this particular reduction plausible. This case is very different from the case in which chemistry is reduced to physics. In the physics case, the reduction is almost coincidental. It so happens that our knowledge of atoms enables us to predict all sorts of chemical phenomena. Hence the reduction of chemistry to physics is helpful to chemistry because it enables us to predict chemical events with the help of physical laws. Not so with climate and governments. Here we have nothing in our knowledge of climate to enable us to predict forms of government likely to occur

in a given region with a certain climate. We are simply expected to consider a certain form of government "explained" by the reduction to the occurrence of given climates.

The poverty of reductionism is also highlighted by a different example. It is in theory possible to reduce all social events in a given region to the laws governing the behavior of the molecules of which the members of a given society consist. Here reduction, however, is not at all a helpful explanation because it would simply amount to a dissolution of the intelligible phenomena of social life and leave us with the laconic insight that molecules are as molecules do even when they happen to appear in the shape of social agents. The poverty of reduction is further underpinned, when one considers reduction in the opposite direction, from physics to history. One can explain the strength of an electric current historically by referring to a magnet revolving inside a coil of wire. But a reduction to history that states that the presence of the electric current is explained because somebody started the magnet turning inside the coil in order to amuse a child does not explain the strength of the current. Whatever is thus added to the explanation, the mere reduction by itself is not as such explanatory.

Lest it be thought that grand reductions are no longer in fashion, we should recall that Kuhn's philosophy of science is a reduction. Kuhn considers that changes in paradigms are explained when it can be shown that they are reducible to sociological changes in the personnel of scientists.

Finally, a reductionist strategy does not explain at all because it leaves the *explanandum* as a totally unintelligible event and places the whole burden of explanation on the intelligibility of the subject the *explanandum* is reduced to. Kuhn, for example, leaves the history of paradigm changes as a completely unintelligible series of changes. The historical sociology of scientific communities, on the other hand, is intelligible and the history of paradigm changes becomes intelligible only in so far as it is made to appear as *nothing but* the historical sociology of scientific communities.

2. The *historicist model* is not only poverty stricken, it is based on the fallacy that we can speak of a law when all we have is a series of events. The very notion "developmental law" is a contradiction in terms. This is well argued by Karl Popper, and there is no need here to rehearse the arguments. The succession: primitive society—feudalism—capitalism—communism may or may not have occurred. In no sense are we entitled to think that there is a law that decrees that it had to occur or, if it did occur, that the occurrence was determined by a developmental law. Hence a location of any event in this series

can be no more than a historical curiosity. It cannot explain anything. It is not an "explanation" of capitalism when we are told that it followed after a period of feudalism. Nor would it be sensible to maintain that capitalistic features of a certain society are not capitalistic because they are not preceded by a stage of feudalism. In historicism we have not only an explanatory strategy which is poverty-stricken as Popper has argued; we actually have a strategy which is a non-strategy.

3. The *colligation model* has very little to commend itself. Its usefulness is based on the assumption that historical events come in clusters and that these clusters are "given." It is usually very hard to find out what the advocates of this model mean by "given" in this context. In one sense they mean that events are linked together into clusters by their temporal succession. It is averred, for example, that the campaigns of Napoleon are colligated with the social dynamics of the French Revolution, or that the corn laws in England were linked into one cluster with the dominance of agricultural, feudal interests. It is then maintained that these clusters speak for themselves and that a historian finds these clusters ready made. One needs very little critical examination to find that these events appear colligated only on certain historical assumptions about a given set of causal laws and that if one changes the causal laws, a cluster easily disintegrates and can, with the help of different causal laws be re-assembled into a different cluster. At best, therefore, this kind of colligation is explanatory only in a derivative sense, *i.e., after* the validity of certain causal laws has been established. By itself, this kind of colligation tells us nothing.

A different meaning of "given" is often put forward by advocates of the colligation model. It is argued that events are colligated by their succession in time. One can take it, it is argued, that events are in a cluster when they are temporally contiguous. I would argue that this notion of temporal contiguity is a fallacy. Every event is made up of sub-events, and every sub-event of further sub-events. All events, in other words, are infinitely sub-divisible and, therefore, in all cases, it is impossible to establish genuine temporal contiguity between events. When a historian feels his way from one event to the next event, the next event is not the event next in temporal succession. There is always, theoretically, at least one event in between. Any temporal sequence, which appears in a historical narrative—even though it may have the commonsense appearance of temporal contiguity—is not really a series of temporally contiguous events. If they are contiguous—and in a historical narrative they ought to be contiguous—they are not *temporally* contiguous. When a historian feels his way forward from the social dynamism of the French Revolution to the campaigns of Napoleon, he is producing a contiguous series. But the contiguity is by virtue of a general law about the nature of social dynamism—not by virtue of temporal succession. The mystery of Napoleon's campaigns is not at all abated when we are told that they are temporally contiguous with the social dynamism of the French Revolution even though they are temporally close together with that dynamism.

4. The *empathy model* sounds, on the face of it, fairly useful. Given the reasonable assumption that when Napoleon started his campaign or when Caesar crossed the Rubicon, they must have had something in mind, it is tempting to imagine that we can explain the campaigns or the crossing if we could empathically enter into Napoleon's or Caesar's mind at that time. We can even conceive or imagine what such empathy might consist of. After all, we all have minds and with some effort, it should be possible to relive the state of mind experienced by Caesar or Napoleon at a certain moment. The poverty of this strategy does not lie in the absurdity of the invitation to perform empathy, but in the impossibility of rational criticism. Napoleon's state of mind was, presumably, known to Napoleon. But whatever it was he knew is not open to a test and therefore not available for criticism. Here, then, we have an explanatory strategy, which looks plausible, but cannot really offer an explanation because it is not available for criticism.

Moreover, this strategy suffers from a second-order defect. Suppose we could enter into Napoleon's mind, and suppose we disregard the impossibility of criticism of what we conjecture to have been Napoleon's state of mind. We would then still be left with a further problem. Did Napoleon really know his mind or was he deceiving himself? He may well have said to himself when he embarked upon his campaign against Russia that he was doing so in order to solve the problem, which had arisen from the fact that he was unable to invade England whose continental blockade was strangling the economy of his Empire. Suppose our empathy gets him right on this point. There is very little or no explanatory force in this empathy because we will be left with the very real doubt as to whether he was suffering from a delusion. His real mental state may not have been, "I cannot cope with the continental blockade," but may well have been, "England or no England, my ambition is towards limitless conquest." Or, alternatively, it may have been, "I must compensate for the inferiority I feel because I am an upstart in France, because I am short, because I am a foreigner."

5. Next we come to explanations by *unmasking*. Advocates of

this strategy contend that it explains because it shows what is behind the surface or the appearance. It explains because it pulls off the veil and exhibits the reality. When the Spaniards went to America to convert the heathen, they really went to get the gold. When capitalists profess a love of liberty, they really mean to exploit the proletariat, and so forth. There is unquestioned value in such moves, for deception and illusion is of the essence of ignorance. But the advocates of such moves are themselves under an illusion as to what they are likely to achieve. The real value of such moves does not consist in the fact that, once the bluff is called or the veil torn off, the reality will exhibit itself. The real value consists in the fact that the move is made and the professed reason or motive subject to criticism. It does not follow and indeed cannot follow that such a move shows up "what really happened," unless one knows *beforehand* what really happened. In other words, the unmasking does only one thing, not two, as the advocates of unmasking allege. The unmasking is a move in the practice of criticism. It does not automatically reveal something behind the alleged mask and can therefore not explain what the phenomenon, once it is unmasked, was designed to conceal. In practice, the advocates of explaining by unmasking are dogmatists at heart and believe they know dogmatically what is behind the mask. If such dogmatism were granted, the unmasking would indeed be at once both criticism and explanation. But since dogmatism is to be rejected on all counts, the explanatory power of unmasking as distinct from the critical import, amounts to nothing.

6. Nothing need here be said about *historism*. The fundamental misconception of the nature of individuality on which historism is based makes historism into a non-explanatory strategy. The only explanatory move open to historists is to refer a small event or part to a larger event or whole. Wittgenstein says that a blunder is always a blunder in a certain game but never a blunder as such. Foucault argues that any method is a method in its appropriate *episteme*. Spengler maintains that any political system is justifiable in terms of the culture it is part of but not absolutely and not in terms of any other culture. These are typical examples of the limits of the explanatory strategy open to historists. At best, "explanations" in historism are referrals.

7. Finally we come to explanation by the *employment of a covering law*. Here we have a strategy which is genuinely explanatory. One starts with the *explanandum* and then seeks, by virtue of a covering law, the *explanans*. Formally speaking, one starts with the prognosis and seeks the initial condition and the covering law. In order to see how this functions in specifically historical explanation, one has to

avoid a common misunderstanding. In its commonest form explanation by covering law resembles the famous syllogism about Socrates and mortality. In this syllogism one starts with the initial condition and then deduces, with the help of the covering law ("all men are mortal") the prognosis ("Socrates is mortal"). This, however, is not the sequence in which the model is employed in historical explanation. In history one starts with the prognosis ("Socrates is mortal") and then seeks an initial condition and a covering law. Moreover, the syllogism as it stands is not an example of a historical sequence. In order to get a historical sequence, one has to assign a time index to both prognosis and initial condition so that the prognosis will be an event that takes place after the initial condition. For example: All men seek gold. Pizarro was a man. Pizarro sought gold.

Once the time index is introduced, one comes up immediately against a superficial difficulty. With time indexes for both initial condition and prognosis, one could still have a covering law that is quite general like "all men seek gold." However, we know perfectly well that there are lots of men who do not seek much gold or do not always seek gold. The covering law's validity on which the explanatory procedure depends will therefore become stronger if we diminish the degree of generality of the covering law and deprive it of its unlimited generality. It will still do its job if we substitute for "all men seek gold" the generalisation "all Spaniards of a certain type in the sixteenth century sought gold."

Such tuning down of the generality of the covering law is often essential. Take, for example, the case in which we want to explain why Jones raised his hat. The initial condition will state that Jones met a friend in the street. The covering law will say something about the general custom of raising hats in greeting. However, suppose somebody else raises his hat in a society in which people greet one another by rubbing noses. In such a situation the original covering law about greeting and raising hats will not help. In order to make sure that we really explain why Jones raised his hat we have to have a covering law of very limited generality, *i.e.*, a covering law that states specifically that in a certain society, certain classes of men greet each other by raising their hats. We have here a covering law of limited generality and can see that its explanatory power is directly proportional to the degree to which it is of limited generality. This matter is really obvious and not in need of elaboration. But in conclusion we must state that the employment of the covering law model in history obliges us not only to reverse the order of discovery so that we start with the prognosis and find the antecedent initial condition (rather than the other way round), but also to provide time and space indexation for both *explanandum* and *explanans* and also, preferably, for the covering law.

In history we are never concerned with the future. Therefore, the covering-law model's ability to provide a prognosis in the strict sense is irrelevant. The event described in the model as the prognosis is an event which has already happened. We do not predict that it will happen but use the model to identify it, pick it up and link it to its *explanans*.

HOW WELL DO THESE STRATEGIES SCORE IN THE SIX REQUIREMENTS?

Let us now try to see how the different models of explanation in history rate in terms of the six requirements listed above.

1. Reductionism scores well on the first and third requirement: its reductions are criticizable and help to reduce the appearance of contingency. It does not score at all on the second requirement, which states that an explanation must remain in a given context; and it scores only moderately on the fourth requirement, which demands that it must be applicable to human and non-human contexts. The reduction from human contexts to physics is, as we have seen, useless; and a reduction from social contexts to biological contexts needs a lot of additional theory. Reduction also comes close to an ontological commitment and scores badly on the fifth requirement but does quite well on the sixth requirement.

2. Historicism does not score on the first requirement. It is not criticizable. The assertion that there is a developmental law, no matter what that law says, is beyond the possibility of falsification. This alone rules it out of court. It is therefore irrelevant if one has to concede that the historicist strategy scores well on the remaining five requirements.

3. Colligation scores moderately well on the first, second, and third requirement but does not satisfy the fourth requirement. For as soon as one moves away from the human context, the belief that there is a given set of events—some of which are colligated inscrutably and unalterably—has to be abandoned. Moreover, in so far as it is criticizable, it has failed to stand up to even elementary criticism. Colligation gets some marks on the sixth requirement because it accounts for change; but no score for the fifth requirement because of its strong commitment to an ontology of time.

4. Empathy fails completely by the first and the fourth require-

ment: empathy is neither criticizable nor applicable outside the strictly human or mental context. There is a good score on the absence of ontological commitment and on the ability to account for change.

5. Unmasking as an explanatory, as distinct from a purely critical strategy, fails partially on the first requirement. It is criticizable in so far as any criticism is open to criticism; but it is not criticizable in so far as its dogmatic component is concerned. It can explain only if one is prepared to consider the reality that is made to appear behind the mask to be a dogmatic certainty. It also fails frequently on the second requirement because the unmasking, more often than not though never necessarily, moves us out of the given context. It scores moderately on the third requirement because—provided one is willing to enter into the inherent dogmatism of the revelation—it helps to make events appear to be less contingent. It scores unexpectedly well on the fourth requirement that a strategy should be capable of being used both in a human and a non-human situation. There is no score on the fifth requirement because there is strong and dogmatic commitment to the reality behind the mask. There is no or little score on the sixth requirement that a strategy should explain change.

6. Historism, in professing that nothing can be explained, gets no score at all. Historists would not consider such failure to be a criticism but an occasion for pride. Moreover, historism has a commitment to an ontology in that it considers individuality a brute fact of reality and fails completely by the fourth requirement that any explanatory strategy should be applicable to human and non-human phenomena, for historists grant that outside the human sphere, individual differences are not brute facts.

7. The covering-law model scores well on all requirements. First, every law or generalisation employed is criticizable. Second, it offers every opportunity for remaining within a given situation unless one has a generalization which leads beyond it for good reasons. Third, it helps to reduce the appearance of contingency; and fourth, it can be used to explain both human and non-human events. The same model is used for physics and for sociology or psychology. There is no commitment to any ontology and a high score for the ability to explain change.

There is no point in providing a formal summary of scored points. Obviously, some of the points scored for, say, criticizability are more telling than others, say for the requirement of remaining in the given context. One cannot even suggest that it would take three points scored for the third requirement of remaining in given context to outweigh one failure to score in the first requirement of criticizability. In this situation, the present survey of relative scores must remain somewhat inconclusive and can do no more than offer collateral reasons for the final rating arrived at by the initial survey.

HISTORY OF THE COVERING LAW MODEL

Having come to the conclusion that the covering-law model (CLM) alone is without blemishes, let us now turn to a fuller investigation of its special value in history. But first a brief word about its history.

The employment of the CLM in the composition of narratives is as old as intelligible narratives themselves. Wherever we find a narrative that is not a recital of disconnected events, we find that the CLM has been used. One can easily put this to a test, and I suggest we try as an example the opening paragraph of Thucydides VI, 9. The general laws used there are not spelled out—largely because they are quite trivial and can be taken for granted. But without the assumption that the reader can supply them, the passage would not make sense. To the best of my knowledge, the first theoretical formulation of the CLM is to be found in the famous treatise on geology by Lyell, first published in 1839. Lyell does not use the label but makes it quite clear that the explanation of the history of the earth must take the form of the CLM. Any change, he states, is to be understood as resulting from the operation of those general laws, which we can observe to be operating today. This famous methodological postulate is spelled out in the title of his book. As a geologist, Lyell was not concerned with the possibility of explaining changes with the help of general laws that are no longer in operation today or that were never in operation but that were in another place and time believed to be in operation. For his purposes, Lyell could afford to be a straight uniformitarian.[5]

The CLM, though it was even then not given its name, was first formally described by Karl Popper in *Die Logik der Forschung* of 1934. Since then, it has found explicit treatment in many papers by Carl Hempel and in many of Popper's works. It was eventually christened CLM by Dray in his *Laws and Explanation in History* in 1957. This label has found universal acceptance.

USEFULNESS OF THE COVERING-LAW MODEL

Next, let us consider its tangible usefulness to the historian. This usefulness is apparent regardless of whether one is dealing with the history of the earth, the history of politics, the history of social structures, *etc*. It is equally useful whether one is dealing with impersonal events such as climatic conditions or with impersonal events and their effects on personal or mental conditions or with intentional and intended activities. The ubiquity and all-pervasiveness of the CLM is very striking. One can often detect its presence even in much Marxian and Marxist history, where it is claimed that events are strung together intelligibly in terms of a developmental law (historicism) and not in terms of the CLM. But in so far as Marx's history is intelligible, it is due to the tacit employment of the CLM and not to adherence to his historicist theory of development. For the sake of simplicity, I will from now on confine the discussion to ordinary history, *i.e.*, to what is colloquially meant by "history" and exclude the history of the earth (geology) and of living cells (evolution) and of the cosmos.

In history the CLM is particularly useful because it does not just provide explanations. The CLM also provides a structure for the narrative. Such structure is a *sine qua non* because there cannot be a narrative that hangs together chronologically. Narrated events are seen to follow one another for reasons other than the fact that they are temporally contiguous. Non-narrative sciences do not have to confront this problem. History, which is an essentially narrative science and which purports to describe the truth about events which follow one another, is in need of a special non-temporal structure. Such structure is provided by the CLM.

1. The CLM provides a direct alternative to temporal contiguity in that it presents events in sequence other than temporal sequences. The *explanans* precedes the *explanandum* in time; but the *explanandum* is not temporally contiguous with the *explanans*. The gap between the former and the latter is covered by the covering law. Causal or genetic explanation is thus seen to be independent of temporal contiguity, but dependent on covering laws.

2. A narrative must be constructed in such a way that a reader can "follow" it. If there are too many surprises, and if a reader finds too many events he could not have anticipated, the story remains unintelligible. W.B. Gallie, *Philosophy and the Historical Understanding*[6] argued that narrators achieve such intelligibility by making the events in the story they are telling less contingent than they really are. As against this, the CLM helps us to understand precisely how intelligibility is brought about. In order to make his story intelligible, the narrator does not, by a sleight of hand as it were, spirit contingencies

away. He strings events together with the help of covering laws that are known to the reader or with the help of covering laws, which— if not known to the reader—are explicitly stated. It is not a question of extruding contingency as such, as Gallie maintained. Any one event can well be contingent relative to the rest of the story. A brick can work loose and kill the hero unexpectedly, or the beauty of Cleopatra's nose can make Roman statesmen linger in Egypt longer than prudence dictates. But both for the brick and for Cleopatra's nose there will be covering laws, which makes it perfectly intelligible why the brick or the nose intruded into the sequence of events at a particular point.

3. Last and not least, the CLM helps the research historian to find events he may not know of. It is a heuristic device. If one assumes that every intelligible narrative must consist of mini-narratives that are intelligible, one can focus on the minimum triad represented by the covering law, the initial condition, and the prognosis. Provided one knows any two elements of this triad, one can search for the third element. One's knowledge of the original two will help to determine where to look for the third, unknown element. In this way, focusing on an initial condition and a prognosis, one can try to find the covering law, which must ideally have been available to the agents involved; or one can use the covering law and the initial condition to look for the prognosis; or one can use the covering law and the prognosis to search for the initial condition. In this way, historical research ceases to be an undirected type of antiquarian pastime and becomes a rational search in certain directions. Such research is based on expectations. If the research so indicated remains fruitless, one can take it that the covering law is falsified or that the particular events (initial condition or prognosis, as the case may be) did not take place. The expectation, in other words, was misplaced.

OBJECTIONS TO COVERING LAW MODEL

As is to be expected, the CLM has found many critics. The following list shows the major and most common criticisms, which have been advanced. The list of critics is taken, with one or two exceptions, from K. Acham, *Analytische Geschichtsphilosophie*[7] although the rebuttals are my own.

1. It is suggested that the CLM is irrelevant to historical narratives because in most cases the laws employed are truisms.[8] CLM advocates are ready to concede that many of the laws involved are

truisms. But this does not invalidate the explanatory power of the CLM. The charge of irrelevance is itself irrelevant.

2. It has been argued that general laws are always laws of physics and that therefore any CLM explanation of social or psychological events cannot hold.[9] This argument is patently untrue for there are lots of generalizations of a social and psychological character.

3. It has been argued that any covering law only states the necessary conditions under which the events would take place.[10] But for an explanation to be intelligible, one has to state the sufficient conditions as well. The sufficient conditions are those that are in fact intelligible to a listener and are more likely to be an immediately antecedent condition rather than a generalization. This second part of the argument, however, is not correct. Even if one is looking for a sufficient condition and finds that sufficient condition in an immediately antecedent event, that immediately antecedent event is only linked to the *explanandum* event in virtue of a covering law. Thus, while the importance of sufficient conditions for an explanation is undeniable, the search for the sufficient condition does not obviate the need for a covering law.

4. It has been argued that covering laws are always atemporal, Platonic forms and therefore commit the employer of covering laws to a Platonic view of the atemporality of universals.[11] This objection is based on a false view of the character of general laws. First, general laws need not be more than generalizations and can be entertained even when one knows that in a different society at a different time they are false. Second, it is questionable whether general laws even of wide validity are atemporal entities. They are in all cases statements of regularities and as such, falsifiable.

5. Some critics believe that the covering law is supposed to be like an umbrella under which events take place so that they can all be deduced from a universal law.[12] Alternately it is alleged, *e.g.*, that the CLM implies that one can deduce and explain Caesar's murder from a general law about the average yearly murder rate in ancient Rome. Such misconceptions of the functions of general laws in explanation need no rebuttal other than an invitation to read the argument in favour of the CLM more carefully.

6. It has also been objected that in so far as covering laws are generalizations or statements of probabilities rather than really general laws, they cannot explain.[13] This objection is based on a mistaken notion of what constitutes an explanation. In many cases we have to be content with uncertainties. It is wrong to suppose that unless we can obtain certainty we have no explanation.

7. The backbone of the opposition to the CLM is formed by

the old argument that human beings, unlike atoms and living cells, rocks or stars, are individuals and that any explanatory strategy that depends on the deployment of a general law must be condemned to failure.[14] Individuals, it is alleged, cannot become the subject of laws without gross distortion. This argument is based on a fallacious estimate of individuality. In one sense, individuality is by no means confined to human persons and to conglomerates like societies, which consist of individual persons. As Darwin observed, there are no two finches alike and the whole motor of evolution depends on the realization that there are no two individual organisms that are exactly alike. (I am not competent to say how far this observation can be applied to inorganic nature.) However, in an important sense, it is possible to gloss over the differences between individuals and to abstract in all cases those qualities that are alike or sufficiently similar. If a finch were so sensitive to individual differences that it could not distinguish between another finch and an elephant, there would be no mating and no differential reproduction rates and, therefore, no evolution. In other words, though individuals are genuinely individuals, if one could not disregard, up to a point, individual differences, we would never have evolved. The fact that we have evolved indicates, therefore, that unquestioned differences are no final obstacle to the formation of general concepts and of general laws. In order to uphold the viability of general laws one does not have to deny the reality of individual differences, as many opponents of the CLM claim; but merely accept that individual differences are not insurmountable obstacle to the formation of general concepts and the formulation of general laws.

THE FRUITFULNESS OF THE COVERING LAW MODEL FOR OLD DEBATES

I have shown so far that the explanatory strategy of the CLM in history shows that historical knowledge is part of the Unity of Science; that the CLM has uses in history, which go beyond mere explanation—*i.e.*, it helps to create the minimum conditions for an intelligible time series and serves as a heuristic device for the researcher. Next, I have shown that the critical charges commonly made against the CLM cannot stand up to scrutiny. Finally, now I want to show that the CLM can make a fruitful contribution to the settlement of several major methodological debates. These debates are very old; but if such recent books as J. Rusen, *Historische Vernunft*, Göttingen, 1983, and

M. Oakeshott, *On History*, Oxford, 1983 are anything to go by, these debates are far from resolved. In resolving some of these issues the fruitfulness of the CLM will become further apparent.

1. It is frequently alleged that the effort to explain is antithetical to or incompatible with the effort to understand. The advocates of the effort to explain are usually aligned on the side of natural science because it is believed that explanation by subsumption under general laws and the employment of a nomological-deductive procedure is, outside the natural sciences, a form of scientism. The advocates of the effort to understand are considered to be truly aware of the fact that in the social and human sciences all events are irreducibly particular events or individual constellations; or truly aware of the fact that in the social and human sciences the objects of knowledge are really subjects who can think for themselves and that these thoughts are for the most part inaccessible to the outside observer. Understanding is therefore considered to be a procedure that is in principle different from explaining.

The CLM can show that there is nothing antithetical in the difference between understanding and explaining and that there is only one strategy involved in both procedures; but that there is, nevertheless, an important difference between understanding and explaining. Using the CLM we say that we understand when we employ only those covering laws that were used or could have been used by the person we are trying to explain. We say that we explain when we are using those covering laws, which we as modern or outside observers believe to be true. The difference between *erklären* (explaining) and *verstehen* (understanding) derives from the differences in the kind of covering laws used; not from a difference in procedure. Thus the important distinction between explanation and understanding is pin-pointed and maintained even though the fundamental unity of scientific method is preserved.

It is helpful to introduce another terminological distinction here. We can say that we explain what actually happened if we confine our explanations to the employment of covering laws used by or known to the people we are explaining; and we can say that we explain what really happened if we confine our explanations to the employment of covering laws that we ourselves hold true. Thus, we can eliminate the seemingly semantic difference between understanding and explanation according to which the former is a mysteriously human and intuitive procedure and the latter an overtly scientific procedure. We replace the distinction by a neutral terminology in that we are using two terms like actual and real—terms, which are semantically very similar, possibly even synonimous. We report about actuality when we understand; and about reality when we are explaining. When modern people talk about modern history, actuality and reality coincide (at least ideally) and explanation and understanding come to the same thing.

2. The CLM also brings a decisive clarification into the never-ending debate about the level of objectivity we are entitled to aim at or expect from historians. With the help of the CLM we can see at once that every historical series—that is, every sequence from initial condition to prognosis—is governed by a covering law. Every such series is a series relative to a covering law. In our quest for objectivity we must therefore focus not on the particular statements by themselves but on the link between them established by the covering law. It cannot make sense to ask whether it is objectively true that Caesar crossed the Rubicon. The correct question to ask is whether the covering law employed to link the crossing to the next event in the series is true or not. In all cases, the concern with objectivity is not to be directed to the particular events but to the covering law that links particular and separate events (in this case, the first and the second step across the Rubicon) to each other. Once this is done, we can see that in demanding "objectivity" we are demanding that a covering law be used that was used or could have been used by the person we are talking about. The question as to whether a newspaper reporter reported "objectively" in stating that Caesar crossed the Rubicon is trivial and concerns nothing more than personal bias, prejudice, or mendacity. But in asking whether the covering law employed in linking the crossing to another event was the covering law used by Caesar himself, we are asking a methodologically important question, which has nothing to do with honesty or bias. In thus redirecting the quest for objectivity, we also make an important methodological contribution.

All historical series are relative to a covering law. *Tot storiae quot leges.* There is therefore no merit in criticizing the particular events linked together by a covering law. If the covering law is granted, the series of events that it produces has to be accepted—provided always that every single event actually did take place. Criticism therefore has to concentrate on the covering law. Seeing that any historical series is relative to a covering law, one is not entitled, as so many historians have done, to throw up one's hands in despair and declare that all histories are relative and that one is as good as any other. One must, on the contrary, pay double attention to the covering law employed and distinguish the true story from the false story by discussing the covering laws employed in the composition of each story. This can be no comfort to relativists.

3. The CLM also makes a vital and decisive contribution to the problem of the so called *hermeneutic circle*. If we want to understand Luther as he understood himself, it is alleged, we have in a different sense to have understood him already. We cannot understand unless we see the world as he saw it, and we cannot see the world as he saw it unless we understand Luther. This is the grand hermeneutic circularity. The CLM can bring clarification and show that there is no real circularity at all. To understand Luther as he understood himself, we have to find the covering law or laws that Luther could or would have used. These laws may well be false and are likely to be very different from the covering laws we would use to explain what happened to Luther. But this insight does not present an obstacle and does not lead to circularity. On the contrary. We are entitled to presume that even though the covering laws used by Luther were different from the covering laws that we would use for his case, Luther and the modern historian have something in common. Both used covering laws. In this recognition there lies an initial comprehension. Though the actual laws used by Luther differed from the laws used by modern historian, we can legitimately rely on the fact that in both cases covering laws were used. And while the surface structures of the two explanations used by Luther and the modern historian respectively are different, the deep structure of the explanations used by Luther and the modern historian must be the same. Given the common deep structure, the circularity disappears. We understand perfectly well what explanatory strategy was used by Luther because that strategy is identical with the strategy used by the modern historian, even though the actual covering laws used by Luther differ from the covering laws used by the modern historian. The CLM enables us to distinguish between the deep structure of explanations (presented by the CLM) and the surface structures dependent on the employment of different covering laws. Thus the CLM enables us to resolve one of the thorniest debates ever to have bedevilled historical understanding and explanation.[15]

4. The CLM can also clarify the debate between Collingwood and Popper about re-enactment. Collingwood suggested that in order to understand how, *e.g.*, the Theodosian Code was produced, he has to re-enact in his own mind what was going on in the minds of the authors of the Code. Popper has suggested that such re-enactment is impossible because most of the acts in question are far beyond the historian's capacity. Popper suggests instead that we consider every task as a problem situation with a variety of choices. The historian, Popper proposes, should reconstruct the problem situation as it appeared to the agent so that the actions of the agent will be seen as

adequate to the situation.[16] In *The Poverty of Historicism*[17] the proposal comes in a slightly different form. Here Popper suggests that the historian construct a model in which all information is available, and then estimate the degree of deviation of actual behavior from model behavior.

Unlike Collingwood, Popper sees that in every human action or performance there is an element of rationality.[18] Popper seeks to track down this element and make it less elusive by measuring it against what would count as a completely rational performance. The effort to figure out what would be a completely rational performance and then define the universally present element of rationality in terms of the deviation of an actual performance from the model performance must remain illusory and theoretical at best. If the debate is restated in terms of the CLM, we can dispense with the notion of a perfect rationality model and yet define the element of rationality in every performance. With the help of the CLM we can say that for every performance there is a covering law at the back of the mind of the performer. This covering law need not be explicit; it can be trivial. It may be no more than an ideal reconstruction; and, to the best of our knowledge it can be false. However, as long as we assume that there is—potentially and theoretically—a covering law for every performance, we can see that in every performance there is an element of rationality. We can even define this element now by saying that every performer has "good reason" for his performance because he must have been able, ideally, to explain his performance to himself with the help of a covering law. The "good reason" quality of every performance is even present when we are dealing with notoriously neurotic behavior. The hallmark of neurotic behavior is not that it has no "good reason," but that what appears as "good reason" to the performer is a "bad reason" to the observer. Thus, we can detect the ubiquity of Popper's element of rationality, without recourse to an allegedly completely rational model of performance.

It is now even possible to reformulate what Collingwood meant by re-enactment. We can re-enact precisely because of the element of rationality in all behavior. All performers used or could have used a covering law. If we re-enact the reasons for a performance, we are simply wiping away the covering laws that we would have used and are replacing them with the covering law or laws that the performer could have used, thus discovering the "good reasons" he had in behaving as he did. Re-enactment in this sense ceases to be the semi-intuitive and uncriticizable activity Collingwood alleged it to be; it becomes, instead, a rational scientific pursuit, the results of which are open to inspection and criticism. For a historian can certainly make a mistake in attributing to a performer the use of a certain covering law. Re-enactments in terms of the CLM are falsifiable.

5. So far, the discussion has assumed that it makes no difference to the explanatory power of the CLM whether the covering laws employed are trivial or not. In practice, however, there is an important difference between covering laws that are trivial ("All men must breathe") and covering laws that are not ("Adolescents tend to seek a moratorium from parental pressure") or "religious beliefs are determined by the mode of production in which the believers are engaged"). The truth value of trivial laws need not be in question. The truth value of non-trivial laws must always be in question. How then can one assess the truth value of non-trivial covering laws? We have here a genuine methodological problem, for the truth of any generalization must be relative to the particular instances it is a generalization of. Historians in particular and scientists in general who are dealing with infinite data (*i.e.*, in the social sciences one cannot claim to be confining oneself to any one set or type of events) are almost always in the position where they are using the covering law as a criterion of selection as well as an essential part of their explanation. In order to weaken the resulting circularity of argument, one has to introduce two Postulates. First, one has to adhere to the Postulate of Sufficient Specification. This Postulate demands that any covering law employed must be sufficiently specific (*i.e.*, not totally general) so that if it is used also as a criterion of selection, one can select events only from a given area. Thus, it becomes possible to discuss the empirical content or truth value of the covering law. For a criterion of selection that yields supporting evidence from a specified area has a higher empirical content than one that yields supporting evidence from anywhere at all.

Second, there must be the Postulate of Sufficient Variety. This Postulate states that the empirical content or truth value of a covering law will be proportional to the degree to which the criterion of selection varies from the covering law employed. In practice, one can give the following example. If one uses a Marxist covering law as a criterion of selection and then invites the reader to accept the events selected as confirmation of the truth of a Marxist covering law, there can be very little confidence in the truth of the covering law. But if one uses Gibbon's selection of events and then finds that they can be explained with the help of a Marxist covering law, one can be more confident that there must be some truth in the Marxist covering laws.

COVERING LAWS INVOLVED IN OTHER EXPLANATORY STRATEGIES

In conclusion, I would stress that not the least merit of the CLM is that it can also be used to underpin at least some of the other six strategies and those strategies become more useful to the degree to which they can be shown to avail themselves of the CLM.

The notion that there is colligation can be derived from the CLM. It is a mistaken notion if the colligation is taken to be elementary, but if colligation is a secondary phenomenon, one can see how the events in any series set up with the help of the CLM must appear to be colligated.

Empathy has to be dismissed as an explanatory strategy because the act of empathy cannot be criticized. However, if one means by "empathy" a summary description of the covering laws available to the person one is trying to empathize with, the project of empathy becomes criticizable for one can certainly decide with the help of records or documents what covering laws could have been made use of by the person one is trying to empathize with. I cannot get into the mind of Charlemagne. But knowing whom he dealt with and what he read or listened to, I can conjecture what covering laws he might have made use of. And a person more learned than I can criticize my conjecture.

The strategy of unmasking also owes a debt to the CLM. In a nutshell, the attempt to unmask can be described as an attempt to substitute one set of covering laws, say about economics, for a different set, say about theology. In so far as the explanatory strategy of unmasking is no more than such a substitution it can be considered as a special application of the CLM. In fact, unmakers, however, claim that their substitutions have a special kind of finality. In so far as they make this claim, their employment of the CLM is pure coincidence, for the heart of their strategy consists in giving unqualified preference to a set of dogmatically asserted covering laws.

This brief survey leaves only three of the seven strategies without obvious debt to the CLM—reductionism, historicism and historism.

NOTES

1. *Analytical Philosophy of History,* Cambridge: Cambridge University Press, 1968, p. 237.

2. Middletown: Wesleyan University Press, 1977.

3. M. Oakeshott, *On Human Conduct*, Oxford: Clarendon Press, 1975, p. 106.

4. For further discussion and elaboration of the details of the laws and the deduction involved, I refer to the classical paper by C. Hempel, "The Function of General Laws in History," *Journal of Philosophy* 39 (1942): 35–48; W. Stegmüller, "Historisch-genetische Erklärungen," in his *Probleme und Resultate der Wissenschaftstheorie und Analyse*, Berlin: Springer, 1969, Vol. I; and R. Weingartner, "The Quarrel about Historical Explanation," *Journal of Philosophy* 58 (1961): 29–45.

5. For further details on Lyell's method of explanation see Ch.C. Gillispie, *The Edge of Objectivity*, Princeton: Princeton University Press, 1960, pp. 299 ff and the same author's *Genesis and Geology*, Cambridge: Harvard University Press, 1951, Ch. V. See also my "Finches, Fossils and Foscarini," *New Zealand Journal of History* 14 (1980): 132–152.

6. London: Chatto and Windus, 1964.

7. Freiburg: Alber, 1974, pp. 164 ff.

8. M. Scriven, "Truisms as the Ground for Historical Explanations," in P. Gardiner (ed.), *Theories of History*, N.Y.: Oxford University Press, 1967.

9. J. Hexter, *The History Primer*, London: Allen Lane, 1972, Ch. I.

10. W. Dray, *Laws and Explanation in History*, Oxford: Oxford University Press, 1957.

11. A. Kuzminski, Review of Peter Munz, "The Shapes of Time," in *History and Theory* 18 (1979), pp. 61–84.

12. B. Barry, "Happiness and Joe Higgins," *London Review of Books*, 20 Oct., (1983), p. 8.

13. M. White, *Foundations of Historical Knowledge*, N.Y.: Harper & Row, 1965, p. 188 f.

14. For a history of this tradition which eventually issued in the non-explanatory strategies of hermeneutics and *Geisteswissenschaften* see F. Meinecke, *Die Entstehung des Historismus*, München: Leibniz, 1936.

15. I have linked the CLM to Chomskyan terminology. For a similar resolution of hermeneutic circularity without Chomskyan terminology see W. Stegmüller, "The So-Called Circle of Understanding," in his *Collected Papers on Epistemology, etc.*, Dordrecht: Reidel, 1977, Vol. I.

16. K.R. Popper, *Objective Knowledge*, Oxford: Clarendon Press, 1972, p. 189.

17. K.R. Popper, *The Poverty of Historicism*, London: Routledge, 1957, p. 141.

18. K.R. Popper, *The Poverty of Historicism*, p. 140.

19

Comments on Munz's Essay

EILEEN BARKER

Munz's interesting essay makes many statements with which I have no difficulty in concurring. I am, however, not always entirely certain what kinds of claims he is making about covering laws and the scope of their use. Sometimes he would seem to be arguing that we *ought* to use the covering-law model, at other times the argument seems to be that we *do* use it all the time, although we may not be aware that we are invoking such a law whenever we explain or, indeed, act. I am quite prepared to accept, at an almost tautological level, that there is probably a CLM crying to get out in most of the explanations (and understandings) we adduce for the behavior of protons, molecules, organs, organisms, kings, peasants, and ourselves. I would also be quite happy to concur with the sentiment that the work of the natural scientist, the social scientist and/or the historian will be enhanced to the extent that he or she is capable of making explicit covering laws, which are relevant to our understanding of the processes (or events) in which we are interested.

My agreement that the employment of a covering law produces the most valuable type of explanation in history, does, however, lead me to ask a few more questions about the status of such laws in history and, perhaps, to question exactly what is implied by the second of Munz's six requirements for an explanation (that the explanation must remain within the context of the matter to be explained, unless a different theory is offered why a reduction to a different context is helpful). This is because I am unclear exactly what his claim to an underlying unity of the sciences is, unless it is merely that some kind of covering law must, necessarily, be invoked. This is not, presumably, meant to imply *sufficient* method? What about the different kinds of law, which require different methods to discover them? I am assuming that a "law" is something that does have to be discovered as an empirical regularity.

Munz opens his paper with the claim that "in an important sense, all explanations are historical explanations." His point is that there always has to be an antecedent condition and a subsequent consequence. This is, of course, perfectly true—although I can never quite make up my mind whether saying that end A of a see-saw is going up because end B is going down could count as a synchronic explanation. Be that as it may, when a covering law is evoked to explain an event, an initial event is also evoked and this event is normally of a historical nature. The point which I would like to pursue is that—apart from exceptional instances such as the creation/evolution of the material world, or, perhaps, quantum physics—it is (to most intents and purposes) irrelevant to the natural sciences whether or not an explanation of the covering law has an historical dimension. This is not inevitably the case in the social sciences—and there are, I believe, some particularly pernicious kinds of reductionism, which can ensue from forgetting this difference, and some instances in which this might seem to argue for a "genetic reductionism" within the social sciences.

Let me try to sketch the argument in terms that are slightly different from (but possibly compatible with) those employed by Munz. Put crudely, a covering law is a description of a regularity—a description of a way in which two or more definitionally distinguishable variables are in some way connected. Generally speaking, so far as those regularities that we refer to as the laws of nature are concerned, it makes little difference whether they are occurring in Asia, America, Africa, or Europe, and we assume that they could have been applied equally in the nineteenth, eighth and first centuries.

There are some regularities in social behavior that have little to do (directly) with the time or place in which the actors involved happen to be living. Such regularities include the structural constraints and potentialities that emerge from the organization of patterned interactions between people; different power structures or different channels of communication will, for example, result in different consequences for those involved. The relationship between the participants in a dyad will enjoy different potentialities and suffer different constraints from the relationships that can exist in a triad—and these differences will have nothing to do with (cannot be reduced to) the individual personalities or genes involved. The "laws" describing such irreducible patterns are almost as non-temporal as those of the natural sciences; A feudal structure will exhibit certain properties that are well-nigh inevitable, whatever the continent or century within which it is to be found. One can think of this kind of irreducibility as being similar to that in the natural sciences.

The existence of people who will behave in certain ways when combined, related, or organized into one type of structure, and behave in other ways when organized into a different type of structure seems analogous to the differences in the properties of hydrogen and oxygen, water (H_2O), and hydrogen peroxide (H_2O_2). The point is possibly obvious enough, but let me spell out these emergent properties—potentialities and constraints—in a somewhat anthropomorphic language in order to make the analogy. When hydrogen and oxygen are organized as H_2O, they can "do" certain things (such as wet a towel at room temperature and pressure) which they would not be able to do were they not so organized—and they cannot do other things which they would have been able to do had they not been combined at all (the oxygen can no longer sustain combustion), or if they had been combined in a different way (water will not bleach in the same way that the combination H_2O_2 will).

Somewhat similarly, people whose relationships are structured in a bureaucracy (in which communication and decision making is organized along hierarchical lines) will be able to perform certain tasks efficiently, while other tasks, which could have been performed more efficiently in, say, a democratically run commune, will become tied up with red-tape. The individual will be constrained from doing certain things—such as telling his superiors what they ought to do—in the bureaucratic structure. But this is not to say that he is physically, or even necessarily psychologically constrained from doing so. The covering law: "Bureaucrats do not tell superiors what to do" is not ontologically comparable to the covering law: "Oxygen does not cause combustion when "in" water," although both types of laws can be used to explain why a particular kind of organization prevents (or results in) certain kinds of behavior.

Some of the regularities that Munz refers to as covering laws and which occur as part of the social world are, however, qualitatively different in their dependence on a human space/time dimension for their existence. Unlike the laws of nature, they have to be subjectively *known* (albeit sometimes only at a subconscious level) *in order that they should exist.* (It can be argued that Popper's "World III" has an independent existence, but it has no *effect* except in so far as it is known.) The regularities to which I am referring are the result of (more or less) shared perceptions of reality creating and (more or less) "upholding" a social reality. Such regularities do have an important historical dimension and are relative to time and culture.

Here I am talking about the phenomenon of a social reality which, while it depends for its existence upon human beings "knowing" it, is social in the sense that it is not reducible to any particular human being, and is a reality in the sense that it exists independent of the volition of any individual; the fact that it is, in one sense, only in the minds of men and women does not mean that *a* man or woman can wish it away. It is the culture—or rather the cultures—of a society, the "out-theres," that confront, influence, constrain, and enable those who share in its knowledge to interact (amicably or with conflict). To ignore this reality is to ignore a reality that is responsible for shaping many of the actions—and reactions—of both ordinary and extraordinary people as they go about their daily lives "making history."

This particular type of social reality has a number of properties which, while not exactly paradoxical, are confusing for the social scientist. Two such properties (which are themselves inter-related in that they are both associated with an historical relativism) are the predictability and the non-predictability to which it gives rise, and the reducibility and the non-reducibility of its nature.

Let me make it quite plain that I am not suggesting that there exists a collective conscience in any Platonic sense: to repeat, a cultural reality is dependent upon individuals at the same time as it is independent of any particular individual. But part of the non-reducibility of cultural reality lies in the fact that it consists of a *Gestalt*—or rather, a series of *Gestalten* (and of *Gestalten* within *Gestalten*). Furthermore, although no two people will ever experience exactly the same Gestalt, there is sufficient inter-subjective sharing of the patterns of reality given by a culture for there to be a culture within which people can interact and, indeed, negotiate to change that culture. The existence of the (more or less) shared Gestalt not only allows a society to function, it can be seen as a crucial factor in the process (socialization) by which the infant grows into a "truly human" person—indeed, it can well be argued that in this respect, to explain the individual (psychology) one has to understand the whole (culture). Knowledge of the "higher" level is necessary to explain the "lower" level.

At the same time, due partly to the slightly different experiences of life that individuals have and which result in their seeing, hearing, and, therefore, "knowing" in slightly different ways, the shared, predictable structure of the culture is constantly shifting and adapting to changing (endogenous and exogenous) circumstances. There is, in other words, enough predictability for social scientists to be able— to need—to take this Gestalt reality into account in their explanations of historical happenings (which will include both change and non-change in the culture itself). And there is a fundamentally historical component of unpredictability inherent within the shared culture, which makes any "covering" law essentially relative to the historical circumstances—which is not to say that we have no means of access to such knowledge, but is to say that the relationship between the *explanans* and the *explanandum* is historically specific.

There is, moreover, a sense in which the explanation of the origin of any particular cultural Gestalt must be reduced to the actions (which do, of course, include the speech acts) of particular individuals (although, paradoxically, these may well be mythical). It is, however, necessary to understand the culture as a Gestalt in order to understand how it works. One needs to look on it as an irreducible whole if it is invoked for explanatory purposes. It is, in other words, necessary to understand the extent to which people throughout history have seen the world through culturally specific spectacles, and that to look at "what they really see" without being aware of these spectacles is to miss out on a crucial element in explaining what they are doing.

But, at the same time, we have to remember that each individual sees reality in different kinds of ways and there will exist a whole battery of different, though inter-related, Gestalten within any particular society—and this is especially significant in modern, pluralistic societies in which there is a high degree of differentiation and in which there exist cultural supermarkets offering a plethora of Gestalten/spectacles/Weltanschauungen (or what-have-you) to provide a variety of social realities that help (or hinder) the individual as he or she tries to make sense of the world. Anyone with the slightest knowledge of history or anthropology is unlikely to be unaware of either the relativism or the explanatory importance of these Gestalten, but it is an interesting fact that most people tend to believe that someone who is looking at the world through a different set of (socially constructed) glasses from their own is wrong. Even more interesting to observe is the fact that one of the current ways of "dealing with" people who are using the "wrong" glasses is to invoke "scientific" reductionism.

There are those who make it their business to "medicalize" the social realities, beliefs, and practices of others. An obvious example is to be found in Soviet Russia, where political dissidents are proclaimed psychologically ill, confined in mental hospitals, and "treated" with drugs until they learn how to see the "true" Gestalt. But it is not only the communists who have sought psychological explanations for "distorted pictures of reality." Take, for example, the reductionist conversion of conversion that is to be found among certain members of the psychiatric fraternity in America who lend support to the practice of "deprogramming."

I do not want to suggest that malfunctioning of the central nervous system may not, on occasion, give rise to strange views of reality, which can, in turn, lead people to behave in strange ways. One can, however, remark upon the ease with which people will believe that other people's acceptance or rejection of certain socially constructed realities (most obviously when these are of a political or religious nature) is "really" a manifestation of some kind of biological malfunctioning, when the only empirical evidence they have is the social behavior of the person concerned. How, I wonder, will future historians explain 20th-century reductionists?

In summary, then, I want to go a little further than Munz in both directions. I want to connect the different levels more than his (albeit limited) anti-reductionism would seem to permit, but I also want to recognize the distinction between different levels as being more fundamental than he appears to consider them to be. A scepticism about the adequacy of reductionist explanations is necessary, but it can hardly lead to a unification of the sciences. I believe that we have to accept both that some psychological phenomena—including some mental illnesses—can, and need to be explained (at least in part) in terms of social factors and that some social phenomena can, and need to be explained (at least in part) in terms of psychological factors. While I certainly have little sympathy for a crude reductionism that rules out the emergent properties of social structures and cultures, it seems to me equally foolhardy to ignore certain elements of reductionist explanations when our subject matter and our "covering laws" are so historically contingent.

Furthermore, it does not get us all that far just to say that both social and psychological (and biological etc.) dimensions are necessary for a greater understanding of history. More work of both an empirical and a philosophical nature is needed to understand the relationship of the interaction between the individuals and the social reality in which they live. This attempt to follow the process of interaction between the two levels is not reductionist in the sense that it denies that the whole is greater than the sum of its parts, but it is reductionist in the sense that it attempts to understand how the whole *becomes* greater than the sum of its parts, how the whole then affects the parts—and what part that process plays in history.

At the same time, we need to be aware of the fundamentally different nature of the regularities that occur in the natural world and those which occur in the social world. In the social world, shared "knowledge" (conscious or unconscious, correct or false) can be the reason for the very existence of the regularity, and, moreover, knowledge of a regularity can itself lead to the disappearance of that regularity. We have to recognize that, although there are some similarities to and connections with the study of the nonsocial world, we are playing (partly because we are looking at) a different ball game when we are "doing" explanations with the use of a covering law in history or the other sciences of social life.

Part IV

THE REDUCTIONISM OF THE SOCIOLOGICAL TURN IN THE PHILOSOPHY OF SCIENCE

20

Explanation, Reduction and the Sociological Turn in the Philosophy of Science or Kuhn as Ideologue for Merton's Theory of Science

IAN C. JARVIE

The general problem that this paper addresses is whether sociological explanations of science can dispense with the independent causal factor of ideas.[1] It will argue that these sociological explanations themselves employ ideas the development of which cannot be explained away.

INTRODUCTION

The scientific ethos was always universalistic: everything has a scientific explanation. Slowly it transpired that scientific explanation was causal, in some sense (and, of course, valid and true or else not explanation or not science). Hence, every event has a cause. The events that look particularly uncaused are inspirations, so those inspired by the scientific ethos took the bull by the horns and declared inspirations to be caused. At first it looked as if religious inspirations were the hardest to explain causally; they turned out to be the easiest, being explicable as hoaxes, or psychologically, or sociologically (functionally). What turned out to be genuinely difficult to explain were scientific inspirations. It is for this reason that the philosopher who attacked the scientific ethos in recent times—Bergson—used scientific inspiration as the paradigm that violates the scientific ethos.

More recently, the scientific ethos has been studied sociologically.

Scientific ideas themselves were by way of a crucial test case. Was the fount of determinism itself determined? Faced with this rather daunting gulf, the founding father of modern sociology of science, Robert K. Merton in his *Science and Society in the Seventeenth Century* followed his mentor Mannheim in not offering any reduction of scientific ideas to social, economic, and military-technological factors. These factors, Merton allows, can make the time ripe for an idea to be taken up or even searched out, but an idea has some sort of separate existence. However, neither in that work nor in his subsequent publications (1973, 1977) has Merton been very explicit about ideas. This may explain why there has arisen at Edinburgh a group devoted to the Strong Programme in the Sociology of Knowledge, *i.e.*, the program of going beyond Mannheim and of condemning anything less than full determinism as idealism:

> because received concepts and beliefs were routinely used to explain the actions of individual scientists, there was a tendency to idealism in the history of science, just as there is always such a tendency in the history of ideas generally. Concepts, beliefs, principles were credited with inherent potency; they were thought of as autonomous entities with power or influence over men's minds. Cultural change was even, on occasion, conceptualized as the unfolding of the inherent implications of ideas. Such a one-sided conception, which ignored the power men possess to extend, adapt, modify or reflect received ideas, was not acceptable in sociology (Barnes, p. 8).

Who is and who is not an idealist need not detain us. But clearly Merton's ambiguity about ideas has left a big hole in his theory that needs to be closed if it is not to collapse towards the Edinburgh reduction.

To close this gap, I shall proceed by way of Merton's 1977 study of the new science of the sociology of science; a text in which, once more, he says very little about the role of ideas, and, within that general topic, concentrates on his case study of the diverging careers of two men whose ideas have influenced the science of the sociology of science although, again, Merton scarcely discusses their ideas. The two men are Karl R. Popper and Thomas S. Kuhn, the latter more influential than the former.

Merton's original study of 1938 looked at the rise of natural science in the 17th Century. His new study concerns the rise of the science of the sociology of science in the period since 1938. In each case his approach is the same. He attempts to explain the rise of science by studying the social formations in which it is embedded. Such an explanation is not necessarily an objectionable reduction.

My *philosophical* thesis will be that sociology engages in illicit reduction if it tries to explain socially the truth or untruth of scientific ideas. My second, *material or sociological*, thesis will be that the ideas Kuhn and Popper put forward are essential to explain what Merton calls their differential "presence" to the sociology of science. Kuhn's ideas, it will transpire, legitimize the social formations in which the science of his time is temporarily housed. Popper, more ambitious, offers an explanation of the success of science that not only transcends the particular social formations of his time, but which also happens to be inimical to and critical of these formations, and thereby of those ideas of Kuhn which legitimate these formations. Kuhn's ideas legitimate science's current social embodiment; Popper's undermine it. These no doubt unintended consequences of each man's *ideas* are, I will argue, integrally necessary for explaining the trajectory of their careers. The American academic and scientific Establishment, sensing these unintended consequences, has naturally preferred to embrace Kuhn and to hold Popper at a distance. An interesting question is whether this "fit" between Kuhn's ideas and Establishment needs was, as Merton has it, a serendipitous mutual discovery, or whether Kuhn sensed and articulated Establishment needs. Popper, by contrast to Kuhn, has always been aware of a normative element in his work, a normative element suspicious, and hence critical of Establishments as such. His increasing popularity with the natural science Establishment of Europe will be touched on later.

REDUCTION OF SCIENCE TO SOCIETY

At least two very different things can be meant by the rise of science: organizational success and intellectual success. Organizational success includes the founding of scientific societies, the introduction of science into the curriculum; growth in the absolute and percentage numbers of people who are scientists; rise in the status of the scientific profession, in the percentage of the GNP spent on research, in Nobel Prizes won, and so on. Intellectual success is the growth of scientific knowledge, whether measured by quantity, quality, or rate of increase. The question of reduction amounts to asking whether organizational success can be explained independently of intellectual success.

Before discussing Merton's specific study of Kuhn and Popper, we need to look at his general ideas on science and on success. Only then will we be prepared for his explanation of Kuhn's influence on, and Popper's relative neglect by, social scientists.

Merton's pioneering 1938 monograph, *Science, Technology and*

Society in Seventeenth Century England did not wholly discount ideas but was primarily a study of organizational success. He set out to test the idea that the growth of science was significantly and interestingly connected with social, political, military and, ideological matters. There was in it an implicit criticism of those historians of science who looked only at scientific ideas in their temporal succession. And one need not be a connoisseur to see immediately that it was incomparably superior to the traditional style of history of science, largely dominated, as it was, by the Great Men, Great Ideas approach. Between 1938 and 1977 the emphasis in Merton's work on organization as opposed to ideas grew stronger, so that when in 1977 he studied the rise of the science of the sociology of science in the mid-twentieth century ideas played very little role.

So far we have discussed success. But it could be argued that, both socially and intellectually, there is more to science than success. Science also embraces failure, routine, hard work. Any reduction of science to social factors that does not comprehend its quotidien and unsuccessful sides as well as its brilliant and successful sides is scarcely adequate. This, I conjecture, is where Kuhn comes in: he makes room for the mundane in the house of science.[2] Indeed, I think he makes scientific mediocrities, to change the metaphor, the salt of the scientific earth. Kuhn is like one of those war-time politicians boosting the morale of face-workers in the coal mines by telling them they are essential to the war effort because their coal heats the blast furnaces that produce the metals that go into the guns, ships and aeroplanes that are destroying the enemy. Much of the stir caused by Kuhn's 1962 monograph *The Structure of Scientific Revolutions* stemmed, I conjecture, from his effort to specify what science was, not in terms of intellectual success, but in terms of current social organization. His thesis was that science is and can only be produced within a scientific community, there is no Robinson Crusoe science. Furthermore, a scientific community comes into being only when individuals and institutions subordinate themselves to the authority of a paradigm (or—in his later preferred usage—"disciplinary matrix"). A paradigm is not merely an intellectual construct such as a theory:

> "paradigms" . . . . I take to be universally recognised scientific achievements that for a time provide model problems and solutions to a community of practitioners . . . (p. 11). In learning a paradigm the scientist acquires theory, methods, and standards together, usually in inextricable mixture (p. 108).

Popper also, as we shall see, proposed a view that excludes

Robinson Crusoe science and gave a crucial role to the scientific community. But his was not a view that gave comfort either to mediocrities or to the established élites who presided over the system. Hobbesian sociologists see the fundamental problem of sociology as "How is social order possible?" In Kuhn's scheme the paradigm and the guardians of the paradigm are what the community depends upon for its very existence. Popper's social and political philosophy is rather different. Communities are not created solely by subordination to authority, to a Hobbesian sovereign paradigm, which must be obeyed until it is overthrown.[3] Instead, Popper sees the fundamental sociological problem as, "How can the social order be reformed?" He urges all scientists to be Trotskyites, apostles of permanent revolution, critical of intellectual as well as social authority. The aim that unites the scientific community is not fear of social and intellectual chaos but devotion to the ideal of truth. Instead of society explaining science, intellectual values explain social formation.

Kuhn, no doubt, would deny any reductionist intent. He sought to specify science as he found it. As Merton suggests, he might say, "je ne suis pas kuhniste" (1977, p. 109). The fact remains that the Edinburgh heresy combines Merton's pioneer work, and Kuhn's paradigms into an over-arching attempt to reduce science to society. What are these reductions reducing? Answer: the traditional intellectualist account of science as a body of ideas, inspirations. Other values traditionally ascribed to this scientific body of knowledge besides truth include: certain, based in experience, reliable, predictability, cumulative, authoritative. Kuhn's social reduction preserves only some of these values as distinctive of science. Truth and certainty he abandons in the course of fitting revolutionary change into his characterization of science. The Edinburgh school go one further: all the traditional intellectual values of science are mere epiphenomena: not they but the social functions of science make it what it is. Science becomes identical with its social embodiment. True, they allow, the social formations of science, like all social formations, have some unique features—and also some features typical of social formations in general. Both unique and typical features are social; ideas, values are epiphenomena. Thus Merton's modest program for examining the social aspects of science can, partly as a result of the ambiguities of its own emphasis, be grotesquely transformed. The sociology of science, which for Merton is a branch of the sociology of knowledge, which is a branch of sociology, can be transmogrified by the Strong Programme into a totalising science—the master science that catches everything in its embrace, including itself (it is declared to be "reflexive").

EXPLANATION WITHOUT REDUCTION

Contrasted to social reductions of science is the long intellectualist tradition that places truth and certainty at the center, where *they* can be used to explain the reliability, predictions, and authoritativeness of science; as well as the rise of scientific organizations; the trajectory of scientific careers; and other matters such as science citations or science indicators. It's not just that a piece of work is good because it is cited; it is cited because it is good; and, moreover, it could be good but not get cited and vice versa. One major reason that this intellectualist tradition has been challenged by the reductionist programs is that it seems to have broken down. During the extraordinary period when Newton's physics ruled virtually unchallenged as a paradigm of science, all epistemological discussion took it and its established place for granted. Once, however, Newton's physics was overthrown, its claims to truth, certainty, basedness in experience, reliability, cumulativeness, predictions and authoritativeness were taken as deceptive. Whatever replaced it, there was no reason that that should not in its turn to be replaced. And if science is identified with Newton, then science comes to seem impermanent.

Intellectualism need not oppose efforts, such as Merton's, to study the manner in which the success of science connects to other events in the surrounding society, to features of the organization of science, and so on. What intellectualism must oppose is the claim that science is *no more than* another, special, social formation. Without denying that science *is* another, special, social formation, intellectualism makes the claim that what explains its specialness is its product. That is to say, science is the social formation that produces scientific knowledge (ideas, inspirations). The success of science is, then, to be assessed neither by its organizational features alone, nor by measures of output or citation alone, but by both of these plus the nonoperationalizable concept of truthlikeness or proximity to truth of the ideas.

More than thirty years before Kuhn's book was published, a young Viennese was trying to fathom the problems of the intellectualist tradition. Reflecting on Kant's view of scientific knowledge and his implicit identification of it with Newton, Popper sought a way in which he could solve two problems.[4] The first was to recast the intellectualist tradition to make sense of Einstein's overthrow of Newton. This he did by making falsification, or the overthrow of ideas, the motor of that tradition. The second problem was to discriminate the progressive character of Einstein's achievement from all the many pseudo-achievements, which filled the Austro-Hungarian intellectual atmosphere. This he also did with falsification, by making it a criterion of genuine achievement, and hence in principle desirable.

A substitute teacher and outsider, Popper tried hard to get the attention of the then ruling philosophy of science establishment, called the *logical positivists.*. If one is to judge by such fashionable measures as the paucity of citations of his work in the literature, the relative isolation and low profile of his career trajectory—of which more below—and the difficulty he experienced in publishing, then it looks as though his ideas were not taken very seriously. Indeed, despite his criticism, which was later judged deadly, the logical positivist movement continued to flourish, reaching its apogee—in science indicator terms—about 1960 or perhaps a bit earlier.

Like Kuhn, Popper wanted to explain scientific success; unlike Kuhn he wanted to do it without abandoning the intellectualist tradition. Not unmindful of the fact that science was a social institution— indeed, he was the first philosopher of science to integrate this point into his philosophy of science, a couple of years before Merton—he yet wanted to claim that its very special aim (namely, the truth about nature) was pursued within a very special social structure. Success was to be measured not by social formations, nor by indicators, prizes, or what not, and certainly not by dogmatic imposition of any ruling idea; rather, it consisted in refutable assertions about the world and such social formations as would foster their production and refutation. Scientific success in Popper's view consisted in an increase in the quantity or in the scope of our knowledge of the world.

MERTON'S STUDY OF POPPER AND KUHN

In a nice reflexive twist, Merton in 1977 ("The Sociology of Science: An Episodic Memoir") made the emergence of the science of the sociology of science a case study for the emergence of science in general and hence a case study in tracing the connections between scientific success and social setting. Merton's own strategic position as a facilitator of the emergence both of the sociology of science and of Kuhn makes his participant observer's report a fine-grained and invaluable document.

Merton's 1938 monograph inaugurated a field in which, he reports, there was little activity for ten years, little more for twenty, and which then began a rapid emergence. What had been lacking was a theory to undergird the sociology of science. To be more precise what was lacking was the coincidence of a theory and the time being ripe.

Two philosophers of science, Merton says, Popper and Kuhn, offered theories of a connection between science and society. Although the presence of both looms large today, Popper, despite publishing nearly thirty years before Kuhn, is less often cited. Popper's 1934 book was widely reviewed but noticed mainly by philosophers of science, being little remarked in the literature of sociology and the history of science.[5]

> In (forty-five journals of) philosophy, Popper is cited some one-and-a-half times as often as Kuhn while Kuhn is cited some one-and-a-half times as often as Popper in the ninety-nine journals of sociology and the seven journals in the history of science covered in the 1973 and 1974 *Social Science Citation Index* (Merton 1977, p. 69)

Thirty years after his first book, with the sociology of science already growing, Popper's 1963 and 1972 works become the route for the eventual osmosis of his ideas from the philosophy of science to sociology, via the sociology of science. This "suggests that delayed cognitive interests wait upon appropriate cognitive and institutional developments in neighboring disciplines before they actually become operative" (71).

This sentence of Merton's is a trifle opaque. It seems to say that Popper's lack of influence was because he was ahead of his time. Being ahead of his time means that there was a lag in the development of cognate disciplines, which made them unable to take up his ideas. Philosophers, by contrast, did take up those ideas. Merton would seem to be arguing that a field of study had to be identified, isolated and mapped out prior to it beginning the search for a theory. Thus, his own (1938) work seeks out patterns or connections which then become data to be explained by theory. Theory that arrives too soon will thus have nothing to explain, and no audience to appreciate it.

In criticism of Merton it should be said that Popper's ideas were in fact not taken up by philosophers of science except in the Pickwickian sense that they were more or less systematically ignored. Secondly, Popper's ideas stipulate that data cannot precede theory. Since Popper's theory denies the time-is-ripe doctrine the problem of why his ideas did not stimulate the growth of the social study of science much earlier remains. To this day he is the inspiration of very few sociologists of science.

Merton is on surer ground with his study of Kuhn, which is based on his insider knowledge. The story according to Merton is that Kuhn came along at the right time, indeed was brought along by the Establishment to be in the right place at the about-to-arrive right time. Merton wants to show how Kuhn stood at an intersection where his own developing interests met those of others, and that his positioning for such serendipity was a sort of Hidden-Hand wisdom built into the commanding institutions of American academic life. These institutions single out a person like Kuhn, offer him opportunities to follow new directions of thought, and, as his work is recognized first at the local and later at the cosmopolitan level, slot him into a process of "cumulative advantage." Hence, while the intellectual public was dazzled by the appearance of *The Structure of Scientific Revolutions* in 1962, the inner circles of the relevant academic élites were not. They had looked on Kuhn as a coming man since late in the second world war and had in anticipation already heaped upon him many of the privileges and advantages available in American academic life.

Merton's story explains the emergence of a key figure in the science of the sociology of science. The science of social explanations is socially explained. Back in 1938 the problem Merton had tackled was to explain the rise of science in 17th Century society. His thesis was that "the socially patterned interests, motivations and behavior established in one institutional sphere—say, that of religion or economy—are interdependent with the socially patterned interests, motivations and behavior obtaining in other institutional spheres—say, that of science." (ix). The interdependencies Merton explored were religious (especially the Puritan value system), economic (especially mining and transportation), and military. "Before it became widely accepted as a value in its own right, science was required to justify itself to men in terms of values other than that of knowledge itself" (xix). Science for its own sake, pure science, came later: "The autonomous case for pure science evolved out of the derivative case for applied science" (xii).

This seems obvious enough. There is a wide constituency able to judge an applied scientist's work. If boats miss their landfall then owner, passengers, crew, and those awaiting their arrival can all judge either the navigation or the navigator to be faulty. But when the problems are pure, the need for a specialist reference group is felt. So a scientist's "claim resides only in the recognition accorded his work by peers in the social system of science through reference to his work" (48). Thus, concludes Merton in 1970, "science is public not private knowledge."

The invisible college of peers is partly housed, nowadays, in élite academic institutions, which attract and reward talent. This enables those on the frontiers of knowledge to engage in interactions far beyond their specialty. If thereby they enrich their field, then it has been serendipitous. This is an expectation, not a demand. Kuhn, in Merton's example, was both slow and reluctant to publish (91). For his legitimation, however, results and reactions were needed: "If one's work is not being noticed and used by others in the system of science, doubts about its value are apt to arise" (5).

So, the "gatekeepers" in the networks of academic privilege in the United States early identified T. S. Kuhn, a "not yet widely identifiable young scholar" (101), "doubly marginal," as a suitable recipient "for valued opportunities in fields widely defined as alien to his own" (96). From graduate study in physics he was inducted into the Harvard Society of Fellows, gave the Lowell Lectures, taught at Harvard, and in the same year was offered both a Guggenheim Fellowship and a Fellowship at the Center for Advanced Study in the Behavioral Sciences—all before he had published his first book (1957).

Merton scrutinizes Kuhn's footnotes and acknowledgements to chart the various people and publications Kuhn's "cumulative advantages" enabled him to bump into, and which fed the ideas of his magnum opus; people and publications across which he might not have come were it not for his positioning in the system of elite academic institutions.

Unlike Popper's work of 1934 Kuhn's of 1962 was timely: a constituency was awaiting it, a growing constituency in the sociology of science. Kuhn's career and this developing constituency intersected as the growing literature and numbers of practitioners came into contact with him. Thus, his crowning achievement was, in a way, the capstone of the sociology of science, offering as it did a major theoretical system for understanding science in social terms.

CRITIQUE OF THE KUHN CASE STUDY

Before offering some critical comments on Merton, it is only fair to stress again that he, unlike some of his intellectual heirs, nowhere actually says that the ideas scientists produce can be explained away or reduced to the study of the social formations to which they connect. Indeed, that will be one of my criticisms, for it seems to me that Kuhn's ideas eerily serve the very social formations amongst which they emerged. I do not say that the social formation caused Kuhn to think the ideas, as Durkheim would. Rather, I suggest that we recall the functionalist insight that the reception of ideas may have to do with their fitting or not fitting into pre-existing social formations.

To speak sociologically, Kuhn's ideas legitimate the system from which he benefited so much; a system moreover, that was relatively new and sorely in need of a legitimating ideology. Although Merton does not reduce ideas to social factors, he does slight ideas by ommission, by not stating his valuation of ideas as ideas. He thus overlooks the explanatory power of Popper and Kuhn's ideas for his problem: the congeniality and uncongeniality of Popper and Kuhn to sections of the American academic élite. I expand this in detailed criticism of Merton.

First, a minor point. Although he mentions Popper's autobiography (1976), Merton refrains from analysing it into a detailed study of Popper's career trajectory. It is, after all, no less sociologically interesting to study what happens to someone for whom the time is not ripe, than to study someone for whom it is.

Next, a criticism that is not so minor. Merton makes much reference to *first class minds, talent* and *brilliance.* These are words which name, presumably, properties possessed by individuals that cause them to produce work of merit. They are independent variables. But since individuals possessed of these properties are identified within a system, what this actually cashes out to is that these individuals have the capacity to jump through certain hoops set up by the system: such as getting high marks in university courses, or impressing senior colleagues. They are dependent variables. The system, so to speak, takes itself for granted; is itself the independent variable. Merton however stresses that sooner or later recipients of the rewards of the system must "produce" or the rewards process will dry up. This is contentious in itself, since tenure is sometimes awarded on promise, particularly Oxbridge and the Ivy League, promise that is never fulfilled—particularly in Oxbridge and the Ivy League. Be that as it may, the question becomes, what is "production," that is to say, what is it that we expect those talents swept into the system to produce? Merton seems to allow that what must be produced are intellectual products: science, i.e., what the peer-review system of science considers to be a fulfillment of its expectations. He fails to consider that the vested interests of the system are such that whatever its creatures produce will be hailed as major new achievements. And here is where the self-exemplifying character of the sociology of science breaks down. Science offers something that might be naively described as conceptions of nature. These conceptions, moreover, can be tested against evidence other than that considered by their creators. What, however, can play that role of independent check on the sociology of science?

Merton is very interested in devising numerical devices to assist in independent checking; but Merton's radical strong program heirs claim there is no such check on their views, that scientific activity is a self-reinforcing system no more subject to the independent checks of some "external nature" than are the speculations of the sociology of science. The institutions of science and of Azande witchcraft are thus on a sociological par.[6] Why, then, were both Merton and the Strong Programme stimulated by Kuhn? Not, surely, because he was a product of the system, science-anointed as it were? For, were that so, then the question would be, how was young Kuhn recognized, what were the signs? Merton's answer is to dispense with such specific signs: Kuhn was not selected like a Dalai Lama, where the transmigrated soul is sought out in a child. Rather, the social system delegates to its élite institutions the task of seeking out talent, selecting its own future leadership in a manner that might variously be called sleepwalking or guidance by the Hidden Hand. But what if Kuhn had not fulfilled expectations? And what if he had produced different ideas? Would a Stalinist theory of science have been accepted from him? Or suppose Kuhn, having once been contaminated by contact with Popper (see below), had produced a Popperian anti-Establishment theory. What then? This smacks of playing with those bogeymen of philosophers, subjunctive and counter-factual conditionals. That, however, is not the case. These are traditional sociological questions, namely, why did *these* ideas find a suitable home among *these* persons and institutions at *this* time. To neglect these questions is to leave a big hole in the explanations of the lack of acceptance of Popper and the acceptance of Kuhn.

Moreover, neglect of these questions also casts doubt on some of Merton's detail. Kuhn's success was not unclouded. His quest for respectability among philosophers did not go smoothly either at Berkeley, or in the reception of his book, some reactions to which were withering. His second thoughts and replies to critics were widely held to be weak and defensive. His output of graduate students has been small, and he seems recently to have thrown in his lot with the philosophy of language.

Parallel to his slightly too rosy account of Kuhn's career, Merton also quite underestimates "the Popperian presence," which is required to explain a great deal of what is happening in philosophy and the social sciences—even though Popper is rarely mentioned.

And now to the meatiest criticism: Merton does not care to explore Kuhn's ideas. He mentions there is a literature critical of Kuhn and notes that Kuhn might well want to dissociate himself from some of the things done in his name. But he overlooks the most alarming and conspicuous fact: Kuhn explicitly abandons the notion of an external nature against which science is checked, and in the understanding of which science claims to make progress. Rather, Kuhn operates with a model of scientists organizing themselves into communities of experts rallying round a paradigm (or disciplinary matrix), serving its ends and defending it to the death (theirs or its). Once a paradigm is overthrown in a revolution no comparisons with the past are possible in terms of progress or depth, the scientists in effect inhabit a new world, a world governed, in another echo of Hobbesian sovereign power, by new laws and procedures. Kuhn's theory is very odd. It postulates science as a series of hegemonies or establishments that perpetuate themselves by indoctrinating students and systematically obliterating the past in textbooks that offer students puzzle-solving tasks. This 1984-type exercise is justified in terms of the (social?) necessity of training people to perform these tasks; this is called "puzzle-solving normal science." It is, he explicitly says, dogmatic and intolerant of questioning of fundamentals. Society rewards scientists with high status and money for this blinkered performance.

The social philosophy is hard to fathom. Hobbes feared the absence of authority, anarchy. But he was concerned with the whole social Leviathan, not with the particular social formations within it. Kuhn gives us no reason to think he is not a liberal and a democrat, a believer, in general, in freedom of thought. Yet his argument is that when it comes to science if we want to make progress (note his contradiction) we have to suppress anarchy and impose intellectual discipline. The power of discipline gets things done, whether it is the Manhattan Project or the trains running on time.

Dare one see elements of autobiography in all this? Is Kuhn describing how he, as a young man with a mind that tended to wander, was forced to discipline himself (no questioning of fundamentals) to get his degrees in physics? Having done that and earned the opportunity to wander, he leaves science, enters history of science and then, lo and behold, produces a theory of science that blends many currents of fashionable ideas (Merton also completely misses the Wittgensteinian veneer) and offers a rationalizing legitimation of the system from which he emerged which simultaneously explains how and why it works and why a free spirit like Kuhn left it. There is no suggestion in Merton that Kuhn carefully refrained from biting the hand that had stroked him. Quite the contrary: Merton treats Kuhn as a naive believer in the system Merton describes. His theory and the system it describes are, however, quite incoherent. It is easy to see on Popper's principles how obviously incoherent it is; but its incoherence is there—one way or another.

Merton needs to explain the establishment's patronage and recruitment of Kuhn, and its initial failure to recruit or even take Popper seriously, by some such general property as their being or not being "talented." To be more precise, Popper may serve as a test case to evaluate Merton's test case as well as his theory. And, clearly, Merton's case study is too thin on Popper to explain Popper's outsider status and his later transformation into the leading philosopher of science he now is. This is why I will make a few remarks about all this later. Here let me round off my critique of Merton's case study of Kuhn and Popper.

At several places in his 1977 paper Merton holds that it is Kuhn's first-class performance and talent that led senior people at Harvard to discover him, promote his "early visibility" and strongly back his accumulation of advantage. This is certainly the manner of self-perception of the establishment and institutions within it; Harvard and other élite institutions see themselves as part of a meritocracy not as merely a self-perpetuating set of institutions. Indeed, they can stoutly defend themselves against a charge of mere self-perpetuation by pointing to the scope of their recruiting effort, the objectivity of their procedures and results—that member institutions of the establishment time and again gain prestigious awards, research monies, and high rankings of their graduate programs. There is a concordance between their local forms of self-evaluation and the cosmopolitan forms of evaluation that are taken to be somewhat more objective. Merton is not unaware of the fact that such an argument is possibly circular and thus a self-fulfilling prophecy; but he does not address it as the possibly serious deficiency I think it is.

Subsequent to the publication of Henry Fairlie's journalistic article "The Establishment," and Hugh Thomas' anthologizing of it, any such self-defense by an intellectual establishment has to be disingenuous. An establishment is a network of self-perpetuating institutions dedicated to maintaining its hold on power on behalf of the current and future membership, yet in full conviction that, as the best and the brightest, it is to the benefit of the society as a whole for it to do so. So strong is the rationale that many members of the establishment are unaware of themselves as such, and even deny its existence.

The Harvard defense need not claim that everyone deserving recruitment has been recruited; so it can allow for some dissatisfaction from those with talent as well as that from those with ambition but without talent. It need not be claimed that the establishment embodies the interests of any class or party or system of ideas. On the contrary, a healthy establishment will be as flexible about ideas as it is about recruitment; it will be disinterested. It is even possible for the establishment to connive at piece-meal attempts to alter its own structure. All that is required for its legitimation is the admission that there has to be *some* hierarchical structure of leaders and followers, experts and laymen, if society is to gain the benefits it wants. An acknowledgement, in other words, that there must be an establishment, is sufficient for the establishment to justify itself by more than its own self-interest. For all of this Merton has to draw on Kuhn who argued that in the absence of an established paradigm there is no science.

Since such a minimum requirement will still result in disaffection and envy by those who want to lead and by those who hate being led, it would benefit an establishment to have an ideology that legitimates the hierarchy of expertise as a hierarchy of power. It is a striking feature of our modern age that there has grown up in the liberal tolerant democracies professions that are structured in an outspokenly authoritarian and illiberal manner. Oldest among these is the law, which was a profession before medicine was even a guild. There followed medicine, obviously still a guild, though pretending to be a profession. Just as law courts insist on laymen employing their officers, so physicians insist that the State legalize their monopoly on drugs and on surgery. Last of the modern professions to evolve are scientists and teachers, which are partially overlapping. Other professions have formed into guilds, notably engineers and accountants, and still others are in the process of formation.

All these professions claim to impart through their training and licensing procedures a form of expertise so essential to society that its acquisition must be supervised and restricted. Its power, then, is accumulated to "protect" society. We see, then, that forms of social organization have been growing that, if challenged, may require some form of general ideological legitimation if they are to explain and defend the power they wield in an egalitarian and democratic society. Kuhn supplied that for science and in so doing papered over the cracks in Merton's theory.

POPPER AS A THREAT TO THE ESTABLISHMENT

Although Merton tells us the citation ratio of Popper to Kuhn is over the range of 1.5:1 positive and negative, in his 1977 paper he devotes three pages to Popper and forty-two to Kuhn, a ratio of 1:14. Such are the rewards of not being ahead of your time. Let me then redress the balance of objective indicators somewhat by offering a few more pages on Popper and his career as part of the process of showing how important his idea is that ideas (including, for my money, his ideas) are important.

In the nineteen twenties a young man was maturing in Vienna who was to subject science and democratic society to unprecedented scrutiny—offering the thought that our fundamental understanding of each was in error and needed rectification. A deep admirer both of science and democratic society, Popper nevertheless detected authoritarian dangers in the excessive respect for expertise in both. By 1934 Popper had published his scrutiny of science (in German) in a manner that insured that it would get limited attention but not be understood as the swingeing attack it was. *Logik der Forschung* was published in a series edited by the positivist Schlick. This falsely identified Popper to the intellectual public as a bright and independent member of the iconoclastic European philosophical group called the logical positivists. On this basis he was offered, as a refugee, a temporary job at Cambridge. He declined, and took a post in New Zealand in 1937 where he was to work out his ideas for democracy, published in 1945 to great if delayed acclaim, as *The Open Society and its Enemies.* The acclaim did not turn into establishment recognition, but rather into establishment disbelief and disapproval by establishment political radicals whose social, political, and academic credentials it challenged. It was almost twenty years more before Popper began to accumulate the academic and political "advantage" that a Mertonian recognition of "talent" should have been bestowing. It is notable that Popper was invited to the new Stanford Center for Advanced Study in the Behavioral Sciences in 1956–57, a year later than Kuhn, who was then 32; Popper was at this time 54. Kuhn declined, Popper accepted.

At the end of the war Popper came to The London School of Economics where he stayed until his retirement. Popper's career as outsider, by no means unknown outsider, but outsider kept at a distance from the intellectual establishment and its networks of power and influence, followed by his absorption in the British establishment networks only at the very end of his career, and his continuing exclusion from American establishment networks can be explained by Merton either by the suggestion that Popper had less talent than Kuhn and hence was not quickly inducted into the system of benefits and rewards; or that his talent was harder to discern; or by the accident of being a Viennese rather than an American, and of being of the generation in Europe whose academic lives were disrupted by the second European war.[7] None of these explanations works, especially when the careers of other Viennese are looked at. Equally poor is explanation by randomizing sample in which one simply allows establishment recruitment and succession procedures to have a certain amount of error, the capacity to miss a certain percentage of good people. Popper's exclusion continued after he was acknowledged as good.

All these explanations are very weak, and could be resorted to only were a better one not available. But Kuhn's career, of rapid induction at a very early age to the establishment, which made available to him all its perks long in advance of him publishing anything of any particular significance, suggests a line of explanation much more powerful than these weak ones. This explanation is that Kuhn was one of the small group of scholars being recruited to the emerging subject of the sociology of science, under the auspices of élite institutions and scientists within them, in recognition of the need of the greying science establishment to find a legitimating ideology. Indeed, the very absence from the social formations of a sociology of science group, yet the strongly felt need for a justification to the public of science's prestige and wealth, facilitated Kuhn's recruitment to take place outside of and prior to the growth of sociology of science. Both sociology of science itself, which legitimized scientific organization as science; and the specific model of science devised by Kuhn; functioned well to buttress the claims of the scientific profession to ever more money and power. These were not by any means the only signs that the establishment was defending itself. A quite systematic muddling of science with technology (both the atomic bomb and the moon landing being taken as vindicating "science"), and aggressive campaigns against cranks (Velikovsky), superstition (astrology) and religion (creationism) are other signs. We might see these as a customs union with the powerful technology, plus strict boundary policing, to keep benefits away from non-citizens.

It may not therefore be quite "serendipitous," to use Merton's word, since it seems that when Kuhn began to publish his ideas, they served very well to legitimize the hierarchy of expertise and its hegemony of power claimed by science in a manner that explains and legitimates Kuhn's own recruitment as described by Merton. Had Kuhn published his *Structure* in 1938, and had it been a standard text in 1950, there would have been no need to recruit anyone. Fleck had in fact published in 1935 and Polanyi in 1958, the one too soon, the other too late, to become the standard text book.

To explain this, we have to explain why it was that in the postwar period the scientific Establishment, especially in America, felt an increasingly urgent need for an ideology.

The first thing to note is that this establishment itself, as well as its money and power, were new phenomena. The growth of R and D during and after the war had catapulted a new class of scientists—normal scientists Kuhn calls them, though their normality is very recent—into the structure of western society. This class had an interest in perpetuating and increasing its power when the Cold War created a situation in which further heavy investment in research and development for military purposes became imperative. The Russian atomic and hydrogen bombs, and their launch of Sputnik accentuated the already strong tendency for the richest nation in the world to tackle problems by throwing money at them. Thus was the situation created for the mammoth growth of the military-industrial-scientific complex, a complex that faithfully obeys the theories of bureaucracy of both Max Weber and C. Northcote Parkinson.[8]

This sheer growth in scale itself made the previously available ideologies for science inadequate. Very little is needed to legitimize the paper and pencils required by a Swiss patent clerk. In truth, the prevalent ideology of the inter-war years—logical positivism—fitted Einstein's work rather poorly. It fitted the mixed technical and scientific efforts of the Manhattan Project much better, and the behaviorist psychology applied to troop morale, home and overseas propaganda, better still. Unfortunately, the cognoscenti knew, although none of them would consciously allow, that logical positivism's intellectual foundations were in ruins, and the collapse of the whole building was only a matter of time. A darker secret, one still not acknowledged in public, was that the one person primarily responsible for this ruin more than any other was Karl Popper.[9]

Any thought that Popper could be the needed ideologist of the new situation was scotched by two considerations. The first was that he had committed the thoughtcrime of attacking logical positivism, a crime not mitigated by the attack being successful. The scientific establishment and its captive audience of normal scientists had all been raised in the heady atmosphere of logical positivism and were not happy to lose their toys (some have yet to admit that they are lost). Bad enough to have to seek a replacement, but to go for it to the very instrument of this fate, Popper, was altogether asking too much. Secondly, Popper's own ideas were quite unsuitable, since, so far from legitimizing an establishment and its perquisites, Popper threw doubt on all expertise and made challenging establishments integral to the scientific endeavor.

It is my hypothesis that Kuhn was aware of all these matters although not perhaps consciously.

Already at Harvard in 1950 he had attended Popper's William James lectures and seminars. He was subsequently recruited by the positivist group who edited the *International Encyclopedia of Unified Science,* to write a volume for them, which is the origins of his *The*

Structure of Scientific Revolutions. One might then conjecture that Kuhn's theory of science serves to describe and legitimize the hegemony of those with expertise—an expertise demanded by a paradigm—and enforced by those who accept and impose it on scientific training. Thus Kuhn's theory allows that scientists develop a faculty of judgement that warrants their dismissing the works of outsiders with at best a cursory examination. He allows that science systematically rewrites its textbooks, ignoring and falsifying history in the cause of training in the paradigm and engendering the puzzle-solving capacity in budding scientists. No matter how inegalitarian, illiberal, or anti-democratic the behavior of scientific elites, Kuhn is able to show openly and in good conscience how to legitimize them by appeal to scientific success and technological success and hence to the benefit of society at large.

KUHN'S FUNCTION FOR THE ESTABLISHMENT

We still need a crucial missing link. Consider the facts. Kuhn was recruited as part of a pool of talent whose job was to reinforce the collapsing ideology of an insecure establishment. Hence Kuhn's rapid elevation from author of an obscure (and, some thought, iconoclastic) monograph to a major figure in American academic life. Although the main theses of his book were severely criticized not to say refuted within a couple of years of its appearance, if anything, attention to it grows as the criticism mounts. Its value as a legitimation charter becomes ever clearer.

The facts being these, the missing link needed is this: how has the boat-rocking Popper been recruited to the establishment? The answer is that he has not. What has been recruited to the establishment is the Popper Legend, a Legend whose contents Popper has himself delineated, and about whose growth and influence he has been greatly exercised.[10] When Popper says he doesn't believe in experts; that Kuhn's normal science is for him a disaster; that what is important is to be critical; it is as though no one hears, certainly not the establishment, which turns its attention rather to the gadfly Feyerabend, or the vulgarizer Lakatos, both easily brushed off *and* incorporated. Kuhn meanwhile goes from strength to strength, redefining his terms, acting as though his work is intact and that most criticism of it is a matter of either misunderstanding or minor disagreement. It is in fact neither, it is rather the detection of vagueness or inconsistencies in his basic ideas.

The sociology of science, then, is a self-exemplifying development, as in the present paper. Kuhn's theory is a theory of science in which the role of ideas is minimized. Most of what he calls normal science is devoid of them. Scientific revolutions are rare, unwelcome, and as much changes of generation and of pedagogy as they are of ideas. Scientific education wants stability in order to know what to teach and to develop standards; it also wants success—rewards for the effort. Only upon education and standards can a prosperous profession be built. Without quite reducing science to society, Kuhn stresses that paradigms or disciplinary matrices and exemplars have only a small component of ideas. His own work is thus the ideal paradigm for the emerging sociology of science.

Ideas, however, will not go away. Moreover, despite the best efforts both of the philosophy and of the sociology of science to ignore Popper's centering of ideas, criticism, the overthrow of establishments, the democratizing of society, severe checks on power, and critique of expertise, he has found, surprisingly, as Merton notes, quite a following among *bona fide* professional scientists, especially in Europe. On Merton's model this is inexplicable. On Popper's, in which science is not a monolith but a battleground fought over by shifting coalitions of friendly-hostile groups, it is. For if Kuhn's theory is correct the neglect of Popper is to be expected to continue. If Popper's theory is correct things need not be, and perhaps are not, near so bad.

NOTES

1. Many thanks to J. Agassi, W. W. Bartley, III, Donald Campbell and Gerard Radnitzky for their critical comments on an earlier version of this paper. The usual warning that this in no way spreads to them responsibility for the upshot, should be taken with unusual seriousness.

2. The metaphor of the house of science comes from Oppenheimer (1954).

3. The Hobbes parallel comes from Geller (1982).

4. K. R. Popper (1976).

5. Popper's claim, that Merton repeats, that *Logik der Forschung* gained a modest amount of attention could, as far as philosophers of science are concerned, be shown, by citation measure, to be false. Popper contrasts this early reception with the paucity and poor quality of the reviews of the translation, published in 1959. Reviews may be poor indicators.

Citation of *The Logic of Scientific Discovery* shows it to be very well known indeed.

6. Evans-Pritchard (1937) showed us how any system of ideas can be self-critical, provided the criticism is internal to the system. It is criticism *of the system* that marks science.

7. This is close to the view of my commentator, Michael Cavanaugh, whom I thank for his critique.

8. Weber (1968); Parkinson (1958). Not to mention "Murphy."

9. See "Who Killed Logical Positivism" in Popper (1976).

10. The great bulk of Popper citations, for example, refer not to Popper but to the Popper Legend.

REFERENCES

Barnes, Barry, 1982. *T.S. Kuhn and Social Science*. London: Macmillan.

Evans-Pritchard, E., 1937. *Witchcraft, Oracles and Magic Among the Azande*. Oxford: Oxford University Press.

Fairlie, H. 1968. "Evolution of a Term." *New Yorker*, October 19, vol. 44, pp. 173–206.

Fleck, L. 1979 (1935). *Genesis and Development of a Scientific Fact*. Chicago: University of Chicago.

Gellner, E., 1982. "The Paradox of Paradigms." *Times Literary Supplement*, 23 April, pp. 451–2.

Kuhn, T., 1972. *The Structure of Scientific Revolutions*. Chicago: University of Chicago Press.

Latour, B. and Woolgar, S., 1979. *Laboratory Life*. Beverly Hills: Sage.

Merton, R., 1938. "Science, Technology and Society in Seventeenth Century England." *Osiris*, vol. IV, Part 2; reprinted New York: Howard Fertig, 1970.

Merton, R., 1973. *The Sociology of Science*. Chicago: University of Chicago.

Merton, R., 1977. "Sociology of Science: An Episodic Memoir." edited by Merton, R. and Gaston, J. in, *The Sociology of Science in Europe*. Carbondale (Ill.): Southern Illinois University Press.

Oppenheimer, J., 1954. *Science and the Common Understanding*. Oxford: O.U.P.

Parkinson, C., 1958, *Parkinson's Law*. London: John Murray.

Polanyi, M., 1958. *Personal Knowledge*. London: Routledge.

Popper, K.R., 1934. *Logik der Forschung*. Vienna:

Popper, K.R., 1963. *Conjectures and Refutations*. London: Routledge.

Popper, K.R. 1972. *Objective Knowledge*. Oxford: Oxford University Press.

Popper, K.R. 1976. *Unended Quest*. London: Fontana.

Thomas, H., ed., 1959. *The Establishment*. London: Anthony Blond.

Weber, M. 1968. *Economy and Society*. London: Bedminster Press.

21

The Philosophical Lure of the Sociology of Knowledge

PETER MUNZ

Thomas Kuhn's philosophy of science is one of the really great successes of the intellectual history of the 20th Century. Whenever there is talk of how knowledge grows, how it changes, and how it is justified, most people reach for their *Structure of Scientific Revolutions.* This success is all the more remarkable as the main contention of that book is that knowledge is a function of social pressures and institutions. Kuhn's philosophy of science reduces the development of science and of knowledge in general to a sociological problem. How can one explain this turn of the philosophy of science towards sociology?

Paradoxically, it is easier to obtain knowledge than to account for the manner in wich it is obtained. In natural as well as in social science we have a lot of progress and many tangible results. But as soon as one asks *why* we have those results, dissension and confusion starts to abound. It may well be true, to use a now famous metaphor, that scientists of both nature and society are like sleepwalkers. They seem to get somewhere even though they do not quite know how.

If one looks at the history of *theories* of knowledge one will get indeed a very strange tale, and if one follows its course over the last three hundred years or so one will readily see what the reasons for Kuhn's astonishing success are, even though one must conclude that his success is mainly *faute de mieux;* that is, though not inherently commendable, in the eyes of many people Kuhn's theory is the best possible explanation. Above all one will see that it is merely the most recent phase in a long intellectual development in the course of which philosophers of science disappointed or frustrated by rationalism and positivism, have searched and found varying degrees of solace in the arms of sociology.

THE QUANDARY OF THE THEORY OF KNOWLEDGE

In order to understand the course of intellectual history which has ushered in Kuhn, one has to get rid of some conventional views about the middle ages and the Enlightenment. According to conventional wisdom about the history of thought, people were very credulous in the middle ages, unable to distinguish between religious knowledge and scientific knowledge, confusing the sources of the one with the sources of the other so that no proper scientific picture could emerge, at least none which would have withstood modern canons of criticism. At best, we get the theories of St. Thomas Aquinas who believed that men can follow reason to advantage because God has imprinted reason on man when He created him. And then, at long last, if we are still following conventional wisdom, there dawned the Enlightenment. The clouds of superstition were blown away and, free of dogma and tradition, men could devote themselves to the scientific search for truth. From Galileo and Kepler to Newton and Einstein there was no stopping them now.

In an important sense this conventional story is actually true—at least, it is true as far as the findings or the content of knowledge are concerned. But in an equally important sense it is false; that is, it is false as far as the *theory* of knowledge is concerned.

When we are looking at the theory rather than the practice of knowledge, we find first of all that in the middle ages, in the very midst of all that darkness and authority and superstition, there was nurtured a fundamental postulate. People believed that God had created the world according to laws or rules and that there were, as a consequence, regularities. We have been made familiar with this pre-scientific belief and its importance by A.N. Whitehead and it has been underpinned by the researches of Zilsel into the development of the idea of *law* and elaborated in that wonderful book by Joseph Needham, *The Grand Titration.* The development of scientific practice was made possible, these scholars and philosophers argue, by the world-view which stated that the universe is governed by laws. It was in this religious world-view, deeply in debt to the Old Testament, that there was nourished the thought that there are regularities, and that thought eventually provided Newton with his vocabulary so that he could refer to his famous *leges.* In the 16th and 17th Centuries, people had wavered in their use of "law"—hovering often between the religious-judicial usage and the philosophy of nature usage. If the culture of the middle ages had been favorable to the assumption that there were regularities in nature, and if that assumption was there, ready to be used for the conception that one can experiment, then that hypothesis must be inter-subjective, and, eventually, for the formulation of a theory of evolution that depends totally on the ideal that any adaptation to the environment must be an adaptation to regularities in the environment.

However, no matter how pre-adapted medieval thought had been for the emergence of critically sustained knowledge, its dogmatism had to be destroyed and the hold of tradition and authority abandoned before critically sustained knowledge could emerge. Even though the idea that there were regularities turned out to be fruitful, the manner in which it had been held was not. For in our modern view of knowledge we are not only aware that one's views as to the actual regularities keep changing, but also have come to accept ever since Hume that the existence of regularities itself cannot be proved. The Enlightenment—and this is the crucial point which is so frequently overlooked—not only sowed doubts in regard to religious traditions but also in regard to knowledge in general. For if there can be no guarantee that there *are* regularities, how can one have any certainty about the allegation that there are some specific regularities? "The philosophers' glorification of criticism and their *qualified* repudiation of metaphysics make it obvious that the Enlightenment was not an Age of Reason but a Revolt against Rationalism," Peter Gay writes on p. 141 of Vol. I of his *The Enlightenment*.

The reason why this point is overlooked is that we have taken our evaluation of the Enlightenment from Voltaire, its greatest purveyor. Voltaire was something of a "catastrophist." In fact, he was a catastrophist long before the catastrophists in geology had established themselves. Voltaire believed that the Enlightenment had suddenly broken upon mankind and illuminated it by its rays like a sudden catastrophe. He believed that its great protagonists were Locke and Newton and that its nurture had taken place in England. For Voltaire, Locke and Newton were the great heralds of science, and before them the medieval world of superstition had suddenly collapsed. Voltaire was the first to introduce the reading public of the European continent to the marvels of England's urbanity and civility, to the generous infra-structure of its towns, to coffee-houses and newspapers, theatres, assembly rooms, philosophical and royal societies and lending libraries. In this atmosphere, he told his readers, the progress of rational knowledge was assured and the rest of mankind would soon benefit by it. The battle against religious superstition was led by the progress of science and reason.

This picture painted by Voltaire is basically false. There is no space to go into details; an outline sketch must suffice. Locke's advocacy of sense observation could not be applied, least of all by Newton. Newton himself was frequently confused as to how he was going about getting his marvelous knowledge, and developed one strategy for gravity and another one for optics. The truth of the matter is that the Enlightenment's main and immediate impact, *pace* Voltaire, was to create doubt and scepticism not only in regard to religion and the middle ages but also in regard to knowledge as such, even in regard to knowledge of the so-called "rational" kind. A dispassionate and non-Voltairean look at the 18th Century reveals immediately the widespread scepticism in regard to scientific as well as religious knowledge. People became (as a result of the absence of old blinders) aware that one could not have confidence in anything— not even in science. There is no need to mention Hume. Goethe in lapidary poetry proclaimed that in the beginning there was the deed; and that whatever we know followed from action and the living situation in which we found ourselves, not from cognition. Rousseau and Wordsworth between them upheld the voice of the heart and the simplistic naivety of children against sophisticated criticism and reason. This is all familiar ground, and we need to remind ourselves of it only in order to show that the grand century of the origin of modern science was presided over by scepticism and by despair: ". . . und sehe dass wir nichts wissen können. Das will mir schier das Herz verbrennen . . ." wrote Goethe. And when Kant came to the rescue, all he managed to do was to assure us that Newton must be right because his laws did not apply to the noumenál world and the thing-in-itself, but only to the conventional world of our experience. This may have been a temporary vindication of Newton in the face of Hume's scepticism about regularities, but was really and deeply a counsel of despair about knowledge. In passing, we might note that Kant was actually on the right track with his view that our knowledge that there are regularities is *a priori*. But since he wrote before the theory of biological evolution as a cognitive process of natural selection had been developed, he could only assert dogmatically that we happen to be born with such *a priori* knowledge, mysteriously so. At the time in which he wrote, there was no way in which he could surmise that all such *a priori* knowledge was part of a genetic program which we inherit, and the adaptiveness of which to the noumenal world, as Konrad Lorenz was the first to point out forty-five years ago, is warranted, up to a point, by phylogenetic error elimination. Without a theory of biological evolution, Kant's attempt to make philosophy safe for Newton must have appeared cold comfort because it drove a wedge between the knowledge we have and any knowledge of the world as it really is.

It is perfectly true that in spite of such despair and lack of confidence, the battle for scientific progress and the hope of knowledge was carried on. But it was carried on by theoreticians, not by the practitioners. Out and out materialists managed to persuade themselves that knowledge of matter would eventually bring real truth. And then there was positivism—the philosophy that said that at long last knowledge was yielding final and trustworthy results because it had rid itself of tradition and dogma and kept on adhering to sense perception and observation and to nothing but sense-experience and observation. But such talk and such hope was armchair philosophy and entirely theoretical. How theoretical and how divorced from the practice of science and knowledge is made clear by the following anecdote.

By 1847 the experiments of Joule had shown that there could be a connection between chemistry, the theory of heat, electricity, magnetism, and biology. Joule had defined a general equivalence between physico-chemical transformations because he had shown that the conservation of what came to be known as energy could be made quite exact as soon as heat was taken into account. Against this background of thought, the German physiologist, Helmholtz, finally formulated the first law of thermodynamics. On the face of it Helmholtz was a strict positivist. But when it came to the crunch he did not hesitate to take a step forward by freeing himself from the constraints, which positivism would have imposed on him and by proclaiming that the principle of Joule's "equivalence" of all transformations of energy obtained throughout the whole of nature. The philosophy of science, known as positivism, could certainly not have allowed such a leap to the view "that the whole of nature in all particulars was dominated by the fundamental principle of the conservation of energy".[1]

To make a long story short: the Enlightenment, far from successfully combating the ignorance due to religion by the confident knowledge of science, had managed to sow doubt in all directions. Scientific knowledge had progressed, but there had not arisen a confidence inspiring explanation as to why it had done or how it had been possible to do so, let alone as to how much confidence one was entitled to place in that progress. Positivism—whether that of Locke or that of Comte or of Mill—did not correspond to the practice of science at all. Kantianism did, but was deeply shot through with scepticism in regard to the *real* nature of things. The most remarkable episode in this long history of doubt generated by the Enlightenment is the emergence of Logical Positivism in the early 20th Century. In the face of all historical evidence to the contrary, the Vienna Positivists believed in the ability to account for the growth of knowledge by the rigorous argument that all knowledge is derived inductively from observation statements. One glance at the history and progress of knowledge would have demonstrated to them that the theory was false. But a lack of interest in history was an essential part of the *credo* of the Vienna Positivists and so evidence from the history of science was ruled out of court. A procedure all the more remarkable as it was upheld by the very advocates of experience. Perhaps the Vienna Positivists surmised or suspected that historical knowledge above all cannot be legitimized in terms of induction and observation, and perhaps it was for that reason that they insisted on its irrelevance. The only attempt to account for historical knowledge in positivistic terms was made by Richard von Mises in Chapter 18 of his *Kleines Lehrbuch des Positivismus.*[2] But even there it is admitted that the criterion of truth of a historical assertion "includes the application of inferences derived from general experience . . . and is never uniquely determined by the facts."

THE SEARCH FOR A NON-COGNITIVE BASIS OF KNOWLEDGE

When one surveys this long history of doubt and the story of the unsuccessful attempts to account for and to explain the growth of knowledge, it can come hardly as a surprise to find that already in the middle of the 19th Century it began to occur to perceptive observers that one might be able to explain the growth of knowledge by relating it to something other than the growth of knowledge. If one could see it as a function of another growth or as a function of other structures one might be able to explain what had so far resisted all explanations. Prompted by such an insight, philosophers and scholars began to wonder whether it might not be possible to explain the growth of knowledge as a function of social structures or pressures. There were two unrelated reasons why, of all phenomena, social phenomena should have been seized on and why the thought that if knowledge cannot be accounted for as a purely cognitive process, it might be accounted for as a derivative or function of social events. At the beginning of the 19th Century sociology and the importance of the study of society as a natural phenomenon was very much in the foreground. The surprising experience of the French Revolution was responsible for this interest. Until well into the 18th Century it had been believed that societies are held together by people's allegiance to monarchy and religion combined in Feudalism. When these institutions were being attacked, most thoughtful people sensibly predicted chaos and the end of all societies. When societies survived the French Revolution, thoughtful people had to take another look. The experience of the Revolution had forced them to conclude that societies were not held together by monarchy and by religion structured around feudalism. At best, monarchy and church were only one of many possible ways of structuring the social order. Hence there emerged an enormous interest in the problem of social organization, and that interest became institutionalized intellectually as the study of sociology. We find, therefore, that just at the time when students of the growth of knowledge had to cast their net more widely than Locke and Comte had done, there also began the serious study of society—that is, the serious study of the real nature of social bonds and of their transformations.

The influence of Comte in this development is crucial. Comte was not only a positivist, but also the first sociologist. Indeed, we owe the words "positivism" and "sociology" to Comte. He developed both the concept of positivism and the concept of sociology in a very specific inter-dependent manner, believing that positivism was a true account of the procedures of science and that sociology taught that societies are subject to a developmental law, which constrains them to develop from a superstitious adherence to the practice of science as advocated by positivism. This argument by itself does, of course, not make up for the deficiencies of the positivistic account of knowledge as the result of nature's causal action upon our body-mind. But it did help to allay doubts in regard to positivism's account of knowledge and tended to explain the difficulties away. How, positivists could argue after Comte, could positivism be a wrong account if it is to be equated with the most recent, the most advanced, the most enlightened stage of human development? The alliance between positivism and historicism may have been an unholy one, but unholy or not, it did the trick. Comte, in brief, provided a sociological (historicist sociology) explanation of positivism, though not of knowledge or science. As a result of this confluence of positivism and sociology, more and more attention came to be paid to the question as to whether the real grounds for the growth of knowledge might not be found in the organization of society. The philosophy of science, in other words, began to turn towards sociology. If the growth of knowledge could not be explained as resulting entirely from the direct application of reason and/or observation, it might be explicable as the result of social pressures or organizations.

The recourse to society and social structures found collateral support from a very different quarter. There is no denying that we can have readier comprehension of the societies we live in—that is, of their rules, the authorities behind those rules, the reasons for obedience, and similar matters—than we can have of atoms, electrons, photons, the forces of gravity or electricity, and so on. The quite radical distinction between the kinds of readiness of comprehension that are available goes back to Vico. Vico had argued that we can know something if we can understand the reasons for which it was made and the intention that determines its existence and the way it functions. Since no human mind had made atoms and electricity, the argument runs, no human mind can really understand how they function. True, he had a special kind of "understanding" in mind. But if that is granted, his distinction between the knowledge we can have of works of art and possibly even of social structures and the kind of knowledge we can have of atoms and photons is quite striking.

Vico's observation was explicitly directed against Descartes' criterion of certainty and self-evidence. But it could just as well have been directed against Locke whose causal theory of perception in opposition to Descartes' theory of how we know was no more plausible than Descartes' own theory. It has always been surprising that Vico not so much as mentioned Locke.

To begin with, it is just as difficult to acquire knowledge of societies and their structures as it is to acquire knowledge of atoms. But when we are dealing with societies, we can at least presume that their structure was "intended" and that we can therefore recapitulate that intention. Such recapitulation in our mind does not amount to an explanation (although that too has been maintained!), but it is a good way in, and it has to be admitted that we have no comparable way in where atoms are concerned. It is true that no society is the result of intentions and plans. This is not because they are not intended, but because all people ever involved in them, even the most distant ancestors as well as the members of both friendly and hostile societies within reach, have also had intentions so that all these disparate intentions tend to cancel one another out and one gets, at any one stage, not what anybody intended but something like an unintended equilibrium, which results from lots of contrary and contradictory intentions. There is no society known that looks as if it were the result of an intention. Every society, however, is the result of crossing and mutually cancelling intentions, and it is these processes, which can be recapitulated in our minds in a sense in which the behavior of atoms and molecules cannot. Societies, therefore, are more accessible to the understanding than atoms and molecules. Hence the notion that if we could show that our understanding of natural phenomena is determined by the social structures we are living in or, at least, functionally related to those social structures, there would be a net gain in understanding. This is the notion all endeavours to explain knowledge as a function of social conditions latched on to. Since knowledge cannot be explained as the effect of observations, and since in pre-evolutionary days there was not available an explanation of how the *a priori* element in knowledge might have arisen, the project of explaining the acquisition and growth of knowledge as the result of social conditions looked promising. In the absence of any other viable explanation of the undisputed fact that we had knowledge, this detour *via* society had a lot to recommend itself.

THE DETOUR *VIA* SOCIETY

Even so, the historian of ideas must detect a certain irony, not to say paradox, in the emergence of such reasoning and in the way in which sociology came to tighten its grip. Vico himself had been something of a purist. He had distinguished carefully between *facta*, (*i.e.*, artifacts) and natural events. By his own standards of understanding he maintained that we can have knowledge of *facta*—but not of natural events. Given his understanding of understanding, the distinction is impeccable. However, less than half a century after his death, the notion that knowledge is derived by observation and by induction from observation (positivism) had gained so much ground, that people began to accept that knowledge of nature was accounted for and that all that needed a reduction to social structures was knowledge of things other than nature—mental, social, psychological, and religious phenomena. Here then we get, with the assistance of positivism, an outlook very different from that of Vico. Now nature is no longer forever a closed book as it had been for Vico. Now nature is something to be known in the way in which positivists said it is known. The scope for the detour *via* societies was now limited to social, mental, and psychological phenomena, and it was in this sphere that the sociology of knowledge scored its first successes.

But finally we arrive at the irony. Finally the fortunes of positivism declined, and the question as to how we can have knowledge of nature was again wide open. With the absence of positivism, one would have expected a return to the agnosticism in regard to nature which we find in Vico. But there was to be no return to agnosticism in regard to nature. Far from it. Since the sociology of knowledge had by now scored so many successes in the field of social, mental, religious and psychological knowledge, there was no holding back. It now came to be believed that one can explain our knowledge of nature by doing sociology, just as one had been so successful in explaining our knowledge of social and mental and religious phenomena. At this stage, the knowledge of nature came to be included among the subjects that might conveniently be explained by a sociology of knowledge.

The root of the error that a detour *via* society is required if one wants to account for knowledge, is the belief that the quality of knowledge depends on its source of derivation. Thus, when revelation was dismissed as a source for knowledge, people had to run to authority. When authority was dismissed or questioned, people ran to innate ideas. When innate ideas had lost their credibility as a source, people looked to induction and observation. And when that too had proved inadequate, people were thrown back upon social institutions or social experience as a source of knowledge—first as a source of knowledge of social experience and social institutions and in the end, as a source of all knowledge of anything.

As long as one is looking for a source of knowledge, the final recourse to society is not as absurd as it may seem. No matter which of the earlier sources one believes to be acceptable, any analysis will show that behind that source there does indeed lie an appeal to social institutions. Take "observation" as an example. The activity "observation" is described and defined by a word which has a place in a language; language is governed by rules; rules are a social institution. The same goes, *mutatis mutandis,* for revelation, intuition, authority, and any other conceivable source one cares to name. Moreover, the designation of the people capable of making observations, having revelations, exercising authority, *etc.,* is a social institution. By whichever route one chooses to go, it is well nigh impossible to avoid the epistemic authority of social life. Man is a social animal in more than one sense, and even the mind of man is that of a social animal.

The correct method would have been to give up the notion that the quality of our knowledge depends on the source of knowledge. Instead, one ought to accept that the *source* does not matter and that the quality of our knowledge depends on what we do with it, how we treat it, and how much we can criticize it once we have it— regardless of the source. It should never be a question of the impeccability of the source but always a question of the amount of criticism we expose knowledge to.

Even then we may be caught in a trap. Naturally, one will ask:

what kind of criticism is to be applied to any hypothesis? Suppose we state that all knowledge must be criticized to make sure it contains nothing but observations. In stating this, we are setting up a standard of criticism so that we can distinguish senseless criticism from sensible criticism. But as soon as we set up a standard of criticism, we are thrown back upon the road to the society we are living in; that is, upon the same road we were on before we had set up "criticism." Taking observation again, this time as a standard of criticism, we will find the same old questions. First, what will count as observation? We must answer that only such observation can be counted as can be classified under the expression "observation." Such classification, how-ever, is a social rule. For this reason, as soon as we set up a standard of criticism, we are pushed back to a sociological explanation of knowledge.

Second, we must ask: whose observation? The answer then must be that only the observation of "qualified" people can count as observation. But the category "qualified" is a social category. People become qualified by passing examinations or by being accorded a special status in a hierarchy, and so forth. Here too, we are pushed back into sociology.

These quandaries which sooner or later must lead the inquiry back to sociology are the same no matter what criterion we choose to set up as the standard of criticism. Try it for "revelation." First, if we accept as valid any criticism that shows that a piece of knowledge is not derived from revelation, we are forced back to sociology, for the term "revelation" is a language expression and languages are social conventions. Second, we come up against the question as to who is a valid judge of what counts as revelation. Here too we are thrown back upon sociology, for the *designation* of people qualified to decide what is and what is not "revelation" is a social performance controlled by a social institution. Or again, try it for "innate ideas," for "intuition," for "dogma" or for whatever. As soon as we are looking for a *standard* of what counts as criticism, we cannot escape from sociology.

One might avoid the recourse to sociology by an ontological *petitio principii*. If one could suppose that the nature of reality is such that revelation, intuition, observation, or whatever, are the ultimate arbiters of judgement, one could persuade oneself that the employ-ment of the respective standard of criticism is a fail-safe and fool-proof procedure for avoiding error. But any such ontological com-mitment would require one to know in advance—at least in general outline—what the broad qualities of reality are. In other words, one would have to know what one is setting out to know. This is a clear *petitio principii* and for that very good reason both Hume and Kant spurned ontology. If ontology does not offer an escape route from sociology, are we then sentenced to a life-sentence with sociology?

In order to avoid the recourse to sociology, we have to grasp that "criticism" is not in need of a standard. In looking for a standard of criticism, we are always looking for a method that will guarantee to lead us to a final rock bottom, which, when reached, will obviate all further criticism. We must therefore abandon the search for a standard of criticism and accept that criticism is, unlike revelation, observation, intuition, innate ideas, dogma, etc., its own justification, so to speak. With unrelenting criticism, we know that we will never strike any rock bottom and when we think we do, we criticize that rock bottom too. There need be no agreement or consensus as to what would constitute agreement. Such agreement (always a social phenomenon) is only necessary when we have recourse to, say, revelation or observation, either dogmatically by itself or as a standard of criticism. Instead, we simply continue to criticize and thus avoid for ever the settlement of the question as to what is the correct source of knowledge. Such unlimited, relentless criticism is itself the only hallmark of rationality.

The problem which has lured us into sociology was the problem of what is the correct source of knowledge. But when we criticize relentlessly and then criticize the criticism, the problem of what is a correct source disappears for good. Thus the lure of sociology disappears.

Unfortunately, pancritical rationalism, as W.W. Bartley III has christened the strategy we must follow to avoid the lure of sociology, has not yet established itself. Instead, the historian can trace the efforts that have been made to explain all knowledge as a social function or as a function of social institutions.

In this effort, which was crowned with varying degrees of success, we can distinguish clearly three different phases. There was first a sociology of science with an emancipatory orientation; second, a sociology of science with an explanatory orientation; and, third, a sociology of science with a deterministic orientation. In each phase a different use was made of the phenomenon of society.

EMANCIPATORY SOCIOLOGY

In the emancipatory phase it was postulated that the only genuine knowledge is the knowledge that all knowledge is a strategy to obtain a non-cognitive end. With this distinction between genuine and false knowledge, the old problem as to how one can distinguish between superstition and truth—a problem which positivism had signally tried but failed to solve—is simply obviated. With emancipation as the chief aim, one simply holds fast to the view that all knowledge is false, except the knowledge that all knowledge is false. The redeeming feature of this position was that knowledge of nature was accorded an exemption because it was believed to have been accounted for by positivism.

This first turn towards sociology as an explanation of the growth of science was meant to be emancipatory. It followed clearly in the footsteps of the Enlightenment itself. Voltaire himself had advanced a sociological explanation of religious knowledge, and Marx extended the scope of such explanation beyond religion. Marx proposed that we treat all knowledge as an ideology propagated in order to serve the ascendancy of a given class and used in order to facilitate the exploitation of those classes which were not in the ascendancy. He applied this proposal with startling and fruitful results to religious knowledge, to aesthetics, to ethics, and to speculative philosophy. He found that in all these cases the pieces of knowledge were really insecure or fraudulent and had little inherent strength to recommend themselves, but could be understood as ideologies designed to validate something other than they purported to validate. To his eternal glory one must add that Marx himself believed that the natural sciences— alone in the realm of human knowledge—were exempt from the taint of ideology. In some way or other, he believed that since they were quantifiable, they were non-sociological. There could be a sociology of religion, of artistic taste, of morals, and of philosophy—but no sociology of natural science. As is well known, Marx's restraint has not been observed by subsequent Marxists. I myself recall, for example, that the German Marxist philosopher Ernst Bloch even described formal logic as an ideology when he told his students (I was an eye-witness) that the syllogism was an instrument devised by Conservatives in that it limited valid inference to bringing out in the conclusion what was implicit in the premises. Logic, he taught, was an ideology to prevent the discovery of the new in general and of revolutions in particular. Deductive reasoning, he explained, was not eternally valid; but only propagandized to be valid in a society dominated by conservatives who enjoyed its benefits at the expense of the lower orders and wanted to prevent change—for any change would be to their disadvantage.

Marx himself wanted to emancipate mankind. His efforts to unmask knowledge and to show what it really was, was a step in the direction of emancipation. The strategy of unmasking and its emancipating function did not have to remain linked to Marx's own political philosophy. It was possible to pry it loose from its original moorings and use it for emancipation in general. The emancipatory direction of the sociology of knowledge has borne many fruitful results and has remained a salutary ingredient in all subsequent sociologies of knowledge. The emancipatory intention came to be followed by Max Weber in his sociology of religion and by Durkheim's theories about the genesis of religion as well as in his theories about the genesis of collective representations and of abstract thinking. It was even used by theologians like Ernst Troeltsch to re-write the history of Christian ethics and by philosophers like Nietzsche to reassess the value of morality in general.

EXPLANATORY SOCIOLOGY

In the explanatory phase the problem is approached from a different angle. If we do not get a standard of "plausibility" from either revelation or observation or innate ideas, where does it come from? In a sense, this orientation of the sociology of knowledge was important because it confronted a real problem. Unlike the emancipatory phase, it kept in mind the distinction between valid and non-valid knowledge and, therefore, had to seek a standard of plausibility to maintain that distinction. Given that religion, innate ideas, and observation had all failed to provide one, philosophers of this phase were now turning towards our experience of society to provide one. The manner in which we experience the society we are living in, the argument ran, determines our standard of plausibility. In turn, the manner of our experience of society depends to a large extent on the structure of that society—though, not wholly so. Because if it did, the old problem which positivism had failed to solve would still be with us. It is not how society is "actually" structured, but how we "perceive" that structure, that determines our standard of plausibility. It is a moot point to what extent the distinction between the actual structure and the perceived structure can be pin-pointed. But it has to be granted that here we have an honest alternative to any positivist account of knowledge. In this phase, the sociology of knowledge provides a genuine alternative to positivism. For example, the theory that matter is passive and that particles do not move themselves but have to wait for the force of gravity to be moved appears "plausible" to people who live in a hierarchical society in which the lower orders are dependent on the initiatives taken by the higher orders. Always note that we are here concerned only with standards of plausibility and that there is no claim that every hierarchically ordered society must produce a theory about the passivity of matter.

In seeking to explain standards of plausibility, the sociology of knowledge in its second phase uses aspects or parts of social order as explanatory models. Standards of plausibility, it is alleged, are not derived from one's experience of social order as such but from one's experience of the particular type of hierarchy that obtains in the society one is living in; or, to use another example, from the manner in which one experiences the tension between a strong social boundary and a weak internal structure in one's society. Needless to say, according to this argument, standards of plausibility change as societies change: there can be no appeal to the judgement of *l'homme moyen sensuel* and not to that of *homo sociologicus;* but only to that of a member of any particular society.

In this stage, the sociology of knowledge does not always accord an exempt status to knowledge of nature. From the writings of Durkheim onwards, there has been a strong temptation to include especially our perception of space and time among the pieces of knowledge that are socially determined. Karl Mannheim sought to exempt knowledge of nature; but more recently, Mary Douglas has argued that our knowledge of pollution is entirely determined by social experience rather than by any knowledge of chemistry. Similarly, she argues that our assessment of witchcraft depends on our perception of the social structure we are in rather than on our knowledge of the physics of broomsticks. Thus she has wiped out any way in which one might have distinguished between the fear of nuclear fall-out and the fear of the polluting effects of the consumption of pork. It may well be true that positivism cannot wholly account for the knowledge that nuclear fall-out is polluting and for our belief that witches cannot fly on broomsticks. But it is not helpful to be told that, therefore, there is no distinction between nuclear fall-out and the consumption of pork and that both the fear of the one and of the other can be accounted for as the result of one's experience of one's society. One can detect here an ironical twist. Those advocates of the sociology of knowledge who are positivists at heart, are willing to grant that our knowledge of nature is accounted for by some form of positivism. Those who are not, maintain that the ultimate explanation of knowledge of nature is sociological. Thus, it looks as if people who are sceptical of a sociological explanation are forced back to positivism, and as if people who are sceptical of positivism, like Mary Douglas, are forced into a sociological explanation. Fortunately, as the argument of section III showed, we have more than these two choices.

This second turn towards sociology as an explanation for the growth of knowledge came with an explanatory orientation. There grew up a vast enterprise known as the sociology of knowledge, which consisted of fragmentary attempts to explain various pieces of knowledge as the result of social pressures or situations. In this sociology of knowledge there was no interest in emancipation, but a desire to account for specific knowledge in terms of sociology when all attempts to account for them in terms of human reason or in terms of revelation had failed. Here we have such enterprises as Merton's work on the science of 17th Century Puritans, and Forman's work on the Uncertainty Principle and Quantum Mechanics, which found the real springs of Heisenberg's thought in the social conditions of the Weimar Republic. People, it is argued in all these works, did not pursue science in the 17th Century or were upholders of Quantum Mechanics because science or Quantum Mechanics had anything to recommend themselves. They pursued science or were upholders of Quantum Mechanics because of their position in certain societies or because of the general climate generated by the societies they were living in.

In all these attempts, the argument turns upon the criterion of plausibility. Given that the Uncertainty Principle in Quantum Mechanics was not wholly convincing, not even to Einstein and Schrödinger, and poses severe problems in our conception of local causality and our conception that any electron must be at a certain place at a certain time, how can we account for the fact that the Uncertainty Principle found so much support?

DETERMINISTIC SOCIOLOGY

Finally we come to the last phase in which scholars turned towards sociology in order to show that social bonds exercised a determining constraint on knowledge. The most influential proponent of this view was Wittgenstein. Having made a brilliant and super-human effort to validate observation in particular and positivism in general in his *Tractatus* through his picture theory of meaning, Wittgenstein did a complete *volte face* and propounded the theory that all meaning is determined by the language rules of a given speech community or a community of the users of certain rules. Within that community, meaning is relative to those rules and can be criticized by reference to those rules. Outside that community, statements have no meaning at all and cannot depend or be determined by non-linguistic events such as observation or revelation or intuition. A blunder, he said, is always a blunder in an established context, but never a blunder as such.

In this third, deterministic phase, the phenomenon of society is thus put to yet another use. This time it is not a question of unmasking the real meaning of a particular piece of knowledge, and not a question of accounting for a particular piece of knowledge by explaining that it is made plausible by the experience of or familiarity with a social structure rather than by the experience of what it is knowledge of. This time, the sociology of knowledge is dominated by a real radicalism. This time it is not a question of who is hoodwinking whom and why (first phase); nor a question as to which specific social experience can account for a piece of knowledge (second phase). This time the fact that human beings live in societies and that all societies are rule-following institutions is equated with knowledge *tout court*. Knowledge, so the argument now runs, is stated in sentences and sentences are controlled by language-rules. Hence knowledge is determined by the rules of language of any one-speech community.

This argument is not nearly as absurd as it sounds. For the old difficulty which had beset all other philosophies of knowledge, had been precisely the difficulty of going behind language, *i.e.*, of accounting for the way in which an observation (that is, a psychological and/or physiological experience) can determine the use of a linguistic expression. Alternately, how an experience of revelation as a non-linguistic event, can determine a linguistic event such as, *e.g.*, the Ten Commandments. Christians have always been very sceptical about the allegation that anything had been revealed to Mohammed because, they said, God could not have spoken in Arabic. But they have notoriously been less sceptical about the possibility that God appears to have spoken to Moses in the language that Moses could have understood. If we now find a sociology of knowledge that simply cuts the Gordian knot by saying that one cannot go "behind" language, and that all knowledge that is going is determined by the rules of the language-game one happens to be committed to by the facts that one is a social being, one ought not to be surprised. As mentioned, no Christian had ever been surprised that there was an intractable problem for muslims. The surprise, if any, comes only now when we find that the problem of how one might go behind language is by no means specific to muslims. Nor ought there to be a surprise when we are being told that the problem is not even specific to revelation but includes the psycho-physiology of observation too.

What is surprising is the simplicity of the suggested remedy. The remedy, we are told, is that in order to distinguish between true knowledge and false knowledge we stop going behind language, be it to observation or to revelation, and that we assess knowledge entirely and exclusively by reference to the rules that govern our use of language. In this sense, in the third phase, the fact of social organization itself is turned into the constitution of knowledge so that any recourse to a non-social event is obviated.

This last turn towards sociology has become very influential, largely because it has been taken up in France by Michel Foucault and in America by Thomas Kuhn. Foucault, to the best of my knowledge, never quotes Wittgenstein and, for that matter, could probably stand on his own feet. But Kuhn makes very explicit the circumstantial reference to Wittgenstein in Chapter V of his *The Structure of Scientific Revolutions.*

Foucault argues that all knowledge is dictated by the adherence to an *episteme* and that in every century European mankind is dominated by a different *episteme.* When that *episteme* changes, all knowledge changes. Each century dominated by an *episteme* forms a language-game—the rules of which are determined by the presiding *episteme.* This is how Foucault's sociology of knowledge would sound if translated into Wittgensteinian terminology. Kuhn is less dogmatic. He argues that all knowledge is derived from a given paradigm and that from time to time in response to demographic changes and social pressures, the paradigm changes.

The ordinary historian must be struck by the fact that in this last, third phase, the turn towards sociology is more comprehensive and therefore more fruitful than the turn in the first and second phases. Indeed, in truly Hegelian fashion, the third phase not only supersedes the other two phases, but preserves and comprehends them. The theory that all knowledge is dictated by adherence to a central paradigm or *episteme* is not only deterministic but also emancipatory and explanatory. If one can see, for example, that the theory of biological evolution is dictated by the *episteme* of the 19th Century, one will be able to abandon it as one passes from the *episteme* of the 19th Century into that of the 20th Century. One does not have to argue against it nor can one hope to argue for it. One simply has to wait until the 19th Century with its particular *episteme* fades away in the 20th Century and all thoughts of evolution will soon fade with it. To the best of my knowledge, Foucault has never confronted the problem posed to his theory of *epistemes* by the extraordinary success story of the theory of evolution in the 20th Century and therefore has valiantly been able to evade the question as to whether that success story would have to be taken as a falsification of his sociological philosophy of science or not.

Kuhn is more pragmatic and more circumspect. He too has an emancipatory mission because he compares resistance to his sociological philosophy of science with the resistance made to Darwin. But his view of paradigm changes is more flexible and less historicist than Foucault's view of *episteme* changes. To begin with, while Foucault's *epistemes* are very clearly defined, there is no real touchstone for what Kuhn considers to be a paradigm, and hence there is considerable doubt as to when paradigms change. Kuhn himself in his latest book on the history of Black Body Radiation theories (1978) has implied that one can only determine paradigm changes by reference to a higher-order paradigm.

Within these pragmatic limits, Kuhn shows further pragmatism in regard to the social reasons for the changes of paradigm. Where Foucault has an explicit historicist pattern according to which *epistemes* change in accordance with the passage of measured time, Kuhn says no more than that paradigms change according to fashions and that the most important factor in such changes is the fact that an older generation of scientists simply die out and that the paradigm they uphold and practice passes into oblivion with them. On the other hand, Foucault is more worldly wise than Kuhn and has a lot to say about the power struggles in societies, and he has been known to argue that questions of knowledge must, in the end, always reduce themselves to questions of power. But whether we are historicists with Foucault or pragmatists with Kuhn, we are here clearly with a philosophy of science that explains knowledge as the dictate of a social constellation.

Neat and rigid, or untidy and flexible—both Foucault and Kuhn are striking examples of the third phase of the radical and final turn of the philosophy of science to sociology. In its third phase the sociology of knowledge explains how knowledge is generated and how it maintains its hold sociologically. It has, however no predictive power beyond the general notion that in the future as in the past, there must always be an intimate connection between the existence of social orders and the presence of societies. It cannot predict what specific features a society is likely to generate or make plausible any particular knowledge. In this respect, it falls short of the predictive power involved in the second phase. In the second phase, which was designed to be explanatory rather than designed to reveal the social determination of knowledge as such, there was a strong predictive element. Every piece of knowledge and every theory was linked to a specific social institution or movement, and a similar institution or movement in a different social order could reasonably be expected to generate and sustain a similar theory. In this respect, the theories of the third phase have no predictive power.

NEGATIVE SOCIOLOGY

These turns towards sociology have enjoyed such a long history because of the realization that no ordinary philosophy of science, which said that knowledge is the result of the application of reason (whatever that might be) or which said that knowledge is brought about by strict positivism, could account for two obvious characteristics of knowledge. One is that most theories are in part immune from falsification and the other, that all theories and/or concepts transcend observation. Hence, the recourse to a philosophy of science that sought to use the social setting *(Sitz im Leben)* of knowledge as an explanation of knowledge. This recourse, in my view, is a failure because no matter what light a knowledge of the *Sitz im Leben* can throw on the emergence of knowledge, it cannot explain its validity. But then, the advocates of the sociology of knowledge in any of its three phases would say: "So much the worse for knowledge." I cannot here go into the question of whether we are forever condemned to the low view of knowledge, which the sociologists of science from Marx to Kuhn would leave us with, or whether there are other roads open to the philosophy of science. For myself, I believe that a recourse to biology offers brighter and more realistic prospects, for the evolution of life is itself a process which takes place through the growth of knowledge about the environment. All selective adaptation is a cognitive process. But in conclusion, I would like to sketch briefly some areas in which the recourse to sociology can be genuinely helpful. In none of these areas can we make a blanket claim to have an explanation of knowledge. But in all these areas we can see that the social setting is not simply irrelevant to knowledge. The sociology of knowledge, in brief, can make a genuine but more modest contribution to our understanding of knowledge than has been claimed so far.

1) *False knowledge has an important society building role.* Cooperation and solidarity and the continuity of such cooperation and solidarity across the generations, are an essential element in the maintenance of societies without which individual human beings cannot survive. *False* knowledge can be used to bind people together, and is, in fact, one of the most commonly used bonding mechanisms in society. People who subscribe to the same belief are held together. Correct knowledge cannot carry out such a bonding function because correct knowledge is the same for everybody and would therefore not serve to define separate communities and distinguish them from one another. But every bit of false knowledge is distinct from any other bit of false

knowledge and therefore can serve as a defining criterion for a particular society. In the bosoms of such societies many techniques like the art of writing can be invented and nurtured and since such techniques eventually tend to survive the societies from which they spring, the *false* knowledge which defined that society and which held it together, has an evolutionary function in the growth of knowledge.

2) *A society held together by false knowledge must protect that false knowledge dogmatically.* It cannot afford to expose it to criticism or to allow it to be measured against alternatives. If a society that uses knowledge as its bonding cement fails to protect knowledge dogmatically, it will fall apart. We have seen at the beginning of this essay that some world-views that grew up in the protection of dogmatism, *e.g.* the world-view that the universe is created according to laws or governed by laws, can exercise a fruitful influence on the growth of critical knowledge. They often serve as a metaphysical back-drop and exert an influence long after they have ceased to be protected dogmatically.

3) *An understanding of knowledge in its social setting can also throw a fertile light on a vehemently debated question.* According to some scholars (Lévy-Bruhl) primitive people have primitive minds. According to other scholars (Lévi-Strauss) there is only one kind of mind and so-called primitive people are operating mentally in exactly the same way in which we modern people operate—that is, by making binary distinctions. Sociology can make a fruitful contribution to this debate. Suppose we assume that all human beings have the same potential. However, that potential is prevented from full development if the human being in question lives in a society in which criticism and free debate must be suppressed because the knowledge to be criticized serves as the bonding cement of the social order. Thus, we get so-called primitive minds in one type of social setting, and so-called modern, logical minds in a very different social setting in which solidarity does not depend on dogmatic maintenance of a shared belief. The real question is therefore not whether there are primitive and non-primitive minds—but whether people live in a closed or in an open society. The debate about primitive minds is thus not a debate about the nature of the mind but a question of the social order in which these minds happen to find themselves.

4) *Given the fact that knowledge advances through relentless criticism, it is possible to ascertain those social conditions in which such criticism can be allowed free reign.* When the knowledge available at any one time in any one society has to be pressed into the service of the social structure and used to keep social bonding up—that is, when knowledge has to

be used to perform a social service—knowledge cannot grow because in such a society it is too precious to be released for debate and subjected to criticism. Only in societies that are held together by a neutral, non-cognitive bond, is it possible for knowledge to be released from social bondage—(*i.e.,* the bondage it is in when it has to provide the social bond)—and exposed to criticism. We can therefore proceed to lay down sociological ground rules for the optimum conditions for the growth of knowledge. In a series of famous essays Jean Pierre Vernant has shown how the coming together of people in the *agora* of the early Greek cities provided opportunities for free debates and set rules for rational discussion because the social structure of these cities, in contrast to earlier more primitive communities in Greece, did not depend on the subscription to and the maintenance of a specific set of knowledge.

I would like to propose that we christen this kind of sociology of knowledge that deals with the four topics here listed "the negative sociology of knowledge." For it does not claim to explain any particular kind or piece of knowledge; it merely claims to be able to isolate those social conditions under which any knowledge can grow or be improved through criticism and debate.

NOTES

1. Prigogine and I. Stengers, *Dialog mit der Natur.* München: Piper, 1980, p. 118.
2. English translation, Cambridge, Mass., 1951.

Notes on Contributors

Marcelo Alonso (born 1921) has been Executive Director of the Florida Institute of Technology Research and Engineering (FITRE), Melbourne, FL, since 1980. In this position his responsibility is to promote the utilization of technical capabilities of FITRE to carry out research and development projects as well as engineering services and feasibility studies, by generating projects of interest to industry both in the United States and in less developed countries. He was Director of the Department of Scientific Affairs, OAS, Washington, DC. (1976–1980); From 1976–1980 he was also Executive Secretary for the Inter-American Nuclear Energy Commission; he was Acting Director, Department of Scientific Affairs, OAS (1974–75). Among his publications are: *Physics;* the three-volume *Fundamental University Physics,* of which volume III *Quantum and Statistical Physics* has been translated into ten languages; *Física Atomica; Introducción a la Física* (2 vols.); and *Quantum Mechanics: Principles and Applications.* He is a member of the American Physical Society (APS), the American Association for the Advancement of Science (AAAS), and of the American Nuclear Society.

Eileen Barker has been a member of the Department of Sociology at the London School of Economics and Political Science since 1970 and is currently Dean of Undergraduate Studies. She has published more than sixty articles in scientific journals and collections, authored *The Making of a Moonie: Brainwashing or Choice?*, and *Science and Religion,* and edited *New Religious Movements: A Perspective for Understanding Society,* and *Of Gods and Men: New Religious Movements in the West.*

Raymond Boudon (born 1934) is Professor of Sociology at the Université de Paris-Sorbonne (Paris IV). He has been Visiting Professor at Stanford University, Harvard University, Columbia University, New York University, the University of Genève, and the University of Stockholm. He is a foreign member of the American Academy of Arts and Sciences. Among his recent publications are: *Education, Opportunity and Social Inequality; The Unintended Consequences of Social Action,* and *The Logic of Social Action.*

Alain Boyer (born 1954) is Assistant Professor of Philosophy at the Université de Clermont-Ferrand. Among his publications are: *K. Popper: une épistémologie laïque?; "La tyrannie de la certitude," (Esprit* 1981); and "Popper et Hayek: Réforme ou Révolution?" *(Analyses de la S.E.D.E.I.S.).*

Larry Briskman (born 1947) has taught philosophy at the University of Edinburgh, Scotland, since 1969; in 1977 he was Visiting Professor at Dartmouth College, Hanover, New Hampshire, U.S.A.; and in 1976 Visiting Research Fellow at York University, Canada. Among his many articles are "Essentialism without Inner Natures?" *(Philosophy of the Social Sciences,* September 1982), and "From Logic to Logics (and Back Again)" *(British Journal for the Philosophy of Science,* March 1982).

Max Jammer is Professor of Natural Philosophy and the History of Science at the Department of Physics in Bar Ilan University, Ramat-Gan, Israel. He studied at the Universities of Vienna, Jerusalem, and Harvard. He taught at the Universities of Oklahoma, Hebrew University, Bar Ilan University, and Columbia University, and was Visiting Professor at numerous universities in Europe, the United States, and New Zealand. Presently, he serves as President of the Association for the Advancement of Science in Israel. He is a member of several scientific academies and learned societies and is recipient of the Science Prize of the American Academy of Arts and Sciences. Among his publications are *Concepts of Space* (with a Foreword by Albert Einstein); *Foundations of Dynamics; The Conceptual Development of Quantum Mechanics;* and *The Philosophy of Quantum Mechanics,* as well as other studies in the history and philosophy of physics, which have been published also in German, Italian, Spanish, Russian, Japanese, and Chinese.

Ian C. Jarvie (born 1937) is Professor of Philosophy at York University, Toronto, Ont., Canada. Before that he taught at the London School of Economics and Political Science, the University of Hong Kong, Tufts University, Boston University, and the University of Southern California. He is author of more than 200 scholarly publications.

Among his books are: *The Revolution in Anthropology; Towards a Sociology of the Cinema; Concepts and Society; The Story of Social Anthropology; Functionalism;* and *Rationality and Relativism.*

Bernulf Kanitscheider (born 1939) has been Professor of Philosophy of the Natural Sciences at the Center for the Philosophy and the Foundations of Science in the University of Giessen, West Germany, since 1974. His main interest is the theory of relativity and cosmology in its physical and philosophical ramifications. Among his publications are: *Geometrie und Wirklichkeit; Philosophisch-historische Grundlagen der physikalischen Kosmologie; Vom absoluten Raum zur dynamischen Geometrie; Kosmologie: Geschichte und Systematik in philosophischer Perspektive.* He edited *Moderne Naturphilosophie,* a collection to which many internationally known physicists have contributed.

Noretta Koertge has been Professor in the Department of History and Philosophy of Science at Indiana University since 1981. After teaching chemistry in both the U.S.A. and Turkey, she did a Ph.D. in philosophy of science at London University, where she attended the famous Popper Seminar on a regular basis. Her current research interests center around theories of scientific method and problems in the philosophy of social science. She has also published two novels. She has published more than fifty articles in philosophical and scientific journals and collections, among them: "Towards a New Theory of Scientific Inquiry," in *Progress and Rationality in Science,* edited by G. Radnitzky and G. Andersson, Dordrecht: Reidel, 1978, pp. 253–78; "The Problem of Appraising Scientific Theories," in *Current Research in Philosophy of Science,* edited by P.D. Asquith and H.E. Kyburg, Jr. East Lansing: Philosophy of Science Association, 1979, pp. 228–51; "Ethical Problems in Scientific Communication," in *Rationality in Science and Politics,* edited by G. Andersson, Dordrecht: Reidel, 1983, pp. 181–93; and "Beyond Cultural Relativism," to appear in *Popper and the Human Sciences,* edited by Musgrave and Currie.

Werner Leinfellner (born 1921) is University Professor of Philosophy at the University of Nebraska, and Affiliated Professor at the Technical University of Vienna. From 1962–1967 he was Lecturer at the University of Vienna; 1962–1967 Professor at the Institute of Advanced Studies in Vienna. He has been Visiting Professor at the Universities of Basle, Heidelberg, Boston, Paderborn, and Vienna. Among his publications are: *Struktur and Aufbau wissenschaftlicher Theorien; Einfuehrung in die Wissenschafts- und Erkenntnistheorie; Die Entstehung der Theorie: Eine Analyse des kritischen Denkens in der Antike; Forschungslogik der Sozialwissenschaften; Developments in the Methodology of the Social*

Sciences; Ethics and Social Sciences; Ontologie, Systemtheorie und Semantik (together with E. Leinfellner); *Die Evolution der Intelligenz.* He is editor of 50 volumes of the *Theory and Decision Library,* and of 18 volumes of the journal *Theory and Decision,* co-editor of over 30 volumes in English and German. He is President of the International Society for Foundations of Risk and Utility; Vice President of the Wittgenstein Society; editor in chief of *Theory and Decision: An International Journal for the Methodology of the Social Sciences;* editor in chief of the *International Library Theory and Decision,* and member of twelve international scholarly societies.

Percy Löwenhard (born 1927) has been Professor of Psychology at the University of Gothenburg, Sweden, since 1973. Originally, he was trained as a chemical engineer, did research in nuclear and solid state chemistry at the Technical University of Gothenburg, and studied medicine. Among his publications are: *Beiträge zur Filteranalyse des menschlichen Enzephalogramms; Consciousness—A biological view; Knowledge, Belief and Human Behaviour.*

Peter Munz (born 1921) is Professor of History at the Victoria University of Wellington, New Zealand, and is one of the very few persons to have been a student of both Popper and Wittgenstein. He is the author of many books, including *The Place of Hooker in the History of Thought; Problems of Religious Knowledge; The Origin of the Carolingian Empire; Relationship and Solitude: An Inquiry into the Relationship between Myth, Metaphysics and Ethics; Life in the Age of Charlemagne; Frederick Barbarossa: A Study in Medieval Politics; When the Golden Bough Breaks: Structuralism or Typology?; The Shapes of Time: A New Look at the Philosophy of History,* and *Our Knowledge of the Growth of Knowledge.*

Karl-Dieter Opp (born 1937) has been Professor of Sociology at the University of Hamburg, West Germany, since 1971; before that he was Assistant Professor at the University of Cologne and the University of Erlangen-Nürnberg, West Germany. Among his publications are: *Soziale Probleme und Protestverhalten; Die Entstehung sozialer Normen; Individualistische Sozialwissenschaft;* (with co-authors) *Strafvollzug und Resozialisierung; Theorie sozialer Krisen; Methodologie der Sozialwissenschaften; Einführung in die Mehrvariablenanalyse; Soziologie der Wirtschaftskriminalität,* and *Abweichendes Verhalten und Gesellschaftsstruktur.*

Angelo Maria Petroni (born 1956) is a member of the Scientific Board of the Centro Einaudi, Turin, founding member of the Istituto di Metodología e Filosofía della Scienza, Turin, and member of the Advisory Board of the journal *Il Mulino* (Bologna). Among his publications are: *K.R. Popper: il pensiero politico;* "Giustizia e consequenze della azioni," in Petroni, A. (ed.). *Giustizia come libertà? Saggi su Nozick; Introduction* to the Italian edition of F.v. Hayek's trilogy *Law, Legislation, and Liberty;* "Explication et indéterminisme dans les sciences sociales. A propos de 'La place du désordre' par Raymond Boudon," (*L'Année Sociologique* 1985); *Studi kepleriani;* "On the Determination of Planetary Distances in the Copernican System," (*The British Journal for the Philosophy of Science* 1986).

Hans Primas (born 1928) is Professor *ad personam* for Physical and Theoretical Chemistry at the Eidgenössische Technische Hochschule in Zürich, Switzerland, where he was Head of the Department of Chemistry 1967–1968 and 1976–1978. Among his publications are: "Theory Reduction and Non-Boolean Theories," (*Journal of Mathematical Biology* 1977); *Chemistry, Quantum Mechanics and Reductionism;* "Chemistry and Complementarity," (*Chimia* 1982), and "Verschränkte Systeme und Komplementarität," in Kanitscheider, B. (ed.). *Moderne Naturphilosophie.*

Gerard Radnitzky is Professor of Philosophy of Science at the University of Trier, West Germany. He is the author of *Contemporary Schools of Metascience, Preconceptions in Research, Epistemologia e Politica della Ricerca, L'Epistemologia di Popper e la Ricerca Scientifica,* and over one hundred papers in the philosophy of science and in political philosophy. He is also the editor or co-editor of numerous volumes including *Progress and Rationality in Science, The Structure and Development of Science* (both also in German, Italian and Spanish), *Evolutionary Epistemology, Rationality, and the Sociology of Knowledge* (LaSalle, IL: Open Court 1987), *Economic Imperialism: The Economic Method Applied Outside the Field of Economics* (New York: Paragon House 1987), and *Centripetal Forces in the Sciences* (New York: Paragon House 1987). Formerly Professor of Philosophy at the Ruhr-University of Bochum, West Germany, and Associate Professor at the University of Gothenburg, Sweden, he has also been a Visiting Professor at the State University of New York at Stony Brook (1972), Fellow of the Japan Society for the Promotion of Science (1978), and Premier Assesseur of the Académie Internationale de Philosophie des Sciences since 1982. (*Festschrift* to his 60th birthday: Andersson, G. [ed.]. 1984. *Rationality in Science and Politics.* Dordrecht: Reidel.)

Erwin Schopper (born 1909) is Professor Emeritus; he was Full Professor of Physics and Director of the Institute of Nuclear Physics at the University of Frankfurt, West Germany, from 1956–1979; 1952–1956 he was Head of the Department of Hochspannungslaboratorium Hechingen in the Max-Planck-Institute for the Physics of the Stratosphere;

from 1937–1945 he was the Director of the Central Laboratory of I.G. Farben Industrie Agfa Wolfen. He was Consulting Member of the Deutsche Atom-Kommission (in the German Federal Ministry of Research), Consulting Member for Space Research of the Council of Europe; he is an external member of the Max-Planck-Institute for Aeronomy at Lindau. He has published many articles on nuclear physics, cosmic radiation, space biophysics, and the physics of the upper atmosphere.

Roman Sexl (1939–1986) was Professor of Physics and Director of the Institute for Theoretical Physics at the University of Vienna since 1969; he was Associate Professor at the University of Georgia in 1968; in 1967 he was Assistant Professor at the University of Maryland; from 1972–1976 he was Head of Department in the Institute for Space Research of the Austrian Academy of Science; from 1974 to 1986 he was a member of the International Committee for General Relativity Theory and Gravitation, and from 1980 to 1986 Chairman of the "International Commission for Physics Education." He published more than one hundred articles in scientific journals. Among his books are: *Gravitation und Kosmologie; Weiße Zwerge—schwarze Löcher* (jointly with H. Sexl); *Relativität, Gruppen, Teilchen; Was die Welt zusammenhält,* and *Deutungen der Quantenmechanik* (jointly with K. Baumann).

Walter B. Weimer (born 1942) is Professor of Psychology at the Pennsylvania State University. His main research areas are cognitive psychology, history of psychology, psycholinguistics, and the methodology of science. Among his publications are: *Notes on the Methodology of Scientific Research;* "Hayek's Approach to the Problems of Complex Phenomena: An Introduction to the Theoretical Psychology of *The Sensory Order,*" in Weimer, W. and Palermo, D. (eds.), *Cognition and the Symbolic Processes,* vol. II, pp. 241–285.

Alvin M. Weinberg is Director of the Institute for Energy Analysis, which he was instrumental in establishing at Oak Ridge Associated Universities in January 1974. After serving briefly as Director of the Institute, he became Director of the Federal Energy Administration's Office of Energy Research and Development, and returned to the Institute in July 1975. For more than a quarter century he was Director of the Oak Ridge National Laboratory (ORNL). He joined ORNL in 1945 where he served as Director of the Physics Division (1947–1948), as Research Director (1948–1955), and as Director (1955–1973). He was also among the first members of the University of Chicago's wartime Metallurgical Laboratory, where the first controlled nuclear reaction was achieved in December 1942. Weinberg was the originator of the pressurized water reactor, and he proposed its use for submarine propulsion in 1944. Among his publications is the well-known book *Reflections on Big Science*. Among the many awards and honors which he has received are: The Atoms for Peace Award, and The Enrico Fermi Award—the highest scientific award given by the Department of Energy. He is a member of the National Academy of Arts and Sciences and of the Royal Netherlands Academy of Arts and Sciences.

Franz Wuketits (born 1955) has been Associate Professor of Philosophy of Science (with special regard to Philosophy of Biology) at the University of Vienna since 1980. He has published about 60 articles in biological and philosophical journals. Among his books are: *Wissenschaftstheoretische Probleme der modernen Biologie; Kausalitätsbegriff und Evolutionstheorie; Biologie und Kausalität; Grundriss der Evolutionstheorie; Biologische Erkenntnis: Grundlagen und Probleme; Evolution, Erkenntnis, Ethik;* and *Zustand und Bewußtsein*. He edited *Concepts and Approaches in Evolutionary Epistemology.*

Index

351